GUNBOAT FRONTIER

GUNBOAT FRONTIER

British Maritime Authority and
Northwest Coast Indians, 1846–90

Barry M. Gough

University of British Columbia Press
Vancouver
1984

Gunboat Frontier

British Maritime Authority and Northwest Coast Indians, 1846–90

© The University of British Columbia Press 1984

This book has been published with the help of a grant from the Social Science Federation of Canada, using funds provided by the Social Sciences and Humanities Research Council of Canada.

Canadian Cataloguing in Publication Data

Gough, Barry M., 1938–
    Gunboat frontier

(University of British Columbia Press Pacific
    maritime studies; 4)
Includes index.
Bibliography: p.
ISBN 0-7748-0175-1

1. Pacific coast (Canada) - History. 2. British
Columbia - History. 3. Great Britain. Royal
Navy - History - 19th century. 4. Indians,
Treatment of - Pacific coast (Canada). 5. Great
Britain - Colonies -America - Administration.
I. Title. II. Series.
FC3822.G68 1984   971.1′02   C83-091467-6
F1088.G68 1984

This book is printed on acid-free paper.

ISBN 0-7748-0175-1

Printed in Canada

To Marilyn

Contents

Page

Illustrations   ix
Preface   xiii

PART I: *Company and Colony*

  1. Dwellers Along the Shore   3
  2. Tide of Empire   20
  3. "This Miserable Affair"   32
  4. The Smouldering Volcano   50

PART II: *Putting Out Fires*

  5. Policy Making   75
  6. Of Slaves and Liquor   85
  7. Among the Vikings of the North Pacific   95
  8. Piracy and Punishment   108
  9. Policing the Passage   129
 10. The Pulls of Alaska   148

PART III: *Extending the Frontier*

 11. The "Customary Authority" Under Dominion Auspices   161
 12. At Heaven's Command   172
 13. New Zones of Influence: Nass, Kimsquit, and Skeena   189
 14. Retrospect   210

Appendix   217
Abbreviations   224
Notes   225
Bibliography   267

Index   271

Photographic Credits

Plates 9, 10, and 13 were kindly provided by F. D. H. Nelson, Base Historian, CFB Esquimalt. Plate 16 is from the National Museums of Canada (neg. 266), and Plate 22 is from the Photographic Branch, Department of Travel Industry, Government of British Columbia. The remaining illustrations appear courtesy of the Provincial Archives of British Columbia.

Illustrations

following p. 46

Plate 1. Fort Victoria with boats approaching
2. Fort Victoria with seamen marching
3. Fort Victoria with seamen in action
4. Clallum chief "King George" and others
5. Richard Blanshard
6. Sir James Douglas
7. Arthur Edward Kennedy
8. Frederick Seymour
9. Fairfax Moresby
10. Henry Bruce
11. Arthur Farquhar
12. James Charles Prevost
13. H.M.S. *Trincomalee*
14. H.M. Paddle Sloop *Virago*
15. H.M.S. *Forward*
16. Albert Edenshaw
17. North Coast of Vancouver Island
18. Fort Rupert
19. Fort Rupert
20. Officers from H.M.S. *Scout*
21. H.M.S. *Scout*

following p. 130

Plate 22. Queen Victoria
23. West Coast of Vancouver Island
24. Sechart Indian
25. Indians on H.M.S. *Boxer*
26. H.M.S. *Cameleon*
27. Henry Richards
28. C. R. Robson and H. D. Lascelles

29. H.M.S. *Rocket,* officers and crew
30. H.M.S. *Boxer*
31. H.M.S. *Sparrowhawk*
32. Israel Wood Powell
33. D'Arcy Anthony Denny
34. H.M.S. *Osprey*
35. Map of Saltspring area
36. Friendly Cove, with officers from H.M.S. *Rocket*
37. Metlakatla, B.C.
38. William Wiseman, on H.M.S. *Ganges*
39. Nass River area

Maps

1.	The Northwest Coast of North America	5
2.	Northwest Coast — Linguistic Divisions	11
3.	Northern Part of Vancouver Island	36
4.	The Cowichan Expedition, 1856	64
5.	The Queen Charlotte Islands	97
6.	Clayoquot Sound, Vancouver Island	110
7A.	The Strait of Georgia, Southern Portion	131
7B.	The Strait of Georgia, Northern Portion	133
8.	The North Coast, showing Skeena and Nass Rivers	191

Aoua!

Don't trust white men, dwelling along the shore.
In the days of our fathers white men settled on this island. They were told: there is land for your women to till. Be honest and good, and become our brothers.
The white men promised, yet they dug themselves in, built a black fort, put thunder into tubes of brass. Their priests tried to give us a God we don't know. And then they spoke of obedience and slavery: rather death! The carnage was long and terrible; but despite the lightning they hurled which crushed whole armies, they were destroyed. Aoua!
Don't trust white men.
We have seen new tyrants, stronger and more numerous, set up their tents on the shore. Heaven fought for us casting storms and foul winds upon them. They are no more, and we live, free. Aoua!
Don't trust white men, dwelling along the shore.

Chanson Madecasses (Maurice Ravel)

The haunting song of Ravel's Madagascar natives crosses distant waters to the Northwest Coast. Locale and circumstance differ widely, for these places lie half a world away from each other. Yet imperial processes and native responses have common denominators, and in the conflict of literate and non-literate societies the strident voices of the vanquished are seldom, if ever, heard.

Preface

This is a book about the Royal Navy and Northwest Coast Indians from the time that Britain and the United States divided the last remaining quarter of the North American continent between themselves in 1846 to the end of British naval patrols on Indian duties in the late 1880's. It enquires into the way in which law, backed by armed authority, was transferred to a maritime frontier, heavily populated by natives and lying eighteen thousand miles by sea from the centre of empire in London. This is a story of gunboats, more correctly, sloops-of-war, corvettes and frigates, some of them steam-powered, some not. Because "Send a Gunboat!" was a cry voiced by British subjects at home and abroad, I have chosen to call this work *Gunboat Frontier*, and because this is a study of the extension of British influences, both imperial and colonial, by means of naval power, I have subtitled it *British Maritime Authority and Northwest Coast Indians* with approximate dates, 1846–90.

This book completes a trilogy on the maritime history of British Columbia. It is a companion to *Distant Dominion: Britain and the Northwest Coast of North America, 1579–1809* (1980) and *The Royal Navy and the Northwest Coast of North America, 1810–1914: A Study of British Maritime Ascendancy* (1971). In the latter I noted that the subject of the Navy's relations with Coast Indians would be a topic of future enquiry. This book may serve to explain the intricacies in white-Indian relations in coastal British Columbia during the nineteenth century, particularly in the 1850's, 1860's, and 1870's. My objective has been to get as close to the historic interface of white and native societies as possible, and to describe and assess how each responded to the other. I have also sought to give this work a sense of *place*—the environment of the natives and of the Navy's actions—and to do this I have visited, wherever possible, every creek mouth and cave where the gunboat frontier was being exercised.

Reading Admiralty, Colonial Office, fur trade and other papers for a fifty year epoch reveals that in British Columbia authorities tended to respond on demand, enquiring into murders, thefts, and piracies, investigating illicit liquor traffic, slavetaking and a few cases of cannibalism, supporting settlers in fear of Indian attack, and aiding missionaries as the need arose. Indian policy was essentially crisis management. London had made declarations of intent towards the Indians, as in the charter of Vancouver Island colony in 1849 and in the statute establishing British Columbia as a colony in 1858, and Whitehall, particularly the Admiralty, was quick to rap the knuckles of its representatives if they did not proceed in acceptable fashion. From time to time, colonial governors, mainly Sir James Douglas, who bulks large in these pages, made statements of intent; but essentially London laid down general guidelines which were adapted as colonial circumstances warranted. British Columbia's "Indian policy" thus developed in its own, unique way.

After an uncertain start during Richard Blanshard's governorship, British Columbia's Indian policy was injected with Douglas's personal enthusiasm during his term of office. He authorized the practice of sending of gunboats, and through experience, he honed the rules of intervention to a sharp edge. During the early years of his governorship, Douglas drew on the Hudson's Bay Company policy of peace for the purpose of profit. But the Company's practice of retributive justice against Indians in retaliation for murders and thefts was also employed by British authorities on many imperial frontiers, most notably southern Africa and New Zealand. Douglas's greatest strength was his adaptability. At the same time, he always understood that he was specially empowered with authority to protect the interests of Her Britannic Majesty, Queen Victoria, from internal and external threats. That he was able to anticipate what London wanted and thereby forego the censure accorded his predecessor, Richard Blanshard, and at the same time act as an agent of destiny for his fellow British Columbians is one of his claims to greatness.

Readers of this book can judge for themselves the quality of the naval service before and after Douglas and its influence on the Indians in question. A cardinal tenet of nineteenth-century Englishmen as the Empire expanded was the extension of law as they knew it. John Stuart Mill stated in *Considerations on Representative Government* (1861) that force could be used legitimately to preserve internal peace and order. The reason for this was that order was the precondition for social progress and representative government. The "peace, order and good government" clause in the British North America Act, 1867, recognized this precept and imperial legacy in principle.

Because this book is based on possibly the last hitherto unused major corpus of documentary materials to tell about Northwest Coast Indian life in the nineteenth century, the Admiralty papers, it contains new findings. It provides the first full report on the "miserable affair" at Fort Rupert and the first investigations of the Cowichan crises of 1852–53 and 1856. It also brings to light Douglas's support for American interests in Puget Sound during the Battle of Seattle, 1856, and British gunboat involvement in Alaskan waters in support of Russian authorities in 1862 and American interests in 1879. It deals, too, with the Indians of Vancouver Island's west coast, particularly the largely unknown encounter between the Ahousat and the Royal Navy in 1864, an event generally overshadowed in much British Columbia history by the story of the Waddington party "massacre" near Bute Inlet in the same year. The Haida, Lemalchi Salish, Tsimshian and Nishga peoples feature in other places in this work as do official attempts to check Indian slavery and liquor selling to Indians and to support missionary efforts, particularly at Metlakatla. I have taken pains to mention individual Indians by name because regrettably all too few of them are presently known by anything other than tribal or village designation. Chapchah, Edenshaw, and Acheewun are among the Indian personalities who became better known in these pages.

The central theme of this book is the extension of law and order on the coast with the aid of maritime authority, and to develop it better, the work is divided into three parts, each beginning with an anchoring chapter. The first part, "Company and Colony," begins with a brief survey of the differences in Indian and white societies in the mid-nineteenth century. It then follows, through the 1850's, the development of the colony of Vancouver Island with particular reference to Fort Victoria, Fort Rupert, and Cowichan. The second part is entitled "Putting out Fires." It commences with a review of Indian policy in the colonial period with specific reference to the colony of British Columbia, followed by an enquiry into British attempts to check slavery and stop liquor traffic to Indians, though legal aspects of liquor prohibition are included in the appendix. Then it surveys, in four successive chapters, the exercise of authority "outwards" from the colonial capitals of Victoria and New Westminster to areas of influence—the Queen Charlotte Islands, the West Coast of Vancouver Island, the Strait of Georgia, and even Alaska. The third and final part, entitled "Extending the Frontier," starts with an analysis of Canadian Indian policy in British Columbia in the first twenty years after the colony became a province. The narrative then moves to a study of naval support for missions. The next chapter, "New Zones of Influence," deals with the last cases of gunboat diplomacy against Northwest Coast Indians—on the Nass, at Kimsquit, and on the Skeena. The book concludes with a retrospective assessment of the subject. By this approach I do not claim to have met all the needs of the subject, but had I used a mere chronological approach, my readers would have been totally distracted by jumps from Clayoquot to Kimsquit and from Capilano to Owekeeno. As it is, they will be obliged nonetheless to follow the chronology, recognizing that the maritime nature of this frontier meant that a piracy in one area could be going on at the same time as a murder in another or a theft or some other problem in a third or fourth.

In the writing of this book I have incurred numerous debts to historians, anthropologists, archivists, librarians and others. In particular I thank my friend and sometime colleague David McNab, whose knowledge of both imperial history and native studies in Canada for this period is without rival. I also wish to thank the late Wilson Duff, Margaret Ormsby, Robin W. Winks, Jean Usher Friesen, John Bovey, Richard A. Pierce, James Stanton, Raymond Dumett, Robin Fisher, Robert Kubicek, James Hitchman, Roland L. DeLorme, James Scott, Phyllis Wetherell Bultmann, David Mason, Kent Haworth, Brian Young, Christon Archer, Trisha Gessler, Barbara Efrat, Alan Hoover, Mary Lee Stearns, Robert L. Spearing, A. Keith Cameron, A.S. Davidson, Edmund Hayes, William Hunt, Laird Christie, James Boutilier, Donald H. Mitchell, Gordon Dodds, J.V. Boys, Melinda and Jason Gough, Douglas Leighton, Donald Bourgeois, Ian Johnson, and P.W. Brock. All of these people, in one way or another, have contributed to the material in this volume though in no way are responsible for its use or interpretation. Indian acquaintances Alex and Nancy of Opitsat allowed me to test the capricious currents at Clayoquot by placing their cruiser at my disposal. Judie DeGuire, Susan Planta, Jean Gourlay, and Margaret Meston provided secretarial support. To these people and others and to the trustees and librarians of the following institutions I wish to give thanks for information provided: The British Columbia Provincial Archives and the Legislative Library, the Maritime Museum of British Columbia, Victoria; the Vancouver Island Regional Library, Duncan; the Directorate of History, Canadian Forces Headquarters, Ottawa; the Toronto Public Library; the John Robarts Library, Toronto; the Oregon Historical Society, Portland; the Beineke and Sterling Libraries, Yale University, New Haven, Connecticut; the Perkins Library and Manuscripts Collection, Duke University, Durham, North Carolina; the Huntington Library and Art Gallery, San Marino, California; the Bancroft Library, the University of California, Berkeley; the University of Washington Libraries, Seattle; the Newberry Library, Chicago; the National Maritime Museum, Greenwich; the Public Record Office; the Royal Commonwealth

Society, the British Library, the University of London Library, the Church Missionary Society Archives, London; the Scottish Record Office, the National Library of Scotland, Edinburgh; the Hydrographic Department, Ministry of Defence, Taunton, Somerset; and the Hudson's Bay Company Archives in Winnipeg.

PART I

COMPANY AND COLONY

I

Dwellers Along the Shore

T HEN AS NOW it was one of the wild coasts of the world. Blessed with a mild climate yet curiously cursed by treacherous weather, it is a land of environmental paradox: its outward, rockbound fringe athwart the open Pacific lies nakedly exposed to gale and fog, and as such is scarcely habitable by humankind save in gentle seasons. Where mountains have intervened, as in the case of the Olympics for Puget Sound, the Vancouver Island range for the Strait of Georgia, and the bulky islands of the southern Alaskan shore for the "inland passage," secure and dry footholds exist for populous human occupation. Thus, in the lee of rock or forest mankind lives and has lived almost from time immemorial. This is the Northwest Coast of North America, a double-land of outward coastal desolation and inshore serene security.

Our stereotype of paradise may well be that provided in the novels of Stevenson, Conrad, or Maugham—of Polynesian islands where slender palms sway to the rhythm of the trade winds, where surging surf drums on coral reefs beyond the lagoon, and where life seems harmonious and easy. However, other paradises existed within the Pacific rim in times past. When white explorers first appeared, the Northwest Coast of North America was, in its own unique way, a Garden of Eden. "A soft warm breeze fanned us," the Canadian George Munro Grant wrote in *Ocean to Ocean* of his voyage through Georgia Strait in the 1870's, "and every mile disclosed new features of scenery, to which snow-clad mountain ranges, wooded plains, and a summer sea enfolding countless promontories and islands, contributed their different forms of beauty." Here men lived in harmony with the environment, enjoying a reasonably satisfying life mainly regulated by their maritime habitat. They put little strain on the land and its resources; they also had little need to modify their ecology or change their landscape.

Sometimes the North Pacific belies its name, and Indian as well as white mariners have had to contend with the squalls, fresh gales, and great storms that lash the outer coast in winter months. But by and large, this ocean affords a salubrious and gentle climate to its southeastern shore, which early British travellers rightly boasted resembled that of southern England. The Japanese current offshore delivers moderate temperatures all along the outer shoreline, and even in high latitudes prolonged cold is infrequent. This same current modifies prevailing winds which carry heavy rains to the outer coastal fringe, and the rising moist air approaching the great mountains of the Coast Range yields a heavy rainfall. The area is drained by major river systems flowing to tidewater—the Columbia, Fraser, Skeena, Nass, and Stikine—all with sources west of the Rocky Mountains. In this well-watered area, often called the Pacific Slope, vegetation is heavy. Only a century ago thick stately primeval stands of coniferous trees such as Douglas fir, spruce, hemlock, and red and yellow cedar stood as testaments to untold years of uninterrupted growth.

Countless islands lie athwart the deeply indented coastline, giving sheltered waterways and protected navigation from the unbroken sweep of the Pacific. With bays and inlets added, British Columbia possesses 4,450 miles of shoreline. These coves and islets are legacies of the earth's foldings and of the great ice age, when a heavy sheet of ice inched across the land, rounded off mountain peaks, gouged valleys, and carried away soil and loose rock. These processes left two distinct terrains: the one mountainous and lying parallel to the Pacific in four great ridges; the other a string of small islands, reefs, and shoals flanked on the southwest by Vancouver Island and farther north by the wedge-shaped Queen Charlotte Islands. All told, this was an island world stretching north and west from Cape Flattery to Asia.

Between Vancouver Island and the continental mainland lies a savage maze of rock and water sometimes called the Inland Passage. This "singular and capricious sea," as an erudite nineteenth-century British yachtsman called it, is about 340 miles long and two or three to thirty miles wide. Here the mariner had to guard against "great and perplexing tidal irregularities," a cautious hydrographic surveyor warned in his sailing directions, and to keep a wary eye on whatever charts and rudimentary tide tables were available. Everywhere rocks, shoals, sandbanks, and currents lie in wait for the careless sailor. At such places as Seymour Narrows, or The Rapids as some called it before hazardous Ripple Rock was dynamited in the 1950's, eddies and whirlpools, locally known as tide-

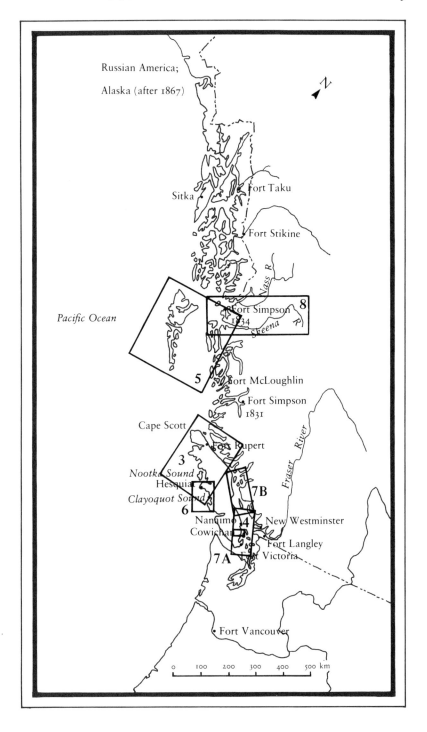

Russian America;
Alaska (after 1867)

N

Sitka

Fort Taku

Fort Stikine

Pacific Ocean

Nass R.

Fort Simpson
1834

8

Skeena R.

Fort McLoughlin

Fort Simpson
1831

Fraser River

5

Cape Scott

Fort Rupert

3

Nootka Sound
Hesquiat
Clayoquot Sound

6

7B

Nanaimo
Cowichan

4

New Westminster

Fort Langley

7A

Fort Victoria

Fort Vancouver

0   100   200   300   400   500 km

rips, posed special dangers; here unless a strong wind was blowing, a ship under sail could be carried helplessly along to destruction. Canoes or ships would be obliged to wait for slack tide before attempting this section of the passage. Even then, floating logs, submerged timber known locally as "deadheads," and gigantic kelp made navigation treacherous in these narrow seas. Sheltered from the North Pacific by the bulk of Vancouver Island, this cradle of Northwest Coast Indian civilization constituted the human highway of coastal British Columbia in times past and present. Here the major weather systems of the North Pacific—the Aleutian low and the North Pacific high—are less noticeable in their effect. Nonetheless, in winter months biting Arctic winds could blow down the great fjords such as Kingcome, Knight, or Bute Inlets, some of which cut eighty miles through the islands and mountains to the northeast. Irrespective of the time of year, at a moment's notice a change in weather pattern could bring on damp and obliterating fog. Seas in the inland straits are roughest in autumn and mildest in spring and summer. But outside the strait to the north, in Hecate Strait and Dixon Entrance, heavy seas and swell from the northeast or southwest make for hazardous navigation in autumn and winter while locally generated weather conditions make for sudden squalls and high seas in late spring and summer.

The first group of people to occupy and exploit this unique maritime environment were the Northwest Coast Indians who inhabited the long crescent-shaped shore of northwestern America from Trinidad Bay in Northern California to Yakutat Bay in southeastern Alaska. The culture of these peoples was not "high" in the sense of an expanded and developed agricultural base and a settled population which gave rise to material and cultural advancement. The livelihood of Northwest Coast Indians did not depend on agriculture: the seas and rivers teemed with fish—salmon, halibut, trout, herring, and oolachan—and the forests abounded with berries and wildlife. For this reason, the Coast Indians were relatively free from the scourge of famine which generally threatened primitive societies. And with their tools they could split and carve the bountiful, beautiful cedar into objects of art and technology.

The dug-out canoe of the Coast Indians typifies their craftsmanship: in fighting, in transporting, in hunting, even in celebrating, their canoes, hollowed with fire and adzes from a single red cedar tree and measuring in some instances to seventy feet and capable of carrying fifty people or more, represented human adaptation to the environment. Carefully shaped by skilled carvers, especially the Nootka, whose vessels were prized up and down the coast, canoes were cherished, protected, and well maintained by their owners. At sea they were propelled by paddles and on rivers by poles, but in historic times many groups used sails woven from mats.

Unlike its deep-keeled or out-rigged Polynesian counterpart, the canoe functioned poorly under sail. It could not beat upwind and would actually make more leeway than headway when the wind was abeam. In fact it operated best with strong arms at the paddles. The Indians depended for success and security on speed developed by oarsmen and by their leader's knowledge of shoals and hideaways. Until exhaustion set in, a well-manned canoe could do 7½ knots and keep pace with one of Her Majesty's paddle-wheel sloops-of-war. A canoe could outpull a frigate or sloop without steam power and could steal away to safety under cover of darkness, fog, or mist. Canoe voyages a great distance from land were seldom undertaken, although the Nootka, for instance, would undertake whaling expeditions in the open Pacific lasting two or three days. Indians of the outer coast, including the Haida, may well have had their own form of celestial navigation.

Yet the canoe with its soaring and sculptured prow formed only one distinctive feature of North Pacific Coast native culture. Craftsmen built rectangular, planked houses and made boxes, weapons, fishing and hunting implements, and ritualistic items such as dance rattles and masks. The "totem pole" is an outstanding example of native artistry: memorial poles placed before a village, house portal poles, mortuary posts, and interior house beams and posts were carved in commemorative themes to represent traditional beings and incidents of importance to family or tribe. And in weapons manufacture, coiled weaving, and salmon weir construction, this culture evidenced ingenuity, hard work, economy, and adaptability.

The society's organization, economy, and art were linked to its systems of belief. The Northwest Coast Indians had a pantheon of beings of the sky, the sun, the shore, and the sea. Some, such as the salmon and whale, conferred benefits. Others, such as sea monsters and the thunderbird, symbolized mastery of the natural world. These supernatural creatures provided the basis for titles, names, crests, songs, dances, legends, and displays. Pride and distinction among societal groups, as shown by material wealth and art forms, were thus related to otherworldly activities. Even the shaman or priest-doctor, in his role as intercessor with supernatural powers, reflected the success and pride of his people.

Along the entire coast the village constituted the autonomous political entity. Unions of such local groupings into larger political units are known in the historical record. However, the names "Haida," "Tlingit" and "Tsimshian" refer to speech communities within which inter-village rivalries and warfare were common well into the 1860's. Thus, in contrast to the Cheyenne or the Crow of the Great Plains, the "tribe" as a unified and self-conscious entity did not exist. The main Indian political organization was the village, numerous in number and various in description, details of which will be provided at the appropriate place in this narrative.

Within and between villages, kinship provided the basis for identity. In the northern area, among the Haida, Tlingit and Tsimshian principally, the kinship group or lineage which might occupy one or more houses within the village, was based upon matrilineal descent. One shared membership in it with one's siblings, mother, her siblings, her sister's children, her mother and so on. In turn the lineage was linked to a larger group, a "clan": two such in the case of the Tlingit (Raven and Wolf), two for the Haida (Raven and Eagle), and four for the Tsimshian (Eagle, Wolf, Fireweed and Frog). The lineage and clan were both possessors of material and symbolic property: rights in fishing, berrying and hunting areas, names, heraldic crest designs, stories, dances and songs. Normally the scion of the principal lineage of a village was its chief. On the basis of locality and dialect, villages sometimes recognized a wider field of identification. For the Tsimshian, for example, there were fourteen or fifteen "tribes" or regional clusters. Like the larger linguistic groupings, these tribes were not political structures.

To the south, on Vancouver Island and the adjacent continental shore, the matrilineal pattern of inheritance and group memberships gave way to a bilateral system in which kin were reckoned on both sides of the family. Thus the Kwakiutl "numaym" resembled a kindred comprising its leader, normally male, possibly his younger siblings and their families, his sons and daughters and, ideally, their spouses and children. The numaym came in time to be identified with a village and constituted the core of the community. Lesser families might attach themselves to the settlement through time. But its name identified it with the founding kindred. In contrast to the northern unilineal kin groups, then, those of such people as the Southern Kwakiutl, Nootka and Coastal Salish were as large and influential as the wealth, leadership, and charisma of the senior kinsmen could make them, growing as they did at the expense of other similar groups of kinsmen who, in the case of the Lemalchi Salish, became outlaws to Indian and white alike.

In other words, though an Indian group might share the language and culture of its neighbour, there was not necessarily a larger political relationship between the two. They held no common interest or unity. To say that the Tsimshian, Tlingit or Haida formed among themselves a basic political or warlike grouping belies the fact that they were internally divided by their economic occupations, political perceptions, territorial divisions, and age-old rivalries. The Tlingit, for instance, consisted of fourteen territorial divisions or loosely related tribes. The possibility of their mounting an armed opposition to the white man was unlikely. Most British, Russians, and Americans, however, did not know this in the 1850's, and, hence, they continually expected a great rising by the northern Indians, that is by the Tsimshian, Tlingit, and Haida, whom European observers customarily classified as the most "warlike" on the coast.

European fears were intensified because they never knew how many Indians they actually faced. They knew there were thousands, but not how many thousands. In 1835, by one recent estimate, there were perhaps 70,000 Indians in the area now called British Columbia. Of these, there were an estimated 13,500 Interior Salish, 1,000 Kootenay, and 8,800 Athapaskan. On the coast, there were about 47,000 Indians. The Straits and Coast Salish, Halkomelem or Cowichan, Squamish, Sechelt, Pentlatch, and Comox linguistic subdivisions numbered approximately 12,000 and lived adjacent to the broad fish-hook shaped waters formed by Juan de Fuca and Georgia straits. At the south end of Quadra Island, where the Inland Passage narrows, the great Kwakiutl area of some 10,700 began. It stretched north and west along both shores of Johnstone Strait and Queen Charlotte Strait and thence to the open Pacific. On the continental mainland, the Kwakiutl lived as far north as the mouth of the Skeena River. Their linguistic subdivisions, the Haisla, Heiltsuk, and Southern Kwakiutl, controlled this vast, indented coastline except for the inner reaches of Dean and Burke Channels where 2,000 Bella Coola lived. Across hazardous Hecate Strait lay the Queen Charlotte Islands, home of the Haida. Divided into two dialects, Masset and Skidegate, the Haida counted perhaps 6,000 in 1835. A smaller number lived on the southwestern corner of the Alaska panhandle. Though small in number by comparison to rival tribes, the Haida were the corsairs of these northern waters. Between Portland Inlet and the northernmost Kwakiutl at Milbanke Sound, the Tsimshian were situated. Numbering 8,500, they consisted of three linguistic subdivisions, the Tsimshian, Gitksan, and Nishga. On the western coast of Vancouver Island were the Nootka, 7,500 strong, and divided by speech forms into northern and southern groups.

This rough estimate of 47,000 coastal Indians seems not at all large by present population figures for British Columbia or for that matter any other part of North America. However, 40 per cent of Canada's Indians then lived within the borders of British Columbia. Moreover, at the time of Columbus's first arrival in 1492, in all of North America north and Mexico, 30 per cent of the two million Indians lived on the Pacific coast on 6 per cent of the continent's land area.[1] Except perhaps for California, the place of greatest Indian population density in North America was the Northwest Coast. And it was here that a foreign society was making a gradual but brutal impact on a culture which in its very complexity made it sadly ill-adapted to withstand a European invasion.

This other way of life invading the Northwest Coast was also maritime, but it was of the deep water variety, capable of sustaining voyages of great distance and danger. By the late eighteenth century, revolutions in agriculture and industry in Britain had produced an expansive society capable of worldwide influence. Through trade and wars, through inventions and devices, by the time Captain James Cook of the Royal Navy called at Nootka Sound in 1778, Great Britain ranked as the pre-eminent power in Europe. No nation, foreign or native, could easily withstand its pervasive influence.

Captain Cook's ships *Resolution* and *Discovery* of the Royal Navy, which stayed for a month within the sheltering, protective confines of Nootka Sound, were symbols of this mastery of wind and gunpowder. Small by comparison to the ships-of-the-line which were to bring Lord Nelson and the British fleet such success and glory at Trafalgar twenty-seven years later, these men-of-war were still far superior in every way, except in mobility in inshore waters, to any seaborne vessel the Northwest Coast Indians possessed. Of 462 and 298 tons burthen respectively, the *Resolution* and *Discovery* could undertake long and hazardous voyages. Neither ship was heavily armed. But their 4-pounders, swivel guns, and musketoons made them superior in gun power to the martial capability of any aboriginal people they were likely to meet during their passage. They actually mounted gun power in excess, making it easier for them to have a psychological impact on various Pacific peoples during their voyage by firing the guns. They also carried fireworks, especially flares and exploding projectiles, calculated to produce awe or, as need dictated, wreak havoc among indigenous peoples.

British warships frequently carried gifts for the purpose of winning friendship and reducing tensions on various maritime frontiers in the late eighteenth century. "You are to endeavour by all proper means to cultivate a friendship with the Natives," the Lords Commissioners of the Admiralty carefully cautioned James Cook in 1768 preparatory to his first voyage to the Pacific, "presenting them with such trifles as may be acceptable to them, exchanging with them for Provisions (for which there is great Plenty) such of the Merchandize you have been directed to Provide, as they may value, and showing them every kind of Civility and regard." The same applied for Cook's voyage to the Northwest Coast. Their Lordships also told him to distribute gifts which would remain as "traces and testimonies of you having been there."[2]

Thus in 1778 the Indians were already being manipulated in a contest for empire between the British and Spanish and subsequently the Russians and the Americans. The natives could not shield themselves against this new and penetrating materialism. As a shrewd observer of trade and empire, Adam Smith had rightly written only two years before, "in ancient times the opulent and civilized found it difficult to defend themselves against the poor and barbarous nations; in modern times the poor and barbarous find it difficult to defend themselves against the

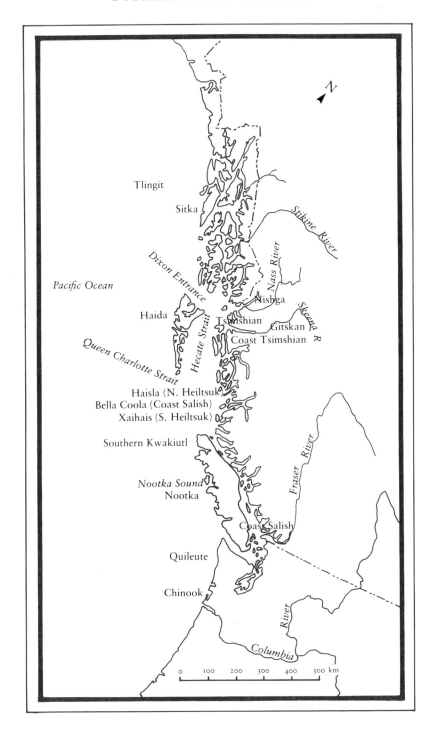

N

Tlingit

Sitka

Stikine River

Dixon Entrance

Nass River

Pacific Ocean

Haida

Nishga

Tsimshian

Gitskan

Skeena R

Coast Tsimshian

Hecate Strait

Queen Charlotte Strait

Haisla (N. Heiltsuk)
Bella Coola (Coast Salish)
Xaihais (S. Heiltsuk)

Southern Kwakiutl

Fraser River

Nootka Sound
Nootka

Coast Salish

Quileute

Chinook

River

Columbia

0   100   200   300   400   500 km

opulent and civilized." In brief, industrial Europe possessed the means to subjugate a non-industrial society.

Later, as the nineteenth century progressed, the industrial revolution changed British naval power and made it more effective in inshore waters. Sail gave way to steam, and England's "wooden walls" yielded to iron and steel ships. On the Northwest Coast, steam added leverage to the growing British influence. As early as 1846 H.M.S. *Cormorant,* a paddle-wheel gunboat mounting six 32-pound guns, navigated the inland waters from Fort Victoria to Seymour Narrows in a fraction of the time it would have taken a sloop without steam. The steamers *Driver, Virago,* and *Devastation,* all of the same class as the *Cormorant,* proved effective gunboats in inshore waters. However, in the late 1840's and early 1850's, owing to the grinding parsimony of the Treasury and the reluctance of the Lords of the Admiralty, most ships in the British fleet did not have steam power. Thus, sloops or corvettes such as the *Daedalus, Daphne,* and *Trincomalee* lacked mobility in the intricate and still largely uncharted inland waters, and often they relied on Hudson's Bay Company steamers *Beaver* and *Otter* to tow them or their boats to scenes of action. Frequently they had to anchor a good distance from an Indian village and send boat parties ashore in the ship's gig, pinnace, or steam launch. To terrorize natives and burn villages the British found rockets which could be fired from these boats particularly handy. Most of Her Majesty's ships carried well-drilled Royal Marines who were sent ashore with sailors for limited periods. They were always well equipped with rifles and small arms. Sometimes they took howitzers and other field pieces when terrain, vegetation, and weather permitted.

The steady rise of industrialization and the need for fast gunboats capable of manoeuvering in shallow, protected waters during the Crimean War, 1854–56, affected white-Indian maritime encounters on the Northwest Coast. The wooden gunboats *Forward* and *Grappler*—whose very names signified advance and aggression—represented this new machine age. Costing £10,000 each, they were built to fight the Russians. But with the war over, in early 1859 they were fitted for service in British Columbia to counter Indian "threats" and American aggrandizement. They measured 106 feet in length and had a draft (when barnacles and seaweed did not increase it) of six feet six inches. They had reciprocating engines of sixty nominal horsepower (206 – 233 h.p. actually developed) driving screw propellers which gave a service speed of 7½ knots. They used coal, sometimes dug by Indian labour on Vancouver Island. But they also had a combination fore-and-aft and square rig which gave them adequate speed under sail. They were designed to carry a 68-pound gun on the forecastle, a 32-pound gun aft, and two 24-pound howitzers or "smashers" amidships.[3] They had an economical complement of thirty-six to forty officers and ratings. In all, these gunboats constituted a cheap and effective show of power.

These two highly mobile vessels, like so many others, were subtle symbols of the British imperial presence in distant seas. For a full century after the Battle of Trafalgar in 1805 Britain stood almost without rival in both her merchant marine and her naval power. Recognizing the various police actions necessary to protect the nation's interests on and over the seas when no European or American rival threatened, the British fleet concentrated less and less on the ship-of-the-line and more and more on small, economical, steam-driven warships. "Send a gunboat!" became an automatic response for London when circumstances required.

The Northwest Coast from the 1850's was one place where the government was convinced such action was necessary. Gunboats were very useful in the inland waters of British Columbia. By 1868, when the boilers of the *Forward* and *Grappler* were beyond repair, the ships were sold and replaced with the two gunvessels *Boxer* and *Rocket*, whose mobility, speed, and gunpower were superior to the gunboats. Later, H.M.S. *Sparrowhawk, Myrmidon, Ringdove, Pheasant,* and others would take their turns on "Indian patrol." These were not the only ships in Her Majesty's fleet to be used on the coast against the Indians. Heavily gunned steam corvettes such as the *Clio* and even more powerful steam frigates such as the *Sutlej* undertook "gunboat actions" on the coast in the 1860's.[4] But because of their availability, size and mobility, gunboats and gunvessels were the warships most commonly seen in the waters adjacent to native villages and encampments. Their psychological impact on Indians was sometimes, but not always, immense. They became the long arm of both imperial and colonial governments in extending the *laissez-faire* principles of the Victorian age. Through their auspices, trade was protected, seas were surveyed, settlement and the rule of law were extended, missions were undertaken, and, above all, the colonies of Vancouver Island and British Columbia (founded in 1849 and 1858 respectively and united in 1866) were made secure.

The customary technique of the gunboat commander involved the use of force as the last resort. He would take his ship into a position where its guns could be used to greatest effect. As a preliminary show of power he might fire his guns or shoot his rockets at a chosen target. In the 1880's he might even show his new searchlights at night. He would parley with the natives. He might flog offenders for petty crimes such as pilfering. He might seize property such as canoes, thereby sealing off avenues of escape. He might take chiefs as hostages. He might employ interpreters and send them with police to shore. He might hire native informants. But, if after a process of escalating pressure was employed without effect, the ultimate arbiter, force, would then be used. This might involve destroying villages, salmon weirs, and canoes and killing inhabitants if any remained in the village. If caught and tried, the guilty would be hanged before the assembled tribe. But in many cases, the smouldering ruins of a village and a scattered village tribe were the telling testaments of the process of keeping Northwest Coast Indians "in awe of British power."

The process of forceful intervention by gunboats came only with colonization. In the late eighteenth and early nineteenth centuries the British were less concerned with dominion than with trade. Private investors and East India Company interests were eager to create a network of commercial alliances in eastern seas and the Pacific; and the Northwest Coast of North America constituted one zone of influence regarded by British policy makers and the leading mercantilist spirits as worthy of government support. British success in the Nootka Sound crisis of 1790 revealed the government's determination to back their pretensions with naval support. In short, London acquired rights of trade at Nootka Sound, a preserve previously claimed exclusively by the Spanish crown. However, an empire of settlement was still a far-distant thought for the English.

At this time of initial European contact with the Northwest Coast Indians, both Europeans and Indians had materials which the other wanted. The British had iron and copper, porcelain and cloth. The Indians had furs, especially the sea otter, for which Cook's crew, anticipating a bountiful market in Japan, Kamchatka, or Canton, traded their possessions—coats, shirts, and even spare buttons. The Nootka had a high sense of ownership of their resources. They objected to the British taking wood and water from the shore without payment. So tenacious were they in this regard that Cook recorded in his journal on 22 April 1778 that never before had he met indigenous peoples "who have such high notions of everything the Country produced being their exclusive property as these."[5]

This did not mean, however, that the Nootka always respected the visitors' property, which they would have regarded as communal. Cook and his men were constantly on the alert against Indian thefts. "We had the company of the natives all day," he wrote on 31 March, "who now laid aside all manner of restraint, if ever they had any, and came on board the ships and mixed with our people with the greatest of freedom. And we soon found that they were as light fingered as any people we had before met with, and were far more dangerous for with their knives and other cut[ting] instruments of iron, they could cut a hook from a tackle or any other piece of iron from a rope, the instant our backs was turned." Cook noted that if the British missed an object just after it was stolen, it could be retrieved: "we found no difficulty in finding out the thief, as they were ready enough to impeach one another, but the thief generally relinquished his prize with reluctancy and sometimes not without force."[6]

In the trading process that began in earnest with the arrival of James Hanna from China in 1785, violence between whites and Indians was frequent.[7] Other traders or observers—James Strange, George Dixon, John Meares, John Bartlett, and Joseph Ingraham, to name a few—record attempts by Indians on various parts of the coast to seize vessels, steal cargo and equipment, or murder Europeans.[8] As William Sturgis, a prominent American trader, put it, the fault was owing to "the lawless and brutal violence of the white man; and it would be easy to show that these fatal disasters might have been averted by a different treatment of the natives and by prudence and proper precaution on the part of their civilized visitors."[9]

In the late eighteenth and early nineteenth centuries individual traders, whether British, American, French, Russian or Spanish, did not have a vested interest in long-range relations with the Nootka or other tribes. Their concern was trade not dominion. They took from the Indians as they could. They introduced liquor and firearms. They did not remain to see the consequences of their work. Some, who would return frequently, might have been of a different mind; to them goodwill between buyer and seller must have been important. Regrettably, they were the exception rather than the rule.

British government policy, however, possessed a different character. Cook's instructions demanded that he be conciliatory and friendly. This same attitude is seen in Captain George Vancouver's orders of 1791. "In the execution of every part of this Service," the Lords of the Admiralty advised, "it is very material that the Commanding Officer should be instructed to use every possible care to avoid disputes with the Natives of any of the Parts where he may touch, and that he should be particularly attentive to endeavour, by Presents and by all other means, to conciliate their friendship and confidence."[10]

During his survey of the Northwest Coast, Vancouver acted with care, for he knew that beneath the fragile facade of goodwill lay racial hatreds that might quickly rise into an incident of serious proportions. He also knew that unscrupulous traders such as the Yankee pedlar John Kendrick were ready to cheat the Indians in trade and provoke their wrath, and he realized that Maquinna of the Nootka, Wicanninnish of the Clayoquot, and other chiefs were rivals. In these potentially volatile circumstances he instructed his officers to take every precaution. Boats leaving his ships, the *Discovery* and *Chatham,* to survey, reconnoitre, or provision were always to be ready for defence. When landing parties went on shore (which they were not to do in the face of large numbers), sentinels were to guard against surprise from the natives and to prevent inquisitive British sailors from straying into the habitations where misunderstandings and disputes might lead to violence. Dependent on Indian goodwill for wood, water, and food, and keeping in mind the British government's

long-range objective of securing accord with the natives, George Vancouver took no chances. In 1794 he remarked that he had been sent none
too soon to accomplish the arduous and hazardous task of surveying the
northern coast: the conduct of some individual maritime fur traders had
so increased the animosity of the Indians that in another year he believed
he would not have had the force on board his ships to repel their
attacks.[11]

By the early years of the nineteenth-century feelings of mutual suspicion and insecurity were well entrenched. They did not bode well for the
future. Accordingly, American traders warned ship's owners not cruise
on that coast without a large complement, swivel guns, and small arms.
The Hudson's Bay Company added thirteen Hawaiians to the crew of the
William & Anne in 1825 in order to make her "perfectly secure" in those
dangerous waters. When the company trader William Fraser Tolmie
planned to sail in a company schooner to Milbanke Sound in 1833, he
noted in his diary that though the voyage would be enjoyable the ship's
crew would be "constantly armed to the teeth."[12] Judge Howay wrote of
the 1820's:

> For years the maritime traders had sown the dragon's teeth, for
> trifling offences, for theft, for failure to aid them in recovering their
> property, for failure to trade with them, they had ruthlessly turned
> their guns upon the Indians and killed them, taken and held their
> chiefs for ransom, taken and destroyed their property. Now the crop
> was appearing. The whole trade was impregnated with mutual dis-
> trust. The Indian, equipped with the deadly weapons of the white
> man, was ready to return force with force. He was ready, too, to
> take revenge for earlier wrongs.[13]

The Northwest Coast of North America, which had been raised from
relative obscurity to prominence in the diplomatic cases of European
plenipotentiaries during the Nootka Sound dispute, was for all intents
and purposes an area in which the first wave of exploitation from
overseas had come and gone.[14] Now the era of the continental fur trade
would advance one step further and British trade ascendancy be established on the coast first by the Montreal-based North West Company
and, after 1821, by the Gentlemen Adventurers of England trading into
Hudson's Bay. For the natives, both "Boston men" and "King George
men" were part of their expanding world. Through the long Victorian
era, some Indians maintained a preference for "King George men,"
perhaps because of the forbearance of Captains Cook and Vancouver.[15]

For a generation the Hudson's Bay Company held sway on the Northwest Coast, keeping Russian rivals at a distance in southeastern Alaska
and out-trading American trappers on Old Oregon's southern frontiers.

Their general Indian policy of fair but firm dealings had the Colonial Office's tacit support in an era when cries were coming from certain public quarters that aboriginal interests were or might be threatened by the growth of white settlement and trade. London sought to avoid a repetition of the violent American frontier experience and trusted to the good sense of the Bay traders, all the while keeping a close watch on any affairs of Rupert's Land and Oregon that might come to the public's attention. The Company's territories were really an empire within an empire. The cases of gunboat diplomacy used by company ships on the Northwest Coast to retaliate against the Clallum in 1828 by shelling their village, to punish the Clatsop near the mouth of the Columbia River in the following year in a similar way, or to threaten the northern Indians by using the "white man's fire canoe," the company steamer and veritable gunboat *Beaver* [16] went unnoticed by humanitarian groups such as the Aborigines' Protection Society, a powerful lobby for native interests in Britain. On the other hand, questions were asked of the Company at the time Vancouver Island became a colony in 1849, when a select British Parliamentary inquiry into the affairs of the Hudson's Bay Company was held in 1857, and when British Columbia came into existence as a colony in 1858.

The British were activated by prospects of trade and of strategic gain. But a desire to eradicate slavery and slave-taking, piracy, murder, theft, cannibalism, and intertribal warfare also formed a strong current in British imperial motivation, and these objectives, each of them rivulets, swelled into the larger stream of law and order.

It was an understood tenet of the British that one of the primary functions of government was to provide a system of law and order to prevent anarchy, chaos and violence among the people of that territorial jurisdiction. Progress could not occur without order. And to enforce law the state must have authority to exercise judicial influence—through courts, magistrates, justices of the peace, sheriffs, and constables.

Nineteenth-century Britons saw it as their mission to extend their authority to the "savage" and the "uncivilized."[17] British imperial administrators, whether in Whitehall or the wilderness, were married to the concept of law and order or, to use the time-honored phrase, "peace, order and good government." The 1837 House of Commons Committee on Aborigines considered it a national duty "to carry civilization and humanity, peace and good government, and, above all the knowledge of the true God, to the uttermost ends of the earth." This somewhat superior and righteous viewpoint nonetheless expresses a strong strain of thinking held by some colonial administrators of the Victorian age. One such, the secretary of state for war and the colonies, the third Earl Grey, argued in 1852 that the extermination of less civilized peoples could be averted by the "enforcement of order." Rather than letting natives be destroyed, the imperial mission of civilization and Christianity, he said, was "a high and noble object well worthy of considerable sacrifice on the part of the British people."[18]

If the British voiced a disdain of lawlessness among the "uncivilized" they also knew that whites on distant, unorganized frontiers would act in lawless ways. Traders, whalers, gold seekers, settlers, missionaries, sailors, and others, were pressing outwards from the home islands to distant frontiers. The acquisitive habits of these persons on the borderlands of civilization, a colonial secretary wrote in 1837, "compelled the strong to encroach on the weak, and the powerful and unprincipled to wrest by force or fraud, from the comparatively feeble and defenceless, wealth or property or dominion, richer pastures, more numerous herds, and a wider range of territory."[19] In these circumstances, the British attempted to prevent turbulence on their frontiers—to control indiscriminate, lawless behaviour by whites against one another and against natives.

Faced with the tricky dilemma of letting those persons police themselves or of intervening through means of authority, both civil and military, invariably the British chose to intervene. "If colonists of European descent," Earl Grey argued in 1852, "are to be left, unsupported by the power of the mother country, to rely solely on themselves for protection from fierce barbarians with whom they are placed in immediate contact, they must also be left to the unchecked exercise of those severe measures of self-defence which a position of so much danger will naturally dictate. Experience shows that in such circumstances measures of self-defence will degenerate into indiscriminate vengeance, and will lead to the gradual extermination of the less civilized race."[20] Thus the extension of law and order was inseparable from native trusteeship. And frequently it led to an extension, despite contrary pressures, of territorial jurisdiction.

In these circumstances London had to concern itself with the welfare of the Northwest Coast Indians. Some critics urged the suspension of the Company's monopoly of trade. Others, however, apprehensively viewed the unrestricted admission of the "free trader" on the western frontier. They anticipated the possibility of the free traders introducing liquor in an indiscriminate fashion. This would mean the disruption of the Indian economy and lifestyle. Land speculators, lawyers, newspapermen, and others would be the vanguard of cultural genocide. They wondered how the free trader would uphold the principles of Christianity. Might not the horrors of the American experience be repeated? To investigate these questions, in 1857 parliament struck a Select Committee "to consider the State of those British Possessions in North America which are under the Administration of the Hudson's Bay Company, or over which they possess a Licence to Trade." The Company's position, as reported in the committee's 550 pages of evidence, was defended as honourable. The hearings cleared the Company of charges of inhumanity in its dealings with the Indians, or rather said these charges could not be proved. This view coincided with the opinion of the colonial secretary, Henry Labouchere, who told company officers that the unique nature of the trading relationships supplied reason enough why monopoly ought not give way before public pressures for free trade.[21]

At the same time, there were champions of the cause that British colonists had rights of determining native policies in their own locales. Increasingly during the mid-Victorian era, the Colonial Office had to acknowledge that colonial self-government meant an end to London's paternalism. Nonetheless, the growing trend towards colonial self-management in Indian affairs did not take root in Vancouver Island or British Columbia. A meagre settlement threatened by American incursions from without, whether real or imaginary, and by Indian disorders from within could not fully shape its own native policy. The stamp and legacies of Hudson's Bay Company *imperium,* the paternalistic action of successive colonial governors on the spot, the very nature of the maritime environment on the Pacific coast, and, perhaps most, the absence of a large white population demanding self-government—all these meant that government action was not to be determined by settlers but by the governor and whatever naval or military assistance lay at his disposal. Of necessity, native policy was forged mainly "on the spot."[22]

British Columbia was only one area of Queen Victoria's Empire which suffered from racial conflict. Empires are based on power. Consequently Victoria's was frequently "at war"—on an estimated 230 occasions during her sixty-four year reign.[23] The *Pax Britannica* constituted a unique system of global dominance. But strangely this peace of empire was maintained only by "Queen Victoria's Little Wars." Peace paradoxically meant war, as the high-minded Lord Glenelg, the colonial secretary, noted in 1838. "The great principles of morality are of immutable and universal obligation, and from them are deduced the laws of war," he wrote with sadness. "Whether we contend with a civilized or barbarous enemy, the gratuitous aggravation of the horrors of war on the plea of vengeance or retribution, or on any similar grounds, is alike indefensible."[24]

Nonetheless, practice frequently departed from principle, for by the very character of empire, the "gratuitous aggravations" of which Glenelg complained were unavoidable on the frontiers of empire. The Maori in New Zealand, the Aborigines in Australia, the Bantu in southern Africa, and the Ashanti on the Gold Coast, to name but a few, were the subject of British concern and of British guns. The Indians of the Northwest Coast were no exception to the prevailing imperial process. Queen Victoria's Little War on the British Columbia coast, which like the others was never officially declared, extended over three decades and more. Establishing the *Pax Britannica* took time, and it took gunboats.

2

Tide of Empire

THE PENETRATION of white settlement into Oregon in the 1840's
foreshadowed the demise of the Indian people's control over the
land which they had occupied and used at least from the historic period if
not from "time immemorial." It marked the rising tide of new political,
economic, and social régimes with which the Indians would have to deal.
London and Washington, the metropolitan centres of two great empires,
agreed to divide Oregon in 1846. In this territorial division the British
desire for trade and navigation on Vancouver Island and its adjacent
mainland north of the 49° north latitude had prevailed. Corres-
pondingly, the United States' desire for lands for settlement in the Columbia, Cowlitz, and Willamette valleys and for ports on Puget Sound
had been successful. The so-called Oregon "compromise" was just that
for Britain and the United States. For the Northwest Coast Indians, by
contrast, it was no compromise; it constituted a takeover of territory
they had long occupied and exploited in their own ways.

On Vancouver Island the signs of occupation had already begun to appear. In March 1843, James Douglas, a "Scotch West Indian" in the Hudson's Bay Company's employ, landed from the *Beaver* at Clover Point,
near the Island's southernmost tip. This thirty-nine-year-old trader was
no ordinary man, and he rose to become governor of Vancouver Island
and British Columbia. His background was unusual "even for that time
and place," a British admiral recalled after his visit to Vancouver Island
in the early 1850's. He continued:

Here indeed was a *man*, middle aged, tall, and well-knit, with keen features, alert and kindly. I recognized the type that has broken out of our island-home in all centuries to colonize and civilise—the born pioneer. His influence over the surrounding tribes was unbounded, and the more so because of his perfect acquaintance with their dialects, and the fact that his wife was herself an Indian princess, and his saviour from death at the hands of her people. Here lay his romance.[1]

Many other observers and his superiors in the Hudson's Bay Company held similar views of him. From the 1830's he had been marked for steady advancement in company service. Sir George Simpson, the governor of company affairs of North America, thought him "well qualified for any Service requiring bodily exertion, firmness of mind and the exercise of sound judgement, but furiously violent when roused"—a compliment from so acerbic a judge of men. Douglas's skills and outlook had ample room for exercise on Vancouver Island. The colony's course of development under company auspices and crown control was very much shaped by his hand and by his opinions about Americans, whom he thought of as dangerous, about Indians, whom he believed would retaliate, and about the Crown, which he lauded and magnified in this remote quarter of the queen's North American dominions. The pioneer gentlewoman Susan Allison gave the following astute assessment of this uncommonly remarkable man: "The Governor himself was a genuine Douglas, kindly and urbane in manner—'A glove of velvet on a hand of steel'—one of the wisest and best Governors we ever had, if he was arbitrary."[2]

Douglas came to North America in 1819 in the employ of the North West Company. But in 1826, five years after that company's merger with the Hudson's Bay traders, he had gone west to Fort St. James, some one hundred miles from the present day Prince George, where he served as assistant to William Connolly, the chief factor. Connolly's daughter, Amelia, was half Cree, and Douglas took her as his wife "according to the custom of the country." In 1828 her timely intervention prevented his murder at the hands of the local Carrier, who were incensed by Douglas's tough-minded killing of one of their kind, a murderer at Fort George. By the time he arrived on Vancouver Island in 1843 he had been living with, or in close proximity to, Indians for a quarter-century. Many company servants and close associates had married Indians, a fact which a visitor to the Island in 1845 said preserved the peace between the races.[3] Douglas was hardly a racist, but as the trusted servant of first the Hudson's Bay Company and then the British Crown, he symbolized the steady thrust of the new *imperium* in British Columbia.

Douglas's founding of Fort Victoria formed a distinct stage in this imperial process. He decided to erect a post on a snug, safe, and accessible harbour called by the Indians "Camosun" or "Camosack," a name probably derived from the tidal rush of water at the harbour's headwaters or "The Gorge." Guarded by nature, yet virtually adjacent to the open Pacific which lay westwards down the mountain-fringed Strait of Juan de Fuca some dozen miles, the place afforded a near perfect location for a company sea depot on the Northwest Coast. Fort Vancouver, upstream on the hazardous Columbia River, had proven to be a dangerous base for the Company's "Naval Department." Ships without steam could be detained for weeks off the inhospitable coast, lying in wait for the brief, favourable opportunity to cross the notorious Columbia bar. Then, too, the Company's northern trade had become more efficient with the introduction of steam navigation. The company steamer *Beaver* could service the Company's posts without large shore establishments being maintained. This floating general store and receiving depot made it possible for the Company to close Fort McLoughlin on Milbanke Sound, Fort Durham on Taku Inlet, and the posts on the Stikine River in 1843 and 1844. The *Beaver* now became the material link between Fort Victoria and the Indian trappers and consumers along the seven or eight hundred miles of the Northwest Coast including southeastern Alaska. Fort Simpson, founded in 1834 near the mouth of Portland Canal, remained the sole maritime trading post of any consequence north of Vancouver Island.

There were other reasons why Fort Victoria seemed essential to the growth of British interests. The Island's southern tip, which appeared to Douglas a perfect Eden because of its luxuriant vegetation, rich soil, and lack of mosquitoes, had lands highly suitable for tillage and pasture, and these could be made productive without costly clearing. The Puget's Sound Agricultural Company, a subsidiary of the Hudson's Bay Company, established large farms to serve settlers, traders, and sailors. Nearby, at the Gorge, water power was harnessed for milling flour and sawing lumber. And, as Douglas foresaw, by virtue of its situation and accessibility, the protected harbour eventually became "a centre of operation, either to ourselves or to others who may be attracted thither, by the valuable timber and the exhaustless fisheries of that inland sea."[4] In short, Fort Victoria promised to serve all the needs of the Company for a depot and agricultural base for its Pacific and coastal trade.

However, the place had to be made secure from potential Indian attack. Simpson, who knew native mores and had visited the place in 1841, believed that a "very large population of daring, fierce and treacherous Indians" inhabited the southern shore of Vancouver Island. Thus, when constructed, this wilderness Gibraltar would require a "heavy establishment" of forty or fifty men for its protection. He believed that in time the *Beaver*, "whose powers and ubiquity have done more... to tame those daring hordes, than all other means to that end that have ever been brought into action by whites," would enable the Company to reduce its manpower at the fort. Contrary to Simpson's expectations, the local Songhees Indians offered no resistance to Douglas and the Company—at least at first. In fact, as Douglas's journal records, they offered all sorts of goodwill and services. When he spoke to the Songhees and informed them of his intention of building a fort there, it evidently pleased them very much. They immediately offered their services in procuring pickets for the establishment.[5]

The original fort, which gave the Company adequate protection on all four sides, consisted of a quadrangle measuring 330 feet by 300 feet formed by an 18-foot timber picket stockade. On the southwest corner, a strong, three-storey octagonal bastion, mounting on two levels six or eight small-bore cannon, commanded the harbour to the west and the agricultural plain to the north and east. In 1847 the fort was enlarged to the north, and a second bastion was erected at the northeast corner. Thirteen neat buildings, most with shaked, pavilion roofs, lay guarded within its protected confines—officers quarters, barracks, stores, warehouses, blacksmith's shop, dining hall, cook-house, chapel, and belfry. But the fort had no regular supply of water, especially in summer, and lacked a powder magazine of any size. Lieutenants Henry J. Warre and Mervin Vavasour, on a secret British military reconnaissance to enquire into the defensive capabilities of the Oregon country in 1845, noted that its six warehouses and two barracks were musketproof and that 300 men could be quartered in the enclosure, but they were not convinced that the fort could withstand a major assault by a disciplined force. Yet they were prepared to say that the place could make a good defence against "an irregular or Indian force." Another visitor there in the mid-1840's thought that these guns made an "attack by savages" to be "out of the question; and if defended with spirit, a disciplined force without artillery would find considerable difficulty in forcing the defences."[6]

No sooner had Douglas's charges completed the building of this outpost of empire than a migration of Lekwungen or, more commonly, Songhees, occurred. This Straits Salish group, which in 1843 was really a cluster of eleven autonomous households, lived at various locations along the coastal crescent from Beecher Bay near Sooke to Cadboro Bay, ten miles by sea from Victoria Harbour. At Cadboro Bay, the largest of their winter villages, they had a small fortress, fringed by stakes, which evidently gave them sufficient protection from warring northern tribes. In certain seasons, during the big fish runs, almost all of the Songhees crossed Haro Strait by canoe to the San Juan Islands where they took salmon in abundance in their reef-nets.

However, the economy and entertainment of the new post at Camosun drew them like a magnet and gave them trade advantages and prestige over rival tribes. Liquor, trinkets, utensils, blankets, cloths, arms, and ammunition were some of the tempting items for sale at Camosun. Most important, the Company needed and was willing to pay for Indian labour to build the fort and the town that was growing outside of its walls. The Songhees chose to build their long, low lodges in the most convenient spot: on the same side of the harbour adjacent to the fort. However, in this location the Songhees, who in the mid 1840's were known collectively as the Swinhon, posed a security problem for the Company. Lieutenant Warre thought the Company lax in controlling the Indians: "The apathy of the Gentleman in charge of the H.B. Cos Posts, in allowing these wild savages to remain so near their Fort is extraordinary whether on account of cleanliness, healthyness or the more alarming danger of fire."[7] Indeed, when a fire broke out in the oak woods near the Indian lodges, the Company had trouble extinguishing it. Roderick Finlayson, in charge of the post, wanted the Songhees to move across the harbour, but they refused. After some "angry parleying," they agreed to do so—on condition that the company men help them.

This relocation, this crossing of the water some four hundred yards distant to Songhees Point, signified the first placement of British Columbia Indians on a reserve. No treaty marked the event, but the Company's intent was clear; at a distance from the post the Indians would be less dangerous. And in the process of relocation, Songhees' mobility and life-styles—already significantly changed through their attraction to Camosun and their growing reliance on the Company's economy—were further transformed.

The Songhees were not the only Indians with whom the Company interacted. Others came from nearby islands such as Whidbey in lower Puget Sound. On one occasion these Indians traded at Fort Victoria and were returning home when they were set upon by the Songhees near Beacon Hill, where they had left their canoes for the short trek to the fort. Robbed of all their possessions and molested by the Songhees, they retreated to the fort's protection and were there befriended by Finlayson. The chief trader summoned the chief of the tribe responsible, explained the Company's free trade policy among the Indians, obtained the stolen goods, and dispatched a canoe and four company servants to convoy the Whidbeys to the safety of their island home.

It would be a mistake to suggest that hereafter such tribes could trade with confidence. Vigilance on the Company's part and a display of naval power were required to afford security to both sides of the trading relationship.[8] "As a general rule, they are cunning in the extreme," a naval officer described the Indians near Fort Victoria in 1846, "addicted to theft; exceedingly filthy in their habits; and often known to commit the most atrocious murders for the sake of plunder." He took pains to state that these Indians gave whites no cause for complaint. Indeed, they were obliging, cheerful, appreciative of a joke, and willing to work if duly paid. In other words, many of the racial tensions were inter-Indian in character.[9].

Intertribal violence was the cause of the first, and most celebrated, case of "forest diplomacy" at Fort Victoria. Tzouhalem,[10] a fierce warrior chief of the neighbouring Cowichan, tried to mobilize the Songhees for an attack upon the fort when their chief Cheealthluc ("King Freezy")[11] was absent. He ordered the Songhees to kill several oxen and horses belonging to the Company. The Company immediately suspended trade and demanded restitution. The Songhees now called neighbouring allies, including Cowichan and Clallum, for assistance. They advanced on the post and for half an hour fired their muskets at the wooden palisade.

Finlayson restrained his men from firing on the attackers. Instead he called a parley with the Indians. He told them that he "was fully prepared to carry on the battle but did not like to kill them without explaining to them that they were wrong and giving them another chance of making restitution." While the Indians discussed the matter, Finlayson employed a ruse; to show his technological advantage he had the fort's nine-pounder cannon fire grapeshot into a vacant Indian lodge nearby. The cedar structure was "blown to splinters" as was, the next day, an old dugout lying in the harbour. This display of power had immediate results. Finlayson entered into discussions with the Indians, the peace pipe was passed, restitution payment was made in furs, trade resumed to everyone's desire, and they all parted friends, according to the trader. Finlayson told the Songhees chief "that our laws were to protect all Indians, no matter what place they came from, for trade with us."[12] By these "judicious and conciliatory advances" this persevering and intelligent Scot won a considerable degree of respect for himself and the fort and allowed for the speedy re-establishment of trade.[13]

While Finlayson was consolidating the company foothold on Vancouver Island, the Foreign Office was undertaking a diplomatic mission with the United States which ended with the division of Oregon by the Treaty of Washington. This accord had not been reached without crisis and threat of war. The Admiralty, on the advice of the Foreign Office, determined to "show the flag" in the Columbia River and Strait of Juan de Fuca in 1844, 1845, and 1846. Some of the British warships made the first surveys of the Strait of Juan de Fuca and harbours on the southern shore of Vancouver Island. Their objectives were to aid British commerce, report on the nearby Indians,[14] and locate a harbour large and safe enough to hold a few British men-of-war. In time, a commodious harbour three miles west of Victoria called Esquimalt, which in Salish means "a place gradually shoaling," became the haven of Her Majesty's squadron in the Pacific and in 1862 the station headquarters. But in the late 1840's it attracted only the occasional frigate or sloop of war sent north by the commander-in-chief, Pacific, for the purpose of protecting the Company, finding spars or coal, or refreshing officers and men in the healthy climate so surprisingly similar to that of southern England. From the first, officers such as Captain John Duntze of the frigate *Fisgard* had instructions to make it his endeavour to preserve friendly relations with the Indians, Canadians, and all others who frequented the shores of the Northwest Coast.[15]

However, these last days of company rule at Victoria were not without trouble. In August 1848 several Straits Salish tribes, including Clallams and Flatterys, who like the Songhees were attracted to Fort Victoria, camped near the bastion and exchanged rifle shots. The frigate *Constance,* mounting fifty guns, commanded by Captain George Courtenay, which had been sent to investigate the seriousness of Indian aggression in Oregon as reported by company traders Peter Skene Odgen and James Douglas, had conveniently made haven in nearby Esquimalt Harbour, the first British warship to do so.[16] Courtenay heard the shots and saw many Indians paddling towards the fort. A tough, decisive man, he sought to stop a serious incident and "very considerately came over with four armed boats." Some Flattery Indians were "haranguing" the Clallams outside the fort's walls, and the captain, taking no chances, ordered a seven gun salute from the boats, which was answered from the bastion. Then all hands, including some thirty marines, disembarked, promenaded around the fort's front yard, and returned in the boats to the frigate. Next morning, the gunboat diplomacy in Victoria harbour continued when Courtenay landed once again, this time with 250 sailors and marines, with the ship's band playing at their head. For a whole day the naval brigade performed various drills in the fort's yard and in the plain behind, while many Company servants enjoyed a day off, watching the novel spectacle. Finlayson told Courtenay he was "surrounded by treacherous Indians" and that if the captain would be so kind as to land some of his men for exercise in the use of arms a due impression would be made on the Indians. A chief told Courtenay that Indians preferred not to fight in the open but rather from behind trees and rocks, implying the stupidity of the British military tactics. "The Captain was not at all pleased with the savage's reply," Finlayson recorded with amusement. Nonetheless, as Finlayson concluded, "This display of arms from the *Constance* had a good effect on the natives, as they were evidently afraid to pick any quarrels with us for some time afterward."[17]

In fact, this seems to have been a benign display of force. Watercolours and sketches of this event by Lieutenant J. T. Haverfield of the Royal

Marines show that in the course of parading around the prairie near the fort, "for a campaign in the Forests of Vancouver's Island," the sailors in blue tunics and marines in red, both with white trousers and webbing, and a field gun crew were surprised by Indians shooting from woods nearby. This skirmish, which is not confirmed by any written evidence, seems to have passed without incident. In a companion sketch, entitled "Bivouac," Haverfield portrays two peaceful Indian chiefs, one a Clallam called "King George," the other the Songhees chief Cheealthluc ("Freezy"), as well as "Tatlea Uncle to K.G." meeting or perhaps trading on friendly terms with two British officers. Nearby stand a field piece and caisson, a cooking fire, a freshly hung deer, and several carts—one carrying a cask about the size of a 45-gallon keg marked H.B.C. and no doubt containing spirits for the ensuing wilderness feast. In the background, a large group of sailors and marines lie reposed before their tents, resting feet and limbs from the day's rough march. A Union Jack, flying somewhat listlessly from a short pole, completes the rather peaceful late August summer scene.

Tempting as it might be to make light of this encounter, beneath this friendly façade lay uncertain feelings.[18] In the following year, 1849, the Company was again assisted by a British man-of-war. The *Inconstant*, a 36-gun frigate commanded by Captain John Shepherd, proceeded to Fort Victoria to secure it against Haida and Tsimshian who had come from their distant northern homes in search of trade items, liquor, arms, and ammunition. Captain Shepherd reported the dangerous nature of the situation to his superior, Rear-Admiral Phipps Hornby, the commander-in-chief on the Pacific Station, who in turn made this report to the secretary of the Admiralty:

> As regards the Colonization of the Island, if such is the Company's object, it is anticipated that much resistance would be offered by the Indians, the Tribes to the northward being described as numerous, well armed, brave and warlike and Captain Shepherd's opinion is, that no colony be established upon it, without being in its infancy rendered safe against the Indians, by the presence of a strong detachment of Troops.[19]

To provide protection and support for the Company, Hornby noted that he would dispatch one of the ships under his command to Vancouver Island.

Here lay the first hint of the threat of the northern Indians, and the information contained in Hornby's letter was passed by the Admiralty to the Colonial Office, which wondered if the colonization of the Island could be undertaken without security. When the question of an appropriate garrison was raised by the Colonial Office, the Company adamantly resisted. They retreated to their ancient policy that civilizing the Indians could best be effected by conciliatory measures and not by bayonets. The Company had no objection to having a British warship permanently on hand. But the idea of a British garrison there was anathema to them, perhaps because they feared interference in the conduct of their affairs on the spot, and perhaps because they would have been obliged to pay, in whole or part, for such a garrison. The Company had no desire to meet the expenses, although, paradoxically, it bore responsibility for the protection of settlement by the charter of grant. On 11 December 1850, the Colonial Office again asked, point-blank, if the Company planned any measures for permanent protection other than that given by the occasional visits of British warships. The reply, similarly blunt and equally measured in tone, read "we have never found any serious difficulty in protecting the Servants and property of the Company from hostile attacks of Indians, and we have every confidence that a continuance of that temperate and prudent conduct towards them, which is the rule and practice of the Service, will be the means of restoring a good understanding with the tribes in Vancouver's Island with whom it may be necessary to maintain intercourse."[20] The Company had its way.

By this time the colony of Vancouver Island had been brought into existence by the British government. In founding the colony, the principal motive of the Colonial Office and the secretary of state for war and the colonies, Earl Grey, was to stay the tide of American settlement. But a second reason, incorporating the objective of imperial trusteeship of aboriginal peoples, lay in the thinking of Grey and of Sir John Pelly, the governor of the Company. The idealistic Grey in particular, as is evidenced by his policies towards New Zealand and Natal, believed that British power fostered peace and order in many distant quarters. Empire provided the opportunity to spread the blessings of Christianity and British civilization among the outlying millions. If for business reasons alone, Pelly held the same altruistic motive with respect to Vancouver Island. In the years 1846, 1847, and 1848 the Colonial office believed that the Company with its capital and its experience in dealing with the Northwest Coast Indians seemed the most suitable of several applicants to receive the charter (or grant) for the colonization of Vancouver Island.

But how, it might be asked, would colonization and trade be balanced with trusteeship? How would the coming of British settlers and the advancement of British commerce not be detrimental to "the protection and welfare of the native Indians"? Some persons already had the answers to these questions. Young Lieutenant Adam Dundas, R.N., on the Northwest Coast in H.M.S. *Modeste* in 1844 and 1845, warned the British government of the Company's "illiberal usurpation of power." "Is it to be supposed," he asked, "that they would aid in the advancement of Civilization when from time immemorial it has been proved that the progress of the one has ever been made at the expense of the other? And should the Native cease to exist, why, their occupation is gone." Ten years later, in 1857, Richard Blanshard, who had previously been the first governor of the Colony of Vancouver Island, advanced a similar view. When he testified before the British Parliamentary Select Committee into the affairs of the Hudson's Bay Company, he suggested that colonization at Vancouver Island would result in genocide. The questions, raised by John Roebuck, M.P., and Blanshard's responses are worthy of repetition:

> Then if colonization were to take place in Vancouver's Island we should hear very little more of the Indian? — Very little more.
> In fact, though it may seem to be an inhuman statement to make, the sooner they get rid of the Indians the better? — I believe it is what the United States, people call improving them.
> Improving them off the face of the land? — Exactly so.[21]

In point of fact, as Dundas had warned and Blanshard had testified, the Hudson's Bay Company on Vancouver Island was not a Christianizing agency but primarily a business concern. Though contemporary hacks in London such as Richard Montgomery Martin praised the Company's work for the advancement of the Indians, critics such as James Edward Fitzgerald complained that the Company wanted to keep Vancouver Island as a vast fur-trading preserve in which the Company maintained a "frightful despotism" over the Indians and kept them in a "state of degradation."[22] In Parliament, as well, the matter was hotly debated. The Earl of Lincoln (later Duke of Newcastle), an expert on colonial affairs, supported the Company's critics and brought before the House of Lords evidence in support of the charges against the Company of "want of morality and feeling" with regard to Indians.[23] Nonetheless, such objections did not carry the day.

If a "state of degradation" existed, then the British government bore no less responsibility than the Company. Crown control through executive powers had been exercised in the newly acquired colony of Trinidad after 1806, to cite one example, in order to prevent a small oligarchy in the colony from developing a native policy not in keeping with London's view of imperial conduct towards people with darker skins. The Colonial Office pursued this form of paternalism with respect to Vancouver Island. The preamble to the charter of grant reflected this principle of imperial trusteeship as Grey understood it. The colonization of the Island by British subjects under company auspices, so it ran, "would conduce greatly to the maintenance of peace, justice and good order, and the advancement of colonization and the promotion and encouragement of trade and commerce in and also the protection and welfare of the native Indians residing within that portion of our North American Territories called Vancouver's Island."[24] The colony was to have a governor and eventually an assembly with powers of self-government. But because the colony had no settlement at the outset, it could have no assembly, and native affairs and welfare thus came under immediate purview of the governor and the Company, with the British government functioning in the background. As Earl Grey had stated on more than one occasion, the "principal bar" to the introduction of self-government in colonial dependencies was "their being inhabited by a population of which a large proportion is not of European race."[25]

Vancouver Island in the early 1850's was a colony of trade and of alien rule. Here the liberal ideas of self-government and self-rule were as far away as the imperial capital. Security could not be counted on, and the government knew that its authority with regard to Indians, Americans, and even Russians was tenuous at best. Thus, though it was tempting for the Hudson's Bay Company to "cry wolf" as they often did, the Foreign Office, Colonial Office, and Admiralty willingly listened. For this reason, they would send gunboats and extend political jurisdiction over turbulent frontiers in the Queen Charlotte Islands in 1851 and New Caledonia (British Columbia) in 1858. Indeed, this Fort Victoria-London axis, the type of centralized administration of which Gladstone and his kind so often complained, gave the governor not a blank cheque but at least considerable latitude to act as he saw fit in the interest of Britain and the colony. "If anything shall happen which may be of advantage or security to Our Island under your Government which is not herein by Our Commission provided for," his instructions ran, "we do hereby allow You, with the advice and consent of Our Council, to take orders for the present herein giving unto Us, through one of Our Principal Secretaries of State, speedy notice thereof, that so you may receive Our ratification if we shall approve the same." In other words, to ensure colonial security against civil insurrection, an unauthorized American take-over, or an Indian raid, the governor could exercise the powers given by his commission in the Crown's name. But still he could not exercise this power without considering or anticipating how ministers of the Crown in far-off London might view such an act. He had no power to commence or declare war without Whitehall's knowledge and consent.

The first governor, Richard Blanshard, a young barrister with frail health, had little if any experience in colonial administration save for travel in the West Indies, British Honduras, and India. He was apparently unknown to Earl Grey immediately prior to his appointment. His main qualifications seem to have been, in addition to intelligence and respectability, that he had no connection whatsoever with the Hudson's Bay Company, and thereby propitiated opposition critics in the House of Commons. Untried and unknown, he was an unfortunate candidate as the Crown's representative on a frontier dominated by the Company and its settlers. At the time of his appointment, the colony had no independent settlers, and the governor possessed no military means to support his authority.

3

"This Miserable Affair"

THE PROSPECTS for the success of British interests in the young
colony of Vancouver Island rested heavily on whether or not a
system of colonization could be introduced in a region inhabited by a
large number of natives and where Hudson's Bay Company servants followed a code of conduct which, although nominally subject to British
authority, was really a law unto itself. Whitehall wished that the colony
would grow in order to offset the possibility of American squatter settlement. Such an objective implied that regulated agricultural settlement
would be instituted to establish the framework and freedoms for the
growth of the new colonial society. And it meant that white-Indian relations might take new, even more violent forms.

Governor Blanshard was committed to planting British institutions on
Vancouver Island soil, which would supply security for settlers. In developing this project, he was thwarted by the fact that the Colonial Office
and the Governor and Committee of the Hudson's Bay Company did not
share an understanding of how to co-operate to assist the governor.
Neither wanted to provide material support for the civil power in the
form of a garrison. That would cost money, and both opposed funding a
force, though for different reasons. On the other hand, neither objected
to the use of naval force whose cost was borne by the Treasury and could
not be charged back to either the Colonial Office or the Company as
colonizing agent. For this reason it was the Navy which provided colonial security that became unavoidably involved in the first sanctioned
use of gunfire against the Northwest Coast Indians. This "miserable
affair," as Dr. John Sebastian Helmcken, a young company surgeon ap-

pointed by Governor Blanshard as magistrate at Fort Rupert called it, was the initial violent encounter between colonial authorities and Indians. It was the first of a long series of gunboat actions wherein officers of the Crown showed that they believed that an exhibition of force was required to uphold English law and that if peaceful means proved unsuccessful, reprisals should be undertaken on the governor's authority.

In 1849, the same year that the colony was founded and plans were drawn up by the Company to send its first emigrant ship, the *Norman Morison,* from Gravesend, England, with eighty colonists, the Company began to operate its first coal mine on Vancouver Island, at Fort Rupert, named after the corporation's princely founder. The place, so important in the colony's early development, lay on the Island's northeastern coast some 240 miles from Fort Victoria by land and half that again by sea via the treacherous, unlighted, and unbuoyed west coast. The usual passage for sailing ships was not by the inside straits, for only steam could conquer the currents at such places as Dodds Narrows and Seymour Narrows, and delays would be encountered by ships under sail in their endless tacking in those island-infested waters. Thus, masters of navy sloops, company barques, and other sailing vessels preferred the considerably longer open passage, entering the inland straits from the north via Scott Channel, Gordon Channel, and then Queen Charlotte Strait to bring them safely to Fort Rupert on Beaver Harbour. Some masters might have been tempted to take the short cut by way of the narrow Goletas Channel, separating Hope and Nigei Islands from Vancouver Island. Customarily, however, ships under sail followed the more open course recommended by various naval officers beginning with Captain George Gordon of H.M.S. *Cormorant* in 1846.

The fort's origins can be traced to 1835 when Indians found outcrops of a substance that they called in Chinook "klale stone" near their ancient sealing place of Suquash and reported the finding to company officers. The *Beaver* was sent to investigate, and her crew located coal at Beaver Harbour, between the present settlements of Port Hardy and Port McNeill. As an anchorage Beaver Harbour is imperfect, except in summer when the sea is usually quiet. In other seasons, northeasterly winds can send in a heavy sea, the breakers rolling in towards the bank which extends almost a half mile off the low lying south shore. During these strong winds, which could last for days upon end, mariners preferred to keep their distance from the "strand" and the man-made ramp leading to the fort's entrance. Even after officers of the Navy surveyed the bay in 1850 and 1851, skippers deemed it unsafe to venture closer than a mile from the beach, even if their vessels had steam power. They preferred to ride at anchor in the south and west parts of the harbour, and to announce their arrivals to the natives and traders ashore by firing a gun.

The naturalist John Keast Lord, a visitor in the company steamer *Otter* in 1859, described how the gunshot echoed through the Indian encampment, the forest and the Seven Sisters Hills beyond, and at once "countless tiny specks were discernible dancing over the waves like birds." Soon the specks grew into canoes of all descriptions as the vessels approached the ship.[1]

Callers such as Lord or the missionary Richard Dowson who was there in 1859 saw this world through European prisms and invariably commented on the nude, filthy, and unkempt natives, whom they habitually and derisively called "savages." They might allow that the Fort Rupert Kwakiutl Indians were "a fine race," yet in the same breath they would denounce them as "woefully dirty" and "uncivilized." As the many British visitors were earnest Victorians who believed in improvement, for them it was a tenet of faith that the Victorian age with its concern for law, order, and industry would bring the "savage" from infancy to a civilized maturity, thus ridding him of his "barbarism."

If the visitors had courage enough to venture into the cluster of about sixty cedar houses that formed the Indian village of Ku-Kultz,[2] they were certain to be the subject of attention from what Lord classified as "the vilest assemblage man ever beheld." This "City of the Redskins"[3] consisted of a long row of square huts, each made of adzed cedar planks about four inches thick and emblazoned on the outside in white, red, and blue heraldic patterns of intricate symmetrical design. The intruder might also note how chiefs and other men surrounded him first, with women and children in the background, and with dogs of all kinds adding to the energetic, unnerving welcoming party. The smell of the place was still less agreeable. Heaps of clamshells and fish offal lay strewn around the encampment and on the beach. Seagulls circled, then dived to help themselves to the pickings. "The fragrance was so strong," a company servant complained, "as almost to require an axe to cut it."[4] Nearby, in a clearing not infested with stinging nettle and blackberry brambles, craftsmen reduced cedar trees to graceful canoes, fashioned by eye without line, model, or measure. As a rule, however, the tribes who came to be known as the Fort Rupert Kwakiutl had no reputation as canoe-builders and were dependent on others to fashion their seventy-foot war canoes.

But more than this, they had brought with them to the fort their renown as great and proud maritime warriors whose territorial aggrandizement had forced the Coast Salish to retreat southwards to Comox. They plundered and took slaves and booty at will on marauding expeditions which took them as far as Nanaimo and the Fraser River. They numbered between 1,100 and 3,000 persons in the late 1850's, though no exact census seems to have been taken.[5] "They were of a fierce and quarrelsome disposition," according to Captain John Walbran, a Canadian coastal surveyor who knew every port of call from Puget Sound to Lynn Canal, "and for a long time the dread of both traders and natives up and down the coast." In 1850 Charley Beardmore, a company servant, told a newcomer that he would grow accustomed to the Kwakiutls returning from their expeditions laden with slaves and the amputated heads of their enemies, which they would arrange along the shore on stakes as a warning to other rivals and as a symbol of their own power and prestige and their noted intolerance of Indian foes. To Beardmore the Fort Rupert Kwakiutl were simply "a precious bad lot, a terror!"[6]

Not surprisingly, the Company stood alert against assault from these natives or from their enemies who might come from afar to seek revenge. Fort Rupert formed a distinct contrast to its neighbour, Ku-Kultz, and as Captain Edwin Augustus Porcher, R.N., observed dryly, it was "built after the usual typical form."[7] Actually it was among the best the Company had ever built. Care had been taken to design an outpost that a handful of employees could defend against overwhelming native numbers. This whitewashed, "square-stockaded" post consisted of an immense 18-foot high palisade with an interior catwalk, enclosing within various houses, trading and artisans' buildings, and a well-kept English gentleman's garden—"a perfect little community in itself," according to the British yachtsman Charles Barrett-Lennard. The place could only be entered by two massive gates, an inner and an outer. Two octagonal bastions "of a very doubtful style of architecture," according to Lord, gave the Bay traders a modicum of defence from an attack outside. The bastions commanded a field of fire along all four sides of the fort's curtain wall. The sole approach from outside of the fort to the traderoom lay by a long passage bent acutely near the traderoom window, sufficiently narrow to admit only one Indian at a time. In these circumstances, trade at gunpoint was virtually impossible for the Indian. And such a trap access allowed the Company to be less concerned about the ordnance needs of its bastions. Thus, when Lord called there, he was surprised to find that instead of "many formidable cannon, with rammers, sponges, neat piles of round-shot and grape, magazines of powder, and ready hands to load and fire" against natives disputing the Company's supremacy, only two small rusty cannonades occupied the old turrets. He wrote, in exaggeration, that tradition held that these guns had once been fired over the heads of rebellious natives and that instead of being terror-stricken, the Indians chased after the cannonball, found it, and brought it back triumphantly to the fort as a trade item that it might be fired again for their amusement.[8]

No doubt Lord did not understand that some years before, in 1850, the place was on a war footing. A good deal of rivalry existed among the

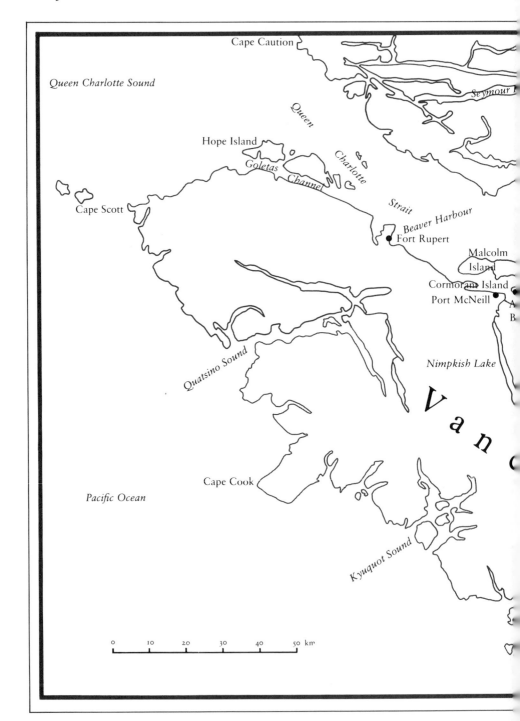

Cape Caution

Queen Charlotte Sound

Seymour

Queen

Charlotte

Hope Island

Goletas

Channel

Strait

Beaver Harbour

Cape Scott

● Fort Rupert

Malcolm
Island

Cormorant Island

Port McNeill ●

A
B

Nimpkish Lake

V
a
n
c

Quatsino Sound

Cape Cook

Pacific Ocean

Kyuquot Sound

0   10   20   30   40   50 km

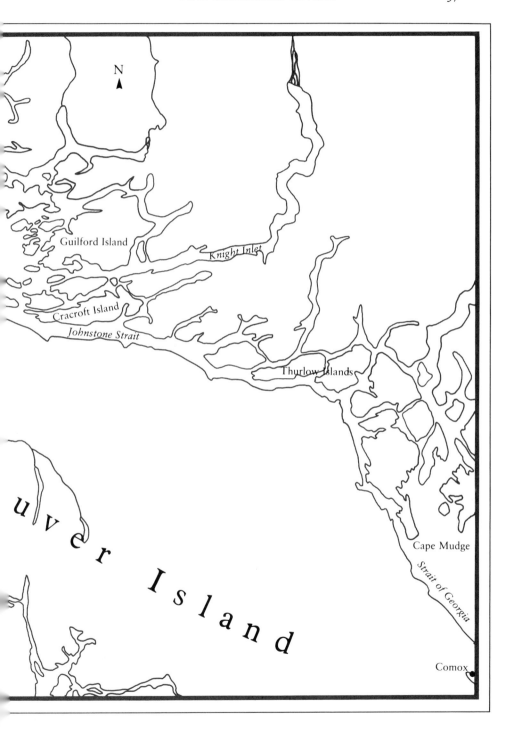

local Kwakiutl. A group of closely related tribes or septs[9] had migrated to Beaver Harbour after the Company built the post, and for a generation the gradations among the various chiefs were confused and procedure uncertain. Potlatches and winter ceremonies, which were associated with warfare in spirit and origin, became progressively more elaborate in the ongoing contest for chiefly prestige and ascendancy.[10] This new village of Ku-Kultz, like so many others built by the natives to take advantage of European economic activity and to adapt to new trading patterns, grew into a great centre of Kwakiutl culture, attracting anthropologists such as Franz Boas and witnessing the development of such artists as Mungo Martin.

Except in its yellowing bastions and the HBC red ensign flying over its battlements, Fort Rupert was different from Fort Victoria. Whereas Victoria had been transformed by European settlement in the 1850's into a veritable little England, Fort Rupert, despite its floral garden, remained an imperial outpost in what the noble Mr. Lord and his kind liked to call "a sea of savagery." Within the palisade lived some sixty individuals — Scots, Irish, English, Canadians, Métis, and Sandwich Islanders or Kanakas — a motley body of men whose motives for enduring the tensions of this remote outpost were altogether uncharacteristic of the alien people living outside the wooden walls. The company servants were a disaffected and unsavoury bunch, provoking the harassed officer in charge to scratch in the fort's journal that never before had "such a misérable set of devils" been congregated.[11] Here the company officers strained to keep strict discipline, a tough order of conduct, Dr. Helmcken recorded, "as necessary as well ashore as afloat, altho' no one felt it, watchfulness having become a mere habit, or second nature, by reason of being constantly surrounded by real or supposed dangers."[12] Living in a small, isolated community on the edge of a forbidding forest, the fort's chief trader and subordinates nurtured a garrison mentality.

The fear grew in intensity as major economic changes brought uncertainty to white-Indian relations. Native labour had been used to dig the surface croppings and carry coal from the beach in canoes to steamers such as H.M.S. *Cormorant* in 1846. However, the Company knew that because surface croppings had been exposed to the elements and might not be the best for steamers, shafts would have to be sunk by experienced hands. And with the Company contracting to deliver from 500 to 1000 tons of coal to the new Pacific Mail Steamship Company's ships at San Francisco at the price of twenty shillings per ton, it sought to put the mines on a more permanent footing. Thus, in 1849 the Company imported Scottish miners (one oversman named John Muir and six miners, four of whom were his sons or nephews) and a blacksmith to mine coal.

From the beginning the mining went poorly, first at McNeill Harbour and then a half mile from the post. The proud Scots, journeymen miners skilled in "working at the face," objected to having to do field and pit work befitting only labourers (a breach of contract) and to being visited by angry Indians threatening to shoot them. Several times, Andrew Muir wrote in his diary, the fort was "having rows with the Indians," and the miners were obliged to put up with "Indian annoyance by day and depredations by night."[13] The miners also complained of poor housing and bad weather. When their frustrations reached a climax on 10 April 1850, they went on strike, demanding assistance, protection, and adequate tools. The discovery of gold in California contributed to their discontent, for the whole coast was alive with rumours of Eldorado and farm labourers, traders, sailors, and miners in company employ escaped their weary indenture in the hopes of becoming rich overnight. For them, Fort Rupert was one of the gates to freedom.

On the Company's part, the miners' activity did not augur well. Fort routine out of necessity was conducted in the rigid ship-discipline established by Captain McNeill of the *Beaver* when he built the place in 1849. George Blenkinsop, the headstrong officer in charge, grew angry with the Scots and antagonized them repeatedly. McNeill himself arrived in the *Beaver* in May and ordered the Scots back to work; they refused and demanded to be tried fairly by English law. Not to be manipulated, the company officers put the miners in chains but finally let them go. The Scots brought charges against McNeill, Blenkinsop and Beardmore for false imprisonment, against the Company for breaking contract and bad treatment, and in the case of Andrew Muir against Blenkinsop for defamation of character. Pending investigation, Helmcken bound them over on their own recognizances to keep the peace.[14]

But the Scots, as Andrew Muir wrote in his diary, decided "to make for some Christian place" where rights and privileges could be regained. The departure of the trading barque *England* from Fort Rupert for San Francisco gave them the opportunity for which they had been waiting. Two of them quit the place by canoe on 3 July to join the vessel in the straits. They were probably aided by some Newitty of the Kwakiutl, who hid them for several days, and then they were picked up by the *England* with several other miners and their families. Only John Muir, senior, his son Michael, and their families remained behind. One of the escapees was the blacksmith. "Fort Go Ahead," as the optimist Beardmore had called it only a few months before, now stood still.[15]

To the problems of labour-management was added the Indian "menace." The possibility of an Indian rising may well have been exaggerated. Nonetheless, several observers, British and American alike, saw such a danger. The captain of the United States warship *Massachusetts,* which coaled at Fort Rupert during the crisis, lingered at the fort in order to give Blenkinsop help against what the captain regarded as possible trouble "with the Indians outside."[16]

This important reference indicates that the British were less concerned with the Fort Rupert Kwakiutl than they were with their near and distant neighbours. They may have been anxious about the hereditary enemies of the Fort Rupert Kwakiutl, the Bella Bella, Quatsino, and Haida. More likely in this instance, they were concerned with other Kwakiutl than those of Ku-Kultz, specifically with the Newitty.

The Newitty were an ancient warrior race inhabiting Vancouver Island's north shore and adjacent islands. Living as they did exposed to continual harassment if not actual fear of attack, the Newitty were tormented with rumours of war and invasion from their powerful neighbours, particularly the Fort Rupert Kwakiutl, Haida and Milbanke Indians, and thus they were far less noisy and boisterous than the Fort Rupert Kwakiutl. They formed two tribes whose principal village in 1851 seems to have been at Cape Commerell, the northernmost part of Vancouver Island, and called Newitty, the name by which these natives were known to the whites. The village stood on a small rocky peninsula on the east side of the cape, and on the south side a moderately well-sheltered bay with a fine sandy beach provided an excellent landing place for their canoes. The Newitty had other fortified villages, six in all, some of them on rocky islets and still others in rock shelters formed by overhanging cliffs, but Newitty was their main village. With a population of about 3,125, according to a Hudson's Bay Company census taken a decade before, the Newitty could claim some 774 fighting men.[17]

In March 1850 Governor Richard Blanshard arrived in H.M.S. *Driver* and made the first of his three visits, this one lasting three days, to Fort Rupert. He gained the opinion that the Fort Rupert and adjacent tribes were "numerous, savage and treacherous." The *Driver*'s appearance, the fort's officer noted, had "a good effect on the Indians." By this time the state of Indian affairs on Vancouver Island required the permanent presence of one of Her Majesty's ships, and Blanshard advised the commander-in-chief on the Pacific Station that the next warship that called should stay longer.[18] He was right. By June, the situation at the fort had changed dramatically for the worse.

In that month the *England* had called at Beaver Harbour to take in coal. The coaling process was long because there was no wharf, and accordingly the crew spent a good deal of time on shore while boats and canoes shuttled back and forth from shore to ship loading coal. On shore the men talked with the company servants, telling them of the riches and pleasures of the California gold fields. They urged some of them to quit the post for San Francisco. The company men, though not the officers according to Helmcken, grew resentful and insubordinate; the contagion mounted as the time drew near for the barque to leave for San Francisco. Liquor was readily available from the ship, quarrelling ensued, and men and women threatened to leave in canoes if they could not go in the *England*. But the officers talked with the Kwakiutl chiefs, and they agreed not to sell canoes to whites or to convey them away. The fort's gates were now more carefully locked than ever before to guard against an eruption of Indians or discontented employees. To Helmcken it was "Dangers within; dangers outside; danger all round."

At this critical juncture the *Beaver* appeared in the harbour, searching for three sailors, deserters from the company ship *Norman Morison*. They had stowed away aboard the *England* at Fort Victoria in the hopes of getting to California. The Company regarded the deserters as outlaws. When the *Beaver* entered the harbour, the deserters panicked, slipped over the side into a canoe, and made their way down Goletas Channel towards the open Pacific, perhaps hoping that they would later rejoin the *England*. They encamped on an island midway between Beaver Harbour and Newitty (presumably Nigei). Old Wale, a Fort Rupert Kwakiutl chief friendly to the Company, brought news of this to Blenkinsop at the fort. Blenkinsop, who did not know of the sailors, thought the men were the missing Scots and promised to pay thirty blankets for the recovery of each of the three men. This information was conveyed to Old Wale through a French-speaking interpreter as thirty blankets *par tête* — which Governor Blanshard later interpreted as meaning dead or alive. It was a large reward, but one which Blenkinsop hoped (rightly it seems)[19] would bring back the blacksmith, a tradesman absolutely necessary for the mining.

But Old Wale did not find the deserters. They had left the island and near Shushartie Bay had fallen in with some Newitty, and, according to Indian evidence, had been killed by three Indians (Tackshicoate, Tawankstalla, and Killonecaulla) for refusing to submit to some extravagant demands. Two of the whites were stripped and buried in hollow trees; the third was weighted down and sunk in the sea.[20]

Dr. John Sebastian Helmcken, who took up his duties as magistrate and justice of the peace in and around Fort Rupert on 27 June, could find no company servants willing to act as constables. By canoe and in difficult weather, Helmcken, Blenkinsop, Beardmore, and Indian aides conducted investigations along the thirty miles of island-dotted coastline, and Beardmore even interrogated the Newitty at Bull Harbour, their main village.[21] They found the remains of the three deserted seamen. Helmcken, however, could find no rationale for why the Newitty would have killed the deserters and tended to side with them in their claim that some northern tribe, perhaps the Sebessa of Kitkatla or some Haida were responsible. The charge against the Newitty seems to have been pro-

moted by their ancient enemy the Fort Rupert Kwakiutl who looked on
them "as dogs." Helmcken, admitting much conflicting evidence, told
Blanshard he could not decide who was to blame.[22]

Helmcken's objective was to get the suspected murderers into custody.
But he had only two options as to how to do this. He would offer a reward and hope that it would induce the Indians to bring forth the suspects or, less agreeably, to use some means of force. He made a dramatic
appeal to Blanshard, saying that if the reward did not succeed "we
cannot go to war, because the distance is great and our men too few to
protect the fort and fight also, even if they were willing so to do."
"Nevertheless," he continued, "something must be done and I should be
glad if Your Excellency would come as soon as possible; because if we
make no demonstration the Indians will lose all respect for us and may
make an attack on our fort, particularly as they well know also, that the
men here are in the greatest disaffection, and whom they despise." The
Fort Rupert Kwakiutl were more than willing to fight the Newitty for the
whites at Fort Rupert and frequently had to be dissuaded from this "but
if we could find out who did it, summary vengeance ought to be taken,
but as I said before, the means are not here." Helmcken was eminently
aware of the hostility of the "saucy" Fort Rupert Kwakiutl towards the
whites, who were outnumbered by three thousand to thirty or forty,
remarking to the governor that it was "not very difficult to imagine who
would gain the Victory." Not least, in concluding his impassioned appeal
for support, Helmcken noted that he was "perfectly powerless" against
the disaffected company people: "the next thing you will hear is that the
Indians have attacked our fort and this only on account of the insubor-
dination of our own people."[23]

In response to this appeal, Blanshard complained that he had no way
to back up the queen's name with the queen's bayonets. The best he
could do was send messages to San Francisco and elsewhere on the coast
for a warship, hoping this would hasten her arrival at Esquimalt from
where she would proceed with the governor "to put matters on a proper
footing at Fort Rupert." Blanshard did not have to wait long; he was
soon on the spot, which he called this "bed of thorns."[24] In early October
the British corvette *Daedalus,* commanded by Captain George Grenville
Wellesley, brought him to Beaver Harbour on a voyage of inspection and
inquiry.[25]

It is important to note that after Blanshard left Fort Victoria on this
mission, Douglas wrote to George Blenkinsop, the company officer in
charge at Fort Rupert, in tones indicating abundant awareness of the difficulties. The Newitty would be "startled," he explained, "particularly if
Mr. Blanshard acts with the decision I expect. Otherwise our position on
Vancouver's Island will be insufferable and the civil government worse

than a dead letter."[26] This indicates how serious Douglas regarded the situation and how necessary he thought it for the governor to take action against the Newitty.

At Fort Rupert Blanshard found the position intolerable to the Company. Coal mining was in a critical state, for the Company was dependent on Scottish and Indian labour, which was not available; and the post was surrounded by three thousand, well-armed Kwakiutl, "one of the most warlike Tribes on the Coast."[27]

Blanshard believed he had cause for alarm and determined to act. On 9 October he instructed Helmcken to talk with the Newitty, camped twelve miles away.[28] Helmcken was authorized to offer a reward of twenty blankets for the arrest of each murderer. But he was thwarted by Indian resistance, for when he visited the camp on 11 October, Blanshard explained to Grey, the secretary of state for the war and the colonies, "the whole tribe took up arms; they acknowledged the murder, and offered furs in payment, but refused to surrender the guilty parties, declaring themselves hostile, and threatened the lives of the Magistrate and his party, pointing their guns at them."[29] Helmcken was content to retreat, "not finding it by any means pleasant to have so many muskets levelled at us by these excited and untamed creatures." But Helmcken had made an important breakthrough in his investigation. Previously he was uncertain that the Newitty could be singled out as the guilty party. Their determined resistance, however, seemed proof enough to him of their guilt. Evidently they had been lying before in blaming the Sebessa and Haida for the murders.

The Newitty's refusal to accept the British terms and offer of furs reflected their traditional form of compensation.[30] Their action led Blanshard on 12 October to send three armed boats from the *Daedalus* to the Newitty. Their object was to secure the actual murderers or take chiefs as hostages and, if that failed, to attack the camp and burn houses and property. The officer commanding the boats, Lieutenant A.A. Burton, found the camp deserted and ordered the burning of deserted cedar houses and the destruction of other Indian property.[31] Blanshard wrote Rear-Admiral Phipps Hornby, that, "The boats of the Daedalus have been employed in an attempt to apprehend the Indian murderers at Newitte, but, though both officers and men showed all possible skill, and doubtless felt the greatest anxiety to punish the perpetrators, I regret to say it was fruitless, as the Indians decamped with the greatest part of their property, the remainder was burnt with the houses of the deserted camp."[32] An extended stay by the *Daedalus* would have been useful, Blanshard said, and he trusted that the next time a British warship visited Vancouver Island it would be for a longer period.

In these strained circumstances, Blanshard appealed to Phipps

Hornby's successor, Rear-Admiral Fairfax Moresby, for help. He explained that the Newitty had been able to flout British authority. The murderers were not likely to be surrendered to the civil authority, the governor warned Moresby, unless intimidated by an overwhelming force such as a warship, and he went on to detail that the only Hudson's Bay Company defences were their stockades and that their only mode of coercion was to stop trade with the Indians.[33]

Perhaps the developing scenario seemed familiar to Moresby who, unlike Blanshard, operated from a position of strength and experience.[34] The spirited Moresby was an old hand in treating and dealing with "natives" and had won recognition from the abolitionist William Wilberforce and the Admiralty in the 1820's for his role in fighting the East African slave trade. He was anxious to settle the Fort Rupert issue and bring security to the colony. Accepting Blanshard's statement that the Company and the settlers seemed far from secure, he determined in July 1851 to replace the influence of the Company by a display of British force. He sent the sloop of war *Daphne,* bearing Governor Blanshard, to Beaver Harbour, where Hudson's Bay Company officers had instructions from Douglas to give every assistance to the governor and naval officers. The governor believed that if the murderers were not given up, the tribe should be punished *as a group*—a tactic which the British believed the Indians understood and used in their own warfare. When the Newitty did not co-operate, Blanshard asked the *Daphne*'s commander, Captain Edward G. Fanshawe, to dispatch a proper force to seize and destroy their encampment, canoes and other property if necessary.[35]

Captain Fanshawe now sent armed boats from the *Daphne* to search for the Indian encampment and arrest the suspects. Lieutenant Edward Lacy, the officer in charge, first ascertained that the camp was at Bull Harbour on Hope Island, apparently from information gathered by a spy. He proceeded there in the boats with about sixty sailors and marines. On the evening of 19 July, they reached a point about a mile away, and the boats anchored for the night. At daybreak, they advanced on the encampment. They found it to be a strong position on an islet, no doubt Norman Island, communicating with the shore by a wooden bridge. When the boats approached, the Indians fired muskets, and the pinnace's gun fired in return. This "nearly silenced their fire," according to Lacy, and the party now landed to take possession of the encampment. The Indians "instantly abandoned it and took to the bush, from whence they kept up an occasional fire, wounding two of the seamen, and where, from the nature of the ground, I did not consider it prudent to pursue them," Lacy noted in his report of proceedings. In keeping with his instructions, Lacy ordered the party to burn the houses and the property in them and to destroy the canoes.[36] Again the Newitty had retreated into the interior, beyond reach of any naval party that Lacy or Fanshawe might send to capture them. George Blenkinsop then offered peace if the three Indians were delivered.

Helmcken, whose version differs slightly, wrote that Blenkinsop accompanied the expedition for the purpose of "getting quiet possession of the murderers." But when the *Daphne*'s boats were fired upon and some of the sailors wounded, they attacked, and soon the Indians ran into the woods behind by way of a narrow causeway. The man-of-war's men wished to get possession of this isthmus, but they were too late. The landing party did not follow the Indians into the dense forest, but the *Daphne*'s men set fire to the village, destroyed the canoes and then left. The Newitty later reported that on this occasion only one man, Chief Lookinglass, was killed and three others wounded. Helmcken provides us with some further details. The Newitty, who were now offered thirty blankets for each murderer captured, determined to give up those who had caused the trouble and thus prevent further British retaliation. Evidently they tried to capture the guilty clandestinely. Failing to do so, they set upon them, "coolly" shooting them. Helmcken says, though, that in the scuffle a promising young chief was killed. One murderer with light coloured hair escaped, and a slave may have been killed and substituted in his place.[37]

In any event, the Newitty desecrated the three bodies and brought the mangled remains to Fort Rupert, where they were buried in the English garden. The encounter with the Newitty was over. In Blanshard's estimation "a most beneficial effect" had been produced on the neighbouring tribes: Fort Rupert remained in safety.[38]

Thus was "this miserable affair," as Helmcken called it, terminated.[39] Its distortions regrettably remain. Hubert Howe Bancroft, in the course of developing his anti-Hudson's Bay Company stance—a position no doubt prompted by his anti-British, pro-American leanings—established a view which has been hard to expunge from the standard historical treatment of the Fort Rupert affair. He argued that instead of proceeding against the real instigators of the trouble, the Company (who it was asserted, but never proved, had offered rewards for the return of the deserted sailors, dead or alive) and "officers of the imperial government" directed "the full force of their vengeance against the natives." Bancroft neglects to mention the several attempts made by all the principal civil, naval, and company officers—Blanshard, Helmcken, Blenkinsop, Wellesley, Fanshawe, and their subordinates—to obtain the murderers by peaceful means and states that the Newitty were quietly holding a potlatch when the *Daphne*'s boats "crept into their harbour, and announced their arrival by discharge of musketry. Men, women, and children were mercilessly cut down, persons innocent of any thought of wrong against

their murderers, and their village again destroyed. Then the *Daphne*
sailed away. Justice was satisfied; and Blenkinsop and the rest of them
went about their work as usual."[40]

Bancroft implies that the British arrived in their vessels of war and
made no attempt to conciliate, but instead they made war upon persons
who had not fired upon them. In point of fact, as shown here, the
Newitty had first fired upon the British. The British had returned the fire
and conducted the reprisal. This was a reprisal conducted with the traditional company method of payment of reward in keeping with Indian tradition of payment for damages.[41] Thus had the matter been terminated.
Of course, "Rule Britannia" was anathema to Bancroft, but to the vener-
able Helmcken, who spent many of his later days trying to correct the
record and protect his public image through a lengthy report in the
Victoria Daily Colonist of New Year's Day 1890, Bancroft had maliciously misrepresented the truth. As Helmcken put it cogently, "That
the navy acted brutally is a lie." A similar view was held by Blenkinsop,
an eyewitness to the *Daphne*'s boats encounter with the Newitty. He objected to the charge of a "massacre of Indians."[42]

A more recent position, taken by Robin Fisher, places the blame
squarely on Blanshard. The young governor regarded the Indians as ir-
rational, appealing to Rear-Admiral Moresby for force on the basis that
"safeguards were needed against any 'sudden outburst of fury to which all
savages are liable.' "[43] Fisher might have mentioned that the governor
knew that the Company was no less sure of the Indian temper there, that
company officers regarded a show of force as necessary to put a stop to
the anarchy then developing within and without the fort, and that it was
Blanshard's duty to protect the settlers in the colony. The British were
not out for vengeance: Blanshard, "aided and abetted" by Moresby, told
Helmcken "to tell the Indians that 'the white man's blood never dries.' "
This was a company maxim. "It has been the uniform policy of the Hudson's Bay Company," Governor Sir John Pelly advised Earl Grey on 14
January 1852, "never to suffer the blood of a white man to be shed by a
savage with impunity."[44] This was simply a varient of the old *lex talionis*
and was meeting the Indians on their own terms.[45] The brutal action that
followed, an action in which the Newitty were neither willing nor able to
surrender the murderers, Fisher says, was uncalled for. "The killing of
the three sailors did not even remotely constitute an Indian menace of
'serious proportions,' nor was the Newitty tribe particularly warlike."[46]
In short, the punishment was out of proportion to the crime, and Blanshard and Moresby are seen as representative of a new set of values im-
pinging on the Indians with the stealthy approach of settlement. Fisher
claims that Douglas contended that Blanshard's tactics were inappropri-

Plate 1. Fort Victoria in August 1848, showing boats from H.M.S. *Constance* approaching the post on Camosun (later Victoria) Harbour, Vancouver Island. The natives watch from Songhees Point. View by Lieutenant J.T. Haverfield of the Royal Marines.

Plate 2. In a display of force 250 seamen and marines from H.M.S. *Constance,* Captain George Courtenay commanding, march from Fort Victoria to keep the Indians "in awe of British power."

Plate 3. During their "campaign in the forests of Vancouver Island," marines and seamen prepare for action, firing their weapons. The field guns were standard issue to H.M. ships, and the gun crews required drill when possible. Another drawing by Haverfield.

Plate 4. In this view Haverfield portrays two peaceful Indian chiefs, one a Clallam called "King George," the other the Songhees chief Cheealthluc ("Freezy"), as well as Tetlea, who was uncle to "King George," meeting with two British officers. Venison is being smoked, sailors and marines rest near their camp, and spirits are provided by the H.B.C.

Plate 5. His Excellency Richard Blanshard, first Governor of Vancouver Island (1849–51), set down the first policies for use of H.M. ships of war on the Northwest Coast in Indian relations. In trouble with the Hudson's Bay Company in Victoria and the Colonial Office in London, he quit the service in 1851.

Plate 6. His Excellency Sir James Douglas, K.C.B., second governor of Vancouver Island (1851–64) and first governor of the mainland colony of British Columbia (1858–64). The dominant figure of British Columbia colonial history, he was not alone in his visions or abilities to extend the "gunboat frontier."

Plate 7. His Excellency Captain Arthur Edward Kennedy, governor of Vancouver Island (1864–66). Knighted 1868. Born 1810, died 1883, he also served as governor of the West African settlements, Hong Kong, and Queensland.

Plate 8. His Excellency Frederick Seymour, governor of the mainland colony of British Columbia 1864–69, was debilitated by drink, slow to act, and died on the job, at Bella Coola, 10 June 1869.

Plate 9. The Commander-in-Chief, Pacific, Sir Fairfax Moresby, K.C.B., a seasoned practitioner of gunboat diplomacy elsewhere, readily supported requests from governors Blanshard and Douglas for aid at Fort Rupert and Newitty in 1851, the Queen Charlotte Islands in 1852, and at Cowichan in 1853.

Plate 10. Rear-Admiral Henry William Bruce, Commander-in-Chief, 1854–56, a veteran of Trafalgar, enthusiastically promoted the advancement of British interests on the Northwest Coast, including effective use of naval force as at Cowichan and Nanaimo in 1856.

Plate 11. "The amount and dreadful character of Social Evil reported to exist among them [Indian women in European settlements] is deplorable," Rear-Admiral Arthur Farquhar advised the Admiralty in 1873.. He praised Metlakatla for its improving possibilities.

Plate 12. Admiral James Charles Prevost, missionary promoter and practitioner of gunboat diplomacy. Commanding officer of H.M.S. *Virago* and H.M.S. *Satellite* he believed that the Northwest Coast Indians would benefit from Church Missionary Society activities.

Plate 13. H.M.S. *Trincomalee,* 26 guns, launched in 1817, and commanded by Captain Wallace Houston, carried landing parties to Cowichan Bay in 1856 to secure the Somenos chief Tathlasut, who had attempted to kill the English settler Thomas Williams when the latter had seduced Tathlasut's intended bride. This ship is still afloat, in Portsmouth Harbour, as the Training Ship *Foudroyant,* the oldest floating ex-warship in the world.

Plate 14. H.M.S. *Virago,* a paddle-wheel sloop-of-war mounting 6 guns, launched in 1842, was at Fort Simpson, Fort Rupert, and the Queen Charlotte Islands in 1852 and 1853. Her commander, James Charles Prevost, investigated the *Susan Sturgis* piracy but could not find any Haida, including Edenshaw, specifically guilty.

Plate 15. The gunboat H.M.S. *Forward,* commander Lt. Charles R. Robson, was engaged in two police actions against the Lekwiltok and the Haida in the area of Cape Mudge in 1861 and 1862.

Plate 16. Albert Edward Edenshaw (1812?–1894), right, celebrated pilot, trader and Haida chief, was involved in the *Susan Sturgis* affair. Navy officers held high opinions of this man who sought to become the greatest of the Haida chiefs.

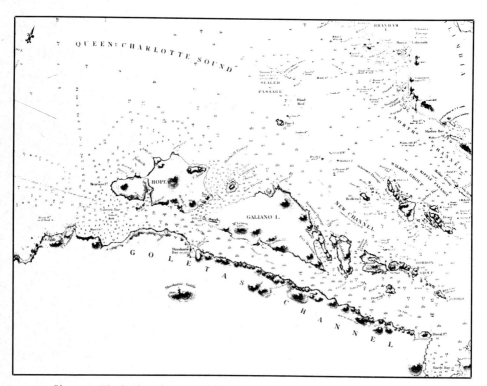

Plate 17. The lands and waters of the Newitty Kwakiutl, showing the north coast of Vancouver Island and Bull Harbour, Hope Island, where boats from H.M. Ship *Daphne* in 1851 "stormed and burned" the Indian village. Detail from an 1864 British Admiralty chart based on surveys by Captain George Henry Richards, R.N., in 1860.

Plate 18. Fort Rupert, Vancouver Island, showing the picketed enclosure and gateway from the beach. Built as a coal mining and merchandising centre, it had a curiously faltering history under Hudson's Bay Company auspices. Photo by F. Dally.

Plate 19. The Fort Rupert Indian village or, as it was sometimes called, Ku-Kultz. With an estimated population of 1500, it was a noted liquor trafficking and potlatching centre. H.M.S. *Clio* destroyed the village in 1865 when the captain could not get "satisfaction" from the chiefs.

Plate 20. Fort Rupert Indians, 1866, with officers and men of H.M.S. *Scout*. The chiefs demanded compensation for loss of their village, but their demands were rejected by the governor of Vancouver Island, Arthur Kennedy. Photograph by R. Maynard.

Plate 21. H.M.S. *Scout,* launched 1856, and on station 1866–67 and 1871–73, was a 21-gun screw corvette. Commanded by Captain J. A. P. Price, she carried Govenor Kennedy on a tour of inspection of Vancouver Island in 1866.

ate, but he does not mention that Douglas believed, as he wrote to Grey on 31 October 1851, that the criminals "met the fate they so justly deserved."[47]

To lionize Douglas at Blanshard's expense is a mistake.[48] Douglas shared Blanshard's concerns about the finely balanced white-Indian interplay at Fort Rupert and on Vancouver Island in 1850 and 1851. More specifically, he did not think Blanshard's actions against the Newitty were either ill-founded or excessive. "It is to be regretted that the Indians were not more severely punished," he wrote privately to Bienkinsop on 15 August 1851, "but I trust they have had a lesson they will not soon forget." He hoped, he told another company servant, that the punishments would "inspire respect" not "provoke ridicule." What he objected to was Blanshard's desire to hold the whole tribe responsible for the crime, because he had more foresight and greater local knowledge. This course, he wrote to Blenkinsop, was "as unpolitick as unjust and might lead to disastrous warfare with these savages." Like Blanshard, Douglas would have preferred moderate measures; by offering a reward the guilty might be brought to trial, and by punishing the guilty alone, goodwill with the tribe might be maintained. For these reasons he continued Blanshard's policy of appointing local magistrates when the colony's revenues would allow it. Like Blanshard he was happy to have the protection of whatever British sloops of war would put in to Esquimalt from time to time. Unlike his predecessor, he opposed the idea of military garrisons on Vancouver Island. As for the Company in London, it delighted in the interest that Rear-Admiral Moresby had shown in Vancouver Island. The Navy's presence, they trusted, would make a "due impression both on the natives and on the Americans."[49]

At the Colonial Office Blanshard found little support and was seen to have exercised his powers in an unwarranted manner. In Earl Grey's opinion, the several reports that had filtered through to him at 13 and 14 Downing Street indicated that the matter was of insufficient consequence for Blanshard to engage in such highhanded reprisals. His stinging rebuke, based on the views of his permanent undersecretary Herman Merivale, served notice that the governor's actions in this case were both unnecessary and out of keeping with British policy. Grey chastised Blanshard:

> At all events, it is necessary that I should state for your guidance on future occasions that Her Majesty's Government cannot undertake to protect, or attempt to punish injuries committed upon British subjects, who voluntarily expose themselves to the violence or treachery of the Native Tribes at a distance from the settlements.

I have no reason to suppose from the accounts which have reached
me both from yourself and other quarters, that the Settlements are
in actual danger. [50]

Grey need not have said more. But his penny-pinching disposition got the
best of him. For imprudence poor Blanshard (who was never salaried in
the first place) would have to pay to Captain Wellesley the £47.15.0.
owing for food, drink, and passage during the *Daedalus*'s patrol. Thus,
injury was added to insult. Again, the Colonial Office had revealed an
ignorance of the difficulties facing their man on the spot, whose relationship with the office was shortcircuited by data supplied by the Company
and no doubt favourable to it. [51]

The resistance of Downing Street was not the only thing taught by the
Fort Rupert affair. Blanshard had been told that British protection did
not extend beyond the frontiers of settlement or the sea-lanes of trade
and especially to deserters who exposed themselves to dangers, a policy
departed from by the mid-1850's under Douglas as governor.

If there were theoretical limits to protection of British subjects in the
Vancouver Island wilds during the Fort Rupert affair, there was also a
new definition of British legal rights for dealing with indigenous peoples
in the Pacific. To what extent, the Lords of the Admiralty asked the Law
Officers of the Crown who advised government departments on certain
legalities, might ships' commanders exact from the natives redress for
wrongs done to British subjects in cases of unprovoked and deliberate
murder? The Empire's ever-expanding frontiers were bringing the British
into contact with natives of all sorts, and as the tool of government the
Navy was seeking a codification of the terms of intervention. The guidelines suggested by the Law Officers were that if a naval commander actually witnessed the murder of a British subject, he could exact redress
from the chief or chiefs of the tribe to which the offender belonged by
first taking hostages and, if that failed, by using violent measures. If,
however, there were no such witness, "the utmost caution and forbearance" was to be used before resorting to any exercise of force. [52]

Accordingly, the Navy became more cautious in its dealings with the
Indians. The governor of Vancouver Island grew more influential in the
direction of Indian policy. Such policy, the Colonial Office believed, had
largely to be generated on the spot. Merivale, the permanent undersecretary of state for war and the colonies, minuted:

To give orders from hence as to the conduct to be observed towards Indians in Vancouver's Island, seems rather unlikely to be of
much service. If the colony is to maintain itself, as was the condition of its foundation, the local government much needs to be left

very much to its discretion as to dealings with the natives in the immediate neighbourhood of those settled parts, although distant excursions against them may be discouraged. [53]

As for Fort Rupert it had a lingering death as a trading post, and its mines never reached their potential, partly because of labour problems. Order was maintained by a granger and twelve loyal men sent by Douglas in order to keep the deserters to their contracts. [54] Soon the miners were transferred southwards to Nanaimo where an excellent coal seam had been located. Ku-Kultz, however, remained as an Indian village. Frequently visited by British warships in the 1860's it was once destroyed by Navy gunfire in 1865 in an action which will be recounted later.

The "miserable affair" marked a major event in white-Indian relations on Vancouver Island. For the first time in the infant colony's history a magistrate had been appointed and sent to a crisis spot. The governor himself had been so concerned with developments there that he had given it his personal attention. Indeed, the Fort Rupert affair was the principal problem that Governor Blanshard faced during his short tenure. In the face of crumbling company authority and of growing anarchy, Blanshard had endeavoured to introduce legal institutions and to provide law and order at this remote frontier post. With the Company pursuing its own course of justice to apprehend the deserting miners and seamen and the governor endeavouring to establish English legal institutions, the symbols and means of authority were confused and divided. The Newitty murder of the three seamen intensified the problem; they took white lives — something which no local authority, whether colonial, naval, or Company could tolerate. In the violence that ensued the Newitty revealed to the whites that they were indeed capable fighters and skilled tacticians. Moreover, they had proudly solved the crisis in their own way — by killing the murderers themselves and in this way suing for peace on their terms.

In this remote territory where British authority was frail, the use of force in support of the civil power constituted a form of "forest diplomacy." The Fort Rupert affair showed that the application of naval power was not always precise, nor was it fully effective. But above all, it indicated that naval authority was becoming a regular feature of British expansion on this maritime frontier and, given the lack of colonial self-defence, that governors would make repeated calls upon the service to support colonial interests and British law and order.

4

The Smouldering Volcano

D URING JAMES DOUGLAS'S governorship British naval power became an integral part of the rule of authority gradually emerging on the Northwest Coast — on both sides of the border. The growth of white settlement on southern Vancouver Island and on the shores of Puget Sound meant that Douglas and his counterpart in Washington Territory grew increasingly alert to what they regarded as an Indian "menace," and they used maritime power — either gunboats or company steamers — in an attempt to provide security for trade, settlement, and commerce. In this distant quarter British armed strength at sea even gave succour to rival Americans, though its main role was to serve British interests.

In the early and mid-1850's, Douglas continued to wrestle with the same problems as had faced Blanshard. Fearful of imperial meddling in this company preserve, he had to be ingenious in providing protection for settlers. He did not want a colonial garrison, for the Hudson's Bay Company would be obliged to pay for it. Thus he relied on whatever meagre means were at his disposal — the Company's French-Canadian and Métis guard at Victoria known as the Voltigeurs, the Company's ships, especially the steamers *Beaver* and *Otter*, and, increasingly important, various British warships that called at Esquimalt. Even in that era, legend had it that Douglas's pacification of hostile Indians consisted in giving them a little bread and treacle.[1] Nonetheless, he always acted as if he were bargaining from strength, exhibiting a grave and singular presence conditioned by lengthy service in a hostile land where white men were few and Indians many. In settling Indian problems his commanding presence and bearing were no small asset.

In keeping with Hudson's Bay Company tradition, Douglas made clear to the Indians that the whites were neither to be trifled with nor intimidated. He pursued such a policy against the Cowichan and Nanaimo Indians during the winter of 1852–53. On 5 November 1852, two Cowichan Indians murdered a Scottish shepherd named Peter Brown at Christmas on Lake Hill, a sheep station kept by the Company some five miles north of Fort Victoria. Brown's associate presumed that the deed was committed by two Cowichan whom he had left at the hut when the sheep had been driven out to pasture.[2] On hearing the news, Douglas immediately stopped the sale of gunpowder to Indians. The settlers were much alarmed, fearing a Cowichan attack on Victoria. But Douglas sensed that the murderers had fled north to Nanaimo and decided to send an expedition of sufficient size to capture them. Douglas has reason to be optimistic because the Cowichan had sent him word that they greatly regretted the event, that they would not harbour the murderers, and that they would do all they could to capture them. Douglas believed that the Cowichan intended to keep their promise.[3]

The British frigate *Thetis*, Captain Augustus Kuper, C.B., commanding, lay at her moorings in Esquimalt when news of the murder reached Governor Douglas at Fort Victoria. Kuper immediately agreed to Douglas's request for assistance. But sending a sailing frigate through the tortuous and still uncharted narrows that led to Cowichan Bay and then Nanaimo was beyond the range of possibility. However, an amphibious force, a naval brigade, could be sent if appropriate transport could be provided by the governor.

Kuper thus dispatched Lieutenants Arthur Sansun and John Moresby with 130 blue-jackets and marines to be embarked in the company brigantine *Recovery*. With the launch, barge, and pinnace from the *Thetis*, with guns ready for service, they would be towed by the steamer *Beaver* first to Saanich Village and then Cowichan and Nanaimo. Twenty men from the Victoria Voltigeurs went also. The governor was in the *Beaver* with a bodyguard of French Canadians and twenty Royal Marines. Sansun, Moresby, and other officers and men were in the *Recovery*, her hold planked over to accommodate the sailors. In all, it constituted an impressive force, Douglas noted, the finest display of force he had witnessed in the Indian country.[4]

The weather was very bad at that season, and the voyage from Esquimalt round the southern tip of the island to Saanich and through Satellite Channel leading to Cowichan Bay suffered delays. It was cold and wet, and the forces were frequently exposed to the elements, but only one or two "trifling cases" of rheumatism occurred.

The suspects were not found at Saanich, having fled to Cowichan, a populous camp on the banks of the fish-rich Cowichan (then known as

Quamichan) and Koksilah Rivers that flowed tortuously eastwards through a densely treed alluvial plain to the inland straits some forty miles north of Fort Victoria. The beach and river mouths were not easy to approach in heavy weather when wind and surf made the upper reaches of the bay dangerous. Even in fair weather the shallows of the river delta and mud flats off the ill-defined shoreline made for tricky navigation. It was no place for a man of war without steam power. Only well-armed boats pulled by strong sailors dared approach the shell-strewn shore, and even then they did so with caution.

Europeans were not welcome in the encampment where the Cowichan lived. Previously, Company officials had been reluctant to tread on Cowichan shores. When Eden Colvile, a company director, had proposed visiting the Cowichan Valley in 1849 to investigate its agricultural possibilities, Douglas had rejected the idea because an adequate guard was not available at Fort Victoria to protect them during the excursion. The place, Colvile was told, was "thickly inhabited by a very uncivilized and treacherous tribe of Indians; and that laying aside the idea of personal risk, any successful attempt to outrage on their part would be attended with bad consequences as regards the business and settlement of the island."[5] The Cowichan demanded to be treated with respect, and Douglas acknowledged this.

Arriving in the bay on the morning of 6 January 1853, Douglas noticed that the Indians were greatly excited and that they "shunned" the British vessels. He sent a messenger to the Cowichan chiefs inviting them to meet as soon as possible. The chiefs agreed to meet the next morning but insisted that the rendezvous be on a rising ground near the river mouth and not on the *Beaver*, which they were afraid to board. Douglas consented and planned to land the men fully armed and prepared for any contingency.

The following morning, the day "broke wet and sullen" over Cowichan Bay, a young lieutenant recalled, "but in order to gain a choice of position we made an early start and landed our forces, anchoring our boats so that their guns dominated the situation." The launch, barge, and pinnace from the *Thetis* and a boat from the *Beaver* had pulled towards the Cowichan River mouth in a line under the lead of the launch, with colours flying and rifles ready. The party landed and immediately, on a "pretty rising oak-ground," a tent was pitched for the governor. Here were deposited presents for the tribe and the governor's pistols and cutlass, "the use of either to depend upon circumstances." A fire was made, and the sailors and marines were put back a distance from the river in order to conceal their numbers, because Soseiah, the Cowichan chief, had indicated that his tribe would be afraid to approach in the face of a large number of whites.[6] Guarded by the French Canadians and Royal Marines, Douglas stood waiting.

The Indians were not punctual and several hours passed before the dull thud of drums heralded the arrival of large canoes from upriver. First one or two appeared, and then they all came down river in line. Anxious moments followed when some two hundred Cowichans landed. "They had a very imposing appearance as they pulled slowly towards us," Douglas wrote, "chanting their warlike songs, whooping like demons, and drumming on their canoes by turns, with all their might. They landed a little beyond, and rushed up the hill, in a state of the wildest excitement, shouting and dashing their arms about, like people who expected to be immediately attacked."[7] Not surprisingly the sailors and marines had to be restrained from opening fire while Douglas waited. The *Thetis*'s gunnery lieutenant, John Moresby, later wrote that Douglas raised his hand and said:

> Hearken, O Chiefs! I am sent by King George who is your friend, and who desires right only between your tribes and his men. If his men kill an Indian, they are punished. If your men do likewise, they must also suffer. Give up the murderer, and let there be peace between the peoples, or I will burn your lodges and trample out your tribes.[8]

Here was Douglas at his toughest and best, exhibiting the old Hudson's Bay Company brand of "forest diplomacy" and bargaining coolly from strength. Though Moresby did not record how many of the natives understood the governor's speech, this show of force evidently had the desired effect. The Cowichan brought forth the accused, Sque-is, who claimed that he was innocent, and he was promised a fair trial at Nanaimo, where Douglas hoped the other suspected murderer would be apprehended.

Douglas then addressed the Indians on the subject of their relations with the Crown and the colony. His diary records the details of the proceedings:

> I informed them that the whole country was a possession of the British crown, and that Her Majesty the Queen had given me a special charge, to treat them with justice and humanity and to protect them against the violence of all foreign nations which might attempt to molest them, so long as they remained at peace with the settlements. I told them to apply to me for redress, if they met with any injury or injustice at the hands of the Colonists and not to retaliate, and above all things, I undertook to impress upon the minds of the chiefs, that they must respect Her Majesty's warrant and surrender any criminal belonging to their respective tribes, on demand of the Court Magistrate and that resistance to the Civil Power, would ex-

pose them to be considered as enemies. I also told them that being
satisfied with their conduct in the present conference, peace was
restored and they might resume their trade with Fort Victoria. The
distribution of a little tobacco and some speechifying on the part of
the Indians, expressions of their regard and friendship for the whites
closed the proceedings and the conference broke up.[9]

The importance of this event bulked large in Governor Douglas's
mind. He considered the surrender of the murderers by the most warlike
tribe on the island, without bloodshed or even a shot being fired, to con-
situte an "epoch in the history of our Indian relations." It augured well
for the future peace and prosperity of the colony. Settlers near Fort Victoria would still have to be "prudent and vigilant," he knew. However,
they could dismiss from their minds the "idle terrors" of a Cowichan invasion. As Douglas noted, the rumours of such a raid were unfounded. In
fact, such false news only "served to elate and encourage the natives to
lead to the evil which the settlers so much dread."[10]

The incident did not end, however, until the force caught the second
suspect near Nanaimo. This place, whose name derived from *Sne-ny-mo*,
a local Indian term meaning "big strong people," was a confederation of
populous Indian villages bound together for protection from rival tribes.
Here the Company's hexagonal bastion signified that the Europeans
were there to stay — to trade and to mine the rich coalfields below the
fort's guns.

When the naval force reached Nanaimo on 9 January 1853, Douglas
called on the natives to surrender the suspect, Siam-a-sit, the son of a
chief. First they consented. Then they changed their minds and three
days later offered to ransom his life by a payment of furs. Douglas utterly
rejected this proposition because it defied English law. On the other
hand, he did not want to pursue a violent alternative that might result in
bloodshed, and he took steps to exhaust every other means before resorting to the "disagreeable alternative." Douglas persisted in the search.
He convinced Lieutenant Sansun in charge of the landing party to carry
on for a few more days in order that the authorities would not lose face
and that the Indians might believe they would not be punished and would
thus be "emboldened. . . by impunity." He dispatched a landing party,
which took the village against no Indian resistance save "noise and
bluster." He secured the chief as hostage and distributed tobacco as an
index of friendly intent. When they learned that the suspect had left
Nanaimo River for a hiding place in the woods of the coast about three
miles distant, they dispatched the pinnace with sixteen seamen and nine
voltigeurs. The landing party made a long and dangerous chase into the
woods and captured "the wretched man," as Douglas called him, and

took him on board the *Beaver*. The force was immediately withdrawn from the entrance to the river, the governor boasted, "without molesting or doing any damage whatever to the other Natives."[11] Skilfully planned and delicately executed, the expedition had reached its hoped-for conclusion.

Now the judicial process must run its course, and at Nanaimo, on 17 January 1853, trial by jury, the first of its kind in the area now known as British Columbia, was conducted on the quarter-deck on the *Beaver*. The accused were condemned by a jury composed of naval officers and sentenced to death. In the afternoon, the two Indians were hanged on Protection Island outside of Nanaimo Harbour at a place still known as Gallows Point. The execution took place in the presence of all the Nanaimo people. "This summary measure," Captain Kuper informed Rear-Admiral Moresby, "will no doubt have a most beneficial effect for the safety of the colonists against attacks from the Indians in future, and it is most satisfactory that the object was gained without bloodshed, as the Cowitzen Tribe is very numerous, and from their proximity to Victoria would probably have caused much annoyance to settlers, had it been found necessary to resort to hostile measures, and thereby excite their revenge." As for Douglas, he reported that the scene appeared to make a deep impression on them. Always pragmatic, he hoped that the event would have the effect of restraining others from crime. But the melancholy event was not without its long range impact. Reflecting on this punitive expedition some years later, John Moresby bemoaned, "I fear the pity of this, one of the myriad tragedies of the red man's collision with civilization, appealed to none of us at the time... I can remember nothing but pleasure and excitement."[13]

The Indians took the dead bodies, and gave them to family and friends for burial. The mother of the Nanaimo Indian had pleaded for her son before his moment of death, as she would now be lonely. Douglas had countered by saying her son had murdered a man whose mother was perhaps crying for him, and sons could not be killed with impunity, a well-adapted argument which was well received by them. The Indian female relatives of the deceased provided a special lamentation for the crew of the *Thetis*, a procedure explained by the fact that they saw this man of war as a "Silax" or "angry ship" and the Royal Navy to be "a separate tribe of King George men (as they call Englishmen) who go about punishing all who offend against other tribes." And as for Douglas, his decorum and his conduct of trial made as impressive as possible, contributed to the Indian acknowledgement of the justice of the proceedings, according to one careful observer.[14]

That Douglas could influence the natives in this fashion owed as much to his experience, determination, and sound judgment as to the fact that he had the Royal Navy at his disposal for making his policy clear. "I feel much indebted," he wrote London, "to Lieutenant Sansun for his perfect arrangements and for the admirable temper and forbearance exhibited by the force under his command in circumstances more trying for brave men than actual conflict." And as he admitted, the Cowichan "troubles" would not have ended in the way they did without an exhibition of force.[15]

However, Vancouver Island colonists, especially the non-Company settlers, did not share Douglas's optimism about security. In the next year, 1854, a group of malcontents hostile to the governor's regime or "squawtocracy," as one wag acidly called it, complained to the secretary of state for the colonies of the disadvantages under which the colony toiled. They argued that no proper court existed at Fort Victoria or else-where in the colony. Nor were their homes and families secure from an Indian raid, being without the "protecting presence of even one of the many of Her Majesty's ships which are now wintering at Valparaiso, Sandwich Islands, and San Francisco." The British government advised Douglas in 1855 that more frequent visits by naval vessels would suffice to protect the colony against hostile Indians and Russian cruisers during the Crimean War. The settlers, however, remained uneasy. They knew they could deal with one belligerent tribe, but a warlike Indian alliance was another matter altogether. Because of this general concern, the Legislative Council of Vancouver Island authorized the raising of a small company of soldiers to be maintained at public expense until "the Northern Savages leave the settlements." They also chartered and armed the *Otter* as a guardship. However, they rejected a proposal from a trusting governor that natives be armed as militiamen, fearing that the Indians might turn their armed might and newly won discipline against the colonists.[16]

Across the straits from Fort Victoria, in nearby Puget Sound, a general Indian war posed a threat to the settlers of Vancouver Island. Governor Isaac Stevens of Washington Territory, a strong-willed man of military background, was anxious to extinguish Indian title, to survey a railway line to the Pacific, and to provide military protection for Puget Sound settlers who now numbered about four thousand. He had to do so in an area populated by some thirty thousand Indians. Some of the natives such as Chief Seattle and his daughter Angeline of the Dwamish, Suqua-mish and allied tribes readily sold their title. But others, such as Leschi, a Nisqually chief, militantly opposed such actions and defended their in-terests against the rising American tide. In 1853, white vigilantes acted against Indians suspected of murder, and the Indians retaliated. In 1854, as violence intensified, the Territory provided a militia for local protec-tion. In October 1855, after the murder of settlers at White River near present day Kent, Washington, troops were brought in from Forts Stela-coom, Vancouver, and The Dalles. In addition, one thousand troops were brought from California and two regiments of volunteers were called up. Authorities declared martial law in Pierce County, and nearly all white males of military age were placed in arms.

American settlers also feared Indians from northern British Columbia and Alaska, who had giant canoes and pillaged and looted at will. Some even accused the Hudson's Bay Company of sending the Stikine Indians to attack Bellingham Bay, a preposterous allegation according to Douglas.[17] They sent a memorial to Congress in February 1855 asking that a United States gunboat be stationed on the sound to protect the settlements against the northern Indians. Governor Stevens and James Tilton, the adjutant-general of Washington Territory, also appealed to Governor Douglas for help. On 1 November 1855, Tilton sent an emissary to Victoria bearing an urgent message that Indians on both sides of the Cascades were acting in combination against the whites, that the American settlers lacked any army protection, and that Tilton knew of Douglas's goodwill towards the Americans. In impassioned tones, he urgently appealed for help so that "the savages upon the sound" would become more aware that the Anglo-American ties of blood and interest were sufficiently strong so that each nation would reinforce the position of the other when threatened. A show of maritime force was needed. He asked that the *Beaver* be sent as a transport for the U.S. Army and to act as a deterrent until the U.S.S. *Active* and *Massachusetts* could arrive.[18]

Despite his anti-American prejudices, now seasoned by his desire to resist American frontier traditions on Vancouver Island, Douglas did not fail to support his neighbours. Aiding his fellow man against the "savages" became his goal, as his correspondence with Tilton shows. He told the Americans that he acknowledged the moral obligation which bound Christians and civilized nations to use their full power to check the "inroads of the merciless savage." He explained that H.M.S. *President* had sailed from Esquimalt a week previously for San Francisco. Otherwise, he might have procured sufficient arms from her commander. He regretted, he told Tilton (quite truthfully), that at Victoria they were unprepared for war. Therefore, from the arms and ammunition available he could only consign to him in care of William Fraser Tolmie at Fort Nisqually, fifty rifles, three kegs of powder, five hundredweight of shot, and some gun flints, of a total value of $811.00. He also agreed to send a company steamer when available, carefully stating that she would not act in the capacity of a belligerent but merely to help protect the settlements against Indian attack. He anticipated that the steamer's visit to Puget Sound would be "powerfully felt" by the tribes and would serve to divide them and break up the confederacy of tribes. And he concluded, "I trust in God that such may be the event."[19]

Actually it was the *Otter* which Douglas sent to deliver the ammunition and to cruise the sound as a display of power. Her appearance, the governor expected, would be a token that company sympathies were on the American side and that the Indians could "expect neither countenance nor support from Her Majesty's authorities in this quarter." As to the Indians in British territory, they remained, he thought, friendly and quiet though evidently "powerfully moved in favour of their race." Such a feeling might act mischievously "on their excitable minds," a fact that made it necessary to watch their every movement.[20]

Douglas had good information from Tolmie at Nisqually about the Indian danger. Both believed it was necessary to show the Indians that the two nations were in agreement and that the Indian "plots and conspiracies" against the whites had to be defeated.[21] Once again, as in Oregon in 1847 during the Cayuse War, preservation of race overcame divisions of nationality. Ironically, for all their appreciation of Douglas's kindness, the Americans were exhibiting a local outburst of Manifest Destiny at San Juan Island under the old pretence that the Hudson's Bay Company was turning the northern Indians against the American settlers on the island.[22]

In fact, it was the Indians within Washington Territory who provided the near and present danger for the Americans. Early in January 1856 settlers at the nascent mill town of Seattle on Elliott Bay suspected a local rising. They hurriedly built a wooden blockhouse with the help of the officers and men of the recently arrived U.S. sloop-of-war *Decatur*. The place was fortified with two 9-pound cannon and garrisoned. On 26 January the Battle of Seattle began: the white forces took the initiative against an Indian hut where the suspected troublemakers were known to be. The *Decatur*'s shot demolished the building and other buildings while the white settlers took refuge in the bastion or were taken to the *Decatur* and the barque *Brontes* in the harbour. By ten o'clock in the evening the Battle of Seattle was over, and the Indians had fled.

Meanwhile the Hudson's Bay Company was employing its own form of gunboat diplomacy against the Puget Sound Indians at the request of American authorities. On 5 January, Leschi and thirty-eight warriors visited the reservation opposite Steilacoom, the army headquarters near Fort Nisqually, to win support from Indians who had not committed themselves to the hostilities. On American request, Tolmie sent the *Beaver* from Nisqually to Steilacoom. There she embarked Captain Maloney and thirty men of the U.S. Army and Judge Edward Lander, on service with the Washington Territory Volunteers. At the reservation, the *Beaver*'s presence did not have the desired effect. The steamer had no guns sufficient to cover a landing party and had only one boat capable of landing more than four or five men. Moreover, Leschi and his well-armed comrades lined the beach. Under such circumstances the *Beaver* withdrew, leaving Leschi in control.

During this tense time Douglas again came under pressure from the

Washington territorial government to lend funds for the purchase of arms and supplies. Stevens sent his commissary and agent, Captain Robinson, to Victoria, and the latter persuaded Douglas to advance $3,535 to Olympia, now bringing the American indebtedness to $7,000. With reference to funds advanced from his private fortune, Douglas wrote to the Colonial Office.

> This is a serious drain on my resources, but in the circumstances I could not with propriety deny the assistance so pressingly claimed, and I confess that it was not motives of humanity alone that induced me to lend such aid... other reasons of sound policy were not wanting... such as the conviction on my mind that the triumph of the Native Tribes would certainly endanger the position of this colony, which in that case could not be maintained without a vast increase of expense for military defences. It is therefore clearly to our interest that the American cause should triumph, and the natives be made to feel that they cannot successfully contend against the power and resources of the whites.

Eventually, Douglas also billed the U.S. Government $40,000 for the services of the *Otter* and *Beaver*, a sum which he had some difficulty in collecting because Washington was not eager to authorize payment for the initiatives of their excited agents on the Pacific Northwest frontier and also because the costs of this Indian war were very high. The delay in obtaining reimbursement, which extended to 1859, the permanent undersecretary at the Colonial Office minuted, was "not very encouraging to English officers who may be inclined to help the U.S. governor in pecuniary scrapes."[23]

By October 1856 the crisis had subsided, but the territory remained on a war footing for at least the next three years. Reflecting on the event, Tilton boasted, "History will present the fact with credit and honour to the volunteer force that during the six months of active service of 1,000 of the citizens of Washington Territory not a single friendly Indian has been harmed in a volunteer camp or scout, no Indian has been plundered or molested, and the captured property of defeated savages has been in many cases turned over to the proper officers and faithfully accounted for by them." Many white settlers and Governor Stevens believed that a "foothold of civilization" had been maintained. But in the process, this so-called blockhouse era in the history of Washington Territory, sixty-one stockades had been built for military protection, many roads constructed for security purposes, and gunboats or "fireships" as the Indians appropriately called them, brought in for the purposes of pacification. Forts Townsend and Bellingham were built to protect against Haida and other northern Indians who arrived in their fifty-man canoes in search of slaves and plunder, camped at places such as Port Gamble on Hood Canal, and refused to leave. On one such occasion in November 1856 gunboat action by the American warship *Massachusetts* resulted in the killing of twenty-seven Indians and the destruction of their encampment and canoes. The defeated Haida were taken to Fort Victoria and placed under British control.[24]

Governor Douglas's sending of the *Otter* and *Beaver* to Fort Nisqually on Puget Sound during the crisis affords evidence that a general Indian rising in Puget Sound had concerned him as well as his American counterpart. Settlers on Vancouver Island shared this anxiety. One colonist at Fort Victoria, R.S. Swanston, held the opinion that Vancouver Island Indians watched with satisfaction the success of the Nisqually, Puyallup, and other tribes in the southern parts of Puget Sound. He knew that Governor Douglas had sent steamers, rifles, and ammunition to aid the Americans. But he feared that the Indians of Vancouver Island would think that the "King George Men" and the "Bostons" had as their common objective "the ultimate destruction" of the Indian. "The whites on Vancouver Island are placed in a very difficult position," he complained, "a position that requires an abler man at the head of affairs than Mr. Douglas. *Nous verrons!*"[25]

However, the objections of a few private interests who urged Douglas's removal did not sway the Colonial Office. It had information from Rear-Admiral H.W. Bruce, who had recently been to Fort Victoria, that Douglas was as capable a person for the governorship as could be found, either in the colony or elsewhere. And London knew that the Company's activities would be investigated before the licence for exclusive trade with the Indians came up for renewal in 1859. Moreover, on the basis of past performance, the Colonial Office knew that the Company, for all its faults, kept the Indians in hand and the expansive Americans in check. They required nothing more. For these reasons, in 1856, the Company was allowed to continue under the terms of the royal grant, while at the same time some meagre representative institutions were granted to the colony, among them a legislative assembly.[26]

Douglas spoke of the northern Indians "menace" at the first meeting of the Legislative Assembly of Vancouver Island on 12 August 1856. He had, he said, great sympathy for guarding Indian interests. He pledged that he would continue treating Indians with "justice and forebearance" and protecting their rights, both agrarian and civil. In his opinion, "cogent reasons of humanity and sound policy" recommended this course of action, a procedure in which he would rely on the support of the Legislative Assembly. The enmity of the Indians he considered more disastrous than any other danger to which the colony should be exposed, and a feeling of insecurity would exist as long as the colony remained without military protection. Further evidence of his concern is revealed in a letter written nearly a month before to the secretary of the Hudson's Bay Company. "The Northern Indians," he wrote, "are still very numerous in the settlements, and though kept under restraint, by constant watchfulness, give much cause for uneasiness. Our position may be compared to a smouldering volcano, which may at any moment explode, with the most destructive effects."[27]

In these trying circumstances, Douglas could find some solace in the knowledge that the Admiralty, on the request of the Colonial Office, had dispatched the fifty-gun frigate *President* to Esquimalt. The Crimean War being over, the commander-in-chief, Pacific, could devote more attention to the pressing question of protecting the colony from predatory Indians. Thus the British warships *Monarch* and *Trincomalee*, at Esquimalt during the late summer of 1856, could supply 437 sailors, marines, and two 12-pounder howitzers for a second punitive expedition to Cowichan.

This far-reaching military operation, larger than that of three years earlier to the same spot, again revealed the British pattern of using force as a threat to effect justice and provide protection. Gunboat diplomacy served a double purpose—at Cowichan and at Victoria. As Rear-Admiral Bruce reasoned, not only was the force indispensible for bringing the delinquent to justice, the measure was necessary "for the safety and repose of this community."[28] Incidentally, it again showed that steam power was essential for the safe and speedy movement of British warships in the confined waters between Vancouver Island and the mainland.

The Indian "outrage" at Cowichan that had occasioned Douglas's appeal for a naval force was the shooting of an English settler, Thomas Williams, by Chief Tathlasut of the Somenos band as an act of revenge for the seduction of his intended bride. Williams had not been killed, but the charge of attempted murder was sufficiently serious in that time and place to warrant the deployment of about half of the officers and of the British warships then lying in Esquimalt Harbour. The act was wanton, Rear-Admiral Bruce said. He quickly instructed Commander Matthew Connolly of the *Monarch* to take a large detachment of marines and seamen from the *Monarch* and the *Trincomalee*, drill them as a landing party, exercise field piece crews, and then put them all in the *Trincomalee*, a heavily-armed ship which, though lacking steam, had very spacious stowage for the personnel and supplies of this expedition.[29] In the previous expedition to Cowichan, in 1853, the *Beaver* had towed the *Recovery* filled with sailors and voltigeurs to the place of action; this time the company steamer *Otter* provided the motive power, tugging and pulling the *Trincomalee* from Esquimalt through the intricate waters and tricky currents to an anchorage a mile and a half from the river entrance at Cowichan Bay.

It seems likely that on arrival in Cowichan Bay on 31 August a council of war was held on board the *Otter*. Here we can imagine Governor Douglas's seasoned opinions were doubtless heard with respect. He had conducted a very similar expedition nearly three years before, and he knew the terrain and the Cowichan. And it is likely that his very presence would have indicated to the Indians that they might expect the same Douglas treatment as in 1853 – "a fist of iron in a glove of velvet." All the principal naval officers would also have been present. These would have included Connolly, in command of all military details, Connolly's second-in-command, Lieutenant Edward Scott, who was gunnery lieutenant, and Lieutenant J.T. Haverfield, R.M., who had charge of the landing party of marines. Several other lieutenants may have been in attendance, as well as budding young midshipmen such as Sir Lambton Lorraine. As commander of the *Trincomalee*, Captain Wallace Houston was there as well and served as aide-de-camp to the governor.

Following this war council Commander Connolly issued instructions. These reflect Douglas's advice and the attention to military discipline in the field that had been the basis of codes of conduct for numerous naval brigades, and they are worth including here in full:

> As it is hoped to accomplish the object of the present expedition without having recourse to hostile measures; and as an untoward act of aggression on our part may cause an unnecessary effusion of blood and plunge the Colony into a disastrous war; at the same time that it is equally necessary to be prepared against surprise or ambush, and to act with vigour if called upon to do so: The following orders are to be most strictly obeyed by the force under my command.
>
> 1. The Order of March is to be strictly preserved, and no person is to straggle, or fall out from the ranks until a halt is sounded, and even then, not until permission is given to do so.
>
> 2. In passing through or halting at the Native Villages or Stockades, the property of the natives is to be most rigidly respected, and no person is to enter into the huts or houses on any pretense whatsoever, without permission.
>
> 3. As a great feature in Native warfare is stealth and treachery and the cutting off of Stragglers etc. in halting for refreshment, or bivouacing for the night, no person is to pass beyond the line of Sentries unless passed out by an Officer or non-commissioned Officer; and in the daytime, the men will take their meals with their Arms

piled in the centre of each section and at night they will sleep with their arms by their side, and on no occasion will they take off their pouch or bayonet.

4. It might be distinctly explained to the men, that on meeting Tribes of Indians which we are likely to do, their mode of friendly greeting is frequently exhibited by discharges of fire-arms, either blank or loaded with ball, shouting, hooting, yelling etc. but none of these demonstrations are to be misconstrued into acts of hostility and not a musket is to be fired or a movement made without the most explicit orders being given to do so.

5. The Commander of the expedition trusts with all confidence to the good order and steadiness of the men under his command to carry out these orders to the letter and to perform with honour and credit to themselves, the Service upon which they are employed.

6. This order is to be read by the Officers in command of the Companies to the men, and clearly and distinctly explained to them.[30]

Some indication of the resistance that Douglas had expected to find is shown in the number of armed men in the land party. Connolly had 159 Royal Marines (officers and men), 254 seamen (officers and men), and 24 in the ambulance party. In all, 437 officers and men, more than three times the number sent to Cowichan in 1853, took part in this singular display of power.

On 1 September, the full force disembarked and camped on Comiaken Hill, which they called Mount Bruce. This eminence, on which a stone mission church was later built, commanded the surrounding country on the left bank of the Cowichan River and provided an ideal bivouac. Indian scouts were sent to determine the disposition of the Cowichan tribes. Governor Douglas tried to find the suspect, and after receiving conflicting statements from the Indians, he determined that he could be found in a large village about five miles up the Cowichan Valley to the west. Orders were given to march there the following morning.

At eight o'clock in the morning, the fully armed expedition crossed the river in canoes, marched through high grass and potato fields, and advanced single file through "bush and jungle," crossed the river again, and arrived at the village just before noon. Proceeding through the village, the brigade marched to a slightly elevated, open space about a half a mile farther west and encamped. Meanwhile, two field guns were being transported upriver by canoe.

Shortly after Governor Douglas and the force arrived at the camp, "a formidable force of armed Indians" was seen advancing from the village, and in the centre of the group was the suspect. On this occasion any parleying that Douglas did was to no avail. The Cowichan, "their faces

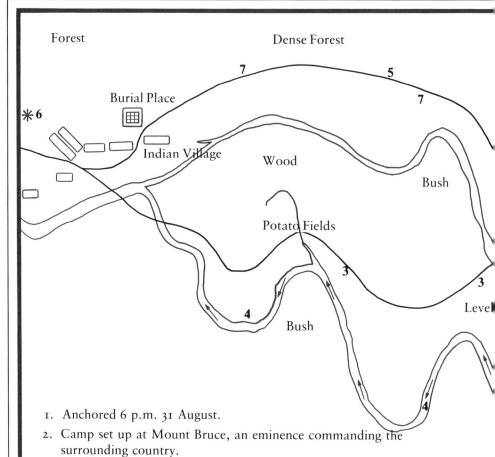

Forest   Dense Forest

Burial Place

✳ 6

Indian Village   Wood

Bush

Potato Fields

Bush

Level

1. Anchored 6 p.m. 31 August.

2. Camp set up at Mount Bruce, an eminence commanding the surrounding country.

3. Track of the main body on 2 September.

4. The field pieces and commissariat were conveyed in canoes from Mount Bruce to the large Indian village by this branch of the river on 2 September.

5. An escort which remained behind at Mount Bruce to embark the field pieces, etc., reached the inland camp by the forest track.

6. Royal Marines and seamen camped here on 2 August on an open space slightly elevated and about a half mile west of the Indian village.

7. Track by which the whole brigade returned to the camp at Mount Bruce, 5 September.

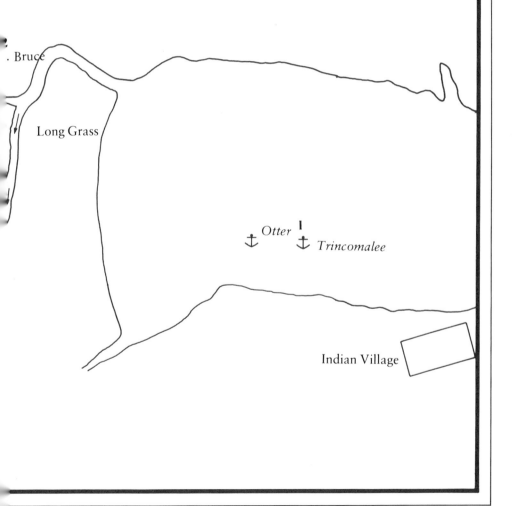

PLAN OF THE COWICHAN VALLEY (from Sir Lambton Lorraine, 1856)

from the mouth of Cowichan Gap to an Indian Village about four miles inland; showing the route of the combined landing parties of *Monarch* and *Trincomalee* against the Indians.

. Bruce

Long Grass

Otter *Trincomalee*

Indian Village

blackened, armed and painted for war, shouting and gesticulating," as William Macdonald of the Victoria militia recalled, would not give up the suspect. The governor and his party with some of the officers were drawn up in front of the camp waiting for their arrival. The two parties gradually advanced towards each other "until within arms' length," Connolly recorded. After a short struggle the culprit was suddenly seized, apparently by Captain Houston, and placed in confinement in the camp.[31]

To return that day to Mount Bruce seemed out of the question, and in the midst of drenching torrents of rain, the men made primitive shelter as best they could. Connolly noted that this tiresome service was most cheerfully performed. In the forenoon of the next day, a court of six officers and six petty officers tried the offender. After a full and patient investigation of the known and substantiated details of the case, the court returned a verdict of guilty. The governor summarily ordered him hanged, and he was executed in the evening. The British took care to conduct the trial and execution on the very spot where the crime had been committed—at one of the majestic oaks that still grace Somenos fields. Captain Macdonald, who was present, recalled that the culprit was hanged before his tribe who, nonetheless, showed "many indications that their approval was withheld and that they yielded only to force."[32] For reasons unknown, the natives did not regard the capture, trial and punishment with the same measure of acceptance as the authorities.

Now the expedition began its tiresome homeward march. The Mount Bruce camp was reached in the mid afternoon of the following day, the passage was considerably more difficult than the way in, and the guns had to be dragged over difficult terrain and through heavy underbrush. On the 5th, the whole party was re-embarked on board the *Trincomalee* for return to Esquimalt "without the slightest accident or casualty of any kind having occurred to mar the success of the expedition."

Captain Macdonald has given an indication of Indian feelings about the event; they did not like it, and they had submitted only to force. Perhaps because of this, self-congratulation seemed the order of the day on the British side. In reporting the event to the Lords of the Admiralty, Rear-Admiral Bruce noted that this "arduous and hazardous" service had been performed without casualty or complaint and that exemplary conduct and discipline had been shown by officers and men. He was particularly pleased with Connolly—"of singular merit and devotion to the service"—and other officers—"all conspicuous for activity, zeal, and watchfulness in their different stations. It was my confidence in them," he reported with satisfaction, "that induced me to consent to their being marched away from the immediate cover of the ship, or boats: a proceeding, which under ordinary circumstances, it would be imprudent to sanction." At the Admiralty, the clerks recorded all the names mentioned in Bruce's despatch and a number of promotions were soon given. Commander Connolly, who was included, advanced to Captain and Midshipman Lorraine to Lieutenant. Their Lordships expressed entire approval of the judgment with which the expedition was conducted and the ability displayed in its execution. As for Douglas, he singled out Connolly and Houston, but asked the admiral to thank all who had performed the great work. And he told Bruce that he was very pleased for the prompt and efficient aid that the commander-in-chief had given, aid which was absolutely "indispensable for the repression of Indian Outrage and the safety of the Colony."³³

Unwittingly, the Cowichan had brought the whites into their midst, for one of the principal legacies of this expedition was the discovery of the expanse and fertility of the Cowichan plain. Douglas predicted the Valley could support fifty thousand settlers. "I have therefore bright hopes for our future," he wrote cheerfully to William Fraser Tolmie, "and no longer despair of the Colony."³⁴ Rear-Admiral Bruce also found reason to be optimistic about the colony. Before visiting Vancouver Island in the summer of 1856, he had prejudged the case by predicting that the country would be "well rid" of the colony, which the Company might sell to the United States:

> Tho' the land is good, timber abundant, coal plentiful and easily worked, coasts swarming with excellent fish, and capital harbours, it is, on the other hand, at immense distance from England, and contiguous to envious, grasping, and quarrelsome neighbours; it is difficult of access, owing to the obscuring and constant fogs which envelop sea and land, and would require the presence of a Naval force to protect it from Indian as well as American aggression.

The whole question, Bruce postulated, was whether or not the British government desired to add to its "very distant possessions."³⁵

But Bruce changed his mind. The threatening attitude of nearby Americans, who were anxious to extend sovereignty to San Juan Island under the pretext that northern Indians were jeopardizing American settlers on Puget Sound, certainly influenced him. The insecurity of the few white families near Victoria was brought home to him, especially in view of the expedition to Cowichan Bay. He did not mince words in telling Sir Charles Wood, the First Lord of the Admiralty, that Vancouver Island should always be protected by a warship to provide it with security for life and property when Indian tribes visit it to "make aggressions upon Indians." Douglas ought to remain as governor for a few years at least, Bruce said. "His knowledge of the Indian character and habits, his influence and command over them, and the respect they exhibit in return for him combine to point him out for that important post." And in conclusion Bruce noted that, paradoxically, though Vancouver Island "leads to no other place, military or commercial, [it] must be its own recommendation; and... everything *has to be done.*" With its coal and agricultural lands and with gold nearby on Fraser River, Vancouver Island could become one of pre-eminence, both from its intrinsic value and its local position between the United States and Russian America.[36]

Bruce put great stock in the future of the Cowichan valley. "Its present population consists of about 14,000 Indians," he told Wood, "who are friendly to the English, and desirous for their residence among them; notwithstanding the summary infliction of justice they so recently witnessed at our hands." Bruce knew of one settler, a Scot, who was anxious to return to Cowichan at all costs.[37] Bruce thought making Vancouver Island a penal settlement to be out of the question because desertions to the nearby United States would be too tempting. Free settlers, free from the influence of the Hudson's Bay Company, were required to develop the colony.

As Bruce correctly described, near Fort Victoria internecine violence was frequent. In the mid 1850's, Indians came to Fort Victoria yearly by the hundreds and thousands, with most estimates ranging from two to six thousand. They were mainly Haida and Tsimshian, but the Stikine (Tlingit), Bella Bella, and Tongass (Tsimshian) were among others who came usually in the winter to trade, to get liquor, to engage in prostitution, and to enquire into the strange ways of the white man and his suspected secret about things external. They did not come with any overt hostile intent. However, they brought with them their feuds, their grudges, and their rivalries. Some, such as the Tongass, sought to use Victoria in 1854 as an advance base from which they could raid the neighbouring American coast in retaliation for their chief's murder. But Douglas could not afford them protection and they left indignantly, wounding a company servant and stealing his sheep. Victoria newspaper reports told of frequent conflict between Songhees and northern visitors such as the Haida. Mutilated bodies floated down Victoria Harbour on the outgoing tide, and it was generally believed that alcoholic beverages were the cause of violence. As a straits settler on the American side wrote despairingly, the northern Indians "never leave without doing something to have us remember them by." Even after the northern Indians left for their distant summer homes, the number of natives at Fort Victoria was "sufficiently great to do evil, if so disposed."[38]

The visiting Indians camped around the shores of Esquimalt and Victoria harbours. They preferred the secluded Gorge area in the arbutus bordered upper reaches of Victoria Harbour, where, even to this day, as if by some curious legacy of past rivalries, the native paddling prowess is still determined by Indian canoe races on the anniversary of Queen Victoria's birthday. Here they potlatched and feasted, fished and hunted, helped themselves to nearby settlers' farm produce, and made a mischievous nuisance of themselves not only to the whites but also to the Songhees.

By contrast, the Songhees were not transients. Opposite the fort's bastion and palisade, their village stood. It resembled a "rancherie," a rude collection of huge, rambling, blackened cedar huts contrasting strangely with the dwellings of the intruding white strangers. On Victoria Harbour a tale of two cities was unfolding, a story of suspicion and prejudice. A non-commissioned naval officer wrote in 1855 that the local Indians had frequently made preparations for attacking the whites but held the guns in great dread. Another visitor, Charles William Wilson, a Royal Engineer lieutenant, believed in the great probability of an Indian war at Victoria in 1859.[39] U.S. Customs agent James Gilchrist Swan wrote from Port Townsend, Washington Territory, "These Northern Indians are not a myth, they are stern realities. They have made themselves formidable at Victoria, where the British Government have a large naval force, and but for the intestine broils among themselves at that place—which have resulted in their being ordered to leave for their northern homes—would long before this have been here in force, and attacked or troubled both whites and natives."[40]

The problem bewildered authorities, who made several attempts to counter the threat as they saw it. First they tried to make all visiting Indians go home—if they outlived their welcome. In these cases, the Navy was called upon to be the armed escort. On one occasion, in March 1859, the Indians escaped from under the not-so-watchful eyes of the Navy: "One of the Men-of-War here," Lieutenant Wilson wrote bemusedly in Victoria, "got a number of their canoes in tow to carry them off, but the rascals soon got tired of that mode of progressing & cut the hawser & vanished like smoke; you have no idea of the quickness of their canoes, with 16 paddles they literally fly through the water."[41] Authorities tried again in March 1860, but with hardly any more favourable result. For though the frigate *Tribune* convoyed twenty-seven canoes as far as Cape Mudge, Quadra Island, from where the authorities assumed, perhaps mistakenly, that the natives would go northwards to their villages, en route Navy lookouts saw so many canoes progressing southwards to Victoria that they realized the utter futility of the "armed escort home."[42]

The colonial government's decision to check the immigration by sending back the Indians to their own country was impolitic and impractical,

Commander Mayne wrote with explicit clarity, and it did not reflect "the judgement that ordinarily characterized the dealing of the Government with the Indians":

> The impolicy of such a measure soon became apparent, to say nothing of the impossibility of carrying it into effect. No one who knew anything of the Indian character would believe that sending a few hundreds back would have the effect of deterring others from attempting the voyage down. Besides which, how could it be expected that men whom we had driven away or kept back forcibly from our towns would permit whites to "prospect" for gold or settle in their country?[43]

Officials realized that "nothing but violent measures of repression, backed by strong military and naval force" could stem the southwards flow of Indian peoples by water, and such harsh measures were not even considered as a workable option.[44]

If the northern disturbers of the peace could not be deported then they must be controlled in and near Victoria, authorities reasoned. Consequently, the colonial government decided to set aside lands for visiting Indians to camp on during their stays at Fort Victoria. The government also issued an ordinance which required them to relinquish their firearms during their sojourn. This annual presence at Fort Victoria of "some thousands" of armed Indians from northern Vancouver Island, the Queen Charlottes, and the North Coast, continued to alarm settlers and authorities, and gunboat diplomacy had to be used in the very harbour where the colony's legislative buildings stood. When some Haidas fired at the schooner *Royal Charlie* in 1860, two boats from H.M.S. *Ganges* went from Esquimalt to Victoria where the Indians were surrounded and disarmed of one hundred muskets, revolvers, and knives. Further disturbance made the presence of H.M.S. *Plumper* essential to show the Indians that their encampment was within easy reach of the warships at Esquimalt naval base. The government continued the practice dating from 1848 of having naval brigades march through town and Beacon Hill Park "to intimidate the Indians."[45]

Governor Douglas and naval officers at Esquimalt knew that the security of Vancouver Island settlers could best be established by telling the northern tribes that they had to stop fighting each other, especially during their annual "conventions" in Victoria. Thus, in 1860 H.M.S. *Plumper, Termagant,* and *Alert* went north to tell the Indians at the Queen Charlottes, Fort Simpson, and elsewhere that they would have to stop their marauding ways and live in peace during their expeditions to Victoria. This masterful stroke of gunboat diplomacy, the subject of another chapter, served to limit slavery in Indian society and to reduce violence and fear in Victoria.[46]

No doubt questions of territoriality caused Indians to war with each other at Victoria. The Songhees had a reservation; the Haida did not. This situation had developed because Douglas, acting for the Hudson's Bay Company, negotiated eleven deeds of conveyance with the Songhees and Saanich tribes by which the Company bought all lands from the Saanich Peninsula to Sooke.

But Indians also had complaints against the white man for taking their lands. Entirely sympathetic to the Indians on the question of compensation, Douglas had company authority to regard Indians as rightful possessors of lands occupied or cultivated at the time that Great Britain obtained sovereignty in 1846. All other lands, his instructions said, were to be regarded as suitable for colonization.[47] Indian ownership was thus recognized, and the Company sought to make purchase. Because compensation in such matters was not uniform within the Empire, one pound sterling per head being the average, Douglas could negotiate the going price with the Indians.

He acquired Songhees' lands for the now seemingly scandalous sum of 371 blankets, valued at 17 shillings each, and one cap for one Tlolemistin, who apparently merited special consideration. Evidently at the time this was a satisfactory price. These eleven Fort Victoria "treaties" and three others signed with Indians in the mid-island region (two at Fort Rupert and one at Nanaimo) are the only treaties signed with British Columbia Indians, apart from Treaty 8 signed in 1899. Douglas saw them as a legal means of extinguishing Indian rights over land to prepare them for future white settlement. The deeds of conveyance guaranteed the Indians village sites and fields for the use of their families; fishing and hunting rights were to be preserved.[48]

These treaties, signed between 1850 and 1852, indicate the growth of European settlement and agriculture on the southern tip of Vancouver Island. They also represent white Victorians' desire to have security in the face of large numbers of Indians nearby. By placing the Songhees on a reserve, for instance, the British could control their mobility and police them in the white settlements, especially the growing town emerging near Fort Victoria. In 1855 certain Songhees living on grounds now occupied by the Provincial Legislature were directed to move to a large reserve on Esquimalt harbour. This they still inhabit, though now in fewer numbers. A government memorandum, dated 1859, noted that the Songhees had become "obnoxious to the inhabitants of Victoria."[49] In other words, the growth of settlement and with it the need for land called for the removal of Indians to the suburbs.

There seems every reason to believe that the Fort Victoria treaties, the establishment of reserves, and the removal of Indians from areas of intended settlement were related to the question of security for the company servants and the few independent settlers making their way to Vancouver Island. As long as the Company remained in a dominant position, as it did until the mid-1850's, its rule was law and it could pacify the Colonial Office about colonial safety. But when settlers, independent of the Company, began to filter in and demand security as British subjects, the age-old relationship between Company and Indians was made less certain and more troubled.

But the burning question of ownership could not be ignored by Douglas. To foster peaceful penetration, it was necessary to provide security for settlers and to satisfy Indian demands. In 1861 he presented to the secretary of state for the colonies from the House of Assembly of Vancouver Island a petition calling for £3,000 for the purpose of purchasing aboriginal title to the Island. The amount was "trifling," Douglas thought, but essential to the interests of the people of the colony. As he said, the Indians regarded the usurpations as "national wrongs," and the feelings of being usurped would increase native disaffection and endanger the peace of the country.[50] The secretary of state did not quarrel with the principle, but believed that the colony should undertake payment itself. Douglas's plan, however, was never taken up by the colony or by successive colonial, provincial and Canadian governments, who sought to avoid this contentious issue.

In this time when the seeds of distrust over compensation for land were sown, the Royal Navy's role in Vancouver's Island development increased substantially. On Admiralty instructions, commanders-in-chief were made aware of the nagging needs of the island-colony's defences. Whether motivated by concerns about turbulence on Puget Sound where a war of races was progressing, Indian murders or shootings of whites at nearby Cowichan, or the presence of large numbers of Haida and other northern Indians on Victoria's doorstep, whites foresaw a danger to their race and their civilization. How much they exaggerated the threat will never be known. In retrospect, Governor Douglas's perception of the "smouldering volcano" and Rear-Admiral Bruce's belief in the colony's future represented two strains of thought which, when combined with imperial support and British settlement, spelled yet another rise in the tide of white influence and institutions.

PART II

PUTTING OUT FIRES

5

Policy Making

IN THE LATE 1850's and early 1860's the growth of settlement in the Strait of Georgia region brought great changes to the white-Indian relationship. At some places—Cowichan and Nanaimo—Governor Douglas had, with Indian agreement, extinguished aboriginal ownership. At other places—in the Gulf Islands and at Comox—white settlers pre-empted land under government supervision and almost invariably without Indian approval. At the same time Victoria and New Westminster were emerging as the colonial capitals of Vancouver Island and British Columbia respectively, the seats of a growing bureaucracy and the centres of a distillery industry whose influence was widespread in the towns and in the Indian villages. New Westminster, on the north bank of the Fraser River, had come into being in 1858, the product of an imperial decision to elevate New Caledonia to a jurisdiction where crown control superseded the ancient Hudson's Bay Company's *imperium*. The British government aimed at providing a regulating authority of law and local government, one which would provide for the eventual growth of political freedoms and traditions. The Colonial Office sought to develop a colony free from the lawlessness of the adjacent American frontier. One intention was to protect the Indians by according them equal protection as British subjects under the law.[1] This position required that the Crown's representative show favour to neither white nor red.

In actuality, the process of colonial development bore with it personal costs for both Indians and settlers. Indians were forced to accommodate themselves, voluntarily or involuntarily, to new political and jurisdictional realities and relationships. The invading settlers had the might of the British Empire behind them. Most of them carried with them an unfailing belief in the superiority of their way of life. They brought with them from Britain, British North America, the United States, and elsewhere the spirit of their race, a disposition quick to ascribe to the "savage" the fault of the cross-cultural violence they saw all around them. The pages of colonial newspapers were peppered with letters from settlers who knew little and cared less about the Indian.

Such views did not go unquestioned. "Nine-tenths of the outrages perpetrated by Natives upon the superior race, and supposed to be the result of insensate cruelty," the Congregational minister Matthew Macfie complained in Victoria in 1865, "can be traced to some wanton violation of the personal or domestic rights of the Indians on the part of the whites." He noted that on the American side of the boundary an Indian was looked on as little more than "a dog." Yet on the British side the same evils occurred—drunkenness, debauchery, increased mortality, syphilis, smallpox, and other diseases. "Appalling as the anomaly may appear," he bemoaned, "it is nevertheless uniform that the nation which professes to bring into a virgin colony the blessings of the gospel in one hand, carries a moral Pandora's box in the other; accomplishing the physical and moral ruin of the primitive inhabitants, whose interests, gratitude and respect should prompt it jealously to guard."[2]

As for the conduct of the Navy, the Service was not free from searing criticism. When bluejackets and marines went on shore they visited bars and brothels. They gambled and drank. They quarreled and fought. Brawling sailors set no example for good conduct. Shore patrols did not always stop Jack Tar when filled with spirit from visiting native villages such as Nanaimo, and from molesting Indian girls and creating a general nuisance of themselves. Reports of such behavior did not reach the Lords of the Admiralty nor were they to be found in the pages of Victoria papers. But occasionally, such as in a missionary account, they appear. And naval surgeon's records of syphilis and other venereal diseases tell of cross-cultural interaction with lethal consequences of an altogether different sort.[3]

These dilemmas of overseas expansion were well known in Britain. For all the government's desires to establish a society free from the contaminating evils of the American frontier, the Colonial Office knew that its native policy could not be promulgated fully from Whitehall. In large measure, it had to emerge "on the spot." London might supply guidelines. Local regulations supplied by willing and compliant governors would be required. Policy cannot operate without practice: material support for British interests would be required. This meant that on this maritime frontier the chief military tool of the Crown, the Royal Navy, had to serve as colonial policeman.

On the Northwest Coast in the 1850's and 1860's the Indian "policy" of the British was to extend the rule of law and order. The method of doing so was essentially crisis management. The British in London were devoted to a high-minded objective of protecting aboriginal peoples within their overseas territories. Hence their desire in 1849 to have strong executive authority (at the expense of local legislative power) in the Colony of Vancouver Island so that Indian "policy" would not fall within the hands of untrustworthy settlers. Similarly in 1858, when British Columbia came into existence, the governor was again provided with wide executive authority in Indian affairs. London instructed Governor Douglas "to pay every regard to the interests of the Natives which an enlightened humanity can suggest" and to employ "the best means of diffusing the blessings of the Christian Religion and of civilization among the natives."[4]

Yet these statements of "policy" were merely declarations of intent, that is, guidelines. London knew that the "man on the spot" was the key to an effective policy-making process, and much depended on the personality, character, experience and health of Her Majesty's representative. In 1858, the Colonial Office placed much confidence in Douglas and did not elaborate on these orders. They thought explicit instructions would only shackle him and were, in any case, because of his intelligence, his skills, and his experience, unnecessary.[5]

In these circumstances, the developing Indian policy was simply "meeting the needs of the day as they arose." Faced with a continuous barrage of problems from various locales on the Northwest Coast, the governor had to respond to pressures from various quarters—mainly from settlers and traders—and to put out fires. Governors of Vancouver Island and British Columbia tried to foresee the consequences of their action and at the same time to reflect on the lessons of the past.[6] They engaged in the policy-making process by responding to emerging problems and in many cases hopped from one problem to another. At the same time that Douglas might be attempting to deal with a piracy on the west coast of Vancouver Island, he might be faced with an Indian threat against white people or property in the Queen Charlotte Islands or intertribal violence on the upper reaches of the inner harbour at Victoria. These crises were sporadic, and the future was not predictable. But past experience demonstrated to Douglas that he required force to maintain his authority and the power and prestige of his office, which was the key to establishing a rule of law within British territory.

The major crisis Douglas faced during his long career was the 1858 Fraser River gold rush. The inrush of thousands of potentially unruly foreigners, most of them American, posed a danger to Douglas's authority. He used every possible mechanism to maintain the Queen's warrant, even employing Hudson's Bay Company monopoly trade regulations to control potential turbulence during the early phases. Because miners in California in 1849 had demonstrated their disregard for Indian lives and property, Douglas was keen to impress on miners "that no abuses would be tolerated; and the laws would protect the rights of the Indian, no less than those of the white man."[7] At this time Thompson River Indians believed the gold in their land to be theirs. They objected to the overbearing attitudes and aggressive acts of the whites, including maltreatment of Indian women.[8] In June, in response to white complaints at Hill's Bar on the Fraser that Indians were threatening to kill them for removing gold, Douglas went to the scene and lectured both whites and Indians on English law. He had British warships and government-hired merchant ships stationed in the river to watch and license miners. He sent parties of sailors, marines and Royal Engineers up the river as needs dictated. These shows of force helped stabilize the frontier, though in actuality the crisis resolved itself in its own way, partly because of Indian willingness to allow whites, as an Indian chief recalled, "to use that country on equal terms with ourselves." The forebearance of one tribe, the Couteau, a chief later claimed, "saved the country from war when the Indians were about to combine and drive out the Whites."[9] Douglas could not countenance lawlessness. He was determined to demonstrate his rule, "laws cannot be disregarded with impunity, and . . . while the intention exists to maintain them, the power to carry out that intention is not wanting."[10] In keeping with this, he appointed prominent members of Indian tribes as magistrates to keep order among the Indians. He also appointed justices of the peace at various places on the Fraser River to whom whites and Indians alike could apply for redress of grievances. The various means employed by Douglas served to resolve a potentially volatile problem, and his diplomacy among miners and Indians alike was exemplary. In this instance he proved a master of crisis management.[11]

A similar instance, though one far less well known, occurred in 1859. Following the discovery of gold, surveyors, traders and settlers continued to move into the lower reaches of the Fraser River Valley and the shores of Burrard Inlet. This migration placed pressure on the various Salish peoples living there, particularly the Musqueam near the mouth of the river, the Squamish on Howe Sound, and various Stalo tribes including the Capilano near the entrance to and on the shores of Burrard Inlet.[12]

On Governor Douglas's request, H.M.S. *Plumper,* commanded by Captain George Henry Richards, was sent to the upper reaches of Burrard Inlet to investigate the reported detention by Indians of a party of Englishmen. He was also to land a party of Royal Engineers to work on a road (later Kingsway) from the inlet to New Westminster. Richards arrived in the outer harbour on 20 August 1859 where he learned from Ki-ap-a-lano, chief of the Capilano, that the Englishmen in question were working at the coal beds unmolested. Richards went to the coal mine and talked with Robert Burnaby, colonial surveyor and leader of the party, who told Richards that he was on very friendly terms with the Indians and, as Ki-ap-a-lano had stated, was quite safe from molestation.

The circumstances of the case as told by Burnaby and Ki-ap-a-lano are as follows. On the 17th, while the party was sinking the coal shaft, they were visited by a large number of Capilano but not by Chief Ki-ap-a-lano, who was absent at Whatcom, now part of Bellingham, Washington. Some of the tribe told the whites that fellow tribesmen had been seized at New Westminster for murders they had not committed. They complained grievously of injustice. From the number of Indians there and the bearing of the whites, the Capilano feared violence. Ki-ap-a-lano said that the murders had been perpetrated by the Musqueams, with whom his people had much "ill feeling." The Musqueams had spread a rumour among the Capilano of the murders and this had been the cause of the demonstration against the whites. As far as his feelings towards the British were concerned, Ki-ap-a-lano categorically denied any hostility by his tribe against the whites. The whole thing, he said, had been a mistake.[13] Captain Richards's explanation to the governor was as follows:

> I impressed upon him through the interpreter that in the Queen's Territory all parties whether English, American or Indian must be subject to the English law which they could not take into their own hands. That certain retribution would follow any act of violence on the part of the Natives towards white men, but at the same time the Indians would receive every protection at our hands.

Richards advised Ki-ap-a-lano to take his complaints to the magistrate or the governor. He also informed him that although he had been sent to help whites "I should have been as promptly sent to afford him and his people protection against our countrymen had they needed it." Ki-ap-a-lano agreed to these provisions and said that he would use his influence among other tribes with whom he was on good terms to convince them to follow a similar course.[14]

At this same time, Richards obtained from Ki-ap-a-lano the names of two Musqueam Indians who had killed whites in the summer of 1858 at a Fraser river sawmill. This was "a most barbarous murder" of four men and one woman whom the Musqueams had evidently killed for their money. Ki-ap-a-lano said that he had withheld this information partly from disinclination to get them into trouble, partly from fear of consequences to himself. However, since then the Musqueams had murdered his own son and now he was prepared to tell of the crime.

On the basis of his enquiry, Richards wrote to his commanding officer, Rear-Admiral Baynes, making specific recommendations about the emerging Indian policy for the colony of British Columbia:

It appears to me that in the present relations existing between our people and the Indians, it cannot be a matter of surprise if many wrongs are committed on both sides, and my opinion is that the Natives in most instances are the oppressed and injured parties. The white man supplies him with intoxicating spirits under the influence of which most of these uncivilized acts are committed. The white man in too many instances considers himself entitled to demand their wives or their sisters, and if such demand is disputed, to proceed to acts of violence to gain their object.

Such acts were not infrequent, Richards remarked. "The Natives can be said to have but little redress in such matters, they are either ignorant of, or discontented with our mode of punishing such cases. Nor can the magistrates who are for the most part unacquainted with Indian character and habits, be expected to be competent to deal with them." In these circumstances, Richards recommended that an Indian agent familiar with Indian people be appointed in that area. This person should be assisted by two subordinates knowledgeable of the different Indian dialects and "the means of maintaining the influence which we already possess over the tribes." If these measures were adopted, such barbarous murders would not recur.[15]

Richards provides the best example of a naval officer determined to resolve white-Indian conflict on the Northwest coast. His competent and sensitive opinions, views he shared with many naval officers, led him to the belief that most of the difficulties lay with the whites, not with the Indians. If, therefore, intermediaries in the form of Indian agents could act as a buffer between whites and Indians, they could prevent further murders and promote white-Indian understanding.[16] Governor Douglas received this information from Rear-Admiral Baynes and thanked the naval officers for this information, though he seems to have done nothing immediately in response to Richards's requests and advice. Nonetheless, in due course, Douglas appointed Indian agents in the area for the purposes which Richards had set forward.

While the authorities could respond to certain needs of the day as they arose, they faced limits. For instance, the influx of European diseases could not be checked. In 1862 the ravages of smallpox reduced coastal tribes by as much as one-third. Victoria, the meeting place of tribes, was also the focal point of disease traffic. Indians also took syphilis home to their villages. Naval surgeon David Walker reported of his visit to the northern coast in 1864:

The extent of this poison is frightful and the results are such as cannot be contemplated without fear...if it were intended to exterminate the natives of this coast no means could be devised more certain than that of permitting these miserable wretches to return home in a state of sickness and disease; wives, husbands, and children become contaminated, and that too in places beyond medical aid, unchecked in its ravages this disease cuts off the prime of the population, and leaves the remainder physically unsuited to continue the habits and pursuits of their forefathers.

A hospital at New Westminster might help "check these ravages" and at least give the sick a chance of cure before starting home.[17] But again, these demands for action did not bring forth action. The governors of Vancouver Island and British Columbia did not regard contaminating diseases as crises threatening their power or white interests. The prevention and treatment of smallpox and syphilis and other aspects of health care lay beyond their immediate jurisdiction, and they watched as the wave of disease continued to engulf native peoples. They pursued no policy in this case, for its magnitude was too great.

Another case of another sort, which explains the variety of official responses, occurred at Fort Rupert in December 1865 and brought forth a minor storm of protest from Vancouver Island legislators against the intervention of the Royal Navy and a concern that Indian affairs be properly regulated. This case, unlike many others described in this book, was one of excessive force being used when circumstances, according to critics, did not warrant it. The use of power was largely covered up by the colonial executive against the wishes of the legislature. But, again, the official response to the needs of the day was at work in the mechanism of Indian policy.

For some years after the "miserable affair" at Fort Rupert, British warships called at Beaver Harbour, sometimes to gather coal, wood or spars.[18] Most often they went there to keep watch on the local Kwakiutl, known for their daring, marauding raids, and liquor traffic. Sometimes ships' captains had to threaten the chiefs with violence specifically destroying their village Ku-Kultz, which was adjacent to the fort, by gunfire, in order to achieve their ends.[19] But the Navy could do nothing in the face of rapid decline in the population from smallpox and syphilis.[20] Indian health care was the responsibility of government, Rear-Admiral Baynes told Douglas after the visit of H.M.S. *Plumper,* Captain Richards commanding, to Fort Rupert in 1860. Baynes understood that Douglas took great interest in improving "the social condition of the Indians" and that he was endeavouring to do so with the limited financial means at his disposal. Under the most advantageous circumstances, Baynes said, this could "only be a work of time" and concentrated efforts should be made towards young Indians.[21]

In investigating cases of slavery, murder and liquor traffic, Captain Richards found that the Fort Rupert Kwakiutl were prepared to resist any threat of force, including the presence of two warships, the *Plumper* and *Alert.* They only wanted revenge for the killing of one of their chiefs,

Tcoosma, by the Songhees in Victoria.[22] "The very decided stand they made in the presence of a force which they constantly acknowledged could destroy them all in a few moments," he advised Baynes, "convinced me that it is the wisest course to lead and teach these people."[23] Missionaries and teachers, native agents or Indian protectors were needed as intermediaries. If these were appointed at every Hudson's Bay Company post, where Richards and Baynes believed harm was being done to Indian interests by the crumbling authority of the Company, "such means would go far to prevent outbreaks extremely dangerous to the whole Indian population, prejudicial to our rule, and calculated to retard in great measure the colonization and advancement of the country."[24] Magistrates could check the liquor traffic, keep order among the settlers, and protect "the Indian against the White man who is generally the aggressor." In Baynes's view, Douglas was reluctant to adopt these measures, and thus offenders had to be brought a great distance to Victoria for trial.[25] "The whole Coast is without any Civil Authority," Baynes complained to Douglas, and except at Nanaimo where there was a magistrate, no civil enforcement existed. Thus, Fort Rupert and Fort Simpson should have magistrates.[26] Law must go to the frontier and not be ensconced only in the colonial metropolis. But this law had to be enforced by the civil authority, not by the Navy alone, whose influence, Baynes noted, had limits of effectiveness. As he explained to Douglas, "The benefit of a ship of war visiting the Northern Ports and other places where Settlers have established themselves is in a great measure neutralized from the officers in command having no control whatever over them, and the White people in the Forts, are very much mixed up with the Indians from the immorality that I fear has been encouraged amongst the servants of the Hudson Bay Company."[27]

Not all naval captains had the tact or the foresight of George Henry Richards. Others were much more hard-headed. One such was Captain Nicholas Edward Brooke Turnour, commanding the steam corvette *Clio*, who had seen action in the storming of Fort Serapequi, Nicaragua, in 1848, at which time he was shot through the body. Turnour reached Fort Rupert on 22 December 1865 to demand the surrender of three Fort Rupert Kwakiutl who had murdered an Indian from Newitty and to search the village for whisky. Turnour sent a landing party under First Lieutenant Charles J. Carey for this purpose. They were met on the beach by Chief Jim (or Gem as he was sometimes called) and fifty Indians while an Indian force of similar size had gathered near the Indian "ranch," armed with muskets and yelling and firing into the air over the heads of the landing party. Carey told the chief to secure the three murderers and to give up the whisky. Jim refused to do so unless the Navy gave two hostages. Carey thought Jim "the prime mover; he appeared to be urging his men to fire on us and was very threatening in his manner." Carey gave the chief the time-honoured ultimatum: unless the prisoners were given up in a certain period of time (which is not specified in Carey's report of proceedings), the Navy would open fire and destroy the village. At the expiration of that time, "we fired upon the Ranch, and totally destroyed it, with 50 or 60 large canoes."[28] Then they imprisoned Jim and ten other Indians.

This bald story of the brutal reduction of Ku-Kultz Indian village does not give a full account of proceedings. Chief Jim told the authorities that once the *Clio* left he would attack Fort Rupert in retaliation, and therefore Carey placed a skeleton marine guard in the fort to reinforce the company garrison. The Indians had sued for peace by hoisting a white flag in place of four flags they had defiantly raised as a sign of their independence, but they would not accede to the appeals from the Hudson's Bay Company officer in charge, Pym Nevins Compton, or from Morris Moss, an Indian agent for British Columbia, to give up the suspected murderers. The *Clio* withdrew for the night to a safer anchorage while the Indians threatened the fort. The next morning, Carey landed once more and appealed to the chiefs to surrender the alleged murderers, while at the same time Chief Jim on board the warship categorically refused to order his people to do what the authorities wished. Twice more the Navy party inflicted damage on the Indian villages, hoping that this would bring results. After no more houses were left to be destroyed, the authorities turned on the canoes, breaking all of them.[29]

In Victoria a major reaction to the Navy's brutality occurred when, on 5 and 6 January 1866, the *British Colonist* published the report of the encounter by the civilian pilot hired onto the *Clio*, Alexander J. Chambers. His report detailed the Navy's many attempts to force the surrender of the alleged murderers by peaceful and ultimately by violent means. Chambers held vehemently to the opinion that the Indians required "a salutary lesson not to play with a man-of-war as they boasted they were doing prior to the shells coming amongst them, or saying that they had seen plenty of men-of-war who always threatened them, but none of them ever fired on them yet. They will not forget the *Clio*, however." Underscoring his belief in the wisdom of retaliatory action, he stated that whites who knew Indian character were convinced that firm action was necessary: "sharp chastisement" brings effects to the Indians in question and to neighbouring tribes; "kindness and forbearance they cannot understand."[30]

Spurred to action, the colonial legislature demanded further details "in regard to the doings of the *Clio* at Fort Rupert; not with the design of condemning the action of Her Majesty's ship, but in order to have such Indian affairs brought under the cognizance of regular authorities." In actuality, Captain Turnour had given the governor, Arthur Kennedy, only the briefest sketch of the affair in writing and had visited him on his return to Esquimalt to explain the circumstances of the retaliation. Kennedy, obviously unwilling to let Turnour be abused by the public or legislature, merely wrote to the legislature that there were no papers on the subject which he could lay before them. And to the colonial executive, Kennedy gave a description of Turnour's terse report. After discussing the matter, the executive decided not to produce the document for the legislative assembly.[31] There the matter rested. Pressures from the public for an investigation into "the doings of the *Clio*" and into Indian affairs died at the highest level of authority in the colony. Nor was the matter taken up by the Lords of the Admiralty or the Colonial Office.

The Navy had exhausted its means of enforcing the law. The Fort Rupert Kwakiutl had defied all demands. The costs of this resistance were great. According to anthropologist Johan Adrian Jacobsen there in 1881, "their strength had been broken," many moved across the strait to the inlets of the mainland while others, 250 to 300, returned and rebuilt the devastated village. "Since then," he concluded in telling tones, "they have become lazy and sullen, impertinent and impolite towards strangers."[32]

In the late 1850's and throughout the 1860's Hudson's Bay Company authority over their own servants and over Indian tribes was disintegrating. The colonial authorities sought to fill this vacuum as best they could with the limited means at their disposal. Gradually a system of magistrates was established as was a colonial constabulary. In the meantime the Navy provided enforcement on the coast and, as has been demonstrated here, was not always effective in its work. The Navy, Rear-Admiral Baynes said, could not do all; the responsibility for civil authority lay with the colonial government. Governor Douglas did not always respond to troubles as they arose. He was active in 1858, as before, in visiting tribes, but by the early 1860's, owing to the press of duties in Victoria and New Westminster, he did not go to the frontiers of influence and turbulence. He was obliged to leave others to carry out the judicial functions of authority.

The Navy could aid him in the Fraser River gold rush, protect coal miners in Burrard Inlet, and investigate murders at Fort Rupert. However, the concept of "Send a Gunboat!" could only have been regarded by Douglas as an interim measure until regular civil authority supported by police could be established. But there was a lag between the needs of the distant frontier, particularly at Fort Rupert and Fort Simpson, and the appointment of police and magistrates. For financial reasons, if for no other, Douglas must have been pleased by the aid provided by the Navy. Baynes and his successors continued to appeal for a suspension of their duties among the Indians. But this cry went unheard by a governor who, one suspects, delighted in having his authority backed up by the force which held the sceptre of the seas.

6

Of Slaves and Liquor

THE WORK of Her Majesty's Ships in British Columbia waters extended to certain social questions that played on the Victorian conscience—slavery and liquor. Neither the anti-slavery patrol nor prohibition enforcement was easy work, for Indian slave owners and sellers and liquor vendors and producers were difficult to locate and even harder to stop. The gradual abolition of slavery was achieved by stopping intertribal marauding, but controlling the liquor traffic proved beyond the power of gunboats already taxed by other duties.

For thousands of years slaves had been an integral part of Northwest Coast Indian life, ideology, and mythology. Slaves were of high economic and prestige value to their owners. The Tsimshian, for instance, used non-Tsimshian slaves captured in battle for gathering and canoeing. In most if not all tribes, slaves were valuable items of property, but they themselves were outcasts (their heads sometimes shaved to identify them) and subject to their owner's disposal. Slaves were acquired by raiding parties or by purchase, and certain tribes—the Chinook, the Makah Nootka, the Newitty Kwakiutl, and the Tsimshian—were well-known slave traders. At various places, particularly The Dalles on the Columbia River and Port Simpson, slaves were bought and sold "after the fashion of dogs and horses," and prized dentalia or "money-shells," blankets, food and other property were used to pay for them.[1] Slavery was widespread for in 1845, by the estimate of two British army lieutenants, 5,146 persons lived in slavery in Hudson's Bay Company territories west of the Rocky Mountains, about one in every fifteen Indians.[2] Other surveys record the percentage of Northwest Coast Indians enslaved as between four and six, perhaps higher.[3]

The slave traffic could not be ignored by British officials who came to colonial British Columbia. Parliament had abolished the British slave trade in 1807 and legislated the end of slavery everywhere within the Empire in 1833. The Foreign Office had conducted an international campaign to rid the world of the institution. In New Caledonia and Oregon, the Hudson's Bay Company tried to eradicate slavery by denouncing it as illegal, by giving runaway slaves protection, and by considering all persons residing in company forts as free British subjects with absolute and legal rights. A "forcible emancipation," trader James Douglas wrote in 1838, was out of the question owing to native feelings. But the "immoral system" of slave traffic could be suppressed by "moral influence."[4] In other words, he trusted that the gradual voluntary extension of British law would eliminate slavery.

Douglas's policy of non-interference in an indigenous institution, and of trusting to the moral influence of law, and presumably of Christianity, for the eventual eradication of slavery showed an appreciation of the strength of Indian societies. Even as late as 1859 the Company did not attempt to free slaves by coercion. Rather, as is shown by the case of a Nanaimo Indian woman who had been captured in a foray by some Fort Rupert Kwakiutl, the Company engaged in the native custom of paying a reward for her return. By British practices this was indeed, as the British Boundary Commission naturalist who witnessed the transaction wrote, "a strange purchase."[5]

The coming of missionaries and legal institutions brought important moral suasion. Missionaries provided much of the remedy, preaching the equality of souls and establishing new native economies free of slavery. They had the support of the Crown and its representatives, who had to at least acknowledge civilly the powerful Aborigines' Protection Society and other British humanitarian groups. They had the support of some naval officers, many of whom like Admirals Moresby and Denman had served with distinction on the African slave patrols, and were themselves committed abolitionists.

On the British Columbia coast, Royal Navy officers were obliged to act to free slaves. Direct action could not be undertaken for a variety of reasons. But they did attempt to stop endemic intertribal warfare, an effort which officers believed would eventually check both slave-taking and slave-trading. And they sought to end these practices by extracting two promises from influential Indians: that they would cease to take or hold slaves and that they would end their marauding ways.

Sometimes the mere presence of whites hindered slave-taking. Commander Mayne wrote that the existence of a white party at Fort Rupert prevented hostility between local Kwakiutl and some hundred Haida.[6] On another occasion, at Fort Rupert, Captain George Henry Richards of H.M.S. *Hecate*, assisted by the presence of H.M.S. *Alert*, forced the ransom for one hundred blankets of a Nanaimo female slave named Husaw-i, whose husband had appealed to the authorities for redress. The Indians had sternly resisted, revealing "the attachment with which they cling to this among other habits of their restless, predatory lives."[7] On the other hand, the chiefs promised that they would willingly abandon their ancient custom of killing and taking slaves if other tribes would do the same.[8] And during Navy patrols or expeditions to the Queen Charlotte Islands, the Nass River, and elsewhere, slaves or captives were freed usually one or two at a time, given protection, and frequently returned to their home tribes.[9] It was not heroic work but one that went on in the usual course of gunboat activities.

In the process of following Douglas's guidelines, Navy officers provided a significant influence in changing native cultural mores. Douglas believed that the abolition of slavery and the security of the settlements could best be achieved by telling the Indians, especially those at or near Fort Rupert, in the Queen Charlottes, in the Nass-Skeena area, and on the west coast of Vancouver Island, that they must stop fighting one another and that they must live by British law. Thus in 1860, when the Indian "danger" had reached its apex, H.M.S. *Plumper, Termagant,* and *Alert*, all under the command of Captain Richards, undertook to take the governor's message to the various warring tribes and to extract promises from their chiefs that they would live according to the law and stop fighting each other, especially during their annual voyages to Victoria. The vessels sailed from Esquimalt on 31 July, proceeded to Fort Rupert, and then, each taking a section of the coast, visited all the main Indian villages north of Vancouver Island as well as those on the Island's west coast.

Everywhere the Indians received them very favourably. At Laskeek in the Queen Charlotte Islands, for instance, the old chief Konyil came on board the *Alert* and got an explanation for the ship's visit. His tribe, he was told, must stop its ancient habit of molesting other tribes. Officers took pains to explain to Konyil the advantages that would accrue to his tribe if they would live in peace and trust to the white man's laws for redress in case of wrong when any of his people should be living in Victoria. The chief, visibly nervous because of the ship's presence, promised compliance and even offered to restore all slaves stolen from Vancouver Island. He agreed to stop any further marauding expeditions, a promise given in order that authorities would permit the Haida to make their annual excursion to Victoria. Konyil's tribe, like others, was undergoing extensive social changes, owing in part to the numerous seductions of

Victoria and the relentless process of acculturation. This exchange between officials and the chief reveals that Konyil wanted to enlist the governor's aid in behalf of his people.[10]

At Skidegate, one of the largest and most important Haida villages, the *Alert's* officers learned just how severely these annual migrations were upsetting the Indian economies. There Chief Nestecanna, himself a one-time slave, told of his sincere desire to live under British rule. "You tell me King George sends you here to talk to all the Indians," he proudly told the British. "I am all the same as King George. Good you write down and tell Mr. Douglas and the Man of War to send all my people home. I wanted to build a large house this summer and nearly all my people are away at Victoria."[11] Near Masset the story was the same. The fact that Edenshaw and the whole of his village were spending their summer in Victoria meant that they would not have put in a stock of provisions, particularly of dried fish, for the coming winter.[12]

Again, at Port Simpson naval officers explained to the Tsimshian "that our visit was friendly and that the British Government was anxious and indeed solicitous for their welfare, that it would be much more to their interest and happiness to live peaceably and orderly among themselves, and of the greatest importance that they implicitly complied with the white man's laws when living among them, and this they were given clearly to understand would be vigorously enforced." They were told that the English "great chiefs" were angry at their ceaseless drinking, a vice which would destroy their whole race. They were also told of the British hatred of slavery, which could not exist wherever the British flag was unfurled. They were instructed to stop molesting other tribes, to be cautious during their excursions to Victoria, and to obey English law. Otherwise, retribution would follow. They were also notified that the "evil deeds" of the Indians and those of their fathers would be forgotten, although as British subjects the Tsimshian would henceforth be held accountable in British law. Lastly, the officers told the Indians that a warship would visit them periodically, it was hoped only on friendly terms.[13]

For their part, the chiefs promised obedience. They blamed their troubles on liquor and appealed to the officials to adopt strict measures to check "spirit sellers" from going among them. Young Tsimshian men and women promised to abstain from drinking, and "this marked expression of good intentions on the part of the Indians was a subject of mutual congratulations." At other coastal encampments captains of the warships announced that the government sought peace with and among the tribes, wanted to abolish slavery there as in other parts of the Empire, desired to end the liquor traffic, and, in general, intended to extend English law to the Northwest Coast. As a further step in this type of forest diplomacy, captains displayed their ships' firepower by exercising their gun crews, firing shot, shell, grapeshot, and canister to impress on the natives the force and utility of Her Majesty's guns.[14]

This cruise helped to put an end to marauding expeditions among Northwest Coast Indians. Governor Douglas's strategy of sending three warships at one time to win the accord of the native élites was particularly adroit. By extracting promises of mutual agreement among the Haida, Tsimshian, Kwakiutl, and other chiefs, the British acted as peacemakers. The chiefs seem to have been more concerned with economic realities and the social consequences of their situation than with the moral implications of slavery as perceived by the British. Nonetheless they apparently agreed to the terms presented. Thus gunboat diplomacy served to reduce internecine tensions and violence, helped achieve security for settlers, and weakened the tendency towards slave-taking and thus slave-trading. After this cruise the Navy continued to investigate cases of slavery and to free slaves.[15]

At the same time as British men-of-war were trying to end internecine violence and its byproduct slavery, they were engaged in attempts to regulate the wide-spread liquor traffic.[16] By the time missionaries such as William Duncan arrived on the scene, some Indians had already begun to distrust their own institutions. A white observer near Nootka in the 1860's ascribed the apathy, withdrawal, and listlessness of the natives to the Indian's contact with white civilization and the native's realization of the inevitability of the white ascendancy.[17] For the Indian, drinking persisted because it was one of the few remaining social activities in which older values could not be easily interfered with or destroyed. And it was regarded as a means of self-validation, of proof of manhood and womanhood. It had also become a way of reducing boredom. Not least, it served as a protest against the rising tide of empire.[18]

However, certain British Columbians of the mid-Victorian age believed that intoxication among Indians led inevitably to alcoholism and economic hardship. Some deplored liquor because of its related evils, particularly prostitution, which occurred in Victoria and other settlements. Mindful of the violent frontier experience in adjacent American territory, colonists wrote impassioned letters to the editors of local papers offering solutions to an Indian "problem" then very much in evidence at Victoria and Nanaimo.[19] Some blamed spirituous liquors for the demise and depravity of Indian populations and urged total abolition.[20] Others planned missions where oaths of abstinence would be taken. Still others, such as the bishop of Columbia and Anglican missionaries, called for Governor Douglas to send gunboats to check the traffic at such places as Port Simpson where a mission had been undertaken in a supposedly "dry" location.[21]

Many British naval officers wrote of the debilitating and evil effects of liquor among the natives. A ship's surgeon blamed "unscrupulous traffickers" for provoking natives, who were normally "quiet and inoffensive to a degree," to violence.[22] Captain W.R. Kennedy of H.M.S. *Reindeer* noted that the Indians were "a very degraded race, especially near the towns, where civilization in the form of whisky and disease have been brought to bear on them."[23] Rear-Admiral Baynes went even further by declaring, in a letter to the Lords of the Admiralty dated 10 September 1860, that the principal if not sole cause of Indian disturbances at Victoria was the ease with which the most deleterious spirits could be bought. In his opinion, the traffic was extensive, the governor reluctant to act, and the offending white traders beyond the Navy's jurisdiction.[24]

Liquor was, in fact, readily available to whites and Indians alike. In northern coastal areas near Alaska in particular, Indians brewed their own fermented beverage *hoochinoo*, or "hooch" as it was frequently called. This was a rough concoction of molasses, flour, berries, potatoes, yeast, water, and, when available, hops or anything that would add protein. Sometimes Indians went even further and distilled the fluid, ingeniously using old oil cans for retorts and kelp for condensing tubes. In addition, a wide and curious variety of intoxicants found their way to Indian consumers. These included whisky, rum, and solutions of camphor, bluestone vitriol, diluted pure alcohol, vanilla extract, colognes and even nitric acid. Mixes with curious names such as Old Tom, Jamaica ginger, and Florida water were highly popular in some native locales.[25]

Port Townsend, the city that whisky made—according to the United States customs informant J. Ross Browne—had its own liquor traffic with the Clallams. One potent concoction of alcohol, red pepper, tobacco, and coal oil, known affectionately as Tarantula Juice, proved particularly attractive to native consumers on both sides of the straits. Generally, traders cared little for the effect of their liquid wares on the Indians.[26] In most areas properly distilled liquors produced in Victoria, New Westminster and Puget Sound ports were considerably less hazardous to health than some solutions peddled by traders. Liquor control in colonial British Columbia thus became to some degree quality control. And it tended to force the Indians into drinking vile, unwholesome mixtures without restricting the quantity they consumed.[27]

Some of the earliest legislation in the colonies of Vancouver Island and British Columbia had made the sale, gift or barter of intoxicants to Indians illegal. In August 1854 the Executive Council of the Colony of Vancouver Island had passed legislation prohibiting the gift or sale of intoxicating liquors to Indians. The rationale for this, the preamble to the act ran, was that spirits were "manifestly injurious to the Native Tribes, endangering the public peace, and the lives and property of Her Majesty's Subjects." But liquor consumption in the white settlements was so widespread and the police forces so small that bootlegging to the Indians was extensively practised. In the region of Port Simpson Indians could obtain liquor from illicit traders or make it themselves, while prohibition tended to put the trade into foreign hands, either American or Russian. Rather than risk seizure in British waters, traders would lie over on the Alaskan side and let the Indian consumers come to them. Thus only foolish traders got caught. In Victoria and its environs, where no less than 149 places had licenses to sell drink in 1864, liquor was also readily available to natives. But here the authorities found their work easier than on the northern coast; in the years from 1858 to 1864, 336 persons were arrested for selling "ardent spirits" to natives and, of this number, 240 were convicted, in other words, there was a 71.5 per cent success rate in prosecutions.[28]

Moreover, colonial income from the sale of spirituous and fermented beverages was high, and in a time of economic uncertainty and high liquor consumption, it could not be frowned upon by legislators. At least twice, in 1861 and 1866, the Vancouver Island Legislative Assembly considered making the sale of liquor to the Indians legal. But such an act, Governor Kennedy acidly wrote in 1866, would have allowed the natives to "execute their own laws, that is, to murder each other without let or hindrance when inflamed by drink." He complained, as Rear-Admiral Baynes had before him, that legislators were reluctant to vote funds sufficient for adequate police control. They looked to the neighbouring American territories for precedents, and found that justice was administered by vigilantes and difficulties were adjusted by revolver and bowie knife. With only five policemen in the colony, Kennedy told the Colonial Office, whisky selling, drunkenness, and prostitution could hardly be checked. He urged union of the colony with British Columbia (a measure which was effected later that year) to aid in the development of a common Indian policy, one necessary for the protection of native interests.[29]

But the legislation prohibiting sale of liquor to Indians was never suspended. Indeed, after the union of the colonies in 1866, the legislative council passed a tougher measure prohibiting the gift or sale of liquor to natives. This ordinance, effective 2 April 1867, increased penalties against offenders, detailed rights of search by customs officers, police and the Royal Navy, and required ships to have bills of lading during their voyages from any port on the British Columbia coast to any other port in the colony or any other port or place on the Alaskan coast. But again the means to enforce these measures were wanting.[30] Overworked magistrates, police superintendents, and constables tried to check the illicit commerce as best they could. Unlike their counterparts in adjacent

Washington Territory or Alaska after 1867, they had no revenue cutters at their disposal. The colonies were too impoverished or, more likely, too ready to let the Navy do this work. In view of the limited number of ships at his disposal and the many calls on his squadron, the commander-in-chief could give little more than casual attention to the problem, despite growing local concern. Gunboats and sloops-of-war were only rarely under specific instruction to police the liquor traffic and then usually in connection with some other matter such as piracy, slavery, or murder.

Nonetheless, in 1862 and 1863, at Governor Douglas's request, Commander John W. Pike of the paddle-sloop *Devastation* took important steps to check the traffic in the Inner Passage near Nanaimo, Port Simpson, and Dundas Island. In September 1862, he had been sent north to Sitka, the Stikine River, and Port Simpson to protect British interests and investigate Indian relations. Near Dundas Island, Dixon Entrance, he learned that the *Hamley*, one of several notorious whisky-trading schooners sailing out of New Westminster, was nearby, having cleared Victoria for Port Simpson. Pike approached the *Hamley* and sent James Cooper, harbour master of New Westminster and a British Columbia colonial agent, to examine her papers. When her skipper could not produce a permit, manifest, or bill of lading, Pike ordered the *Devastation*'s master to pour into the sea that part of the cargo consisting of three hundred gallons of "vile spirits" including fourteen five-gallon tins of pure alcohol. On this occasion Pike chose not to seize the *Hamley* (a treatment not accorded less fortunate liquor traders), for it would have interfered with the *Devastation*'s more pressing duties. He justified his decision to destroy on the grounds that its distribution among the Indians at that time of excitement would have been followed by violence among native peoples.[31]

On the Nass River, Pike had a different sort of experience with whisky traders. In October 1861 the schooner *Nonpareil* had been doing business on Nass Bay, exchanging pure alcohol and camphine, "by no means uncommon articles of trade" according to Pike, for mink, bear, and blankets. She had secretly deposited immense quantities of spirits in various creeks for safekeeping while she replenished her cargo. During the trading much drinking ensued, and a quarrel developed between a Tsimshian crew member and some Nishga over a local chief's wife. The Nishga robbed the schooner. Pike believed they had been provoked and was inclined to dismiss the skipper's complaint. Nonetheless, he explained to the Nishga that they had no right to steal property and must return it, which they later attempted to do.[32]

Early in the next year, 1863, Pike intensified his attempts to suppress the liquor traffic. At Hornby Island, a known Strait of Georgia re-ship-ment point for spirits destined for Indians on the North Coast, he seized the liquid cargo of the wrecked schooner *Explorer*. She carried three or four hundred gallons of spirits from Victoria for sale on the Stikine River, where a gold rush was in progress. Pike knew that the Anglo-Russian Treaty of 1825 specified that British liberty of commerce on the Stikine did not extend to liquor, and he believed that the liquor was destined for Indian consumption. Therefore he impounded the cargo and sent it in a hired sloop to customs officers at New Westminster.[33]

In other cases, Pike was able to halt the traffic at the place of trade. Fort Rupert, he knew, served as the major bootlegging centre. At this native crossroads Indian middlemen from up and down Johnstone Strait rendezvoused with traders in hidden coves or picked up caches sunk at river mouths. Pike's close watch over Fort Rupert brought results. In April he seized seventy gallons of pure alcohol and mixed spirits. He sent the *Devastation*'s cutter to nearby Bishops Cove to bring down two hundred gallons of alcohol. He detained vessels and interrogated traders and consumers. It was a busy round of work in petty cases of illicit trade. Yet on Portland Canal, at the entrance to the Nass River, he made a major seizure of two vessels, the *Langley* and *Petrel*. The *Langley*, a floating distillery, had been selling alcohol and rum made by her master that very morning, and Pike found the Indians impoverished, having bartered away all their furs and blankets. During the trading the Indians had become divided. Some, fearing the evil influence of the liquor, wanted the *Langley* to set sail. Others, who had protection of the ship, refused to allow her to do so. Pike responded by impounding the *Langley,* and he towed her, with two other seized vessels, the *Petrel* and *Kingfisher*, to New Westminster.

There, on the basis of testimony supplied by Indian witnesses brought from the northern coast, the court fined the masters of the vessels heavily — $500 each in the case of the *Langley* and *Petrel*, with forfeiture of vessels and cargoes. Under terms of a British statute regulating seizures, the vessels and cargoes were sold, and a small portion of the prize money (£201.9s.6d.) went to the officers and ship's company of the *Devastation*.[34] It was not a large sum but a reward for hard work brought to a successful conclusion.

Pike's zealous activity did not go unnoticed by Governor Douglas, the British government, or the colonial press. The governor thought his work "judicious and thorough" and very satisfactory, for it would have beneficial results in the colony. When news of Pike's work reached the desks of the secretary of state for the colonies and the Lords of the Admiralty, both offices issued statements of approval.[35] The *British Colonist* noted that Pike's seizures were an index of "the unhallowed trade."[36] Pike won no medals for this peacetime service. Exhausted and in poor health, he was invalided home to England before his regular commission could be completed.

For a decade or more after the *Devastation*'s cruises, the Navy continued its patrols to check the liquor trade to the Indians. Warships watched schooners coming south from Alaska and north from Washington Territory, particularly from Point Roberts, the rendezvous for American liquor traffickers supplying consumers from Cowichan to Comox. Sometimes the search for the ubiquitous smugglers took gunboats to seldom visited bays, where landing parties raided Indian villages and seized or destroyed whatever spirits could be found. Such was the case of the steam corvette *Clio* during a successful cruise to Port Simpson and vicinity in 1865 and 1866 during which at least three whisky schooners were impounded.[37] To convict offenders in court, witnesses were needed. Thus on one occasion the Reverend Robert R.A. Doolan of the Church Missionary Society's Nass post, a horrified observer and strong opponent of Indian liquor feasts, proceeded on William Duncan's orders from Metlakatla into Indian dwellings to secure witnesses.[38]

Despite these successes by authorities, Indians on the Nass were able to get liquor, a whole village would be intoxicated, and, as Doolan noted sadly, fighting continued.[39] The trade was so extensive, so all pervasive in the straits and on the north coast that the cruise of one warship, the *Myrmidon* in 1873, could by no means police it.[40] Missionaries appealed for naval support and the justice of the peace at Port Simpson dealt out severe punishments to bootleggers, but legislators granted small sums for police, and Justice Matthew Begbie in New Westminster tended to reduce sentences against offenders.[41]

Checking slavery and policing the liquor trade were two duties which occupied the Navy in British Columbia waters. They bore on larger questions of bringing the British variant of civilization to the ocean's farthest shore. Their activities reflected aspects of the Victorian conscience. They aimed at suppressing an indigenous activity that had been almost universally deplored by the British nation, and in the other, the extensive operations of unprincipled traders whose work officials regarded as evil. The Navy's influence in the first was more effective. Slavery could be reduced by stopping intertribal violence. Liquor trafficking, however, could not be restricted given the consumptive desires of natives, the elusive tactics of vendors, and, perhaps above all, the inadequacy of colonial control over a trade that many argued was beneficial to some and harmful to others.

7

Among the Vikings of the North Pacific

A T THE SAME TIME as settlers and traders were making inroads into native territories on Vancouver Island, the Queen Charlotte Islands continued largely unknown to whites and remained that way for almost a generation. An insular empire, the rain forested, triangular-shaped archipelago lies 50 miles from the nearest continental shore and 550 miles northwest of Victoria. It was known in the colonial capital of Vancouver Island as the home of the Haida, the place from where the great chiefs and seamen came in their majestic canoes, defying the rough open passage across Hecate Strait and Queen Charlotte Sound and risking death at Kwakiutl hands in order to visit Fort Victoria. But it was also known for its gold, discovered in 1851, which made the Islands a place of concern in the colonial affairs of the United Kingdom. And, not least, it had acquired a reputation as a pirates' nest, where casual naval patrols gave fragile support to British pretensions of sovereignty and freedom of the seas.

"More than any other land upon the northwest coast," the anthropologist John Swanton wrote, "the Queen Charlotte Islands are homes for seamen."[1] The Haida Indians[2] regarded the archipelago and its resources as their own. "Haida," in fact, means "the people," an appropriate and noble appellation for persons splendidly secure in their idea of self and place. They knew intimately the seas, hidden haunts, inlets, and terrain of the islands. They were a distinct and homogeneous breed living in comparative isolation from their brothers on the mainland. They were the consummate Indian sea-rovers. The fabulous stories of their exploits and wars against the Tsimshian and Fort Rupert Kwakiutl reminded the

Anglican missionary W. H. Collison, who lived at Masset on Graham Island, of the sagas and deeds of the Norsemen in ancient times. Not surprisingly, whites frequently called them the "Vikings of the North Pacific."[3] Violence was an integral part of Haida life. Killing, beheading, and enslaving remained the traditional way of Haida warfare. These were horrible and offensive modes of conduct to white observers with different codes of warfare.

Whites also feared the Haida perhaps because invariably they knew them only by reputation. They had heard of the fate of whites during the era of the maritime fur trade. They had also heard of cannibalism and of the forbidding landscape. The Bostonian Robert Haswell pondered what would happen if his ships were wrecked on the Islands in 1789. He wrote that even if they could have hoped for life at the hands of "a most horrid race of savage cannables [sic]," the islands were destitute of the requisites needed to sustain humans. "All was solitary grandeur in this most desolate spot we had yet visited," an awe-inspired navy captain recorded in 1853 of his visit to Gold Harbour—"its very appearance would drive away civilized beings."[4] It was customary for white mariners to believe that if they were shipwrecked they would die at the hands of the barbarians. Or, if they were spared that fate, they would perish in a hostile landscape. These views, accurate or inaccurate, lingered for years.

Nonetheless, because of native strength and capabilities, white visitors to the Islands needed to exercise great caution. Since George Dixon's discovery in 1787 that a profitable commerce could be undertaken with the natives on the Islands' more sheltered and populated eastern shores, traders had come in increasing numbers. They would anchor in the narrow, deep bays and coves, sometimes securing their ship with hawsers to trees on either side. The Indians would then come alongside in their canoes, and not uncommonly as many as twenty canoes of male and female traders would begin to barter. A small ship of sixty or one hundred tons might carry only a crew of five or six; and when they were surrounded by ten times as many natives, it was necessary to be alert against pilfering or attack. One widely adopted technique used well into the late nineteenth century was to employ wide boarding nets about ten feet in width running all round the ship at the gunwales. These allowed strict control over the number of Indians who could enter the vessel. But the ship's crew had to be vigilant. In advising the Lords of the Admiralty that the *Beaver* had traded in the Islands for seventeen years, Captain Prevost explained that her officers and men had always dreaded Indian assaults during barter or even inland navigation. "No vessel," he cautioned, "should be allowed to trade in any part of these waters inhabited by Indians without being properly armed and manned, and in readiness to defend herself from their insidious attacks."[5] His recommendation was

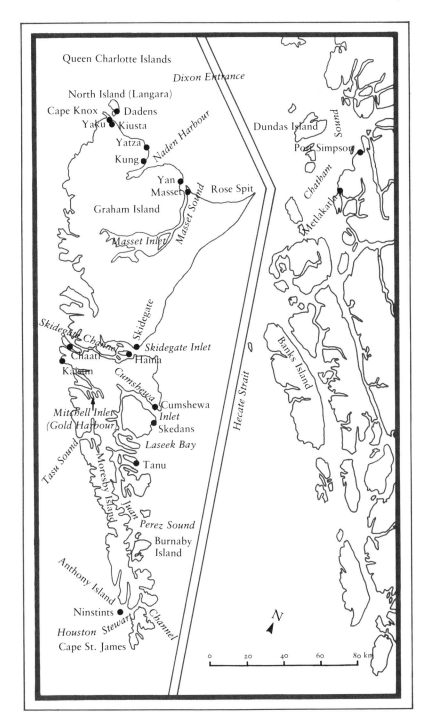

Queen Charlotte Islands

Dixon Entrance

North Island (Langara)

Cape Knox   Dadens

Yaku   Kiusta

Yatza

Kung   *Naden Harbour*

Yan

Masset   Rose Spit

Graham Island   *Masset Sound*

Masset Inlet

Dundas Island

Port Simpson

Chatham Sound

Metlakatla

Skidegate

Skidegate Channel

Chaatl   Skidegate Inlet

Kaisun   Haina

Cumshewa

Mitchell Inlet
(Gold Harbour)   Cumshewa
Inlet
Skedans

Laseek Bay

Tasu Sound   Tanu

Moresby Island

Juan

Perez Sound

Burnaby
Island

Banks Island

Hecate Strait

Anthony Island

Ninstints

Houston Stewart Channel

Cape St. James

N

0   20   40   60   80 km

justifiable because in November 1851 the sloop *Georgiana* had run aground in the Islands, and her Haida capturers held the twenty-seven passengers and crew ransom for goods worth $1,839, which was paid, as was customary in these cases, by the Hudson's Bay Company at Fort Simpson.[6] Further evidence for Prevost's caution was that in June 1853, near Stikine, Indians friendly to the Hudson's Bay Company had warned of the planned piracy of the *Beaver*, a timely act that had helped prevent her capture.[7]

Haida piracy against the American vessel *Susan Sturgis* brought the Royal Navy to the archipelago to engage in the first case of gunboat diplomacy in those seas at about the same time as officials in Fort Victoria and London acquired an interest in the future of the Queen Charlotte Islands. This 150-ton schooner, sailing out of San Francisco under American registry, was a familiar sight in the Queen Charlotte Islands. She was one of several vessels that had gone north in 1851 from California and Oregon ports after the discovery of gold. Governor Blanshard had reported the find to the Colonial Office, and his successor, Douglas, had tried to keep foreign vessels out of these British seas (an unwarranted act, London thought). Douglas had aimed to get a monopoly on gold extraction by sending the Hudson's Bay Company ship *Una* with miners to blast for ore and to trade with the natives. Douglas feared that if the Californians came in great numbers they would subvert British interests, plunder company posts, and raise the Stars and Stripes. Perhaps in that age when Americans, uncontrolled by their government, were sending armed parties to Nicaragua and Hawaii, his apprehensions were justified. In September 1852, the British government extended the jurisdiction of the governor of the colony of Vancouver Island by making Douglas lieutenant-governor of the Queen Charlotte Islands. This action originated the pattern, followed in 1858 when gold was discovered in tributaries of the Fraser River, of extending British authority to "turbulent frontiers" adjacent to existing jurisdictions.[8]

In the Queen Charlotte Islands, where the Hudson's Bay Company had no post and there were no British settlers, authority had to be shown, and hence a series of warships beginning with H.M.S. *Thetis*, a 38-gun frigate, Captain Augustus Kuper commanding, arrived in 1852 before annexation and again in 1853 to show the flag and prevent any American takeover, however real or imagined. Kuper found the navigation difficult, his charts were sketchy, and his pilot, a company servant who supposedly knew those seas, proved useless. But Kuper located Gold Harbour (now Mitchell Inlet) on the west shore of Moresby Island and discovered that generally the reports were true; Americans had been there, but the reports of gold were exaggerated. Anxious to defend their interests, the Indians collected in sufficient numbers to prevent the gold diggers from a second company ship, the *Recovery*, from working the vein. But certainly the precious metal existed there, for the local chief had a piece weighing twenty-two ounces which he was willing to trade for fifteen hundred blankets, an exorbitant price, Kuper thought. He found the Haida in that locale most friendly and generally well-disposed towards the whites. Even the Company, in spite of the threat mentioned above, told Kuper they rarely had trouble with the natives.[9] "Beyond the noise they made," Kuper said, they "caused us no annoyance whatever."[10]

Indeed, Kuper's concern was less with the Indians than with the American trading vessels and miners. He had heard that the *Susan Sturgis* had been in those waters, having left seven British miners to search for gold near the Company's Gold Harbour operations, and that she was expected to return to take them to San Francisco. When she came in sight, he sent a boat to her to warn her master, Matthew Rooney, that all speculators on that coast could be there only upon sufferance.[11] By implication, the Royal Navy could not afford protection to such shipping in these seas. These vessels were there without right and at the mercy of the Indians whom Kuper classified this time as "numerous and warlike."[12]

Rooney flagrantly ignored this warning, and the *Susan Sturgis* continued to trade in the Islands, and on her next voyage out of San Francisco, she called at various harbours trading for fish and looking for Chief Edenshaw. He was a young, powerful, crafty, boastful and energetic chief whose seat of power was then the new fortified village of Kung at the narrows leading to Naden Harbour on Graham Island's north coast. Chief of the Sta Stas Eagles, he was perhaps the most ambitious chief in the area. His predecessors had a longstanding history of dealings with Europeans that provided his Sta Stas Shongaith lineage with prestige and substantial trade advantages. This heritage dated from 1788 when a former chief of Kiusta, Blakow-Coneehaw, had exchanged names with the British maritime fur trader William Douglas as a compliment to one another. Successive chiefs, including Edenshaw, were proud of this fact.[13] In 1850, Edenshaw had led the Hudson's Bay Company to the gold discoveries, a further index of his commercial aggressiveness.

Above all, Edenshaw was a superb sailor who had an excellent reputation as a pilot, and he was much in demand by ships' captains and traders. For this reason the master of the *Susan Sturgis* was obliged to find Edenshaw before trading. At Skidegate, Edenshaw, his wife, and child were received on board the schooner for return to their village. The Skidegate Indians observed the defenceless state of the ship, but Chief Nestecanna, one-time slave and now a great ruler, warned Captain

Rooney "not to stay so long as he intended as the Indians were talking bad, or to tell them he was going to sail on a certain day and to leave earlier." Somehow, when the *Susan Sturgis* did sail, the Indians communicated overland with the Masset people and advised them that it would be easy to capture her.[14]

The schooner's cruise was uneventful until she rounded Invisible or Rose Point Spit, known to the Haida as Nai-Koon, or long-nose, an immense and dangerous sandpit running northeastward from Graham Island. Here a Masset canoe came alongside the vessel. Rooney may have been culpably careless, but he did not know the native language and could not understand what Edenshaw said to the Massets. Indian testimony states that the chief advised them of the ship's defenceless state and said that he would capture her as soon as she arrived at his harbour, then only a few miles away. Edenshaw claimed he told them to bring barter items alongside. The next day, when she lay becalmed off the western point of the harbour, twenty-five canoes came alongside, apparently to barter dried fish. But here was no usual trading party. Rather the Massets, led by old Chief Weah, were all well-armed, their faces were painted black (a signal for war), and no women were on board, an unusual event because no barter was carried on without them. Rooney foolishly took no notice of these details, and all at once the vessel was boarded by about 150 natives. In a very short time the whites were made prisoners and stripped of their clothes, and the vessel was wrecked and burnt. Her strong box, containing $1,500 in gold and silver, was pillaged. What happened between Edenshaw and the attacking chief, Weah, will never be completely known. However, certainly Weah was persuaded to spare the lives of the whites when Edenshaw intervened and told him the Hudson's Bay Company would pay a handsome ransom in blankets for the men delivered safely to Fort Simpson. Rooney later wrote that he and his crew owed their lives to Edenshaw, which may well be true. Nonetheless, Edenshaw and his party shared with the Massets in the spoils. This confused, dual role remained a puzzle to Rooney and to naval officers who investigated the case.[15]

After the whites were ransomed at Fort Simpson, H.M.S. *Virago,* a powerful paddle-wheel sloop, James C. Prevost commanding, was sent to inquire into the circumstances. The difficulties of the *Thetis's* passage had revealed that the next warship to visit the Queen Charlottes should be steam-powered so that she could reach the numerous west coast bays where trading vessels and miners' parties could be secreted and where prompt and vigorous action could be taken. It was not British policy to exclude foreign ships, as Douglas would have liked, but instead to protect British persons and property against depredations by Indians or unwarranted intrusion of foreigners in the queen's territories by sending a naval force.[16] Clearly the government gave equal weight to the Indian and American threats. There was no hint of humanitarianism here, only the necessity of securing national interests.

Prevost knew that he must find Edenshaw and question him on the details of the *Susan Sturgis*'s plunder and he found him trading at Fort Simpson.[17] The Indians there knew of the piracy and were afraid that the *Virago* had come to punish them for their involvement. "We found the natives armed in great numbers prepared to make some resistance if we have come for the purpose of punishing them," Henry Treven, the ship's surgeon, noted in his diary. "On finding we were not come for anything but a friendly visit, we were soon surrounded by upwards of fifty canoes. Our arrival was a great novelty being the first man of war Steamer that has ever been here." Prevost detained Edenshaw on board the *Virago* to prevent any treachery on the Indian's part at the Queen Charlotte Islands. The British officers therefore had ample opportunity to judge this now legendary chief. Prevost thought him the most advanced Indian he had met with—"quick, cunning, ambitious, crafty, and above all anxious to obtain the good opinion of the white man."[18] The ship's surgeon thought him "a sharp fellow and known to be a great rogue" and "a great vagabond."[19] These officers had no doubts as to his slyness or motives. They believed that he planned to continue his attacks on shipping and even to capture the *Virago* by luring the ship into some navigational snare and then attacking her with his men. Because Edenshaw knew the local waters so well, he was valued by Prevost, as by Rooney before him, as an able pilot. But at the same time they knew he could put the ship in jeopardy by a mere turn of the helm. Edenshaw seemed very eager to take the steamer close to land, Treven said. "We told him to be careful where he took the ship, that we drew 16 feet of water and if the ship grounded or struck a rock we would hang him immediately to the yard arm." They showed him the hanging rope, but at first he laughed it off as a joke. However, the chief looked alarmed when a Hudson's Bay Company trader on board told him that he would die if the ship got on shore. He "begged that the ship be brought to anchor when we were about four miles from the land," Surgeon Treven gleefully recorded. Prevost did not include this incident in his report to Rear-Admiral Moresby, perhaps because he continued to remain uncertain about Edenshaw's paradoxical character. "I have no doubt," he informed Moresby, "that he was with men assisting in the plunder [of the *Susan Sturgis*], and was greatly enriched by his share of it but at the same time I believe he knows too well the power white men possess of punishing such crimes to be guilty of this himself."[20]

In these still confused circumstances, Prevost could not take action against the enigmatic Edenshaw. As for the Masset Indians, he believed that they deserved punishment. However he decided not to take coercive measures because many of the tribe who had plundered the *Susan Sturgis* were absent at Sitka, as were all the chiefs, and because those remaining behind promised that they and their brothers would never be guilty of a similar crime again but would give up their lands to Prevost and become "King George's subjects" and also would restore some of the plundered property. He believed that the demonstration, made without any hostile act "towards defenceless savages," would prevent them from committing similar atrocities and satisfy the commander-in-chief and the British government. Had any lives been taken, Prevost told the Masset, they would have been severely punished and the murderers given up to justice.[21]

In deciding on what sort of punishment should be exacted, Prevost had had to determine whether the crime had been against property or life. "Providentially," he told Moresby, it had not been against life, and he hoped that the *Virago*'s visit "though not marked by any sanguinary result, will be the means of preventing these ignorant but treacherous creatures from committing any further acts of plunder." Moresby was gratified by Prevost's judicious and firm demands upon the pirates. He was genuinely pleased that satisfaction had been obtained without resort to bloodshed. He hoped, he told the Lords of the Admiralty, this forebearance would restrain the Masset from committing further acts of plunder. At the Admiralty, Their Lordships approved Prevost's able report.[22]

Meanwhile, ten thousand miles away at his station headquarters at Valparaiso, Chile, Rear-Admiral Moresby grew increasingly concerned about the *Susan Sturgis* affair, the gold rush, and possible American annexation. In keeping with London's decisions, he sent Captain Wallace Houston as senior naval officer to Esquimalt in H.M.S. *Trincomalee*, with instructions to keep an eye on British interests in the Queen Charlottes. At that time the Navy's watch on Russian movements in the North Pacific was intensifying owing to rumours of war, and Moresby had determined that the *Trincomalee* should visit the great Russian American port of Sitka on a voyage of inquiry. Thus it was left to Houston's discretion as to whether he should call at the Islands.[23]

With a thoroughness admired by his fellow officers, Houston called at Virago Sound, Graham Island, in September 1853 and took the opportunity to check on the state of the gold rush, to search out Edenshaw, and to make a visible display of force. Houston had been led to understand that the Haida "held great guns very cheap, that many believed they were of no use." He took the occasion to exercise his gun crews, who fired shot, shell, and rockets at distant targets. The Indians were surprised at the accuracy and explosive capabilities of the projectiles, whose improvement over the eighteenth-century cannon ball was evidently not appreciated locally. They told Houston that one or two shells could blow them all up. Captain Houston gave Edenshaw, who arrived later, a special demonstration on request, the latter having doubted the word of other Haida who had told him of the devastating qualities of the ship's guns. "This very intelligent chief," Houston told Moresby, "was perfectly satisfied and fully understood the nature of these projectiles."[24] The British believed they had made their point.

Houston's opinion of the Haida as corsairs differed little from that of Kuper or Prevost before him. He concluded that it was unsafe for whites to trade with the Haida, and he pointed to the case of the Hudson's Bay Company's brigantine *Vancouver* as sufficient reason. This nearly new vessel was wrecked on Rose Point Spit in August 1854, the second company vessel of that name to be lost on the invisible spit, the first having been wrecked in 1834. The *Beaver* arrived before many Indians knew of the disaster, and yet those natives who were attracted to the scene "behaved as badly as possible," taking liberties by conducting their own salvage operation before the ship was abandoned. The Company officers considered it their duty to set fire to the brigantine and sacrifice the cargo worth £4,000 rather than let it fall into Indian hands.[25] In reporting the wreck of the *Vancouver* to the Company's Board of Management in Victoria, Captain W. H. McNeill wrote from Fort Simpson:

> I must mention that after all had been done possible to save the *Vancouver,* Captain Reid set fire to her, as he says she was breaking up and the sea making a complete breach over her. The Indians had begun to plunder and break up the vessel. Those Massets again, as it was they gave some annoyance. It is now time that this Edenso [Edenshaw] and his gang were punished.

Prevost's expectation that the Masset would cease their piratical ways following his forebearing treatment of them after the *Susan Sturgis* affair had proved to be woefully unrealistic. The Haida apparently would attack any shipping, company or non-company, which fell into the lair of the legendary spit.

Houston had no doubts about the piratical capabilities of the Haida. In the case of the second *Vancouver*, the company officers knew Indian ways. What would have been the result, he asked, if the officers of the vessels had been strangers? The Haida, he knew, would have hesitated to take life because they knew that the Hudson's Bay Company would always ransom white people. Yet he believed that the *Susan Sturgis*'s loss the year before would prevent all vessels with small crews from trading with the Haida, because such attempts would always end in the loss of vessel and cargo. And Houston knew that the whites could not always expect to be given passages of safe conduct in view of the state of internecine struggles. "The different tribes are in a perpetual state of warfare," he advised Moresby, "shooting and robbing each other, taking prisoners for slaves, etc. Why should the white stranger expect any other treatment, unless he goes amongst them well armed and prepared?"[26]

With the gold rush in decline after 1852, the British control of the archipelago existed in name only. Yet the mere act of annexation meant that the colonial authority and the officers of Her Majesty's Navy felt obliged to protect British subjects who went there. Thus, in 1858, when the gold fever flared up again, numerous adventurers were attracted to other places in New Caledonia and eventually to Cariboo. They went as well to Moresby Island where gold was already known to exist. In 1859 the Hudson's Bay Company sent another expedition from Victoria, and although very little gold was discovered, once more with Edenshaw's help, they located some iron and much copper at the Copper Islands on the east coast.[27] This new discovery resulted in the formation of a new company, the Queen Charlotte Mining Company, and Francis Poole, a young geologist, was sent to investigate the riches of Burnaby Island.

Before leaving Victoria, Poole had paid his respects to Governor Douglas, who informed him that he regretted not being able to supply him with the protective arm of a gunboat and a detachment of marines. Douglas told Poole that the hostility attributed to the Haida was well-founded, and he advised him to supply himself with plenty of arms and ammunition. But Indian consent was necessary and advisable. And in Douglas's presence, Poole extracted a promise from the great Gitkins (or Kitgnen as he spelled it), the hereditary Raven's crest chief of the Kloo tribe of Tanu, Laskeek Harbour, who was then visiting Victoria, that he would bring his power to bear so that Poole's party would not be molested in their landing or occupation at the mines.

When Poole reached Laskeek Harbour, he found the Kloo in council. They were worried that a gunboat or two from Esquimalt might visit them and use coercive measures. They asked Poole to give them a reference or protection note. This meant that the Kloo had heard of what the Navy had done elsewhere, perhaps at Newitty, and might do again where resistance was encountered. On the other hand, internecine rivalries, which were still more important to the Haida at this time than the white-Indian relationship, meant that Poole's position remained tenuous. Thus, when the Kloo heard that a neighbouring tribe intended to attack their village, "booty being their undisguised motive," Poole sent off a despatch to Victoria asking that a gunboat be sent. The timely appearance of Captain Richards commanding H.M.S. *Hecate*, "left a most wholesome impression" on the Indians. "For a long time after her visit," Poole wrote, surely with some exaggeration, "whenever the Indians showed disposition to be saucy, we had only to glance with a smile towards the Northwest (the direction in which the gunboat steamed off), and their bodies would quake from head to foot, whilst they rolled their eyeballs wildly."[28]

Actually, Poole had no difficulty with the Haida who were often co-operative and seldom dangerous. The threat of coercive measures by the Royal Navy may have been enough to have prevented them from retaliation against the obvious white intrusion. On the other hand, they may not have been in any position to meet the white influence in their islands. Their population dramatically declined as smallpox and other diseases did their fatal work. Illicit whisky sales and internecine violence intensified. Moreover, they no longer had the sea otter as a resource, and the Haida had reverted to a seasonal cycle of fishing, hunting, and gathering. Indians left ancient village sites and migrated to others, new and old; by 1876 only eleven villages were occupied whereas in 1834 there had been thirty-four. One estimate shows the population diminishing from 10,000 in 1774 to 4,400 in the 1860's.[29] In short, these were tragic years for the Haida and ones of great social readjustment. Totem poles reached their zenith in size and complexity and potlatching increased in the ongoing rivalry among the Haida subdivisions for power, prestige, self-validation, and even survival.

In these circumstances, certain people offered solutions to the Haida plight. Prevost, whose missionary activities are detailed elsewhere, dispensed New Testaments to Edenshaw's sons. Poole, for another, thought the Haida could be saved and elevated by the immigration of industrious Britons and that the Queen Charlottes could be elevated to become one of the "brightest and most precious jewels in the British Crown."[30] This was not the first call for an island mission,[31] but the publication of Poole's *Queen Charlotte Islands* in 1872 resulted in further interests in the Islands, and in 1876 Anglican mission enterprise extended to Masset where the Hudson's Bay Company had established a trading post in 1869. Other missions were founded by Anglicans and other denominations, and these had a marked effect on the Haida economy, leadership, and culture.

Yet the Haida population decrease could not be immediately reversed, and in 1876, Collison at Masset estimated that only 1,300 lived in the northern and 500 in the southern parts of the Islands.[32] By this time most of the natives of Edenshaw's legendary Kung had left, leaving substantial, well-constructed houses to decay or be engulfed by the advancing forest. At Edenshaw's seat of empire only low trees and a protecting sandbar now remain where the fortress had commanded the narrows. As for Edenshaw, he seems to have cultivated the arts of peace, much to

Prevost's pleasure. In 1878, when Prevost once more visited Masset, Archdeacon Collison took Edenshaw and his son to see the officer, now an admiral. The chief had not seen him since the *Virago*'s visit, Collison wrote. "But now he no longer feared to face a naval officer, as he had learned not only to obey the law himself, but to lead his tribe to do the same. The Admiral was delighted to learn that the Haidas were abandoning the warpath and devoting themselves to follow the path of peace."[33] The Canadian government gave him a reserve, but he migrated to the town of Masset and died there in 1894, long remembered by a much-photographed monument presented by a grateful British government and erected outside of the house of his relative Henry Edenshaw. The inscription on his tombstone states that he was a staunch friend of the white man who had heroically saved the captain and crew of the *Susan Sturgis*.[34] This does not tell all. His plots, which may well have been taken to advance his position in relation to other Haida chiefs, clans, and families, were known to Prevost, Treven, and others. Kuper did not exaggerate when he wrote that Edenshaw was "a man of great influence in the neighbourhood" and one worth treating "with every consideration."[35] The *Susan Sturgis* affair doubtless contributed to the stereotype, long-sustained, that the Haida were, as a navy lieutenant-turned-police superintendent put it, "a fierce and wild race."[36]

The Haida and particularly Edenshaw rightly deserved the title Vikings of the North Pacific. They were a seaborne people with immense warlike capacities. They were pirates capable of luring maritime wayfarers into their dens and laying plunder to their ships and then enslaving or ransoming their crews. Their piracies, though few in number, continued at least as late as 1868.[37] These acts left a deep imprint on the minds of certain whites who fell prey to the Haida or endured captivity among them.[38] Thus, in the early literature of British Columbia frequent references are made to the Haida as the most warlike on the coast, "a kind of sea coast Blackfeet," one writer said.[39]

The Navy's role in Haida history in the early 1850's was hardly violent. Kuper, Prevost, Houston, Richards, and other officers never took punitive measures against them. Prevost came as close to any in being obliged to do so. Yet he proved the point to his satisfaction and his superiors' by a display of power and by careful explanation to the Masset that the British were acting without violence for specific reasons. Subsequent visits by gunboats and warnings of officials—that the Haida were to stop their marauding ways and trust to the white man's laws for redress of grievance rather than continuing their internecine violence—contributed to the peaceful course of Haida change.[40] The Navy worked to police the liquor traffic in the Queen Charlottes, and to stop slavery there as well. However, they found the Haida a breed apart, and much of this was sustained from the legacy left by Edenshaw and the *Susan Sturgis* affair. Edenshaw won the admiration of British naval officers, who wondered at the exercise of his power and extension of his influence by whatever means were required. Here was a chief intent on becoming the greatest of all Haida chiefs. But no sooner was this done in the 1870's than the Haida were already, like other Indian peoples, bound on a course of economic, religious and political change in which the chiefly ambitions of an Edenshaw were facing severe tests.

8

Piracy and Punishment

A S IN THE QUEEN CHARLOTTES along the west coast of Vancouver Island the British faced difficulties in protecting settlers and traders and property and in maintaining order among fiercely independent Indian tribes. In the deep arms of the Pacific Ocean that penetrate far into the Island and in the interlocking channels and numerous coves that were the natural habitat of these vigorous seafaring peoples, the west coast Indians possessed a maritime environment that provided wealth, prestige, and security. North and west from Fort Victoria, the shore is virtually unbroken except for Port San Juan opposite Cape Flattery at the entrance to Juan de Fuca Strait. But at Cape Beale, Barkley Sound and its annex Alberni Canal affords a vast, navigable highway into the Island's heartland. From Amphitrite Point to Lennard Island the shore is again relatively unbroken, but at Lennard Island Clayoquot Sound begins—a maze of channels and islands not as spacious as Barkley Sound but still a domain unto itself. Farther northwest again, beyond Hesquiat Harbour and Estevan Point, lies legendary Nootka Sound, another extensive marine access into the Island's interior. Northwest once more the mariner finds in turn Esperanza Inlet, Kyuquot Sound, Quatsino Sound, and the Island's northwesternmost tip, Cape Scott, which points to the broad reaches of the North Pacific stretching across to Asia. Barkley and Clayoquot, Nootka and Quatsino—these were the seats of empire of peoples who differed as much from each other as Latvians do from Russians or French from English—with different languages and modes of behaviour that they prized and defended.

From the time of earliest European contact, especially after James

Cook's 1778 visit, whites had shown a preference for the Nootka, who were skilled diplomats and traders. The Kyuquot to the north were more difficult to deal with, as they were reluctant to welcome foreigners. So were the Clayoquot, including the Ahousat tribe to the south, who acquired a reputation as aggressive and dangerous. They were regarded as such by their native enemies, the name Clayoquot having been given them by their neighbours. The term meant that they were different from what they had been; and the Indian oral tradition held that the Clayoquot had once been quiet and peaceful but that later they had grown troublesome and treacherous.[1] Even their appearance frightened some intruders: one trader thought some of these tribes "really looked as if they had escaped from the dominions of Satan himself."[2]

From the late eighteenth and early nineteenth centuries, this maritime frontier had a violent history of white-native contact.[3] Such events as the captivity of the English carpenter John Jewitt in 1803 and the loss of John Jacob Astor's *Tonquin* in 1811 among the natives were celebrated stories at Victoria. In these inshore waters, piracy had been frequent. Captains and crews of trading vessels on the coast sought to avoid the tribal rivalries and relentless warfare that existed among the west coast Indians, particularly the Clayoquot and Ahousat peoples, that continued through the 1850's. "They are a most treacherous, thievish lot of rascals that cannot be trusted out of sight," the master of H.M.S. *Hecate* there on survey in 1861 wrote of the Ohiet Indians living near Port Effingham on the outer reaches of Barkley Sound, "altho' civil enough for us being man of war's men; but poor lost away ships crews have been dreadfully maltreated by them." He held similar views of the neighbouring Sechart and Uclulet, remarking of the latter that "they would be only too glad to murder all the boats crew for sake of the utensils in her; only knowing us to be a man of war — of which they have a wholesale dread, are afraid of the consequences."[4] Moreover, these Indians' concept of property contrasted sharply with that of the whites. The American trader John Boit claimed that these Indians would pilfer whenever they had the chance.[5] They did not acknowledge rights of salvage of wrecked vessels; Vice-Admiralty courts were unknown to them. Any whisky trader or sealer sailed this coast at his own risk, aware of the consequences if his vessel ran aground on a hidden rock or was dashed to ruin in a gale.

Captain Vancouver's surveys, though important, had actually given navigators only a modicum of data on the Island's waters. The jagged shoreline remained largely unsurveyed until Captain Richards examined Barkley Sound in 1859 (the Admiralty published his chart of the area in 1861) and completed the rough features of a cartographic outline as far north as Cape Scott in 1862.[6] Thus in the late 1850's these largely uncharted, unlighted, and unbuoyed waters were a veritable graveyard of

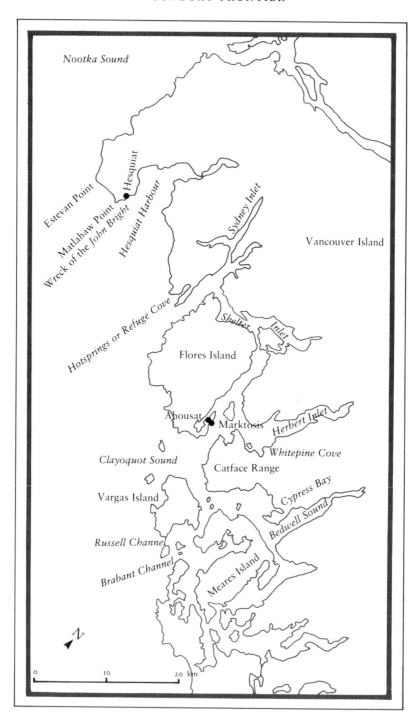

Nootka Sound

Estevan Point

Matlahaw Point

Wreck of the *John Bright*

Hesquiat

Hesquiat Harbour

Sydney Inlet

Vancouver Island

Hotsprings or Refuge Cove

Shelter   Inlet

Flores Island

Ahousat

Marktosis

Herbert Inlet

Whitepine Cove

Clayoquot Sound

Catface Range

Cypress Bay

Vargas Island

Bedwell Sound

Russell Channel

Brabant Channel

Meares Island

N

0   10   20 km

ships, ready to entice to destruction the ignorant or distressed mariner. For this reason, Rear-Admiral Baynes declined to put one of his squadron's ships needlessly in jeopardy. For this reason he would not answer Governor Douglas's urgent plea of 28 October 1859 to send a warship, whenever convenient, to an unsurveyed shore where navigation was, in Baynes's opinion, "dangerous and intricate."[7] For the time being, the west coast of Vancouver Island was out of bounds for British maritime authority.

Despite these obstacles, the profits of trade were sufficiently large in the 1850's to attract a few coasting vessels. In 1852 the Hudson's Bay Company ship *Eagle* was lost and plundered at Clayoquot; and Douglas, regretting the "bad conduct" of the Indians on this occasion and having no force at his disposal to prevent such acts, could only report the event to the Colonial Office with the hope it would bring some imperial intervention.[8] On another occasion, Trader Barney, sailing from Victoria in a schooner, was killed by some Clayoquots at Manhouisaht village in Hot Springs Cove. Captains of trading vessels raised a general alarm. As one skipper declared, the coast from Clayoquot Sound to the Island's northwestern tip appeared absolutely unsafe for traders. He warned that the natives arrogantly boasted that they cared nothing for British gunboats, for Governor Douglas, or, for that matter, for anyone else.[9]

In 1859 the destruction of the *Swiss Boy* intensified the fears of coastal mariners. This American brig, outward-bound from Port Orchard, Puget Sound, to San Francisco laden with lumber, began to take on water through her worm-infested hull, and was beached for repairs at what became known as Robbers Bay, Trevor Channel, Barkley Sound.[10] The vessel was defenceless, and on 1 February local Indians—some Ohiet, others Sheshat—boarded her. They destroyed masts, rigging, and sails; they pillaged the cabins; they robbed the sailors; and they carried ashore everything of value. Her master, Weldon, and crew took refuge in the forecastle where they stayed unmolested for a few days, and escaped an unknown fate by the timely intervention of a young, highly intelligent and widely respected Makah or Cape Flattery chief, pilot and interpreter called Swell, or more correctly (by his kin) Wha-latl.[11] While the waterlogged brig lay on the beach, Weldon and the crew made their way in the schooner *Morning Star* to Victoria. There Weldon made it widely known that only Swell's assistance had saved them.[12] Under the uncomfortable pressure of Weldon seeking help from United States officials in San Francisco, Governor Douglas decided to ask the Senior Naval Officer at Esquimalt, Captain James C. Prevost, to investigate the *Swiss Boy* affair.

Ordered to Barkley Sound to investigate, Captain James C. Prevost of H.M.S. *Satellite* went first to Ohiet. The Indians seemed unconscious of the object of the ship's visit and were "apparently ignorant of having committed any crime." They wanted to trade. By winning the natives' confidence through trade and with the help of the Cape Flattery Chief Swell who had been taken on at Neah Bay as interpreter, the British secured and brought to the vessel the ringleader, "George," and three fellow Ohiet suspects. A landing party recovered some stolen property at nearby Ohiet village. Prevost learned that the Sheshat were implicated and accordingly he visited their village and two others in Barkley Sound, Uchucklesaht and Opetchesaht at the head of Alberni Canal. Yet Ohiet was the place of the captain's concern, and he returned there to show the flag. "I had no sooner anchored," Prevost recorded, "than a subordinate chief came alongside deputed by the tribe to say they were anxious to have a meeting with me, now they understand King George men were not come to knock down their homes and take their lives."[13]

Prevost believed that the presence of a large warship such as the *Satellite* "would strike terror upon their ignorant minds" and also would prevent the recurrence of piracy should another merchantman be forced into the sound under circumstances similar to the *Swiss Boy*'s. After the *Satellite*'s two-week visit, the Ohiets, he wrote, seemed "well disposed, quiet, inoffensive and easily led by anyone capable of gaining their confidence. If this be true how much evil may be prevented by the presence of one who would watch over their interests for good." Other vessels would come under stress of weather, or for trade, or for prospecting, Prevost reasoned, and under the circumstances the association of whites with "ignorant simple-minded Indians unrestrained and unprotected" would be undesirable. Thus Prevost believed that the colonial government should appoint an Indian agent for the Island's west coast from Port San Juan to Cape Scott where five thousand "souls" lived under "no control or restraint."[14] By diplomacy and forbearance Prevost made the British position clear at Barkley Sound, and Prevost, whose name appears elsewhere in these pages in connection with sending missionaries, not gunboats, to the natives, never forgot the wisdom of this peaceful display of power.[15] As for George and the miscreants in the *Swiss Boy*'s case, they were taken to Victoria, and though jailed, they were not convicted for lack of evidence. They were released, much to the fury of the traders.

In the course of Prevost's proceedings much information was gathered concerning why the natives plundered the *Swiss Boy*, an event demonstrating the aggressive salvage tactics of Nootkan peoples all along that shore, from Cape Flattery to Cape Scott. The Ohiet subchief explained to Prevost that the *Swiss Boy* was in such a disabled state that the tribe at once considered her their property (in his words property "coming into their hands") and in these circumstances, their first thought was "plunder."[16] It was customary, the anthropologist says, for one tribe to take the property on another tribe if they thought it safe so to do, and the property became the chief's bounty.[17] The boundaries between tribes were not strictly honored, which explains why the Sheshat joined the Ohiet, and apparently without conflict. To these peoples the *Swiss Boy*'s arrival was an unexpected opportunity, and the vessel was "fair game" for what the natives regarded as legitimate "plunder" by headmen such as George bent on benefitting himself and his people.

The government's failure to adequately punish natives for these continuing depredations led traders to complain bitterly to Governor Douglas once more. They requested that gunboats be sent—when circumstances warranted and also on regular patrols—to provide the authority that Indian and colonial agents, missionaries, and magistrates could not exercise without material aid. Thus in 1862, H.M.S. *Devastation* went to investigate the causes of complaint.[18] With steam power and Richards's new charts, she was able to reach most places where her presence was thought to be useful.

At this time the number of whites inhabiting the shore could still be counted on the fingers of one hand. At Clayoquot a Dane, Frederick Christian Thornberg, married to an Ahousat, ran a trading post. At Barkley Sound, William E. Banfield, a ship's carpenter who had taken his discharge from H.M.S. *Constance* on the station in 1848, and who had been appointed magistrate and Indian agent on Prevost's recommendation, traded with the Indians. On Banfield's advice, Captain Edward Stamp, an English shipmaster and commission agent, began a flourishing lumber export business at Port Alberni at the head of Alberni Canal, Barkley Sound. Timber also brought Scottish-born Gilbert Malcolm Sproat, lumberman and ethnologist, to the Island's west coast. In August 1860, on Banfield's urgings, Stamp and Sproat occupied Port Alberni under force of arms. They arrived in two heavily-armed vessels manned by about fifty men. The local Indians, the Sheshat, threatened resistance, and in particular wanted compensation for lands occupied. They had no objection to the coming of the whites on a permanent basis; in fact they "professed entire satisfaction," according to Banfield. The site chosen for the mill was not the usual camping ground of the Sheshat, but since the first party of artificers had arrived to build the mill, the Sheshat had erected temporary lodges. And they had done so on the very site the new lumber barons wanted most.[19]

In response to these native demands, Stamp made the Sheshat presents of some fifty blankets, as well as some muskets, molasses, food, and "trinkets." Then negotiations proceeded, and on 2 September Stamp and Sproat made a treaty with the Sheshat chiefs. The arrangement was amicable and satisfactory, Banfield said. On the other hand some natives objected. They complained that the coming of more whites would mean that they would "have to do everything according to the 'fancies of the

King-George men.'" Sproat thought them rather "saucy" in their behaviour. From his perspective, the intrusion of a superior people into a land that had not been properly brought into production was fully justified, provided the newcomers purchased the land and acted with "justice, humanity and moderation."[20] Banfield would not be intimidated, and told the Sheshats that they would be "visited with chastisement" if the whites were annoyed or injured.[21]

From Victoria, Douglas watched the progress of these developments as best he could, relying on Banfield's periodic reports and other casual information brought to his attention in times of crisis. Once a rumour reached him that the Alberni colonists had been attacked, and, on his request, the gunboat *Grappler* was sent to investigate. She remained near the settlement for a short time as security for Stamp's men and convinced the Indians, Sproat said, "that the King-George men were in earnest."[22] But more serious was the death of colonial agent Banfield under mysterious circumstances on 20 October 1862. An Indian reported that he had accidentally drowned. However, in the course of H.M.S. *Devastation*'s investigations at Barkley Sound a year and a half later, authorities learned that Banfield had been stabbed to death by an Ohiet chief named Klatsmick. The chief was taken to Victoria for trial. The judge, however, found he could put no credence on the evidence provided by the Indians and dismissed the case.[23] Klatsmick returned to Barkley Sound and boasted that he had killed Banfield.[24] Again, when the schooner *Trader* was seized and an Indian crew member murdered by Nootka Indians, authorities sent the gunboat *Grappler* and corvette *Cameleon* to enquire into the circumstances and investigate the "threatening attitude" of the natives. Douglas recommended that the senior naval officer warn the Indians that they would be held responsible if anything were to happen to the settlers at Alberni, Nootka, and Quatsino.[25]

Prevost had believed that "showing the flag" would prove a deterrent to future piracies. However, traders and the governor in Victoria could not countenance what they regarded as the growing arrogance of the Barkley and Clayoquot Sound natives. Their frustrations grew, and the Navy came under pressure to exact justice at the cannon's mouth.

The piracy which brought forth the Royal Navy's most extensive punishment occurred at Matilda Creek in Clayoquot Sound, a place of trade in seal, seal oil, and deer and elk skins. Ahousat means "people living with their backs to the land and mountains," an accurate appellation since at one time these people inhabited the ocean side of Vargas Island. They were a close, enlarged family numbering five hundred whose chiefs were close kin. In 1864 they lived at seven village sites, one of them being Marktosis ("a coffin") near Matilda Creek.

In August of that year the sloop *Kingfisher*, trading in seal oil, was attacked in Matilda Creek by a piratical band of ten Ahousats. Fearing retribution from the Navy, the Ahousats as a tribe were upset with the pirates since the action could only bring trouble to them all. Word of the crime reached Victoria on 10 September. It was a foul deed, the local press reported: the bodies of the skipper, Captain James Stevenson, his mate and crew, including a Fort Rupert Indian, had been mutilated and, weighted with stones, sunk in the creek. The *Kingfisher* had been pillaged and burnt.[26]

On the request of the governor, the commander-in-chief on the Pacific Station, Rear-Admiral the Hon. Joseph Denman, immediately sent the paddle wheel sloop *Devastation* from Esquimalt to investigate. Her captain, Commander John W. Pike, had orders to steam for Clayoquot Sound to enquire into what the cautious Denman was obliged to classify as the *alleged* capture of the *Kingfisher* and the murder of her crew. Pike also possessed instructions to call at Barkley Sound, where Banfield had been murdered and where native threats against the crew of another merchant vessel had occurred at Toquart and a pistol had been stolen.[27]

Pike went first to Barkley Sound and anchored off the village of Humukanis, near Banfield Creek. He discovered that three hundred natives were armed and ready for battle, for the incautious master of the trading schooner *Surprise* had blatantly misinformed the Indians that when a warship visited them she would at once fire upon them. Pike did not take a violent course. He seized canoes and took the local chief's daughter hostage, a method which enabled him to secure three suspects (Suchkool, Hoth-lu-arta, and Klatsmich) without a shot. To repair the damage caused by the *Surprise*'s master, Pike took pains to explain to the Indians the intentions of the government. The Indians blamed traders for physical and verbal abuses.

> They complained much of the behavior of the traders to them, saying that frequently any wrong they did was provoked by the bad language used towards them, and in some cases by their being pushed and struck by the men in the trading schooners.
>
> They all begged that I would bring this matter to the notice of His Excellency the Governor, and request him to issue a warning to the Masters of trading vessels visiting them, to be more circumspect in their language and behavior to the Indians, when trading with them.[28]

After he crossed the sound to Toquart, Pike recovered the stolen pistol, again without resorting to violence.

Yet Pike found the Ahousats quite different to deal with. At Matilda Creek he found about 195 Indians prepared for war. "Their tactics were truly Indian," Pike reported to Denman, "50 men were placed in ambush at the extreme point of Matilda Creek, 40 were concealed round the village, 30 in Bawden Bay and the remainder were a short distance up Herbert Arm, and every endeavour was made to draw our boats into these ambushes." Pike had no doubts that the guilty persons could be taken captive, but he was certain that it could not be done without loss of life—"considerable on their side, and possibly some on ours." The chief of the Echachets of Clayoquot Sound had even offered to place Indians and canoes at the disposal of the British, should they be required.[29] Yet Pike did not assume the offensive. Owing to Denman's injunction that he was to undertake no hostile measures until the admiral himself reached the scene or "some signal opportunity should offer," Pike cautiously withdrew to await his superior's arrival.[30]

The Hon. Joseph Denman, Fellow of the Royal Society and Rear-Admiral of the White, was no neophyte in dealing with natives or governors. Like Rear-Admiral Moresby who had preceded him in command of the Pacific squadron, he was a seasoned veteran of the slave patrols on the African coasts. The son of a distinguished abolitionist, Lord Chief Justice Thomas 1st Baron Denman, he himself held a passionate hatred of the evil slave trade. Not content to cruise the coast and chase slave-carrying ships, in 1840 he had determined to strike hard, totally on his own initiative, and to face the censure of the Admiralty if he failed. At the mouth of the Gallinas river, the most notorious slave station coast southwards of Sierre Leone, and now renamed the Kerefe, Denman had showed equal toughness against a Spanish trader, Blanco, and a native king, Siaka, who secreted and dealt in slaves. Denman and his men left their ship, crossed raging surf, secured an island base, and meted out punishment against installations of trader and ruler alike. It was a bold little imperial action. With much the same incendiary rockets[31] that he would later use in Clayoquot Sound, Denman burnt all the barracoons or slave pens. By so doing he had for the first time struck at the root of the problem, not being content to capture a slaver at sea but to check the trade on land and to force the chief to sign an abject treaty of renunciation. Denman was generously rewarded by Parliament and promoted to the rank of captain. Lord Palmerston at the Foreign Office advised the Lords of the Admiralty that Denman's tactics were to be employed against all piratical slave establishments. Such actions appealed to Palmerston, but his successor, Lord Aberdeen, had the practice suspended on the advice of the queen's advocate that such actions against nations with which Great Britain was not at war were contrary to international law.[32] But Denman carried with him the reputation of being a ruthless fighter for just causes.

At Esquimalt in 1864, Denman was beset with all too many problems, none of them of easy solution. In addition to keeping a sharp lookout for Confederate commerce raiders or Yankee cruisers that might embroil Britain in the War for the Union, Esquimalt had to be guarded. Ships on Pacific Station had to be stationed at Panama, San Francisco, and Honolulu to watch for potentially hostile vessels. The calls for gunboats to show the flag seemed incessant. In 1864 Denman had fourteen ships of various classes at his disposal, not a large number considering the squadron's diverse, far-flung duties.[33] From these meagre resources he was obliged to spare his flagship and a corvette or two as well as the gunboats *Forward* and *Grappler* for his duties on the Northwest Coast. He warned the Lords of the Admiralty on 15 September that a large number of small vessels would be absolutely required "to keep order amongst the Native tribes on the coast."[34] "Native outrages" had become numerous, but white offenders had to be met with equal determination, especially when natives employed in the British service had suffered at the whites' hands. In the case of the sloop *Random*, in which some native constables had been fired on, and one of them killed, near Port Simpson, Denman had dispatched H.M.S. *Grappler* to investigate.[35] On another occasion, west coast outrages had been caused by the misconduct of white traders.[36] As on the African coast, Denman knew, abuses might be caused by whites or natives. But in any event, supporting authority and maintaining law and order would require the constant employment of Her Majesty's Navy.

On 27 September, the same day that Pike's report of the Ahousats' determined resistance reached Esquimalt, the governor of Vancouver Island, Captain Arthur Edward Kennedy, C.B., appealed to the commander-in-chief for aid to the civil power. Appointed governor of Vancouver Island in November 1863, Kennedy was seasoned, and boasted a proven record of performance to match his hard-headed points of view. Irish-born, he had previously held commissions in the British Army, served on the Irish famine commission, and been governor of Sierra Leone, 1852–54, and of Western Australia, 1855–61. In Victoria he soon earned a reputation as "a soldier-like man" and was well known for saying that it was better to be decidedly wrong than undecidedly right.[37] To his aggressive and uncompromising way of thinking, British interests had to be made safe at all costs, even at the risk of alienating Indians, a course his predecessor Douglas would deftly have tried to avoid. Kennedy believed adamantly that the "atrocities" and the "defiant demeanor" of the murderers and their tribe left no question about what measures should be taken. "There could be no future safety for coasters frequenting that part of the island," he warned Denman, "if the perpetrators of this diabolical crime are not brought to justice with a view to deter them and afford a warning example to neighbouring tribes." He thought that every effort should be made to capture the suspects, who should then be quickly and effectively punished. "Humanity and sound policy alike demand this," he said. He was prepared to accompany Denman on his voyage to deal with what he called "these misguided savages" but for reasons unknown he did not go to Matilda Creek.[38]

Kennedy stood for immediate action, but Denman, keeping in mind October's dangerous fogs, thought the season too far advanced, a fact which did not go unquestioned by the anxious and impatient Lords of the Admiralty, who in far away London showed no appreciation of the dangers of navigation on the west coast of Vancouver Island. He thus prepared to leave Esquimalt in his flagship, the steam frigate *Sutlej*, when weather permitted. Anticipating a protracted stay, he sent the merchant ship *Kinnaird*, to take government supplies for the expedition to the same place. The superintendent of police at Victoria, Philip Hankin, a retired Royal Navy lieutenant, and an Indian interpreter known as Friday embarked on board the *Sutlej*. On the morning of 2 October she sailed from Esquimalt and towards evening of the same day she joined the *Devastation* in Clayoquot Sound.[39]

Denman went first to Matilda Creek where Pike had faced such determined resistance. But he found that the village Marktosis had been abandoned and that the suspects, including the Ahousat chief Chapchah, a principal in the piracy and "a fine athletic strapping fellow about 6 feet high," had escaped. Thus, he proceeded to Siktokkis, on the north arm of Clayoquot Sound, where a native named Ea-qui-ok-shittle was secured. Under questioning, he admitted being a witness to the *Kingfisher* massacre. Ea-qui-ok-shittle testified that Chapchah came to Matilda Creek from Ahousat village with ten men in a canoe. Chapchah deceived the *Kingfisher*'s master into believing that he had seal oil to trade. Chapchah intended, Ea-qui-ok-shittle said, to kill the crew in order to take possession of the schooner's valuable cargo. Ea-qui-ok-shittle detailed to the British the actions of the murderers and the cargo seized by Chapchah and his accomplices.[40]

On the basis of this invaluable data Denman began his search for the suspects. He sent the *Devastation* to Mooyahhat, or as it is now shown on the chart, Moyeha, at the head of Herbert Inlet. Here the Indians, taking the offensive, fired on the ship and her boats. But, obedient to his instructions, Pike withdrew and returned to report to Denman. At this stage, Denman decided that Siktokkis and two Indian villages on Shelter Inlet, Nahpook and Nahtay, where several of the principals lived, should be destroyed by the *Devastation*.

Now knowing that the centre of Indian resistance had shifted to Mooyahhat, Denman proceeded there himself, in the *Sutlej*. First he sent

Friday ashore with the promise to the Ahousat that if the guilty were surrendered, the Navy would not fire on the village. He also offered the Indians the safety of the ship. They defiantly refused. They said that if Denman burned the village, they would soon rebuild it and that if he interfered with the canoes, they would shoot every man who landed.

The swift flame of war now ran round Clayoquot Sound, licking even the most remote of settlements, the fishing stations, and the canoes of the local Indians. The first natives to feel the heat were those at Mooyahhat. Denman's reply to the testy Mooyahhat was immediate and uncompromising and is not at all surprising in view of his West African experience. From the *Sutlej* he opened heavy fire on the surrounding bush to clear it. Then he sent the gigs in to burn Mooyahhat by rocket fire and to bring off the canoes under cover of the ship's cannon. Guns from the launches and pinnace covered the shore to the right and left of the village where the ship's guns could not bear. As the British approached the beach, the Indians fired at the boats, but their fire was silenced by accurate hits from the boats' guns. Under this successful blanket of fire and flame the boat crews were able to seize twelve canoes as well as the *Kingfisher*'s boat, and to do so without loss on the British side. Denman estimated that several Indians had died.

This action, similar in many ways to those which would destroy eight other villages in the course of these reprisals, began at 10:20 in the morning. By 3:30 in the afternoon the village was engulfed in flames and by 4:00 the *Sutlej* was steaming down Herbert Inlet in search of the pirates and murderers. The frigate's last act of the day was to destroy the already deserted and dismantled Marktosis, the village near Matilda Creek where the piracy and murders had been committed.

Now the frontier war was quickly spreading. The next day, 4 October, Denman sent the *Devastation* to punish by burning Chief Chapchah's two villages—one at the mouth of Trout (now Cypre) River in Cypress Bay, the other at the head of Bedwell Sound where the *Devastation* had received such a hostile welcome the previous day. Commander Pike's orders called for him to bring off all canoes, a move calculated to reduce the Indians' chance of any seaborne escape and confine them to the steep and exposed rocky shore. At Trout River, Pike spotted the unrepentant, defiant Chapchah at the head of his men, sporting one of the blue jackets stolen from the *Kingfisher*. Pike pursued his quarry. The Indians "made a regular stand," but the Navy suffered no casualties when boat parties destroyed and burned the village. Chapchah fled into the bush; the *Devastation* steamed to her next assignment. At the head of Bedwell Sound, Pike fired and burned the other village, seized canoes, and, in this case, destroyed them. Again, the natives fought back, firing at the ship and boats in response to the *Devastation*'s guns and rockets, which made short work of the place, the resinous cedar houses making a fantastic fire and billows of smoke.

At every turn Chapchah skilfully eluded his pursuers. Without canoes or succour from any allies he might still have in the sound, resistance would become more difficult, or so his opponent Denman thought. Denman knew that Chapchah was at Catface Point, a gaunt and relatively high peninsula lying between Herbert Inlet and Bedwell Sound. Flat-topped Catface Range dominates its rocky extremity, but on the landward side the peninsula narrows with the northeasternmost slope of Catface leading to a forest-choked swamp drained by Trout River into Cypress Bay, Bedwell Sound. On the other side of the peninsula at Whitepine Cove, a secure anchorage on Herbert Inlet, a somewhat befuddled Denman planned his advance.

How was he to capture the wily and elusive Chapchah? Denman knew that shot and shell could not bring the desired effect. He thus decided to strike "a more severe blow." On the morning of 6 October an armed party of forty seamen, thirty marines, one Ahousat and six Clayoquot Indian guides landed at Whitepine Cove under command of Lieutenant Hugh Stewart. Their object was to move stealthily across the three miles of bog and tangled underbrush separating the cove from Trout River and seize Chapchah and his people by surprise, and if possible to take them prisoner. All went according to plan until the British got within twenty yards of the temporary huts of the refugees. An alert dog, placed as sentinel, gave a warning bark, and an Indian nearby, fashioning a canoe of escape, "raised the warhoop." The Indians took to the bush and returned a heavy fire, but they were soon shot at by the sailors and marines.[41] In a few minutes, the Indians fled, leaving ten comrades killed. Chapchah, who evidently did not fight, was wounded in two places as he ran away but managed once again to find welcome refuge in the forest. The thickness of the bush rendered pursuit impossible. Denman was foiled again.

Though the *Devastation* lay in Whitepine Cove and the *Sutlej* was now on the opposite side near Cypress Bay, the firepower of these vessels was useless against Chapchah and his compadres. Nor could a landing party secure them. The thick forest and difficult terrain provided as good a cover as the wounded chief needed. Thus Denman remained reliant on Indian guides and interpreters to make known to the Indians that a truce had been proclaimed and the *Sutlej* was flying a white flag—not as an act of surrender but to bring the punishment to an end. The Indians were told that Chapchah and the other accused persons were wanted and would be found. During the next few days, small arms parties landed at several places in Clayoquot Sound and on 12 October captured one suspect. Denman now quit the Sound in the *Sutlej* and returned to Esquimalt in the company of the *Devastation*. H.M.S. *Forward* kept her station for a week, and although the remaining suspects were not found, her commander, Lieutenant the Hon. Horace D. Lascelles, believed they would be captured when the Ahousats, who had sought the shelter of the woods in twos and threes, would gather together at their village sites during the next two months.[42]

Reflecting on the episode, Denman believed he had triumphed. Nine Indian villages and sixty-four canoes had been destroyed, and at least fifteen Indians had been killed. "The success of this attack," he boastfully told the Lords of the Admiralty, "conducted after the fashion of their own tactics, has produced profound discouragement, Chapchah being in hiding and pursued by his own people, who had abandoned all ideas of resistance and look on him as responsible for all the evils that have befallen him."[43] He believed the guilt had been widely shared by the tribe because the *Kingfisher*'s effects had been found in so many villages. He evidently cared nothing for the proposition that the goods and chattels might have been traded from one Indian's hands to another; English law specified that possession of stolen goods was a punishable offence, a fact the Ahousat and Clayoquot would not have acknowledged.

At Victoria, Governor Kennedy expressed thanks to the Navy for the "forbearing and effecive manner" in which the service and punishment had been performed. He confidently maintained that the measure would promote the colony's security and check the "piratical and bloodthirsty attitudes of the Coast Indians, which have been left too long unpunished."[44]

The Supreme Court in Victoria, however, did not act in the way the officials hoped or wanted. Accused Indians brought to trial for both the *Swiss Boy* affair and the *Kingfisher* piracy were acquitted by Chief Justice David Cameron on the ground that the Indian witnesses, the only ones available, were incapable of giving evidence on account of their being supposed to have no belief in a future state. Ironically, under an imperial statute of 1843, colonies could legislate the admissability of such unsworn evidence in criminal and civil proceedings, subject to crown consent. But neither Blanshard nor Douglas had brought forward enabling legislation; indeed, in 1852 Douglas received instructions from the Colonial Office that he should accept Indian testimony, swearing witnesses to tell the truth according to whatever form was held most solemn among the Indians; at the same time, courts and juries would determine the testimony's worth. Cameron was rightly criticized by colonists for not knowing the law, a fact which led to his forced retirement shortly thereafter. In the interim, much damage to the British quest for authority had been done, as Denman complained, and would continue until such time as remedial legislation was brought forward, as it was in February 1865.[45]

"From this refusal to admit Indian testimony," Denman wrote Governor Kennedy with bitter indignation, "it follows, that as long as Natives, in attacks upon British Traders, take care to leave no survivors to give evidence, they are perfectly secure from conviction and punishment in the Supreme Court of Victoria." He did not question the court's ruling, because it was not his position to do so, but he hoped the governor would take steps to investigate the legal ramifications. "Your Excellency has determined," he pointed out to the governor with precise clarity, "that the Lex talionis, which has hitherto been the rule amongst the Indians in their dealings with each other, shall cease, and that every case of murder shall be brought before the Courts of Victoria for trial." Now, he warned, the Indians would not cease their violent ways, for there was no punishment.

> In the meantime, I can conceive nothing more mischievous, or calculated to multiply the already frequent atrocities committed by the Natives, than the return to their tribes of these avowed and notorious murderers with perfect impunity; as it cannot fail to produce in their minds an absolute contempt of British Law.

The admiral faced an unfortunate and unavoidable dilemma, for as he explained, if he returned to Clayoquot to seek Chapchah and the remaining suspects he knew that they would be liberated if arrested, and if he did not keep his promise of returning there, the Navy would lose face with the natives.[46] However, Denman was obliged to follow the civil authority; and in the circumstances of confused legalities the governor could do nothing more than call off the hunt for the Ahousat pirates.

As Denman had foreseen, the Navy did lose face. He had threatened to return to Clayoquot in one month to resume his forcible measures. The Ahousats consequently believed, Gilbert Sproat at Alberni observed, that they "had gained a victory over the ships, and, in consideration of such a triumph, all the trouble of making new canoes has been forgotten. Chapchah has added to his reputation; he is the great chief who defied and baffled the English on King-George war-vessels."[47] The Ahousat thought the Navy's "random shooting with great guns" and attacking by daylight contrary to good military conduct.[48] They classified the loss of their sixty-four canoes as "misfortunate" and the loss of half a war canoe of men as a matter of no consequence. Several years later, Father Augustin Joseph Brabant, a Roman Catholic priest at Hesquiat, learned of the event from the Indians and summarized the native interpretation of the event as follows:

> The Indians had not given up their chief to the white man; they

had lost their houses, canoes and iktas [i.e., things], but these they could and would build again; some of their number were taken prisoner, but were afterwards returned to them... therefore they claimed a big victory over the man-of-war and big guns.[49]

Nevertheless, the Clayoquots grew fearful of the British naval presence, as Father Brabant observed in 1874, a fear which diminished with time and as the missionary presence became more permanent and the Indians grew more accustomed to the peaceful calls of British warships on patrol.[50] An immediate effect on the Ahousats was that without their canoes they could not lay in store their usual food supply for the winter of 1865–66. Thus they dispersed to live among friendly tribes until the spring fishing season made them less dependent. During that same winter they built new canoes and eventually re-established themselves at Marktosis and at Ahousat, the former an Indian reserve and the latter a sort of Indian refugee camp and subsequently a Presbyterian mission with a population of 263 in 1906.[51] These settlements had later reminders of the Royal Navy's punitive expedition, for a number of unexploded shells at Catface Point were subsequently discovered. One unexpectedly exploded, killing two Indians. Several cannon balls were also discovered, and as late as 1960, a small one was used as a shot-put in local school athletic events, a curious remnant of the Pax Britannica.[52] And to this day, West Coast sawmill blades are damaged when British lead intended for Chapchah but instead imbedded in fir or cedar passes the inspection of unsuspecting timber surveyors.

The Lords of the Admiralty had no quarrel with Denman's actions. In point of fact, they actually expressed pleasure at the able and satisfactory manner in which the operations had been conducted.[53] The Colonial Office, apparently considering the matter rather routine, similarly approved of the proceedings.[54] Perhaps it reflected their political persuasion because their Liberal successors during Gladstone's first administration did not agree with the tactics of the punitive expedition taken against another tribe farther north on the same coast during the *John Bright* affair. Clearly, Denman was a tough commander-in-chief. Acting on the governor's instructions he employed tactics, some of them borrowed from the Indians themselves, which he believed would bring the guilty to justice and ultimately secure British trade from piracy. As for Philip Hankin, his actions at Clayoquot won Denman's admiration; indeed, Denman's report to Their Lordships was so high in praise that they reinstated Hankin in the service with all arrears of pay. He accompanied Governor Kennedy during his circuit cruise of Vancouver Island in August 1866 in the H.M.S. *Scout* to win accord with the west coast Indians and to tell them "to remember to behave themselves." He remained in the Navy until his retirement as commander in 1870 when he went on imperial service as private secretary to the Duke of Buckingham, the governor at Madras. Hankin later wrote that the Ahousats had received a lesson which they never forgot. Thereafter, he noted, they never dared attack any small trading schooners—which was true in this particular locale.[55]

The *Kingfisher* affair intensified the interest of colonists in Victoria in the future of the west coast. In certain quarters there was a desire for fair play and support for the Navy. The *British Colonist* of 12 October 1864 championed the idea that the loss of Indian life, canoes, and houses would be a lasting "lesson" to the Ahousats. This newspaper praised the Navy firstly for "exhausting every peaceable means" before resorting to "extremities" to bring the Indians to terms, and secondly for the fact that the destruction of property had preceded the taking of life.

> We have demonstrated our power, we have shown our inflexible determination to carry out the law and to punish the aggressors; let us see that we fail not on the other side—that we leave the Indians no reasonable complaint against us; but carry out our responsibilities toward them by improving their condition, protecting them from injustices on the part of the whites, and, in fact, giving them every legitimate return for the lands of which we have despoiled them.

Such a policy would require more constables, magistrates, and Indian agents, and, of course, more gunboats to show the flag at the numerous settlements on the west coast. As Denman knew, another gunboat, superior in armament and steampower to the *Forward* and *Grappler*, was needed to visit the natives on a regular basis. "The aggressions on the coast of Vancouver Island and British Columbia against British traders by the Indians has by degrees increased to a formidable account by long continued impunity," he advised the Lords of the Admiralty, "and though the severe examples I have felt myself compelled to make in Clayoquot Sound will probably for a long time prevent their recurrence, yet it is most desirable that such cases of murder and piracy should be prosecuted, and the painful necessity of such examples avoided." He argued that such a gunboat, under command of an officer who knew Indian ways and languages, such as Hankin, and operated by the colonies of Vancouver Island and British Columbia, would greatly increase the ability to police the tribes and reduce the necessity of employing such large ships as the *Sutlej* in narrow, dangerous waters.[56] Denman hinted to the Lords of the Admiralty that the colonial governors in Victoria and New Westminster favoured the funding of a colonial gunvessel. In fact, the two colonial legislatures or executives never took up the proposal, mainly for financial reasons. Royal Navy ships out of Esquimalt continued to be employed on the west coast as needs dictated, and gunvessels larger than the gunboats, such as the *Sparrowhawk, Rocket,* and *Kingfisher,* were sent from England.

The Navy's actions against the Ahousat pirates and murderers, though extensive, did not convince all west coast tribes to abide by British laws. In most tribes word of the Navy's retaliation may have made the Indians more cautious. At Hesquiat, however, less than thirty miles from the Ahousat villages, the local Indians undertook a different kind of action against shipping which was also a case of piracy but more exactly bore on the question of highly prized salvage rights.

When the barque *John Bright,* outward bound from Port Ludlow, Admiralty Inlet, Washington, with a cargo of lumber, struck a reef during a heavy southwest gale near Estevan Point, north of Clayoquot Sound, on 4 February 1869, certain Hesquiats plundered the ship. The site of the wreck was one mile west of Boulder Point, outside of Hesquiat Harbour. Of the twenty-two people on board the vessel, ten escaped drowning only to fall victim to the Indians. When they reached shore they were shot, and their bodies were hacked to pieces and mutilated. The trading schooner *Surprise,* calling at various places on the west coast, gained information about the *John Bright*'s fate; and five week after the wreck, on 13 March her master, John Christensen, brought news of the disaster to Victoria. The tale created "a rich theme" to talk about in the colonial capital, and became the subject of sensational articles in the local press. In Victoria, a strong appeal was made to the governor to send a gunboat "to punish the heartless savages and teach them a lesson for the future."[57]

However, Christensen's appeal and public pressures brought no response from Governor Kennedy's successor, Frederick Seymour. Possessing a wide range of experience as a colonial administrator in Tasmania, Antigua, Nevis, and particularly Honduras and the Bay Islands, where he was governor from 1857 to 1863 before he took up the post, Seymour had (or so he told an Anglican missionary) received his appointment to British Columbia because of his knowledge of and experience among Indians, presumably meaning (by Colonial Office miscalculation) that the natives of Honduras were in some way similar to those of British Columbia.[58] That aside, for several reasons including a growing attachment to drink, Seymour's responses to native "problems" were by no means as immediate as any of his predecessors—Blanshard, Douglas, or Kennedy. On first hearing about the *John Bright,* he had rejected the idea of sending a warship to Estevan Point on the grounds that coastal traders were forever, on one pretext or another, demanding a gunboat's presence for their own protection. Christensen returned to Hesquiat and found the beach littered with human remains, and he again appealed to the governor to act. By this time the Victoria press was out for blood and it reported that fifty armed whites were ready to leave Victoria to annihilate the Hesquiats.[59] The Victoria *Evening News* charged Seymour with "disgraceful and criminal neglect." Under these pressures Seymour finally took action and requested that the Navy investigate.

On 3 May, fully three months after the murder, H.M.S. *Sparrowhawk*, Commander Henry Wentworth Mist, was ordered to Hesquiat. Commander Mist carried instructions "to be active yet friendly, firm yet conciliatory." He took from Esquimalt a larger number of marines than was customary on such expeditions, for he intended to establish an unquestioned military predominance during what were expected to be dangerous, even violent, operations on shore. Also on board the *Sparrowhawk* were the civil authorities Captain H.M. Ball, the magistrate of New Westminster, and the Attorney-General of British Columbia, H.P.P. Crease.[60]

The Hesquiat offered little resistance. Mist found that they were "utterly unconcerned either at our arrival, or at the landing of so large a force," which had been drawn up in fighting order before the village. The Indians showed no difficulty whatsoever, and offered everything that they had taken from the wreck. Some of the suspects came forward voluntarily, while Indian witnesses proved easy to interrogate. Mist learned that the object of the murders was piracy, and that the Indians were under the apprehension that if any of the white survivors reached Victoria that a gunboat would be sent to wreak retribution. Moreover, they also complained that on previous occasions they had saved lives and had been promised certain rewards for those saved, but that these promises had not been kept. One Indian even produced a promissory note for 10 blankets of which he had been defrauded. In other words, the whites had broken their promises to the Hesquiat.[61]

A board of inquiry and coroner's jury was struck. They found the bodies of eight persons, some decapitated, and were able to account for six others. The wreck of the *John Bright* lay in three fragments. The ship's boomboard bearing the motto *Neminen time, neminen laede* (fear none, injure none) was among the more perverse relics that the beachcombers discovered, providing a curious twist to the episode. Peter Combie, the ship's surgeon, had to decide whether the victims had been murdered or had died of natural causes. Some cases could not be determined, but in others it was clear that murders had been committed.

This finding led to more forceful measures being taken. The Hesquiat would not surrender the murderers, and the authorities responded with their customary threat of violence. Peaceful efforts failed. Accordingly, the landing party forced the surrender of two suspects by burning houses and shelling canoes.

This constituted a fair and necessary procedure in the circumstances, according to the civil authorities on the spot. Moreover the senior naval officer of Esquimalt, Captain William Edge, believed that Mist "acted with great judgement." And, because the whole tribe was implicated, he supported the policy of punishing all of them by destroying their canoes. Neither the brutality of the action nor the wisdom of these 'on-the-spot' views found support in London. The Lords of the Admiralty, dominated by the humanitarian spirit of Gladstone's first administration, quarrelled with the "wholesale destruction of the villages and boats of these savages," in the words of the First Lord, Hugh C. Erskine Childers, M.P. Their Lordships sent their views to the Colonial Office, expressing the hope that an enlightened policy for dealing with Indian problems in colonial British Columbia would soon be forthcoming. Nevertheless, the two Indians, Katkinna and John Anietsachist, were tried in Victoria for murder. The old Katkinna, who was chief, admitted his crime, but Anietsachist persisted in his claim that he had dissuaded other Indians from committing murder. Evidence provided by Katkinna's supporters against the ambitious Anietsachist, who aspired to be chief, served to condemn him. Both were found guilty. On 26 July they were returned to Hesquiat in the *Sparrowhawk* and were baptized by Father Seghers enroute. Three days later they were placed on a portable scaffold, previously used at Nanaimo and Victoria, and were hanged in the presence of the whole tribe and others collected from the neighborhood to witness the event. The authorities hoped the punishment would be a salutary warning to the Hesquiats and to others.[62] The Victoria press, pleased that their proddings had brought results, also supported tough measures. "If we treat with savages," said the *British Colonist* on 31 July, "we must act in a manner intelligible to them." Force must be met with force. "It is absurd to suppose that our views of equity and justice can apply to people ignorant of the commonest sense of humanity, because they do not comprehend our social laws."

Yet the Indians were not convinced of the correctness of the British course. For many years the Hesquiats maintained that the people in the shipwreck had not been murdered. They told their priest, Brabant, that the bodies had been mangled by surf, rocks, and boulders and that, as was customary, they had moved them above the high water mark in order that the fish on which the Indians lived would not feed on the dead bodies.[63] "The Indians also say," Captain Walbran (who was among them many times) noted, "that the executed men were the victims of an interpreter's mistakes, false accusations of hostile tribes and too credulous white people."[64] If this interpretation is to be believed, in the oral tradition of the Hesquiat the story of the *John Bright* must long have remained as a sad, fatal encounter with British law and order. The Navy and the civil authorities may have felt that the punishment met the crime. They may, in their own minds, have satisfied themselves that justice had been served. They were in this case evidently unable to convince the Indians of the judiciousness of their actions.

By the late 1860's, as in the case of Commander Mist, the Navy's encounters with natives such as the Hesquiats and Ahousats were resulting in rules of conduct being explicitly defined. Admirals or senior naval officers at Esquimalt took pains to be present whenever possible and to be accompanied by representatives of the civil power during punitive actions. They also detailed instructions to their subordinates so that abuses such as flogging and beating Indians aboard warships might be avoided.[65] For example, Lieutenant D'Arcy A. Denny commanding the *Forward*, had instructions from Denman "to endeavour to impress them [the Indians] with confidence in the good intention of the Colonial Government towards them, but at the same time to maintain due attention to the Laws of Civilization."[66] He was told nothing more. He and other officers would have to walk the delicate tightrope of commonsense and try to anticipate whether or not Their Lordships of the Board of Admiralty in the secure and prestigious confines of Whitehall would approve of their actions, taken in the name of Queen Victoria, on a remote maritime frontier some eighteen thousand miles distant by sea from the seats of power in London.

9

Policing the Passage

IN THE STRAIT OF GEORGIA separating Vancouver Island from the continental shore, the Navy was at the cutting edge between two societies, enforcing a rule of law virtually unknown to Indians and, at the same time, not always obeyed by whites. The strait was a crossroads for whites and Indians alike and a place of constant tensions. Internecine warfare continued to exist in the early 1860's: Salish fought against Salish; northern tribes such as Kwakiutl, Bella Bella, and Haida preyed on the Salish. Peaceful northern Indians coming south to Victoria and Puget Sound required security while passing certain trouble spots such as Cape Mudge, Cowichan, and Kuper Island. Settlers on the Gulf Islands or eastern shore of Vancouver Island sought the Navy's protection. So did gold seekers and traders who entered the Fraser River or who went north through the strait bound for the Stikine River and Alaska. In all these ways the strait was a critical area both in inter-Indian and in white-Indian relations.

White inroads into the lands bordering the Strait of Georgia grew in intensity from the early nineteenth century. In 1827 the Hudson's Bay Company had founded Fort Langley on the Fraser River to provide a transhipment point for trade goods entering and leaving the continental hinterland. Salmon runs of the river were exploited by the Company as they had been for centuries by the Stalo Salish living near the fort and their kin Salish living in the strait, Puget Sound, and Juan de Fuca Strait. The new fort gave the Stalo welcome security from Cowichan and Kwakiutl marauders. Then, for almost thirty years, a state of relative peace reigned on the lower Fraser as it did across the strait at Fort

Nanaimo, built in 1852 to mine steamer coal for export. In 1858, however, thousands of miners of various nationalities entered the Fraser in search of gold. While Victoria remained the administrative locus, Britannia's sceptre was borne up the Fraser River and north through the strait, particularly among islands and adjacent to coastal plains where settlers were encroaching on aboriginal lands, not always without paying the cost of their lives.

From Victoria north to Discovery Passage, ship channels wind their way tortuously through more than a hundred islands, islets and reefs that comprise the Gulf Islands. In the south, hard by Vancouver Island, Saltspring Island, one of the largest of the Gulf Islands, lies across the entrance to Cowichan Harbour; it was known to the Indians as Tuan, "facing the sea," meaning in this case, Haro Strait. Flanking Saltspring's eastern shore is a chain of long, narrow islands, including Saturna, North and South Pender, Mayne, Galiano, Valdes, and Gabriola, which stretches northwesterly and forms a narrow wall between Vancouver Island and Georgia Strait.

This island barrier leaves another island cluster to the west, adjacent to the present towns of Chemainus and Ladysmith. Here Thetis and Kuper Islands, joined like Siamese twins at low tide, were the home of Halkomen-speaking Salish peoples. The Lemalchi, a fierce and predatory band numbering less than a hundred who were outcasts from other tribes, lived on Kuper Island at Lemalchi Bay (formerly Village Bay), a small cove relatively free from the seasonal southeaster. On the island's eastern shore lived the more populous Penelukuts, who occupied a village site just south of a remarkably white, clam-shell strewn and hook-shaped spit point bearing their tribal name. Farther north, on Vancouver Island's eastern shore, the Nanaimo Indians, "big, strong people," lived in close proximity to a small, rising town born on the crest of a coal-mining boom. North again, the strait's main channel trends towards the island shore with Lasqueti and Texada and then Denman and Hornby Islands punctuating the ever-constricting passage before it reaches Cape Mudge, the southern extremity of Quadra Island.

Cape Mudge differed from other locales in the strait in two ways. For one thing, it was, according to Captain Vancouver, the meeting place of two tides. Here a vessel could be opposed by "strong wind & disagreeable sea." The navigation in nearby Discovery Passage posed many hazards for vessels, especially for those without steampower. At slack water the sea, as Captain Prevost observed, could be a glassy smoothness, but minutes later it might become a rush. An English engineer wrote that it was reducible to submission only by steam.[1] Cape Mudge also marked the southern extremity of the Kwakiutl, the home of the Lekwiltok or, more commonly a century ago, the Yaculta. Their village

Plate 22. Victoria Regina, the Queen Empress whose ships patrolled the oceans in the age of *Pax Britannica* and whose gunboat commanders extended the authority of government, by peace or by war, on the Northwest Coast. This statue faces the Inner Harbour, Victoria, Vancouver Island.

Plate 23. This 1865 British Admiralty chart shows the west coast of Vancouver Island, an area of active British "gunboat diplomacy."

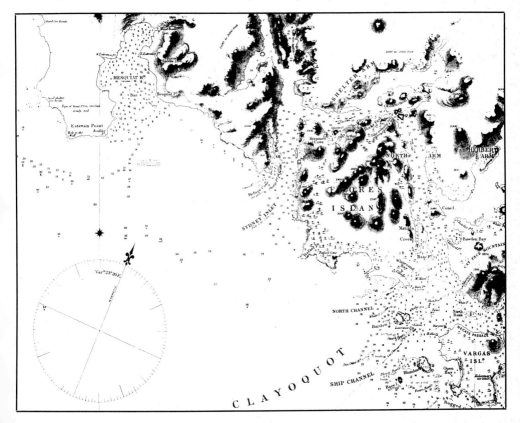

Plate 24. This Sechart Indian came from Clayoquot, Vancouver Island.

Plate 25. A study in contrasts. West Coast Indians and men of H.M.S. *Boxer* on board the gunvessel.

Plate 26. The screw-sloop H.M.S. *Cameleon*, 17 guns, 952 tons and 200 h.p., she served on the Pacific station 1861–65, 1867–69, and 1870–74. During the first period she was commanded by Edward Hardinge, and contributed to the capture of Acheewun in 1863.

Plate 27. George Henry Richards (later Admiral, K.C.B., F.R.S., and Hydrographer to the Admiralty) directed the survey of the British Columbia coast which resulted in thirty-six charts and the first *Vancouver Island Pilot,* published 1864. "My opinion is that the Natives in most instances are the oppressed and injured parties."

Plate 29. The officers, men and mascots of H.M.S. *Rocket,* a gunvessel stationed at Esquimalt 1875–1882. This 1877 photo shows Sergeant Bloomfield of the Victoria police leaning on the rail and Lieutenant Charles Reynold Harris, the commanding officer, sitting front and centre. At the back left, sitting on either side of the marine may perhaps be seen the Tsimshian informant Alfred Dudower (left) and the young George Hunt, taken on at Fort Rupert as interpreter. The *Rocket* destroyed Kimsquit village in punishment for the plunder of the *George S. Wright* and for the murder of survivors.

Plate 28. Two hard-headed British gunboat commanders, shown here in riding attire. Yorkshiremen Charles Rufus Robson (left) of H.M. gunboat *Forward* and his successor in command of the *Forward,* 1862–1865, the Hon. Horace Douglas Lascelles, seventh son of the third Earl of Harewood.

Plate 30. A familiar sight in coast Indian village harbours, H.M.S. *Boxer* was "on station" from 1869 to 1874. Built in 1868 and carrying four guns, she was a "gunvessel" and had better steam-power than the gunboats *Forward* and *Grappler* which she replaced. H.M.S. *Rocket* was of the same Beacon class, and was "on station" 1875–1882.

Plate 31. H.M. screw gunvessel *Sparrowhawk*, on station 1865–1872 commanded by Edwin Augustus Porcher and, after July 1872, by Henry Wentworth Mist. Investigating the horrors of the *John Bright*'s wreck in 1869 she carried police and portable gallows to Hesquiat, where two guilty natives were hanged in the presence of the assembled tribe.

Plate 32. Dr. Israel Wood Powell (1836–1915), M.D., C.M., first Superintendent for Indian Affairs in British Columbia, 1872–1889, continued using the Royal Navy as "the customary authority" among Coast Indians. He greatly admired and followed the policies of Governor James Douglas. First Grand Master of B.C. Masons, he was responsible for early public school and medical practice legislation. This photo taken in 1874.

Plate 33. Lieutenant D'Arcy Anthony Denny, in command of the British gunboat *Forward* 1866–1868, brought 16 years of experience in gunboat operations to British Columbia. A career professional in "inshore gunboat activities" he was spirited and determined, operating as he did from a strict mindset of legalistic rationality, as on the Nass River in 1866.

Plate 34. Celebrated in Alaskan history, the composite sloop H.M.S. *Osprey*, launched in 1876 and equipped with gatling guns (among other weapons), was commanded by Captain H. Holmes A'Court, Senior Naval Officer at Esquimalt, who answered an urgent plea from threatened Americans at Sitka who faced Indian insurgents in 1869. The *Osprey*'s presence, A'Court said, prevented a "serious calamity."

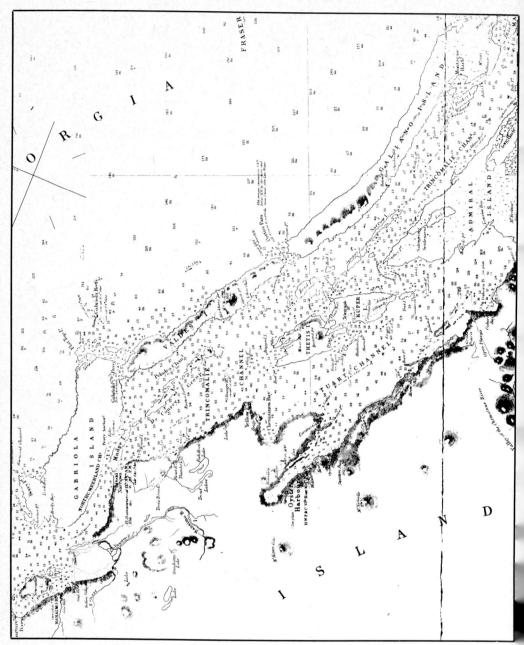

Plate 35. Between Saltspring Island (shown here in this 1865 chart as Admiral Island) and Nanaimo, the east coast of Vancouver Island and its offshore island dependencies form a series of ridges progressing northeastwards towards Georgia Strait and the mouth of the Fraser River. Inhabited by Salish peoples at various coastal locations, it was the area heavily searched by the Royal Navy in 1863 to find the Lemalchi chief from Kuper Island, Acheewun, and his accomplices, suspected of multiple murders. Acheewun was finally captured near Montague Harbour, Galiano Island, was tried in Victoria, found guilty, and hanged.

Plate 36. Indians of Nootka Sound, 1881, showing Indian Commissioner Israel Wood Powell (in uniform as Colonel in the Canadian Militia), Lieutenant-Commander Vere Bernard Orlebar of H.M.S. *Rocket* (centre) and Fisheries Commissioner A.C. Anderson (in boater hat). Note barefoot sailors of boating party and chief, in foreground, with new naval cap presented to him as an ally.

Plate 37. The Church Missionary Society's mission at Metlakatla showing Indians and whites, the houses, church, warehouse and other industrial buildings of this "model Indian village" headed by William Duncan.

Plate 38. William Wiseman, later Sir William Wiseman, Baronet. Shown here in 1862 as a midshipman of H.M.S. *Ganges,* he first visited British Columbia in 1858. He returned in command of H.M.S. *Caroline,* and in 1888 was involved in the last "gunboat action" — an effective show of force at Port Essington during the "Skeena War" upriver. The *Caroline* carried eighty officers and men of Royal Garrison Artillery, twelve police, officers of the civil power, and a Victoria *Colonist* "war correspondent."

Plate 39. The treacherous Nass River from near its serpentine-like entrance on Nass Bay (not shown) to the Lower Nass villages. H.M.S. *Forward,* commanded by Lieutenant D'Arcy A. Denny, first "showed the flag" at the Lower Nass villages in 1866 to stop liquor traffic on the then unsurveyed and unmarked river. In 1868 the lower river was surveyed by Staff Commander Daniel Pender, R.N. This is from an Admiralty chart, 1872.

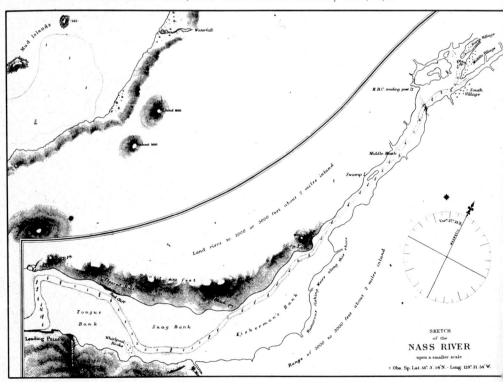

SKETCH
of the
NASS RIVER
upon a smaller scale
+ Obs. Sp. Lat. 55° 3′ 54″N. - Long. 129° 31′ 54″ W.

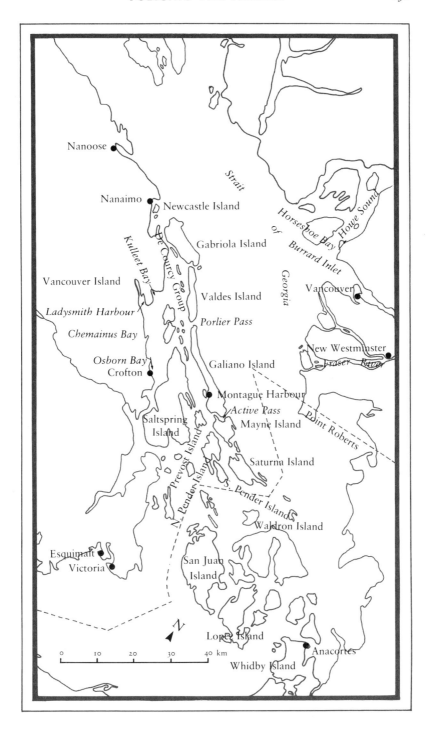

Nanoose

Strait

Horseshoe Bay

Howe Sound

Nanaimo

Newcastle Island

of

Burrard Inlet

Gabriola Island

Kulleet Bay

De Courcy Group

Georgia

Vancouver

Vancouver Island

Valdes Island

Ladysmith Harbour

Porlier Pass

New Westminster

Chemainus Bay

Fraser River

Osborn Bay

Galiano Island

Crofton

Montague Harbour

Active Pass

Point Roberts

Saltspring
Island

Mayne Island

Prevost Island

Saturna Island

N. Pender Island

S. Pender Islands

Waldron Island

Esquimalt

San Juan
Island

Victoria

N

Lopez Island

0   10   20   30   40 km

Anacortes

Whidby Island

on the favourable western side of Quadra Island, a short distance from Cape Mudge and opposite the Yaculta Rapids of Discovery Passage and the present town of Campbell River, was called Tsqulotn, a Salish name meaning "playing field." It was known by others generally as Yuculta Village. Sometime after Vancouver's voyage the Lekwiltok, bearing fire-arms, had pushed southwards into Coast Salish territory, and between 1841 and 1846 and numbering about 4000, including slaves, they established their village at Cape Mudge as well as at other points on Johnstone Strait.[2]

Without doubt the Lekwiltok seemed to outsiders a fierce race. They exerted a strong territorial prerogative over Cape Mudge and nearby waters, including both sides of Johnstone Strait north to within twenty miles of Fort Rupert. They exacted tolls on northern Indians who passed Cape Mudge. They terrorized Salish tribes to the south and ravaged natives living on the Fraser near Fort Langley. For this reason the master of H.M.S. *Plumper* thought them "a very warlike savage race; always fighting with their neighbours and mostly gaining the advantage." Commander Mayne held a similar view, terming them "the Ishmaelites of the coast, their band being literally against everyone's and everyone's against them." "The most wild and savage looking set we had yet seen" was Commander Prevost's assessment. James Douglas, whose opinion is particularly to be respected, called them "decidedly the most daredevil, forward and saucy Indians" he had ever seen, "unreclaimed by the discipline or influence of the whites". Because of the Lekwiltok reputation as "the worst Indians" to be met with and because of the hazards of navigating the narrows, Cape Mudge acquired the dubious distinction as a "death-hole."[3]

No one dreaded the Lekwiltok more than the Comox, the most northern Coast Salish, who had fought an unsuccessful action to prevent the Lekwiltok from invading their territory. These Salish retreated southwards to make Comox Harbour their northern outpost on Vancouver Island, living there for only a generation or two before H.M.S. *Grappler* brought the first white pioneers in 1862. Northern Indians such as the Bella Bella and Haida also knew the power of the Lekwiltok. In the course of their summer visits to Victoria they had to run the gauntlet at Cape Mudge. Still, the Lekwiltok's reputation did not deter these northern tribes, and their determination to reach the colonial capital or Puget Sound, their daring, and their love for wandering won the admiration of at least one naval officer.[4]

The Navy engaged in two police actions against Indians at Cape Mudge, incidents that reveal the utility of one gunboat, H.M.S. *Forward,* in that locale. The first, in the summer of 1860, was against the Lekwiltok themselves and served to strengthen the prevailing white per-

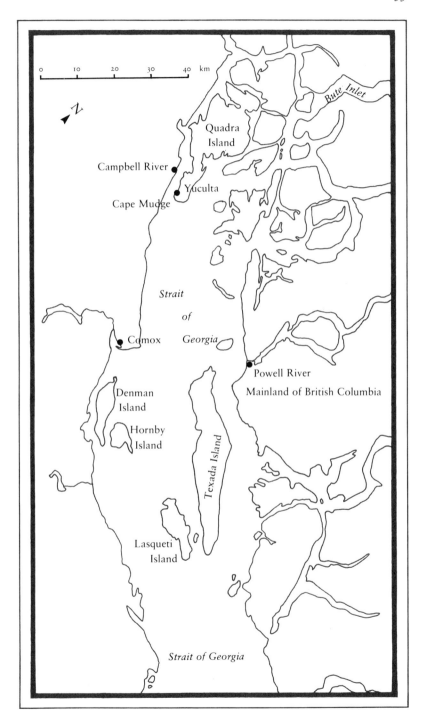

ception that this tribe was "bold as well as bloodthirsty, and by no means disposed to yield, as Indians generally do, to the mere exhibition of force." Off Saltspring Island, a party of these Indians attacked and robbed some boats owned by Chinese and escaped with their booty to Cape Mudge "which, being stockaded for protection against the other tribes," Commander Mayne wrote sarcastically, "they no doubt thought would be equally efficacious against white men." The *Forward*'s captain, Lieutenant Charles R. Robson, could get no satisfaction when he demanded that the property be returned. Consequently he ordered his gun crew to fire one or two shells over the stockade, then at the canoes, and lastly at the stockade itself. During the encounter, the Lekwiltok mounted an extensive musketry fire, but the gunboat's crew were protected by armour mounted along the gunwales, known as rifle plates.[5] Thus was the reprisal concluded with the stockade in ruins and the natives momentarily scattered.

The second action occurred in May 1861. The *Forward* had been sent north from Victoria on government request to patrol the Island's east coast as a precautionary measure to protect settlers at Saltspring Island and Nanaimo from a large party of northern Indians who had left Victoria for their villages in thirty canoes. Governor Douglas's fears were well founded. At Nanaimo, the local magistrate, William Hales Franklyn, appealed to Lieutenant Robson to assist in capturing several Haidas who had boarded and stripped the schooner *Laurel* at Victoria and, besides, had ransacked several houses on Saltspring Island, stolen a great deal of private property, and threatened the lives of settlers.[6] At Nanaimo they had then tried to sell the stolen goods. In Franklyn's opinion, the Haida were not only thieves but marauders and pirates, having systematically plundered all they could lay their hands on en route home.

In appealing for a gunboat, the magistrate impressed upon Lieutenant Robson that danger of Indian attack greatly alarmed settlers at Saltspring Island. "Life and property will not be safe," he warned, "if such things pass unnoticed." Robson was not one to shy away from responsibilities; he believed, as did many fellow officers, "that the Indian Savage fully appreciates prompt retributive Justice" and that the authorities could best be served by providing support "against such desperate and overwhelming numbers." Accordingly, he proceeded north in search of "these marauding villains," taking with him Franklyn and five representatives of the civil power.

On 17 May the *Forward* arrived near the encampment of the Haidas on the beach of Vancouver Island a mile or two south of Cape Mudge. Lieutenant Robson was not out for vengeance and blood. In order to avoid a collision or lead the Indians into believing that they were being coerced, Robson tactfully sent two unarmed civilian officials to shore. They were Edwin Gough, a constable, and Adam Horne, a Hudson's

Bay Company trader, both well known to these Indians. On Robson's instructions, Gough and Horne asked the chief to attend an enquiry on board the *Forward*. To the request, the authorities added their traditional threat: if the Indians failed to comply, the gunboat would fire on them.

The Haida not only refused to obey the request, they also treated the threat with "the utmost derision," boasting that they had their own guns and could fight and that, in reference to the gunboat, they "were not afraid of a schooner like that." Then they became, in Robson's words, "greatly excited, flourishing their weapons." They took Horne prisoner. Robson then steamed close to shore and told the Indians through Horne, in what must have been a very confused exchange, the consequences of their refusal. Their reply to this second chance was to shout defiance. Because all other means had proved to no avail, Robson ordered his gun crew to fire a shot high over the Indian encampment. The Haida immediately answered with a volley of musketry directly at the gunboat, "the balls whistling through the rigging over our heads and striking the side."[7]

Robson now opened direct fire, ordering the *Forward*'s guns to be laid for the canoes, which he intended to destroy in preference to carrying out any indiscriminate slaughter. After considerable firing, the Haida fled to the bush and for some time kept up a vigorous musket fire. At this juncture, Robson saw several canoes fleeing to the northwest. He therefore ceased firing and gave chase in the gunboat. The Indians in the canoes realized that they would be trapped and returned, hugging the shore in order to avoid capture by the warship. Momentarily Robson saw a large canoe with a flag flying coming off the shore. This contained Chief Jefferson of Skidegate, the principal chief of the party. He told Robson that the Haida did not want any more fighting, that four Indians had been killed and several canoes broken, and that the violent encounter was the fault of about forty of their young men who wanted to fight. As for himself, he confessed, he was "no 'fool-man.'"[8]

At this juncture, Robson attempted to determine who the guilty were, both in the piracy of the *Laurel* and in the theft of property from Victoria and Saltspring. Each of several Indians interrogated confessed that the crimes had been committed. But in an act of solidarity, none would identify the guilty. In fact, they even furnished contradictory evidence. Some said that the guilty had been killed in the action; others, that they had returned to Victoria. The authorities persisted and after a "wearisome investigation" extracted enough telling testimony from Chief Jefferson for Magistrate Franklyn to arrest two Indians as principals and two others as accessories to the crimes. Chief Jefferson was to be taken to Victoria as a witness and informant on other Haida suspected in the piracy who might still be in the colonial capital.

Robson's method for compelling the Indians to submit had succeeded.

Peaceful negotiation had failed; so too had threats of the use of force. In this case, a selective, measured use of violence primarily against property rather than persons had resulted in capture of the suspects. The stolen property, including navigation instruments, carpenter's tools, food, liquor and clothes, was relinquished to the Crown. During the engagement eleven Lekwiltok canoes had obligingly come to assist the *Forward* against their old enemies, but Robson had ordered them to stand off until the fight was over. Further inquiries revealed that the "rascality" was not exclusively confined to the Haida. Chief Jefferson, charged with the attack on the *Laurel*, told authorities in Victoria that the whisky sold to him and his "tillicums" (people) by traders had been adulterated with salt water.[9]

Robson sensed the seriousness of his actions, for the official use of violence against Indians might invite censure from certain quarters, both in the colony and in Britain, and he justified his actions in a communication to his commander-in-chief, Rear-Admiral Maitland:

> I am fully aware that I have incurred a grave responsibility in having taken so decisive a part, but after mature deliberation I came to the conclusion that acts of this sort, partaking more of the nature of a piratical foray than anything hitherto attempted must for the safety of the settlers and small craft navigating these inland waters, be met by prompt and decisive action. And I am equally of the opinion that whether there be sufficient evidence or not to convict the actual perpetrators, the moral effect of the lesson they have received will operate in a salutary manner upon the Northern Indians for the future.[10]

Robson won support for his firm actions from both his superior and colonial authorities. Maitland took pains to point out to the Lords of the Admiralty that Robson properly laid his guns for the canoes rather than firing into the encampment. Happily, he added, no one on board the *Forward* had been wounded or otherwise injured and, moreover, the Indians suffered not more than four casualties.[11] The colonial government also supported Robson's successful use of force to compel the Indians to submit. John Work, senior member of the Council of the Colony of Vancouver Island and administering the government in Governor Douglas's absence, thought Robson acted with "much firmness and discretion." The "lesson" given the Haida was "much needed," he added, and for the future would doubtless have a salutary effect. On his return, Douglas objected to the Haida firing on Her Majesty's flag. He fully supported Robson's prompt, vigorous action. "These measures meet with my entire approval," he wrote to Maitland, "and I consider the punishment inflicted upon the Indians was merited and necessary, and the unavoidable consequence of their own rashness." These statements, sent to London, did not bring any complaint from the Admiralty or the Colonial Office.[12]

Such uses of official force were related to the question of security for settlers in and near Cowichan, Nanaimo and Comox. In the same year, on Governor Douglas's request, a gunboat was stationed at Nanaimo, a crossroads of Indian travel, to follow observantly the movements of Indians proceeding to Victoria or returning northwards.[13] Colonial security came first; thus Douglas placed a higher priority on sending a gunboat to Comox to help the nascent settlement against real or imagined dangers than on dispatching a warship to Sitka and the Stikine in August 1862, when Anglo-Russian tensions over the gold rush were developing. By juggling the resources at his disposal, Rear-Admiral Maitland managed to meet the needs of the day in both places.[14] Twice in the next year, 1863, the Navy received requests from Government House for support at Comox.[15] In 1865, another appeal for a gunboat in the northern waters of the Strait of Georgia reached Esquimalt. In the last case the inhabitants needed to be protected "from a most dangerous tribe of Indians called Euclataws."[16] By this time, a colonial official observed, encounters between natives and whites at Comox and Cowichan were "daily assuming larger and more serious proportions." But with the colonial government woefully lax in raising funds for police protection or even magistrates, local officials were few and far between. At this time, a critical need existed for "nipping in the bud," the same official wrote, "the ill-blood and disputes continually arising between the Indians and the white population, and which, I regret to say, are daily assuming larger and more serious proportions."[17] But again the colony's financial difficulties made the devolution of imperial responsibilities to the local level an impossibility. Thus, the metropolitan influence in the form of Navy police actions continued, with ships' commanders being made stipendiary magistrates[18] and police officers from Victoria or New Westminster being employed on naval "flying squads" sent to crisis spots such as Cape Mudge and Comox.

Farther south, at Saltspring and nearby islands such as Pender, cross-cultural conflict continued. As early as 1859 a committee for the settlement of Saltspring Island had been formed in Victoria and enjoyed the colonial government's support.[19] English, Scots, Australians, Hawaiians, Americans, Portuguese, and others were attracted to the island where water and arable land could be had and where few Indians lived. After the island was surveyed in 1859, settlers pre-empted land under claims granted from the recently established colonial lands office in Victoria. Saltspring's earliest settlers comprised a curious collection of individuals—some sought the opportunities of the soil, others an escape from the noise and violence of Victoria that reminded one writer of Dante's Inferno.[20] Still others sought political freedom. One body of settlers, a group of blacks whose origins can be traced to slave families in Missouri, came to Saltspring in 1858 from California, where legislation had been enacted against blacks. Douglas's encouragement that they would be welcomed in British territory was also an inducement to migrate north.

For centuries various Indian tribes had used Saltspring as a stopping point in the course of seaborne travels in the Strait of Georgia. They were used to roaming the island's shores and forests at will. At the time settlers arrived, there were three Indian villages on Saltspring Island. According to pioneers, the Cowichan regarded the island as their own and had actually established one village on Saltspring as a claim for compensation.[21] The Cowichan felt aggrieved: the settlers were usurping their land with the colonial government's aid, and the settlers were using Cowichan territorial waters. The Indians, Cowichan and others, despoiled crops and ransacked cabins. They murdered settlers, black and white. However, the Indian aggression did not come from one particular tribe: the Cowichans were as likely to raid the island as were migratory northern tribes.

The first celebrated case of violence of this sort was against a black family by the name of Stark. No sooner had they landed near Vesuvius Bay than they were stopped by a large number of Bella Bellas en route to Victoria to sell their furs. These Indians robbed the Starks and threatened to kill them. But the immigrants were aided by a Hudson's Bay Company servant named George McCauley who acted as an intermediary and by a Penelukut woman who stole away to her kinsmen at nearby Kuper Island and returned with a large number of armed Penelukut, who chased the Bella Bellas in their canoes and captured them. Oral tradition holds that the Penelukuts told the Bella Bellas that they would not kill the white man but that they would kill the Bella Bellas.[22] The Penelukuts subsequently conveyed their captives to the head of nearby Ganges Harbour. There they fought a desperate battle from which only one northern Indian escaped alive.

This episode again reveals the intensity of rivalry among the Indians themselves.[23] As for the settlers, they feared they would become embroiled when the Bella Bella came to take revenge on the Penelukuts and the Cowichan. They urgently appealed to Governor Douglas for protection.[24] Again, in 1860, some Cowichan singled out blacks, "to whom they considered themselves superior," as targets. Several murders and assaults by Indians against blacks occurred during the 1860's. As a black settler recalled, "the shadow of the Indian seemed destined to cross the threshold of that Mountain home with tragedy." These events led some blacks, who were widely dispersed throughout the island, to move to safer locations on the island such as Ganges or to seek refuge in towns such as Nanaimo or Victoria.[25]

These Indian "incidents" were not undertaken solely against blacks. Whites shared similar fears and frustrations. In 1861, as already mentioned, Haida who raided Saltspring homes were apprehended at Cape Mudge. On 4 April 1863, to cite another case, Indians killed Bill Brady, an American, and badly wounded his companion John Henley, a half-breed Cherokee from Texas, at Bedwell Harbour, Pender Island. These men, both hunters, had befriended three male and two female Cowichan Indians; yet after supper, when Brady and Henley had retired for the night and were asleep, the Indians shot them. Brady eventually died of his wounds but Henley, who after a fierce struggle forced the Cowichan to flee, lived to travel in a boat, aided by the tide, to Oak Bay, near Victoria, from where he was taken to hospital in Victoria.

On Governor Douglas's request, H.M.S. *Forward*, Lieutenant the Hon. Horace D. Lascelles commanding, went to investigate. The gunboat searched Piers Island then anchored off Cowichan Harbour, where Indians returning from a potlatch were stopped by the firing of guns loaded with blank charges only. The Indians were interrogated. The search then took the *Forward* first to Chemainus, where two suspects were seized, and then to several islands, including Portland and Moresby. In company with H.M.S. *Devastation*, the *Forward* returned to Pender Island where Brady's body and possessions were discovered at Shark Cove and he was buried. At Cowichan two other suspects were delivered over to the Victoria police superintendent, Horace Smith, without the Navy taking any coercive measures. Commander Pike of the *Devastation* visited settlers at Cowichan and found them apparently "free from uneasiness or fear of the Indians, all of whom as far as I could judge, seem very well disposed, though some soreness of feeling seems to have arisen among them from the fact of the compensation promised them, for certain lands not having yet been paid them."[26] The "judicious manner" in which Pike and Lascelles completed their assignment won Douglas's acclaim.[27] Such gunboat actions, effected without bloodshed, seldom passed the notice of the grateful governor. As for the suspects, three Indian men and one woman were tried and convicted at Victoria. The men were hanged in Victoria, but the woman was reprieved by a lenient judge and committed to life imprisonment. The judge's sentence did not go unquestioned by her angry accomplices who passed her on the way to the scaffold and futilely told police that in fact she was the most guilty of all, having incited them to commit the murder.[28]

In reporting this and similar acts of violence or "outrages" to the Colonial Office, Governor Douglas took care to note that these were sporadic cases, that they had no pattern except that they seemed motivated by plunder, and that they exhibited nothing resembling "anything of a national character" on the part of the Indians. He feared that local newspaper reports, wrong in substance and inflamed in tone, would give the Colonial Office the impression that an Indian war was in progress; and he advised the secretary of state for the colonies, the Duke of Newcastle, that the police assisted by the naval forces provided by Commodore Spencer, the Senior Naval Officer at Esquimalt, would soon complete a task designed to stop such wanton acts. In the governor's views, these were "very active measures for the punishment of the criminals as a public example for the prevention of crime."[29]

In actuality, such measures failed to provide immediate security the authorities desired. This was again demonstrated by a major crisis in white-native relations in the Cowichan-Saltspring region that occurred in the same year, 1863. This protracted and wearisome affair involved at least two tribes of Cowichan, the Cowichan themselves and the Lemalchi of Kuper Island. The former, Commander Mayne wrote, were "a badly-disposed set." They had shown no favour to settlers who had come to their valley. They were, he continued, "unwilling to sell, still less to be ousted from their land." Resentful and suspicious, they feared outsiders, white and red alike. In the early 1860's the settlers of Cowichan Valley like those of Saltspring Island made persistent appeals to the governor to have gunboats sent to provide security.[30]

Their concerns, and those of Gulf Island settlers, became particularly intense on 8 April 1863 when Frederick Marks and his young married daughter Caroline Harvey were murdered by Indians while they were moving in boats to Mayne Island from Waldron Island in American territory. One Mayne Island resident, their friend Christian Mayers who was helping them, told authorities that when a southeast wind blew up, his sloop was separated from Marks's boat. Marks and his daughter had landed at Saturna island. The Indians shot Marks dead and chased Caroline Harvey along the shore and brutally killed her. Mrs. Marks and her five other children who were in Mayers's sloop, arrived safely at Miners Bay, Mayne Island.

When news of this double murder reached Victoria, the community was outraged.[31] It was a particularly atrocious deed and the worst of a series of murders in the area. Governor Douglas took immediate action, and on his request the *Forward* proceeded on 15 April to various Indian settlements on the east coast of Vancouver Island to seek out the "perpetrators" and bring them to justice. Douglas's instructions to

Lieutenant Lascelles specified that if any tribe refused to comply with his wishes, he could seize their canoes and other property and destroy their villages. But, since the Indians were British subjects, he was cautioned "not to visit them with undue severity." In short, Lascelles had official sanction to engage in an action against Indian property but he was to avoid taking Indian life. This delicate demarcation explains his careful conduct, which one Victoria newspaper came to regard as too gentle.[32]

In the course of seeking out the murderers, Lascelles took the *Forward* into several native villages near Saturna Island and met with no success. On 25 April the *Forward* steamed into Lemalchi Bay, Kuper Island. Lascelles knew that several Indians who were involved in the murders were there and that the Lemalchi intended to resist. Expecting that there would be an exchange of fire, he ordered the gunboat's rifle plates placed along the gunwales as protection for riflemen and had any gaps and spaces between them tightly stashed with seamen's bags. Lascelles could see that the Lemalchi had a substantial log house in the centre of the village "loopholed." If the stronghold resembled that of the Semiahmoo near present day Blaine, Washington, it consisted of a stockade surrounding two plank houses, with tunnels leading from the houses to loopholes in the bank in front of the stockade. These typical Salish fortifications date from 1820–30 and were probably built as defences against increased raids from the northern tribes and may have been inspired by Hudson's Bay Company forts such as Fort Langley on the Fraser River.[33]

Lascelles sent a message to shore stating that he wished to speak to the chief and to do so on board ship. The chief replied that he would neither board the ship nor surrender the murderers. Through Iomo, a half-breed Cherokee interpreter hired at Cowichan, Lascelles told the chief that if he was not on board before the red flag which was hoisted for the purpose was lowered (thereby giving the chief a quarter of an hour to comply) Lascelles would fire on the village. The chief was not to be intimidated. With defiant pride he told the British that he was not afraid of them.[34]

At the end of the appointed time, Lascelles hauled down the flag and fired into the village. The Lemalchi immediately deserted it. They speedily clustered thickly on two points at the extremity of the bay. They replied to the ship's guns by opening a sustained and well directed fire on the gunboat, raking it bow and stern. Exposed to this fire was a boy, Charles Gliddon, who was serving as powderman at the pivot gun. He was killed by a shot through the head. The gunboat was hit in several places but sustained no other injury. For half an hour the exchange continued. The ship's guns "knocked the village down as much as possible" with shot, shell, grape and cannister and fired a few shells into the surrounding woods. The Lemalchi fled to the forest. Next morning, after returning from the night's anchorage at Chemainus Bay, the gunboat fired into every part of the island with the hope of dislodging the Indians from the woods. Lascelles completed the destruction of the village with a few shot and shell. During the night apparently all the Indians had left the place.[35] None of the suspects were captured.

Lascelles continued to comb the islands for the Lemalchi murderers and was joined in the search by the *Devastation*, Commander John Pike. The wandering nature of the Lemalchi frustrated Lascelles and Pike. "From all the information I have been able to gather respecting the above named Indians," the senior naval officer at Esquimalt, Commodore the Hon. J.W.S. Spencer, wrote to the Lords of the Admiralty on 4 May, "they appear to consist of the outcasts of all the different Tribes on the Coast; and are, in fact little better than a nest of Pirates."[36]

Governor Douglas was anxious to bring the Lemalchi to terms. In his opinion they bore "a very bad character."[37] Not only did he want to bring the murderers and accomplices to trial, he wanted to teach them a lesson about British justice and to pacify the settlers in the region. The Lemalchi, he feared, would continue their "murderous and piratical practices" and the lives of white settlers would be in constant danger unless "decisive and vigorous measures be adopted immediately." Since the Lemalchi had fled "to a stronghold from which they can only be suc-cessfully dislodged without great risk of bloodshed by those who are accustomed to their haunts and mode of warfare" Douglas planned to assemble a small militia force of half-breeds and Indians.[38] However, he could not raise the force. Instead, he decided to send Police Superinten-dent Smith to talk with the Lemalchi, and if peaceful measures failed, "there is no alternative consistent with our dignity, and with the safety of other men's lives than to resort to coercive measures." Douglas did not want bloodshed but he did want the Navy's support. He suggested that a very large force should be employed. Smith was to take Indians allied to the government's cause who were also familiar with the Lemalchi haunts. Douglas did not question the abilities of Pike or Lascelles. Yet he cau-tioned Spencer not to send any landing parties from the ship unless the exact position and number of the Indians had been ascertained. Iomo and other interpreters were to accompany the expedition to provide in-formation about the Lemalchi. The object was to drive the Lemalchi out of their stronghold.[39]

In keeping with the governor's recommendation, Commodore Spencer sent a large force under Commander Pike to bring the accused to justice.[40] The *Devastation*, in company of the gunboats *Grappler*, Lieu-tenant Verney commanding, and the *Forward*, with the launches of the flagship *Topaze* in tow, left Esquimalt on 15 May. At Miners Bay, Mayne Island, an Indian volunteered to aid the authorities, but he could provide no evidence about the whereabouts of the Lemalchi. At Chemainus, Vancouver Island, the authorities sprung the trap. Two Chemainus chiefs were taken hostage when it was learned they had been harbouring Acheewun, the principal suspect. In fact, Acheewun had fled from Chemainus the night before when he learned that the warships had anchored nearby. Instead, the Chemainus delivered to the authorities Acheewun's relatives: his father-in-law, uncle, wife, and child. Thereupon the chiefs were set free, to return to their tribe.

After laborious inquiries Lascelles learned that Acheewun and the Lemalchi were encamped in Chemainus Bay, about nine miles north of Chemainus River. The *Forward* and *Devastation* anchored in the bay and searched methodically by armed boats and a shore party under Smith. When the Lemalchi were discovered, the British gave chase but could not secure them. The party destroyed seven canoes secreted in the woods. They burned provisions, cedar mats used for making temporary dwellings over a framework of poles, and any other property they discovered. The landing party went next to nearby Tsukmeen village, captured a principal suspect named Shahkutchsus and imprisoned him on board the *Devastation*. He confessed to being an accomplice and provided key evidence in the case, stating that his brother and his brother's wife had killed Marks' daughter, the man holding her while the woman struck her with an axe.

The hunt continued at Thetis Island, where a landing party combed the bush while boats searched the shore and creeks. The Navy found and destroyed two canoes belonging to one of the suspects, Tishtan, on top of a high cliff. At Chemainus Bay, a landing party searched the area behind the Indian village, a movement co-ordinated with armed boats working along the shore.

At this stage the authorities received welcome help from the Penelukut who, though living near the recently destroyed Lemalchi village, owed no allegiance to their neighbours. Fearing the Navy would retaliate for the crime, the Penelukut had first taken refuge with the Musqueam tribe at the entrance of the Fraser River. Now prepared to co-operate with the authorites, they delivered to the Navy three Lemalchi witnesses of the murders and Acheewun's sister. Despite this aid the search remained incomplete, the mission unaccomplished, and the *Grappler* gave chase to a Lemalchi party known to have been in Osborn Bay, Vancouver Island. Again the Navy located the Lemalchi camp but, once more, the Indians fled into the bush. On this occasion twenty-three Chemainus Indians aided in the hunt, but the search had to be abandoned. Again, the British destroyed canoes, five this time, and other property left behind by the fleeing Lemalchi. At a Penelukut village the Navy stealthily made a night raid and seized six suspects, one of them Allwheuck, known to have killed Marks' daughter, and Skullowayat, believed to be the man who had shot Marks.

Though many suspects had been apprehended, the Lemalchi as a tribe had not been communicated with directly. Their chief, Acheewun, remained at large. The authorities could not bring the search to a satisfactory conclusion without dealing with the tribe as a whole, not necessarily to seek revenge or to employ coercion but to discuss with chiefs and with tribe members the nature of their responsibilities and rights under the new system of law then being spread in British territory. Acheewun had proved extremely elusive, and the British were much frustrated by the protracted affair. They had achieved only a half measure of success—their task remained unfinished as long as Acheewun was at large.

As far as technique was concerned, Pike reported to Spencer that during the whole of his eleven-day cruise he had been denied any parley or even indirect communication with the phantom-like Lemalchi. Two parties of five Lemalchi each had retreated to places so inaccessible to the Navy that he felt compelled to stop the search. Apart from two canoes known to have escaped towards Fraser River, all the Lemalchi canoes, seventeen in number, and a large quantity of property had been destroyed. In his opinion, the Lemalchi would commit no further "outrage" unless under Acheewun's direction. This seemed unlikely, he argued, for Pike had detained enough hostages to provide "sufficient surety" to keep Acheewun quiet.[41] In frustration, Pike returned to Esquimalt to seek instructions from Commodore Spencer on what measures should be taken "to prove to this piratical tribe that the authority they refuse to acknowledge must be respected."[42]

Early in May the Victoria press's impatience with the Navy's inability to bring the Lemalchi to terms led to an episode of comic and almost tragic proportions. Charles Wilson Allen, proprietor of the *Evening Express*, singled out Lascelles with the offensive lines "He who fights and runs away/May live to fight another day." Lieutenant the Hon. Horace Douglas Lascelles, seventh son of the third Earl of Harewood, took objection or perhaps thought he would have a little fun at Allen's expense. Some spirited sailors from the *Forward*, with Lascelles' tacit acknowledgement, inveigled Allen aboard the gunboat and took him for an involuntary sail off Victoria. Frightened, Allen jumped overboard, nearly drowned, and was rescued and returned to shore near Clover Point. Allen retaliated by pressing a charge of false imprisonment against Lascelles, and the officer settled out of court by paying $1,000 in damages.[43]

As in Victoria, citizens at Cowichan, Chemainus, and Saltspring grew anxious about the Lemalchi pirates. A nervous Cowichan resident wrote a letter, published in the *British Colonist*, referring to the "villainy" of the Indians and the murder of "a fine English sailor." "Where is the great Governor's excellent treatment of Indians now?" he asked, "Where is the unpaid constable?" Such letters pointed to the lack of police and magistrates. They also provided sensational reading for the colonial public and at the same time served to heighten the uneasiness of citizens in the capital and outlying settlements. Navy investigations, however, revealed that the Cowichan pioneers were perfectly secure.[44]

Meanwhile, the Royal Navy's detective work continued. At Dodd Narrows, Chemainus, Osborn Bay, Oyster Bay and elsewhere, officers and police took Indians into custody and extracted information by blockading bays and shelling canoes and other property. They offered rewards for clues leading to the arrest of the suspects. By this time their most wanted suspect was Acheewun, a great seaborne warrior reported in the Victoria press as "a perfect fiend and the terror of all the tribes." It was rumoured that if he aimed his gun, death was certain. Any threat from him spelled doom to his enemies. His hand-picked crew of oarsmen made his war canoe the fastest, most elusive in the straits. He boasted he had killed eleven whites and numerous Indians. For all these reasons he was the dread of enemy tribes.[45]

The Navy watched all of Acheewun's possible haunts including Chemainus, Kuper, and Galiano Islands. Indian evidence pointed to Galiano, but that island had many natural obstacles, including thick woods, high mountain caves, and steep rocky shores that made approaches from the sea difficult. On the south, turbulent Active Pass hindered gunboat operations. Acheewun had selected an excellent hidden haunt. Because the Navy knew that most, if not all, of the Lemalchi canoes had been destroyed, the senior officer, Commander Edward Hardinge of the steamsloop *Cameleon*, determined to seal off all sea escapes. He positioned the *Forward* and steam launches from the *Topaze* in Active Pass on the south and Porlier Pass on the north end of the island. The *Cameleon*, with formidable fire power from her seventeen guns, could be employed in flushing Acheewun and his comrades out of the woods if a landing party could not do so.

At the foot of a mountain near Active Pass scouts discovered fresh footprints, and a landing party under Lieutenant Pusey from one of the launches went in pursuit. The party scaled the back of the mountain, found the suspects, and forced them at gunpoint down the mountain face to the shore of Montague Harbour. Rifle fire from the landing party brought the *Forward* and the second launch into the harbour to give assistance. Just as the second landing party arrived, Acheewun and his two aides were captured by Pusey and taken to the gunboat. Acheewun was brought on board "to our great satisfaction," Commander Hardinge wrote in a restrained tone.[46] Acheewun and his brother, Shunaseluk, were the first on board followed by a third, Walleshuk, together with his wife and three children. One suspect remained at large and authorities posted a $100 reward to Indians who could bring to Victoria any suspects. The *Cameleon* returned to Esquimalt with the prisoners, leaving the *Forward* to continue the search and "show the flag."

In all, the authorities took eighteen Lemalchi prisoner. They included Acheewun, two suspects and an accomplice in the murder of Marks's daughter, two suspects in the murder of Marks, and seven known to have been on Pender Island when the murder was committed. They also included Acheewun's sister, a suspect's wife, and three hostages detained for having harboured Acheewun and the murderers at Chemainus. Acheewun clearly was not guilty of murder. He was, however, charged with aiding and abetting those who were guilty of resisting authorities at Lemalchi Bay. Six of his relatives were incarcerated by the authorities: his father-in-law, uncle, wife, child, sister, and sister-in-law.[47]

Acheewun's relationship to the four murderers and one accomplice is not entirely clear. However, they were Lemalchi, a group consisting of outcasts from other Salish tribes. Their sustained unified resistance in support of others of their village demonstrates their zealous tribal solidarity. As was their custom against Indian enemies, they banded together in support of the murderers. And, also true to custom, they had banded together against outsiders—in this case, the authorities.

That the Lemalchi were brought to trial cannot be said to have been the Navy's sole responsibility. The Chemainus, perhaps allied with the Penelukut, aided the British by providing an armed force to comb nearby woods. But only on pressure, when two chiefs were taken hostage, did the Chemainus deliver four of Acheewun's relatives. The Penelukut, by contrast, perhaps fearing that their village would be fired on, perhaps wanting no more middle-of-the-night raids by the Navy on their village, proved the most willing allies in the strait. They delivered to the authorities two murderers, seven suspects, and Acheewun's sister. Other Indians, including Iomo, acted as informants, guides, or *voltigeurs*.

The Navy delivered Acheewun and his fellow captives to Victoria for trial. The court reporter for the *British Colonist* described as follows the legendary chief's response to British justice: "the great pirate robber, who is not by any means of forbidding appearance if we accept his piercing, wicked eye, was perfectly self-possessed and betrayed no concern whatever for his fearfully precarious position."[48] At the trials, begun 17 June, four Indians, including Acheewun were found guilty of complicity in the celebrated double murder and were executed in the early morning of 4 July on a scaffold erected in front of the police barracks.[49] As for Mrs. Marks and her five children, they were brought from Mayne Island to

Victoria where citizens' donations provided a widow's endowment. The Lemalchi quit their cove where the violence with the *Forward* had begun their encounter with British naval power and joined with the larger Penelukut band residing at Penelukut Spit, now an Indian reserve.[50]

The Lemalchi affair had been a protracted gunboat action, the longest undertaken by the Royal Navy to that date on the Northwest Coast and one which required more than one warship to bring the murderers and the elusive Acheewun and his accomplices to trial. For some time thereafter gunboats looked in at various Indian and white settlements in the Strait of Georgia for the twofold purpose of giving confidence to whites who feared Indian retaliation after the great encounter and of warning Indians that they were "not unwatched."[51]

The activities of gunboats such as the *Forward* were hardly prosaic.[52] Calls for protection from settlements adjacent to the Strait of Georgia such as Cowichan, Saltspring Island, Nanaimo, and Comox seemed incessant, and to Governor Douglas particularly, the Saltspring troubles "must have seemed like the buzzing of some persistent mosquito."[53] The Lemalchi and Yaculta were highly mobile and militarily capable enemies, and in the 1860's the calls on the Navy for protection against them were not without foundation. The number of murders of whites and blacks and the molestation of people and property by Indians in the Gulf Islands and elsewhere justified the pleas for a protection which those living under the British flag had reason to expect was their due.

IO

The Pulls of Alaska

COMMANDERS and men of British warships had more than enough responsibilities in British Columbia waters in the 1860's and 1870's without being burdened by Alaskan duties. Yet affairs on the northern fringe of British interests were turbulent enough to draw British warships into foreign waters. Not until the 1880's did the United States government have adequate naval force in Pacific waters to protect national interests in Alaska. And, for a hundred years before that time, both during the Russian and American periods, the imperial power controlling Alaska never had sufficient naval force to support its traders against Indian interference. Although the Alaska shoreline north of Dixon Entrance and Portland Canal was nominally Russian in sovereignty until 1867 and American thereafter, it was actually a region where the powerful Tlingit, Tsimshian, and Kaigani Haida were virtually a law unto themselves. Here also the two imperially chartered business firms, the Russian American Company and the Hudson's Bay Company, traded cooperatively in neighbouring spheres of the panhandle until 1867.

From its founding in 1799, the Russian American Company experienced difficult relations with the Kolosh (Tlingit) living at and near New Archangel (or Sitka), the company headquarters in Sitka Sound, Baranov Island. In June 1802 the great chief Skayutlelt, in an act of revenge against the English arms and liquor trader Henry or Harry Barber of the London ship *Unicorn,* led an attack on the Sitka stockade, burned it, took furs, killed or tortured defenders, and enslaved women and children. A few survivors reached two trading ships, one American and the other British, whose captains ransomed several prisoners. Alexander

Baranov, the Russian chief trader, needed two years to marshal enough force to retake Sitka and used violent measures only after peaceful ones had failed. In 1804 he sent landing parties to shore after company ships and the Russian Imperial Navy's *Neva*, Captain Iu. F. Lisianskii commanding, had bombarded the Tlingit fortifications. The Kolosh doggedly defended their fort, but eventually they went over the mountains to the north.

This legendary event of cross-cultural violence on the Northwest Coast had one outstanding result. Whites living in the Sitka area remained conscious of the warlike capacities of the Tlingit and took steps to maintain security. Baranov erected a strong fortification at Sitka and always kept it well garrisoned. The visits of Russian warships were few and far between, and like the Bay traders at Forts Rupert and Simpson, the white lords of Alaska remained reliant on a rigid mode of discipline, similar to that of the Hudson's Bay Company, to maintain their tenuous position in relation to the natives.[1]

The British had a longstanding interest in Alaskan affairs by virtue of the Foreign Office's desire to check Russia's southward expansion in the early years of the nineteenth century. In 1821 Tsar Alexander I had declared territorial sovereignty along the Alaskan coast from Bering Strait to 51° North latitude and dominion over adjacent seas 115 miles from the continental shore. With Hudson's Bay Company ambitions of trade to consider, Whitehall could not accept this bold extension of empire. Moreover, the Admiralty's interest in the possibility of a Northwest Passage and freedom of the seas could not be discounted. The United States also opposed the tsar's attempts at aggrandizement, though for different reasons. Both Britain and the United States undertook diplomatic initiatives with the Russian court. The resulting conventions, signed between Russia and the United States in 1824 and Russia and the United Kingdom in 1825, established the southern boundary of Russian America at 54° 40′ North, defined an awkward eastern limit to the Russian panhandle, and acknowledged that British subjects had the right of navigating rivers or streams that crossed the *lisière* or border, whether these subjects came from the sea or from the interior. One of these rivers was the "great river" of the Tlingit, the Stikine, in about 57° North latitude. The British could also trade, except in liquor, at Sitka and on the Alaskan coast south of Mount Saint Elias for a ten-year period.

These treaties checked Russian progress to the east and south, restored British and American maritime rights, and allowed the British and Americans to strengthen their position and claims to the remaining portion of the Northwest Coast, a matter eventually resolved in the Oregon Treaty. In the interim, the contest for control of the rich trade of the Stikine River and hinterland continued, and in the 1830's the Hudson's

Bay Company disputed with both the Russians and the Stikine Indians. The Russians wanted no interference. Neither did the Indians. As middlemen to the Hudson's Bay Company trade in the interior, they did not want to be removed from this position by the establishment of a new post to which the interior Indians could go directly. In 1834 the British company sent their brig *Dryad* to establish Fort Stikine, but their efforts were stopped by the Russians at Redoubt St. Dionysius (now Wrangell) near the mouth of the river and by the presence of a Russian warship *Chichagoff*, mounting fourteen guns. But in 1840, under an agreement reached between the companies in 1839, the Bay traders took over Redoubt St. Dionysius and developed it as British headquarters for trade on the Alaskan coast, more particularly up the Stikine River into the present northwest corner of British Columbia and the Yukon.

The Anglo-Russian exploitation of the coastal strip continued uninterrupted until the early 1860's, and might have persisted thereafter had not the region's affairs been influenced by factors beyond Russian or British control. Though the region had grown increasingly unprofitable to the Bay traders, they feared problems when gold seekers entered the Stikine in 1862 in search of deposits in the Cassiar country. Port Highfield, near the northern end of Wrangell Island and just south of the river's entrance, became a staging ground for miners. The gold rush was watched with suspicion by Finnish-born Governor Johann Furuhjelm at Sitka. It also brought an extension of British jurisdiction without Russian protest to the hinterland adjacent to the panhandle: London annexed the Stikine Territory by extending British Columbia's boundaries northwards to the sixty-second parallel and put the region under the supervision of the governor of British Columbia.

Meanwhile, British authorities had grown anxious about the increasing incidence of violence between whites and Indians on the Northwest Coast. The commander-in-chief, Rear-Admiral Maitland, was an experienced practitioner of gunboat diplomacy.[2] As early as 10 June 1861 he had appealed to the Admiralty to station a military as well as naval force at Vancouver Island. The discovery of gold on the Stikine in that year meant that whites would be sailing the waters between Puget Sound and the river entrance, a hazardous route given the warlike nature of the Indian tribes inhabiting the straits. Governor Douglas warned Maitland that the Indians were becoming more dangerous and difficult and that the British would have to be ready for any Indian outbreak. On 3 September 1862 Maitland reported to London that in addition to two gunboats used for various coastal duties, two small warships were needed, one near Fort Simpson on the northern frontier and another near Nanaimo, and, in addition, a large gunboat should be added to the force for the protection of the colony. The extension of British control to the Stikine Territory, Maitland observed correctly, had actually, though not legally, increased the extent of coast to be protected by Her Majesty's ships "by upwards of seven hundred miles." Given the scant resources at his disposal, Maitland could not be expected to provide protection for all gold seekers and traders bound for Stikine. Hence he advised Douglas to issue a proclamation cautioning all British subjects against travelling between Victoria and Stikine in canoes and not to travel that part of the coast at all except in well armed coasting vessels that were prepared for attack by Indians.[3]

The immediate cause of Maitland's alarm was information sent him by Douglas that two white miners bound from Stikine River to Victoria had been murdered by four Tsimshians in the neighbourhood of Fort Simpson near the mouth of the Skeena River. At the same time, the captain of the schooner *Native* warned company servants at Fort Simpson that the Stikine Indians had "been most troublesome demanding all manner of things and threatening to shoot a white man because 'Old Shakes' son-in-law died a short time back." The company servants concluded that whites travelling in waters between Fort Simpson and Fort Rupert near the northern end of Vancouver Island were now "quite unsafe unless adequate measures were taken to punish the guilty parties and protect whites."[4]

Douglas urged Maitland to send a warship to northern waters to investigate the murders, supply assistance to whites, and make known to the Indians, that bloodshed must stop. In Douglas's words, the northern tribes near Fort Simpson and in southeastern Alaska had grown "daring and troublesome." Maitland decided to dispatch the *Devastation* from Esquimalt on this service. Douglas recommended that her captain, Commander Pike, should investigate the matter thoroughly and act in a firm and decisive manner so that the Indians in question could not carry on their lawless acts with impunity. Douglas appointed Pike a justice of the peace of the colony of British Columbia in order to give him added authority in his relations with the Indians.[5]

The British understood that naval intervention in the Stikine River might result in Russian protests. On the advice of the Foreign Office, the Admiralty had advised Maitland not to raise the question of British rights on the Stikine. Consequently, he instructed Pike to proceed to Sitka to discuss with the governor of the Russian American Company, Furuhjelm, Maitland's desire to prevent any misunderstanding occurring concerning British or other subjects who had been drawn to the river by the gold discoveries. He was also to explain Maitland's readiness to co-operate in any way possible to preserve order and prevent infringement of the treaty of 1825 or the lease arrangements of 1839.

Pursuant to these orders, H.M.S. *Devastation* sailed from Esquimalt on 10 August 1862 and arrived at Sitka on the 23rd. The Russian governor appeared co-operative and grateful for the interest Douglas and Maitland had shown for the security of white lives on the Stikine. Furuhjelm expressed his concern about the still unresolved matter of rights of navigation and trade on the Stikine to Commander Pike. Yet he remained content to let these be resolved in Europe by properly delegated officials of the respective governments. Meanwhile, however, he was appreciative of British aid but, at the same time, keen to point out that Russian interests were being watched. As he explained to Pike he had already, in May, sent Prince Maksutoff to ascend the river in a small steamer, though currents nine miles upriver forced him back. Later, an engineer named Andrieff had ascended the river 175 miles in a canoe and reported that he had found four hundred people and "great distress" among them. The governor expected a Russian warship would soon arrive. Meanwhile, an armed company steamer under command of Lieutenant M. Chackloff of the Imperial Russian Navy had gone into the mouth of the river with provisions and clothing to be sold to miners who would be coming down the river. Furuhjelm did not admit to Pike that he did not have adequate forces at his disposal. However, the appearance of the *Devastation* must have gratified him, for, as he wrote to Maitland, he was ready "to cooperate with [him] in anything which may tend to prevent crime and collision" on the Stikine.[6]

The *Devastation* left Sitka on 3 September and arrived at the mouth of the river on the 5th. The following day Pike received many applications from British and other foreign subjects at Port Highfield, Wrangell Island, for protection. These people feared Indian militancy. They claimed that they owed their safety to a native Indian woman who was living with an old Hudson's Bay Company servant and whose adroit diplomacy with neighbouring tribes resulted in their forbearance. She had warned them that a British warship would be certain to visit Stikine River. The British were also aided by an Indian who served as an Indian constable. Pike learned that farther upriver a notorious Indian desperado named "Snooks," already well known in Victoria for his troublesome behaviour, was inciting Indians to fire on miners navigating the river. He evidently hoped his tribe would see him as a great warrior. To accomplish this he killed two whites as an act of revenge for the white killing of his two Indian friends. Pike's response to Snooks was to provide armed boats to convoy miners safely past the supposed ambush. On 12 September at Port Highfield Pike warned natives invited on board the *Devastation* that they would be severely punished if they committed violent acts against white people or property. Forty-four whites of various nationalities boarded the warship for safe passage to Victoria. When the Russian American Company's steamer *Alexander* arrived at the mouth of the Stikine River on 13 September, Pike thought it advisable to leave management of the Indians to the Russian officer in command, Lieutenant Chackloff.[7] Eight months later, in May 1863, the Russian corvette *Rynda* reached Sitka from Japan and proceeded to the Stikine to provide protection for Russian interests and investigate the possibilities of mining.[8]

After the departure of the *Devastation,* the display of the white ensign was not required in the river, for the gold rush declined. But the *Devastation*'s visit contributed substantially to stabilizing the Stikine frontier at a troublesome time for Russian authorities when they had no adequate defence. Like the co-operative nature of Russian American-Hudson's Bay Company exploitation of the Panhandle after 1839, the Russian and British authorities in 1862 were providing mutual support to safeguard interests, protect whites, and show local Indians that they had to act peacefully.

Meanwhile, H.M.S. *Devastation* sailed from the Stikine on 14 September and reached Fort Simpson on the 15th. Here Pike learned about suspects in the murder of the two whites. Taking immediate action, he sent five armed boats from the *Devastation* on the 16th, to surround the village of the Ginakangeek tribe of Tsimshian. The Navy seized eight leading chiefs and others on board the warship as hostages. However, when this did not result in the surrender of all the suspected murderers, the warship proceeded to Dundas Island in British waters, under direction of Captain Richards of H.M.S. *Hecate.* On the 18th, near Dundas Island, fifteen canoes escaping from the warship failed to stop when shots from a broadside gun were fired across their prows. Rather than firing on the canoes, Pike sent armed boats to chase them. The Indians reached the beach first and climbed trees for better protection and aim. However, they were finally seized by the sailors and marines after a skirmish in which no lives were lost on either side. Afterwards almost all the suspects were surrendered, not least because Pike had held important hostages and captured all the native provisions and canoes. But Pike and Richards did not destroy the Indian village since they feared that doing so might cause native resentment. Their conduct of action won Governor Douglas's unequivocal approval and the suspects were brought to trial.[9]

At Fort Simpson, with the aid of missionary William Duncan, Captain Richards gathered the chiefs of the different tribes to tell them, as Pike had done earlier at Port Highfield, to refrain from violent acts or suffer the consequences at the hands of the Navy. In this case, Richards pointed out to the chiefs that the presence of a second warship in the area was proof of British determination. He said that it was the chiefs' duty as well as in their interests to assist in bringing the murderers to justice. In Richards's opinion, the British position had to be very firm. "The natives are," he wrote, "a large and powerful body of eight different tribes, with a certain sympathy connection existing between them, and have always considered themselves, and really been, superior to any European force that has hitherto been brought into contact with them."[10]

Though Indian strength was clearly present, these gunboat actions, including some successful diplomatic discussions with various Indian chiefs, enabled the British to make their point. The straits were to be made safe for the passage of Stikine miners and others. The Navy would enforce that law whenever required. Of course the presence of the *Devastation* and *Hecate* did not altogether stop Indian violence. But without the display of power by these two warships at Fort Simpson and in nearby waters, continued wanton acts would probably have occurred. In this way, British naval influence in northern British Columbia waters also had influence in adjacent Alaskan waters.

Farther north, at Sitka, a change in sovereignty over Alaska affected the course of white-Indian relations and in its own way prolonged the northern duties of the British squadron, as Rear-Admiral Maitland had foreseen. In 1867 the United States purchased Russian America, and British Columbia now found it had American neighbours on both its southern and northern flanks. Despite fears of an eventual American annexation, the Foreign Office instructed the governor of British Columbia to help American authorities in Alaska in their relations with Indians if requested. In short, this might mean sending a gunboat.[11]

Under United States jurisdiction, the new territory was ruled by the sword. Washington placed Alaska under control of the Treasury Department and the War Department and established six garrisons as symbols of authority along the shore. The change of status brought American traders, settlers, missionaries and others to the northern frontier, and this unorganized, unpoliced migration intensified the growing anarchy. As early as 1867 the disposition of the Indians and their attitude towards the new white population made it necessary for the United States government to consider whether a warship should not be permanently present on the coast for "the safety of traders. . . and for the dignity of American institutions." In 1868 the U.S. flagship *Pensacola* took Rear-Admiral Henry K. Thatcher north to Alaska on a tour of inspection, and subsequently the U.S. commander-in-chief, Pacific, instructed ships under his command to cruise in Alaska waters whenever convenient. Soon after the reorganization of the U.S. Pacific station in 1878, American warships visited key ports from Valparaiso to Puget Sound and all main island ports, including Honolulu and Apia, Samoa.[12] But Alaska was without any local government whatsoever, and was, a United States Navy officer wrote, "almost as free from the operation of civil law as the interior of Africa."[13] Customs officials had orders to prohibit the importation of firearms and liquor, but trade in these commodities continued unabated.[14] Tighter regulations through the Customs Act of 1868 prohibited the use of firearms or of distilled liquors but violence remained a common occurrence at Sitka. In 1869, the commanding officer, General Jefferson C. Davis, resorted to gunboat activities against the Kakes Indians of Kou Island in which twenty-nine houses were razed to the ground and a number of canoes were destroyed. On another occasion, in July 1877, European settlers at Sitka lived "in hourly fear of their lives" from the drunkenness and hostility of the local Indians. A show of naval force seemed necessary, especially during October when the Indians held their annual "liquor festival." Yet officials knew that order and good behaviour among the whites and natives also had to be preserved. The problem may have been absence of government rather than misgovernment, and in 1877 a new form of administration came into effect under Treasury and Navy Department jurisdiction.[15]

These attempts towards greater stability could not counter lawlessness. In 1877 the collector of customs bemoaned the fact that the Indians indulged in threats, which in time they would put in practice when they found that no gunboat would appear on the scene. Soon thereafter local Indians began to attack government buildings and blockhouses, thronged aboard the monthly steamer from Portland, and behaved in an "insolent manner." They hauled away parts of a stockade separating the town from the Indian village. "The inhabitants of Sitka," an anxious Treasury agent wrote, "are slumbering on a volcano."[16]

Yet officials lacked force to make their position clear. The principle of protection ranked second to customs revenue. The United States Navy, taxed by duties elsewhere and limited by insufficient units, gave scant attention to Sitka. Instead the American power at sea had to be exercised by the revenue cutter *Oliver Wolcott* and regular mail steamers. In these circumstances the closest place for assistance was Esquimalt from which, in times past, the commander-in-chief had sent British warships to aid American merchant shipping in distress off the Northwest Coast. Some Americans, for patriotic reasons, were loath to call on their old rivals for support, but national antipathies were overcome in the face of apparent peril at Sitka in 1879.

The Indian grievances had deep roots. But they were intensified by two occurrences. In February an Indian demanding his loss of wages be made up could gain no redress. Concurrently, United States officials had imprisoned two Indians on the charge of murdering a white. The issues became one and the same. Indians of the Kiksatis tribe, headed by Chief Katlean, whose ancestor and namesake had led the attack on the Russians in 1802, wanted compensation and justice. When the Sitka authorities failed to pacify them, Katlean and his men plotted to attack the town. Heavily-armed citizens, aided by Indian informants and a local chief named Annahootz of the Kokwantons, withstood Katlean's first assault and prepared for a second. Some residents, including the Russian Orthodox priest N.G. Mitrapolsky, discussed the propriety of appealing to Esquimalt or even to the Tsar for assistance; and after agreement was reached to ask British aid, they signed a petition and sent it to Esquimalt by mail steamer. The document noted that application had been made to the United States government for protection but that they expected American action would take too long to be of use. "Her Majesty's Government," the Sitka residents appealed with a touch of flattery, "has been ever known for its promptness in assisting the oppressed of any nation and we hope our appeal may not be in vain."[17]

On receiving this urgent appeal, Captain H. Holmes A'Court of H.M.S. *Osprey,* the senior naval officer at Esquimalt, immediately sought advice from the American consul in Victoria. He had to be certain that the Sitka citizens were in "immediate and imminent" danger, and he had to have the consul's concurrence, or at least approval, in order to act in a manner which would avoid any possible and predictable charges that the British lion was interfering in the American eagle's affairs. The consul wired Washington for advice. The State Department had no objection to "asking [for] or receiving the protection necessary" if the situation seemed urgent, thereby adroitly delegating authority to the consul. Subsequently, in the best bureaucratic tradition, the consul passed the responsibility to A'Court, who, on the face of the evidence, decided that protection of the Sitka residents was clearly necessary. His decision was subsequently approved by his immediate superior, Rear-Admiral Algernon de Horsey, and by the Foreign Office in London.[18]

On his arrival at Sitka on 1 March, A'Court found the white inhabitants in a state of alarm. They expected Katlean to attack the next day. A'Court believed that the *Osprey*'s presence prevented violence, and he decided to remain there until sufficient American naval strength arrived. The *Oliver Wolcott* appeared on 22 March, and with the approval of United States officials, A'Court placed British sailors and a Gatling gun on board her. A'Court reasoned that she was not powerful enough to protect the inhabitants, though with her three twenty-four-pounders she was capable of destroying the Indian village. On the other hand, with a crew of only thirty-six, she could not protect the women or children or prevent the Indians from sacking the town. "I am also of the opinion," he wrote, "that the destruction of the Indian village is a matter that admits of a question, as there are a great number of friendly Indians, who have lodges and property there, the destruction of which, and possibly the loss of some of their lives, would tend to make them cast their lot with others." And on the matter of Alaska's government and protection, he believed that a "government having authority" would be needed to keep the whites free from molestation. To this end a visible military presence was of paramount importance, and he suggested that men-of-war were preferable to troops "as being moveable, a ship could, at various times, visit the numerous tribes and villages scattered along the coast."[19] He seems merely to have been suggesting that the Americans adopt the same mode of procedure that the British had been using on the British Columbia coast for two decades. The United States corvette *Alaska* reached Sitka on 3 April, and the *Osprey* returned to Esquimalt. Later, on 14 June, the U.S. sloop of war *Jamestown,* Commander Lester A. Beardslee, sent by the Department of the Navy to protect the residents, reached Sitka from San Francisco. Beardslee carried orders to restore harmonious relations between settlers and natives and, in the absence of law and authority, to use full discretionary powers in any emergencies that might arise.[20] But the *Jamestown* lacked steam power, and during her entire service there she lay quietly at her moorings in Sitka Harbour while steam launches with small detachments of officers and men went to various flash points. "The seat of Government," a United States naval officer noted, "was shifted from the quarterdeck of the *Jamestown* as occasion demanded."[21]

In the interim, the timely presence of the *Osprey* and *Oliver Wolcott* had prevented a "serious calamity," in A'Court's words. This fact was never contested by critics, whose real complaints were with the United States government and navy's lack of interest against the fractious Sitka merchants, who may have trumped up the need for protection by misrepresenting the motives and strength of the hostile Indians. But, as the American historian of this incident has written, the petition to seek British aid was "actuated by a real fear of the Indians."[22]

The issue had gone to the root of whether or not American citizens in the United States overseas territories could count on the U.S. Navy for protection. "Here is a chance for the ardent defender of the American flag," the *New York Times* commented acidly, "Citizens of the United States, living on the soil of the Republic, are obliged to appeal to a British officer to see that they are not annihilated by a savage foe."[23] Subsequently, the U.S. Navy, perhaps embarrassed by its inability to concern itself with Alaskan affairs even though the territory was under its jurisdiction, gave more attention to that distant shore. Ships of the U.S. Navy's Pacific squadron made Sitka a customary port of call, and warships were stationed there until the turn of the century. In 1884, Alaska Territory acquired a government under civil authority. Nonetheless from Sitka several gunboat actions were taken against hostile Indians in southeastern Alaska and these were events requiring judgement and discretion on the part of commanders.

In its own way the Royal Navy had contributed to securing the American frontier. In 1856 Governor Douglas had supplied arms to his American counterpart to guard against an Indian rising in Puget Sound. The so-called *Osprey* incident at Sitka was hardly any different. Nor was the support given by the U.S.S. *Massachusetts* at Fort Rupert in 1851 or by the *Oliver Wolcott* at Metlakatla in 1882. Ancient rivals found that blood was thicker than water when faced with a threat to their race. On the Northwest Coast the influence of "Rule Britannia" sometimes spread beyond British colonial jurisdictions. Sometimes, though less frequently, it was aided by American influence within the same sphere.

In the case of Alaska, British warships contributed to the extension of law and order on a frontier that actually lay beyond their immediate jurisdiction. Naval officers were cautious of interfering in what were Russian or United States government matters. Yet they made two displays of naval force. In 1862 they did so on their own initiative in order to protect the lives of Britons navigating from British waters to and from the Stikine River. But again, they acted cautiously and with the understanding and support of Russian authorities. In 1879 they responded to a request from Sitka citizens on humanitarian grounds. Their actions in this case did not appeal to all Americans, some of whom were zealous to protect their own interests, but in the end the British contributed to the maintenance of peace. Despite antipathies between British and Russian and, after 1867, British and United States interests in Alaska, authorities of the respective spheres of sovereignty tended towards co-operation in extending stability and the rule of law when faced with real or possible Indian violence. Indian responses towards these cases of gunboat diplomacy tended towards accommodation in the face of overwhelming military predominance.

PART III

EXTENDING
THE FRONTIER

II

The "Customary Authority" Under Dominion Auspices

FOR AT LEAST TWENTY YEARS after British Columbia's incorporation into Canadian Confederation on 25 July 1871 the objectives and
methods of conducting Indian affairs changed hardly at all from those of
the colonial period. Though Britain actively attempted to disengage itself
in British Columbia and elsewhere in Canada and the Empire, imperial
obligations on the Northwest Coast continued. This was owing partly to
continuing conflict between British Columbia and Canada over Indian
affairs, chiefly on the contentious matter of ownership of crown lands.[1]
The Dominion wanted to create large reserves as was the practice in
some other areas in Canada. However, in order to do so, the Dominion
had to obtain cessions of provincial crown lands, a virtually impossible
undertaking given the attitudes of local politicians. Under the 13th article
of the agreement of union signed by the province and the Dominion, the
latter assumed "charge of the Indians, and the trusteeship and management of the lands reserved for their use and benefit." The Dominion also
agreed to continue an Indian policy "as liberal as that hitherto pursued by
the British Columbia Government."[2] By these provisions the young province's Indian affairs were subject to the British North America Act of
1867, section 91, subsection 24, wherein Ottawa possessed legislative authority over "Indians, and lands reserved for the Indians."[3]

As before 1871, Indian policy remained a local concern. Both the administration and control of crown lands and the maintenance of law and
order under the lieutenant governor, attorney general, and provincial
sheriff's office continued to be provincial responsibilities. Since Douglas's
retirement in 1864, alienating land from Indians had been the main pre-

occupation of Joseph William Trutch, the chief commissioner of lands and works. Similarly, legal enforcement had been the concern of successive governors and attorneys general. However, after 1871 Victoria could neither control all appointments nor appropriate Indian lands and make reserves at will. Neither could it misappropriate Indian monies as Trutch had done in 1869 in respect to the Songhees reserve near Victoria.[4] Provincial authorities and politicians felt aggrieved that matters previously within their own immediate jurisdiction were now managed by people who they thought were ignorant of them and who were unsympathetic to or unaware of local needs.[5]

Despite the shift of authority from London to Ottawa, Indian policy under the Dominion took no adventurous departures in British Columbia. As elsewhere in British North America, a potential British withdrawal of garrisons or gunboats would leave the colonies or provinces with little or no means of self defence. The Dominion provided no gunboats. Rather, it continued to sanction gunboat diplomacy by the Royal Navy. Nor did the Dominion adopt new policies of law enforcement. It tended to maintain the existing practices of peaceful resolution where possible, violent action when necessary. The major disputes between Canadian and British Columbia governments occurred over the appropriation of land for Indian reserves, a subject of intense and ongoing controversy between Ottawa and Victoria. But policy really continued to be made "on the spot." During the first twenty years after the province's entry into Confederation, the traditional patterns of law enforcement among "unlawful savages" were maintained by gunboats, what the commissioner of Indian Affairs for British Columbia, Israel Wood Powell, adroitly called "the customary authority."[6]

Indian affairs in the province were managed by the commissioner of Indian affairs for British Columbia. He answered directly to the deputy superintendent-general of Indian affairs in Ottawa, who in turn reported to the superintendent general of Indian affairs, a member of cabinet. For the period from 1867 to 1873, the superintendent general was secretary of state for the provinces; from 1873 on, he was also minister of the interior. Under his auspices, Indian affairs was virtually tied to the settlement and development of the west under the emerging national policies of Sir John A. Macdonald. From 17 October 1878 to 4 August 1885, Indian affairs were administered by Macdonald himself as president of the Privy Council, a duty added to those he held as prime minister. From 1873 to 1880, when the Department of Indian affairs came into existence, headed by the deputy superintendent-general, it was attached to the Department of the Interior.[7] These changes were not numerous, but they were balanced by the stability of two loyal individuals: Lawrence Vankoughnet, deputy superintendent-general, 1874–93, and Israel Wood Powell, commissioner of Indian affairs for British Columbia, 1872–89. During the fourteen years their service overlapped, they formed a working team, mutually respecting each other's abilities and integrities.

Powell, born in 1836 in Port Colborne, Simcoe County, Upper Canada, of Conservative and United Empire Loyalist stock was a graduate in medicine from McGill University and arrived in Victoria in 1862 as a curious visitor.[8] Rather than proceeding to New Zealand as planned, he remained in the colony, built up an extensive medical practice, and in keeping with family tradition, involved himself in politics supporting the causes of responsible government and confederation. First elected to the legislative assembly of Vancouver Island in 1863, he introduced legislation for general education in British Columbia. Like many of his contemporaries, he also amassed much wealth in land and resources. Whereas his political views endeared him to his old friend Macdonald, his political stance in favour of Confederation was hardly acceptable to certain local politicians who eyed Ottawa with severe suspicion, and when he was defeated in 1869 along with his celebrated co-confederate Amor de Cosmos, Powell retired from active politics. Occupied by family responsibilities and medical obligations, he had refused Macdonald's offers to be the province's first lieutenant-governor and then a senator. In 1872, however, Macdonald offered him the superintendency of Indian affairs and a lieutenant-colonelcy in the Canadian militia in order to give his position some military authority and, should he choose to wear uniform, some ceremonial presence in treaty-making or present-giving activities. Powell accepted, ignoring petty slanders of jealous local politicians and even the lieutenant-governor, Trutch, who thought him "entirely without any knowledge of Indian matters."[9] Macdonald, too, had reservations about Powell's knowledge of Indians, but the appointment was nevertheless secured through the pressure of British Columbia members of Parliament.[10] These political realities remained doggedly with Powell, and he had to endure repeated attempts by Trutch and others to frustrate his work.

For seventeen years, Powell persevered in an assignment that others might have approached halfheartedly, and for many years he also maintained his medical practice. By gunboat and canoe, on horseback and foot, he travelled tirelessly throughout the vast territory which he administered. He advised Indians to obey the law. He persuaded them to allow their children to be educated. He encouraged native peoples to trust medical doctors instead of medicine men. He cautioned against whisky and drunkenness. He awarded medals to Indians who saved vessels and crews. He dispensed Navy buttons, caps, and braid as presents to chiefs and others—all with a view to winning accord with native leadership, gaining allies, reducing tension between races, and freeing the coast from the few marauding Indians who still remained in the 1870's, mainly on Vancouver Island's west coast. Powell accepted this difficult assignment at a time when native economies,[11] supported or sanctioned by tribal unity and authority, were rapidly being supplanted by a new wage economy that was foreign to native tribal structures. Capitalism afforded a new system in which an individual Indian could actually acquire wealth for himself and supplant tribal, village authority. Powell dealt tactfully with certain Indian issues at a time when native peoples were disenchanted with the white man's mounting presence. During Powell's superintendency, native marauding expeditions ceased and slave-taking virtually disappeared.

At this critical time, Powell assumed the prominent "on the spot" role that Douglas had skilfully exercised in Indian affairs as governor of Vancouver Island and British Columbia. Powell kept a steady hand, exerting government influence over Indian affairs. On the coast he continued to maintain authority by gunboat diplomacy. When, for instance, in January 1873 local authorities in Victoria successfully requested the senior naval officer at Esquimalt to detain H.M.S. *Petrel* on the Northwest Coast to deal with expected disturbances with the Indians, the Colonial Office accepted this measure as a temporary expedient. The secretary of state for the colonies, the Earl of Kimberley, wrote to the governor general of Canada, Lord Dufferin, with easy-going optimism, "I am satisfied that the Canadian Government will be prepared to take such steps as may be necessary for the permanent preservation of order and protection of life."[12] The Dominion took no permanent action, leaving the Colonial Office to maintain its vigil. And the Colonial Office kept a ready eye out for what was transpiring in British Columbia. When, for instance, the *Petrel* left Esquimalt on duties other than Indian patrol assigned by Rear-Admiral Hillyar, the Colonial Office thought the action a bit sudden. The Admiralty then had to satisfy the Colonial Office that the vessels *Tenedos* and *Scout*, then at Esquimalt, were sufficient to meet local needs and, moreover, that the *Boxer* had been recommissioned for further service in British Columbia and that the *Reindeer* was on her way as reinforcement.[13]

Apart from this intervention, the Colonial Office took no active position relative to the affairs of Indians in British Columbia, other than acting as a clearing house of pertinent information. The Colonial Office clerks dutifully read copies of reports from naval officers customarily sent to them by the Admiralty. They systematically relayed copies to the governor general in Ottawa. However, the Colonial Office really preferred "to let sleeping dogs lie." In 1873, for instance, a secretary in the Colonial Office minuted in rather laconic tones on a copy of an in-letter from the commander-in-chief, Pacific: "The Indians who are rapidly diminishing in number seem on the whole to be a singularly harmless and inoffensive race."[14] The matter went no further—Ottawa and Powell were in charge.

The working mechanism of Indian policy on the coast remained essentially the same as during the colonial era. The Royal Navy was now the Dominion's tool. An example from 1874 shows the usual method. Powell needed to visit Cowichan and other coastal locations to discharge his duties. He asked the Indian Department in Ottawa to recommend to the secretary of state that he "move" that the lieutenant governor of British Columbia "request" the senior naval officer at Esquimalt to "place" a gunboat at the disposal of "Mr. Commissioner Powell"—a tediously elaborate but nonetheless technically necessary process for requisitioning a gunboat. Powell's recommendation for the exercise of what he called "the customary authority" went unquestioned by the federal cabinet in Ottawa. By the authority of an order-in-council a gunboat was ordered to be sent.[15]

To cite another example, about this same time the Department of Public Works in Ottawa needed a gunboat to be stationed in Dean Channel to protect a Canadian Pacific Railway surveying party under Marius Smith against certain local Indians who were "well known to be of a troublesome character."[16] The cabinet adhered to the opinion, long acknowledged since the murder of Alfred Waddington's Bute Inlet surveying party in 1864, that a show of force by a gunboat would prevent molestation. By another order-in-council Ottawa authorized it. This constituted the first time in which Ottawa ordered the use of a gunboat in British Columbia for its own reasons, that is, for reasons independent of those of the British Columbia government or of the Indian superintendent.[17]

Somehow the telegram from the Admiralty to Esquimalt became public knowledge, and some rabid provincial patriots envisioned that Ottawa was sending the gunboat to coerce them to agree to terms regarding the building of the railway. "People misinterpret telegram," the senior naval officer at Esquimalt, Commander Richard Hare of H.M.S. *Myrmidon*, cabled London, "imagine gunboat proceeds Victoria to intimidate." Hare hastily offered to withdraw the gunboat's services if that were London's wish. But the Colonial Office, though eminently aware of British Columbia's bitterness against Canadian delays in building the railway to the Pacific, was furious. "None but very ignorant and unscrupulous persons could believe such a thing even when under the influence of political excitement," one official noted in anger. His superior, Lord Carnarvon, dismissed British Columbia's response as "a most childish misunderstanding." In the end, on Carnarvon's recommendation, the Admiralty dispatched another telegram, ordering the gunboat be sent.[18]

Again, however, the Colonial Office's importance was diminishing over time. In 1876 London newspapers carried complaints by the Aborigines' Protection Society against the Indian policies pursued at that time and during the previous colonial period in British Columbia. Such information, if widely believed, might damage British Columbia's ability to attract colonists. Gilbert Malcolm Sproat, agent general for the province in London and author of an emigrants' guide published in 1873, advised the permanent undersecretary at the Colonial Office of the injustice of the society's charges. There were, he wrote:

> more natives in proportion to whites in British Columbia than in any other colony, and they are not a simple, docile people who can be dealt with anyhow, but are a people with some idea of their rights, and considerable ruggedness of character.
>
> They, fortunately, are much scattered and separated by tribal feuds and on the coast the tribes are overawed by gunboats, and a fair settlement of the land question should enable us to get on comfortably with them in the future.[19]

However, again the Colonial Office took no initiative and made no response, for the direction of Indian affairs in British Columbia rightly lay beyond London's immediate concern. Because of the implications of responsible government and confederation, the Colonial Office accepted and in fact encouraged the idea that the character of Indian affairs must develop on-the-spot under Canadian authority.

Despite the fact that in the 1870's the lieutenant-governor of British Columbia readily sanctioned gunboat diplomacy, complaints periodically appeared against the practice. One such came from no less than Sproat, who was back in British Columbia in 1879 as commissioner of Indian reserves. Enigmatic and phlegmatic, interfering and egotistical, this pioneer, who himself had made inroads into native hunting and fishing grounds by force of arms, complained to Macdonald as superintendent-general of Indian affairs in Ottawa about "the invariable ship of war which visited the villages to admonish or threaten and sometimes to destroy." The practice had prevailed since the Hudson's Bay Company era, Sproat claimed, though to a lesser extent since 1871. He doubted that the government thought fit to sanction a practice of "terrorism and repression" in the future. He classified gunboat diplomacy as "an inveterate custom and a common sentiment among the white population of British Columbia." But history showed, he said (without providing example), that during the company era the Navy had actually bombarded the wrong villages. Moreover, Navy officers possessed articles they had plundered from Indian sites, which they had fired on or forcibly entered. The fallacy of such diplomacy, he argued, was that it "punishes many innocent persons for one who is guilty." The Department of Indian Affairs, whose humanitarian objectives required patient and kindly intercourse with Indians, should disassociate itself from the Navy with its threatening and warlike techniques. Instead of gunboats, the Indian commissioner and his agents could conduct their duties by a small sailing schooner, Sproat concluded.[20]

To these charges the Indian Department in Ottawa did not reply directly. Rather, it sought Powell's opinion. Distrustful of Sproat's meddling and infuriated by what he regarded as Sproat's blatant misrepresentations Powell wrote his superior in measured tones that Sproat's arguments were both extraordinary and impractical. The suggested use of a schooner bordered on the absurd. Gunboats were the most economical and efficient mode of transport. They had demonstrably aided missionaries of various denominations; they had also helped government agents in disputes with Indians, and Powell noted that in 1877 Sproat had himself called for a gunboat, H.M.S. *Rocket,* at Chemainus to aid authorities in the speedy resolution of the problem of surveying the boundaries of this Indian reserve.[21] Not least, Indians would despise "the 'white chief' who ceases to maintain an air of respectability, and dignity — presenting himself in the garb and with the air and habits little above their own." The respect of the Indians must be maintained. This could hardly be done, Powell wrote, if the Indian superintendent joined the family of "lotus eaters" and drifted lazily from place to place in a sailboat at a time when his duties were extensive and increasing.[22]

Above all, Powell objected to Sproat's charges that the Navy's visits to Indian villages were events of threat and reprisal. In Powell's view, Sproat deliberately misrepresented the facts and conveyed a false impression of the custom of governing Indians during and after the colonial era. "The mode of treating Indians, inaugurated by Sir James Douglas, was one founded upon broad principles of common justice," Powell wrote sharply. Under this system Indians felt their equal rights. On the one hand, they were defended in time of injustice against them, on the other they were punished when found guilty of an offence. This policy was pursued at a time when a very large Indian population had to be kept "in order" by a local government possessing only limited powers. "The manifestation of Her Majesty's ability to enforce obedience to her laws was necessary," Powell concluded his report in obvious admiration of Douglas, "and constitutes the chief reason for the prevalence of law and order now among a population which has only been obtained in other parts of the Dominion at enormous cost and the very questionable system of gifts and annuities which this country could never have afforded." Contrary to Sproat's representation, Powell thought that no other government officials were more greatly respected, indeed no more kindly received by Indians anywhere on the coast than British naval officers. The friendly visits of British warships actually helped "cement the good feelings now prevailing," and he reminded his superior in Ottawa of his recent report and photographs of his most recent coastal tour. These, he stressed, exhibited not "fear of terrorism" but good feelings on the part of Indians. Sproat's complaints, systematically and judiciously answered, died with Powell's reply.[23]

The clearest expression of British Columbia's support for the policy of retaining gunboats came in 1882, when the Admiralty attempted to reduce the number of ships stationed at Esquimalt to deploy them elsewhere on Pacific Station. This proposed measure greatly concerned the provincial government, which petitioned the secretary of state in Ottawa to pressure the British government to maintain the squadron in British Columbia waters.

The province's extensive and forceful appeal had its roots in the argument that the Indian population in British Columbia was the largest in Canada, by at least 10,000. Moreover, this population resided mainly in scattered coastal settlements where the Navy had been "of the greatest importance in maintaining peace and order amongst the native coast tribes, and in protecting life and property." "The Provincial Government," it continued:

> have habitually acted promptly in punishing crime, and it would have been impossible to carry out that policy amongst the Indians on the coast, if the assistance of one of Her Majesty's Ships had not been readily obtainable. In early days the crews of vessels wrecked on the West Coast of Vancouver Island were not infrequently murdered by the natives, but experience has now taught the latter that deeds of violence will not go unpunished.

Moreover, the comparative security afforded by an enforcement of the law was good for investment in fisheries and other economic developments and had fostered beneficial employment for natives. Not least, the presence of warships had "an impressive moral effect on the native mind," and for that reason their withdrawl "would tend to disturb the peaceable attitude now maintained by the Indians."[24]

Though on this occasion the appeals from the frontier, so to speak, yielded a review of how many warships ought to be stationed in British Columbia waters, the Admiralty was obliged to scale down its commitments in the Pacific. Commanders-in-chief had more pressing issues to concern themselves with, including the United States' possible cession of Hawaii, the protection of the Victoria sailing fleet in Bering Sea, and the

Anglo-American dispute over the Alaska boundary.[25] Indian affairs in British Columbia were a dominion responsibility respecting "Indians, and lands reserved for the Indians," but they were equally a provincial responsibility in matters of justice and law enforcement. Admiralty practice was to "send a gunboat" only if circumstances warranted. Their Lordships and the Colonial Office clearly wanted Canada to provide defence against possible Indian attack. Thus, in 1883 when Ottawa requested a warship to protect Port Simpson against threatening natives, the Admiralty observed that if Canada held serious apprehensions about a possible attack, its government should take steps to place an adequate garrison in the "fort." The suggestion was based on the principle of colonial self-defence, and the Admiralty's position received the backing of the Colonial Office.[26] Actually, this crisis passed without incident, and when Rear-Admiral Lyons investigated the state of affairs there some months later he found everything quiet.[27]

In the 1880's Canada undertook its first measures to reduce the need to call on the Royal Navy for other than emergency duties. By this time British authority did not have to be exhibited by a show of pomp and power in every creek mouth, cove and harbour from Cowichan to the Nass. The Navy could provide the force if and when necessary. Meanwhile, however, Indian agents needed appropriate means of conveyance. Before 1890 they had used the sole dominion vessel on the coast, the *Sir James Douglas*, on hire from the Department of Marine at $70 per day.[28] A six-week cruise in this lighthouse tender and fisheries patrol vessel might cost the Indian superintendent upwards of $2,000 — if the *Sir James Douglas* was actually available for hire at the requisite time. Thus in 1889 the Indian Department requested, and was granted, $5000 for the purchase of a strongly-powered steam yacht capable of eight or nine knots for work on a coast where currents were strong and weather boisterous.[29]

The *Vigilant,* a fifty-five-foot schooner-rigged vessel with a crew of two and ample accommodation for department agents and assistants, began service in 1890. Her name was neither accidental nor flippant. The deputy superintendent of Indian affairs, Lawrence Vankoughnet, skilfully shied away from a junior colleague's suggestion that she be called after his wife. He thought "Inez" scarcely suitable for a steamer "designed for such a job." After considering commissioning her the Tsimshian equivalent of "vigilant," but not being able to find such a Tsimshian word, he then ordered that "vigilant" be used. Until 1901 when she was replaced, this vessel worked her beat steadily. But like the *Sir James Douglas* she was constantly in demand by other Canadian officials, including the dominion astronomer and the commissioners of the Alaska boundary inquiry. The Indian agent Charles Todd complained to Ottawa when the *Vigilant* lay at the disposal of others, a frequent occurrence, while he was unable to tend to his duties in his department's vessel. However on at least one occasion, in 1894, his legitimate objections were muted by the imposing influence of his superior, the acting deputy superintendent general, Duncan Campbell Scott.[30]

From the time British Columbia joined Canada to the last decade of the nineteenth century, "the customary authority" was maintained in Indian relations on the coast. H.M. gunboats provided Indian Superintendent Powell's position with prestige and authority where a canoe or even a schooner would scarcely have sufficed. Powell's commission bore little weight without a display of power. On three occasions, 1873, 1879, and 1881, Powell made extensive coastal inspections in British warships, the first in H.M.S. *Boxer*, the others in H.M.S. *Rocket*.[31] At other times he also requisitioned a gunboat. Eventually, agents and constables took his place. But at least once, during a crisis on the Skeena River in 1888, the provincial premier, Alex Davie, appealed to Powell, then desperately ill, to accompany the expedition of police and militia departing Esquimalt in H.M.S. *Caroline*. "We think that there are few if any in the Province," Davie wrote Powell, "whose presence is likely to exert as beneficial an influence upon the Indians as your own and that they will recognize you as being first authority."[32] Powell did not go and retired later next year in poor health. The Skeena troubles recounted in a subsequent chapter were resolved peacefully under a show of force by the British Columbia police and a detachment of Canadian militia delivered safely to the mouth of the Skeena by the Royal Navy.

Thus, the method of dealing with Indian affairs touching on legal questions of persons and property remained essentially unchanged during the early national period. The most important difference was that Ottawa had assumed certain responsibilities and was party to decision making. Admittedly, the process of approving or requisitioning a gunboat became slightly more complex than before, as the examples given in this chapter indicate. Misunderstandings could and did occur. By and large, however, the mechanism worked smoothly. As British Columbia extended its judiciary and constabulary, as Canada developed its militia, and as both governments showed a willingness to use the new officials, gunboat diplomacy became less necessary. This change came at a time when Britain was reluctant to bear costs of policing the seas and "putting out fires" in self-governing colonies. By 1890 gunboat diplomacy in British Columbia had virtually stopped altogether, though it was later exercised in 1911 by one of the first ships of the new Royal Canadian Navy, the *Rainbow*, in Vancouver harbour to stop the landing of illegal Sikh immigrants from the Japanese vessel *Komagata Maru*. Other means—amphibious provincial police in particular—took the place of gunboats, and even today "the customary authority" may be said to be exercised by seaborne detachments of the Royal Canadian Mounted Police enforcing Canadian law.

12

At Heaven's Command

EVEN BEFORE the Spanish corvette *Santiago* carried two Franciscan friars to Nootka Sound in 1774, certain Christian missionaries and philanthropists gazing at maps of the wider world, eyed the Northwest Coast as a place where they believed countless pagans needed salvation, education, improvement, and conversion. Sir Francis Drake, who laid first English claim to the Pacific Coast of North America in 1579, said when speaking of the heathen, "their gain shall be the knowledge of our faith, and ours such riches as the country hath."[1] By the mid-nineteenth century some Englishmen passionately believed that the Empire existed for the good of the governed and that the British, under the peace established by their power, had a special obligation to pursue God's work among their subject peoples. The missionary William Duncan of Metla-katla, who holds a central position in this chapter, thought that the pride and pomp of "Rule Britannia" would not please God. "Rule Britannia" was not consistent with the British position as a nation, he said.[2]

From the perspective of authorities in London and Victoria and in Ottawa after British Columbia became a province of the Dominion of Canada, the Pax Britannica constituted an imperial mission. In keeping with the tenets of the Victorian age, that is, free trade, settlement, industry, law and order, and Christianity, officials provided support for missionaries, British or otherwise. They did so irrespective of whether they thought spreading the gospel and "civilizing the natives" in British Columbia brought good results.[3] They usually gave support of an indirect or moral nature. They preferred to allow missionaries to fend for themselves and usually provided direct or material support only at times of crisis. They tended to leave the law and order on this frontier to captains of the few Royal Navy vessels that patrolled the coast.

Church of England missions on the Northwest Coast commanded most of the Navy's attention—not so much because of national identification with the established church but because of difficulties which arose in the course of their development. These occurred rarely in the 1850's and 1860's when the missionary intrusion was relatively recent, but much more frequently in the 1870's and 1880's, when the question of native identities and imperial jurisdictions had become frustratingly complex to all parties concerned. Ministers of other denominations—Roman Catholic, Presbyterian, Methodist, and Congregational—also received the Navy's support. A case in point is that of the Reverend Augustin Joseph Brabant, who left his account of his ordeals on Vancouver Island's west coast. For thirty-three years, beginning in 1874, this Belgian-born priest ministered to a seaborne parish stretching two hundred miles along this dangerous and desolate shore. From his Hesquiat headquarters in the lee of Estevan Point, he visited his parishioners by canoe and gunboat, sleeping in tent or hut and sometimes, as at Kyuquot, with knife in hand. He faced Indian hostilities at various places, including Kyuquot and Hesquiat. Occasionally a schooner from Victoria would call with supplies and word from his superiors and friends from the outside world. Every year or so his bishop would appear for the apostolic laying on of hands, when new communicants would be added to the faith. And, from time to time also, one of Her Majesty's ships of war would call—on patrol or on a mission of mercy.

Brabant, a sharply independent priest, first encountered a British gunboat at Refuge Cove, Clayoquot Sound, in September 1874. H.M.S. *Boxer,* carrying Dr. Israel Wood Powell, the superintendent of Indian Affairs, was visiting native villages such as Refuge Cove on a coastal inspection. Brabant had arrived by canoe with his bishop, Charles Seghers, and several Indian companions, since the sealing schooner in which they had sailed from Victoria had foundered off the treacherous coast. Tim Scanlan, an Irish steward, came ashore from the *Boxer,* told them of the dangers of canoe travel in that season, and added that the captain hoped to assist them. The bishop did not want his existence known to the captain, perhaps for fear of government interference. On his urging, the apparently trustworthy Scanlan promised to keep their presence secret and returned to his ship. Soon he was once again on shore, this time laden with provisions, rum, and brandy.

The next morning, after the *Boxer* steamed out of Refuge Cove, the bishop, priest, and their Indian associates resumed their canoe passage across Hesquiat Harbour in heavy surf and burning sun. After considerable sea sickness and hard paddling, they reached Friendly Cove, Nootka Sound, where to their "horror" the *Boxer* lay at anchor. Scanlan was soon among them again, with more brandy and word that his captain, Lieutenant-Commander William Collins, R.N., and Dr. Powell would be coming ashore in a boat to invite them to make use of the warship's accommodations.

Brabant and his superior had misunderstood Collins's good intentions and misjudged his character. They seemed surprised to find him a staunch Anglican who daily held divine service on board and had established a bank and a temperance society for his men. The Roman Catholic fathers, now reassured, took Collins's advice, and the captain provided the weary travellers with accommodations: a hammock for the bishop, a bed for the young missionary, and space for their Indian comrades in the marines' quarters. Through foggy, uncertain weather the *Boxer* inched her way northwest to Kyuquot Sound. There the missionaries and Indians lowered their canoe, which had been taken on board the *Boxer* at Friendly Cove and filled with so many provisions from the *Boxer*, that it was dangerously overloaded. They said goodbye to the gunvessel, and continued their visitation to native villages.[4]

The *Boxer*'s timely assistance may have been typical of the Royal Navy's support for missionaries of whatever Christian denomination. Of course, the Navy could not protect Brabant in every circumstance. For instance, when smallpox spread from Nouetsat, fifteen miles away, to Hesquiat in 1875, an excited Hesquiat chief named Matlahaw had contracted the dread disease. Twice vaccinated but without success, he was not appeased by promises of further medicine.[5] He and his people were full of fear and discouragement. They were alarmed by deaths attributable to "memaloose'—smallpox. Townissim, his father, a chief whom he had succeeded, killed the husband of one victim and murdered a slave. Like his father, Matlahaw was tormented. He fired a shotgun at Brabant, wounding him in the hand. When the priest was washing his wounds in a stream, Matlahaw shot him again, this time in the right shoulder and in his back. In serious condition, Brabant managed to crawl to the safety of his house. Loyal men of the tribe, bearing axes, knives, and guns to kill the chief, hunted him in woods nearby and presently plotted to revenge the crime against the priest by killing Matlahaw's unsuspecting sister. However, Brabant used his influence to have a chief appointed as her guardian.

Though the Indians tended to the priest, his condition deteriorated, and a deputation from the tribe told him they intended to send a canoe to Victoria with a report to his bishop and to the police. Brabant advised them to do as they wished, and ten of them left immediately, carrying two weakly-scribbled notes from Brabant. Eight days later H.M.S.

Rocket steamed into Hesquiat Harbour, carrying Bishop Seghers and a doctor from Victoria, W.W. Walkem, who had volunteered to come to the priest's aid. The *Rocket*'s surgeon, Thomas Redfern, also gave his opinion on the victim's rapidly failing health, and it was decided to take Brabant to hospital in Victoria and to amputate his wounded hand if necessary.

The captain of the *Rocket*, Lieutenant Commander Charles Reynold Harris, carrying a magistrate's commission, proposed to arrest the assailant, and told Brabant that doing so was part of his object in coming to Hesquiat. The priest, who knew the terrain, implied that Matlahaw might be hidden far away in the mountains. Because Brabant needed immediate hospital care, it was arranged with the Indians that if Matlahaw were arrested they were to take him to Victoria, where provincial police would pay them a hundred dollars and a supply of provisions for their trouble. Thereupon, Brabant was embarked on the ship. Next day the *Boxer* reached Victoria, and with medical aid and rest the priest returned to health. Once back at Hesquiat he established, on request of the Hesquiat and with Bishop Segher's approval, a three-man Indian constabulary. All desired to live in harmony.[6] Matlahaw was never taken into custody.

Henceforth, the priest seems to have worked in relative peace, pursuing his project of an industrial school at Hesquiat. Isolation continued to plague him, and days passed into weeks on that remote, rainy coast. At one point he lost the run of the days of the week. H.M.S. *Kingfisher*'s arrival in November 1883 was literally "a Godsend," he wrote. Now he could remedy the loss of days and keep the Lord's Day. On other occasions, missionary and naval captain would work together to aid the shipwrecked.[7] Divine intervention nothwithstanding, Brabant owed his life to the Royal Navy's timely rescue, and, by implication, his work among the Indians, which expanded with the years, owes something to British gunboats.

Men such as Commander Collins of the *Boxer*, reflecting in their own way the improving instinct of their age, were well aware of what they regarded as their divine mission — to improve the lot of mankind on earth irrespective of colour. Some were sufficiently sympathetic to the misfortunes and needs of the Indians and dutiful enough to the church that they assumed an active role, dispensing Bibles and New Testaments published by the Naval and Military Bible Society to the natives and, in one case at least, motivated a missionary society to undertake responsibilities on this particular frontier.

Doubtless the best example of this type of naval officer is James Charles Prevost. Prevost first came to the Northwest Coast in 1850 in the *Portland*, flagship of Rear-Admiral Fairfax Moresby, whose daughter

Prevost had married. He was then forty years old, a seasoned officer and a dedicated Christian. In 1852 he assumed command of the paddle-wheel sloop *Virago* and took her to the Queen Charlotte Islands where gold had recently been found. His object was to protect national interests from American threats. Prevost engaged in a peaceful display of power against some Haida suspected of having captured, pillaged, and burned the schooner *Susan Sturgis* and of enslaving her crew. During this cruise he acquired a good deal of information concerning the condition and disposition of the northern Indians.

Prevost was greatly struck by what he saw: sixty thousand natives living in an apparent state of "barbarism" and yet uncared for by the British who gained so much from them in trade. Thus far, he believed, no benefits had accrued to the natives by British possession of the area. He argued that the British Columbia Indians under proper missionary instruction could form as valuable a population as the New Zealand Maoris. He was impressed by the highly intelligent character of the Tsimshian in the region of Fort Simpson. Moreover, he believed, they were populous there and relatively free from growing white influence and liquor, with all its attendant evils. The northern coast offered an excellent place for Anglican missionary enterprise.[8]

Upon Prevost's return to England in the *Virago* he set about gaining support from the Church Missionary Society, a highly influential body which considered "the heathen" as its principal care. Born of a request for a mission from three Britons living in India in the late eighteenth century and formed in 1799 by Anglican clergymen with the aid of the commercial and professional middle class, the Society was already established in Sierra Leone, India, Mombasa, New Zealand, Red River, and elsewhere, and had become one of the most active British missionary societies.[9]

By the mid-nineteenth century, the British portion of the Northwest Coast had become an appropriate locale for the society's attention. Perhaps the cost of such a mission, obligations elsewhere, and the distance from home constituted stumbling blocks. But after Prevost made a personal appeal to the society's secretary Henry Venn, and to his own vicar Joseph Ridgeway of Tunbridge Wells, a campaign was initiated to raise funds for the mission.[10] Prevost's persistence paid off, for the society asked him to put his ideas into writing. His memorandum on the subject was published in the society's *Church Missionary Intelligencer*, edited by Ridgeway.[11] Two or three months afterwards Prevost was appointed British commissioner, a position in which he and his American counterpart were to determine the boundary between British and United States possessions on the Northwest Coast, as indicated in the Oregon Treaty. The Admiralty gave him command of the corvette *Satellite* and instructions to sail from England in December 1856. This gave him his opportunity. He must have approached the First Lord of the Admiralty, Sir Charles Wood, or some other person of influence at the Admiralty. His father-in-law, Fairfax Moresby, who had won distinction in the 1820's for his activities on the west coast of Africa in suppressing the slave traffic and who commanded great respect in the right London circles, may have given weight to Prevost's case. In any event, the Lords of the Admiralty authorized Prevost to take a missionary chosen by the society to the Northwest Coast in H.M.S. *Satellite*.[12]

Though Prevost had recommended that an ordained minister be sent among the Tsimshian to extend God's kingdom, the society called on William Duncan, a young student then in training for missionary work in the society's Highbury College. Never taken into holy orders, Duncan was a Yorkshireman imbued with lower middle class cultural attitudes, and a great admirer of the currently preached values of hard work, thrift, and duty. He was a practical, adaptable, and intelligent individual with a strong streak of independence. Prevost thought him "very young, full of love and zeal."[13] Duncan arrived at Esquimalt in the *Satellite* on 13 June 1857 and four months later reached Fort Simpson.

This environment was home to the Tsimshian. But Fort (later Port) Simpson,[14] since its founding in 1834 as part of a chain of trading posts stretching from the Columbia northward to Russian America, remained a less than agreeable place for European visitors and for Hudson's Bay Company employees obliged to endure at once its loneliness and its hostilities. Though it possessed an excellent garden and a good harbour, Europeans perceived the landscape as dreary and forbidding for most of the year. Like Hesquiat, the dark forests and heavy clouds depressed the whites. The seemingly incessant rains brought no psychic relief. Added to this was Indian "pilfering" of potatoes for the purpose of brewing "hooch."[15] Tightly surrounded by Indian lodges and protected by gates which had to be locked from sunset to sunrise and even during meals, it was, one European said, a "most miserable place." Another, exhibiting a variant of garrison mentality, recalled in the 1850's that the fort remained in "a constant state of siege and suspicion." Yet a third remembered the Indians to be "the worst lot of cutthroats I ever had to do business with."[16]

It was in this place that the Church Missionary Society had decided to establish its Indian utopia. Governor Douglas attempted to prevent its founding there because of the dangers from potentially hostile tribes and its enormous distance of nearly a thousand miles by a warship under sail from Esquimalt. Perhaps Captain Prevost's opinion on the importance of the site bulked large in the perseverance which Duncan exhibited. In his memorandum and letters to the society and in letters to the Admiralty,

Prevost had reasoned that great work could be done at Fort Simpson because little white influence existed among the Tsimshian. These natives were the most important commercial nation on the coast. Furthermore, Fort Simpson, the trade centre, the London of the northern coast, was central to many populous Indian villages. And each spring when the oolachen fishing occurred, "a kind of great national affair" attracted coast and interior tribes. Thus, from a missionary viewpoint there were good strategic reasons why Prevost singled out Fort Simpson for the society's first mission station on the Northwest Coast.

At Fort Simpson, as at Fort Rupert, the gathering of many tribes had brought rivalries of rank and prestige to the surface and thus potlatching and ceremonials increased. A smallpox epidemic had claimed one-third of the natives after its outbreak in 1836 and added further to social readjustments by dispersing tribal groups. But the basic structure of this society, its fundamental rules and modes of conduct still existed at the time of Duncan's arrival.

The missionary worked slowly and surely at Fort Simpson. The Company gave him quarters inside the fort, and when he had learned the Tsimshian language, a school was arranged outside of the walls and his teaching of young and old began. Gradually he came to realize that only with a new economic base and in an environment free from contaminating social influences could his charges be elevated permanently. Thus on 27 May 1862 he led four hundred followers twenty-four miles south to "Metlakatla," a Tsimshian word meaning a place between two bodies of salt water. Some of his Tsimshian followers used this ancient winter station before in their migration to Fort Simpson in 1834. Metlakatla, on Tugwell Island, was shielded by Dundas, Stephens and Melville Islands from the violence of the open Pacific, and it possessed potential for agriculture. At this place, Duncan built on the Tsimshians' spirit of "coming home." He and his charges set about with great energy and determination to construct rows of comfortable, clapboard-sided houses, a school, a wooden church reputed to be the largest in western North America, warehouses, wharfs, and other buildings including a store, set up to rival the Bay traders. For a time they operated a trading schooner, the *Caroline*. A brass band, a well-drilled guard and constabulary, a fire-brigade, separate schools for boys and girls, a dispensary, a jail and more—all had been built or founded to do God's will.[17] Later, street lamps, donated by Prevost, illuminated a spacious esplanade overlooking the bay and wharfs.

Duncan's success in this venture was partly owing to his knowledge of the Tsimshian language, culture, and behaviour. Moreover, he was willing to accommodate his ideas to Tsimshian needs and values. But the Tsimshians as coastal traders had long been in contact with neighbouring tribes and had integrated features of other cultures into their own. Wealthy and acquisitive, they were predisposed to accept Duncan's attitudes, goals and expectations.

Visitors such as Molyneux St. John, who arrived in the H.M.S. *Amethyst* in 1876 in company of Lord Dufferin, the governor general of Canada, marvelled at this unique village. Here eight or nine hundred Tsimshians were learning self-help, thrift, work, industry, and charity towards their fellow man. And their success was resulting in better security for Indian seaborne commerce in the immediate region. These were optimistic signs to the white visitors. Dufferin, who thought the Metlakatla maidens as modest and well-dressed as any in an English parish, told a crowd of British Columbians in Victoria that if the province's thirty thousand natives (by his estimate) could be raised "to the level Mr. Duncan has taught us they can be brought. . . consider what an enormous amount of vital power you will have added to your present strength." Metlakatla had become a model community. "I have seen Missions in various parts of the world before now," Lieutenant Edmund Hope Verney, R.N., told the bishop of Columbia, "but nowhere one that has so impressed me with the reality of what has been accomplished."[18]

This young officer was not alone in praising the mission and William Duncan. Even before Duncan relocated at Metlakatla, Commander Richard Charles Mayne of H.M.S. *Plumper*, an astute judge of men and one who knew Northwest Coast Indians well, wrote that Duncan "impressed me as a man of ten thousand, possessing, with abundant energy and zeal, that talent for acquiring the confidence of love of his fellow creatures, which all who came in his way, were they whites or Indians, could not fail to acknowledge and feel subject to."[19] Few contemporary accounts of early British Columbia fail to mention the man or his work, for Duncan had become a legend. Equally important, he had won the confidence of certain Tsimshian, and by a rigid code of regulations he had obtained their allegiance.

Indians up and down the coast knew of Duncan's skill and influence. When H.M.S. *Plumper* called at Beaver Harbour in August 1860, the Fort Rupert Kwakiutl chiefs complained to her captain, George Henry Richards, that the Tsimshian at Fort Simpson were learning so much while, by contrast, they shamefully remained untutored, ignorant, and ignored. Richards heard their complaints with sympathy. He assured them that he would tell Governor Douglas in Victoria of their needs.[20]

Richards, who was not unlike Prevost, was captivated by the idea of sending missionaries and native teachers, not gunboats. On 19 August of that year, Duncan arrived at Fort Rupert and found the *Plumper* at anchor. Duncan's journal for that date tells of this meeting with Richards. It is worth quoting here at length:

Went on board and was warmly greeted by Captain Richards, who astonished me by saying he had just been writing about me to the Admiral. I read his despatch.[21] It stated that he had had some trouble with the Indians of that place, and at a large meeting they had asked him why Mr. Duncan was not sent to teach them, and then insisted on the injustice of my being sent over their heads to the Tsimshean Indians. During my conversation with Captain Richards, he said the business he had just had with the Indians convinced him that it was not our ships of war that were wanted up the coast, but missionaries. The Indian's ignorance of our power and strong confidence in his own, in addition to his natural savage temper, render him unfit to be dealt with at present by stern and unyielding men of war, unless his destruction be contemplated, which of course is not. "Then," asked the captain, "why do not more men come out, since your mission has been so successful; or, if the missionary societies cannot afford them, why does not Government send out fifty, and place them up the coast at once? Surely it would not be difficult to find fifty good men in England willing to engage in such a work? And their expenses would be almost nothing compared with the cost which the country must sustain to subdue the Indians by force of arms."

Of this, Mayne wrote, "Such are the earnest sentiments of one of Her Majesty's naval captains while among the Indians. And such, I may add, are the sentiments of myself—in common, I believe with all my brother officers—after nearly five years' constant and close intercourse with the natives of Vancouver Island and the coast of British Columbia."[22]

Richards's private feelings may well have been held by other British naval officers such as Mayne. However, the official capacities of these men did not allow them the latitude to extend missions as a public duty. They could, however, convey missionaries to their station or come to their succour or protection. In this way they were aiding God's empire on earth and obeying "Heaven's Command." It was not within their legal province to assume a missionary stance. That function they were obliged to leave to the private religious bodies such as the Church Missionary Society. Metlakatla's success led the society to establish missions among the Nishga at the Lower Nass villages in 1864, among the Haida at Masset in the Queen Charlotte Islands in 1876, among the Kwakiutl at Fort Rupert in 1878 and at Alert Bay on Cormorant Island in 1880, and among other Indians at a few other locales on the northern coast.

Yet, paradoxically, Duncan and the Church Missionary Society were embroiled in a protracted dispute over doctrinal and policy matters. Duncan grew increasingly unorthodox in his theological ideas. He would not permit the Tsimshian to take Holy Communion because he thought the living presence of Christ's body and blood might stimulate Indian cannibalism. He found co-operation with fellow missionaries difficult. His will had become supreme in the settlement. The effects of his megalomania on the Metlakatla Tsimshian were frightening to some; as the Right Reverend William Ridley, the newly appointed bishop of Caledonia, who visited there in 1879 remarked tersely, "This righteous autocracy is as much feared by the ungodly as it is respected by the faithful."[23] Ridley found Duncan's conduct unsuitable, and he discovered that Duncan resented any questioning of his authority at Metlakatla. On Ridley's advice, the Church Missionary Society issued an ultimatum to its recalcitrant agent: he must return to England for a conference, implement the bishop's plans for religious instruction, or hand over the mission to the bishop and quit the place. Duncan did none of these things; instead he used his Tsimshian allies in order to resist the society's demands. No longer willing to serve the society in its ends, he had embarked on a course that involved conflict with provincial and dominion officials over questions of land tenure. They preferred not to interfere with Duncan's authority, having made him a magistrate and allowing him to appoint Indian constables. They did, from time to time such as in 1862 and 1864, send gunboats to watch the settlement and investigate cases of murder and theft. As Lieutenant D'Arcy A. Denny found from his visit there in H.M.S. *Forward* in September 1866, Duncan wanted the Navy to intervene although he was actually able to settle several murder cases to his own satisfaction.[24]

In 1868 Duncan asked for support when nine Indians were murdered by rivals at Metlakatla, noting his "helplessness to carry out British Law in such cases as this without British aid."[25] The appearance of the gunvessel *Sparrowhawk* bearing Rear-Admiral the Hon. George Hastings, C.B., brought some degree of authority.[26] Nonetheless, no permanent measures were taken to establish order on the spot. Governor Seymour actually thought Duncan "too fanatical" to be allowed the direction of gunboat proceedings.[27] In short, by the late 1860's, authorities watched Metlakatla with a wary eye.

By 1871, Duncan was appealing to Victoria to send Her Majesty's gunboats to Metlakatla and other coastal settlements on regular visits. As he rightly insisted, it was far easier to prevent lawlessness by a display of naval force than to solve and punish crimes after they had occurred.[28] Later, as his anti-authoritarian views grew, he would change his opinion about the necessity of using gunboats. By the early 1870's, in the Metlakatla area, the nefarious liquor traffic, the increased mobility of warring tribes, the growing disenchantment among Indian societies about the white man's presence, the dispossession from tribal land, the changes in

Indian economies, and at Metlakatla itself, the pronounced rivalry between factions favourable and opposed to Duncan, made for a potent combination threatening people and property of both races.

The commander-in-chief on the Pacific Station, Rear-Admiral Arthur A. Farquhar, learned of these mounting dangers and determined to visit the north coast to ascertain the general condition and feeling of the Indians at Metlakatla and elsewhere. Proceeding from Esquimalt on 17 September 1873 in the gunvessel *Boxer* to investigate previous reports of intended violence to settlers and to obtain personal observations on Indian conditions and feelings, in the course of his 18-day cruise Farquhar heard no complaint of Indian conduct towards whites at Nanaimo, Fort Rupert, Knight Inlet, Skidegate, or Metlakatla. Neither did he learn of any Indian ill-feeling towards government or settlers. At Duncan's mission station he found great promise of "good progress being made in the speedy amelioration" of the native "condition." Indians living in "well-constructed, commodious plank houses" were being taught trades, education, and religion. By contrast, at many other Indian settlements he found declining populations as a result of disease, intemperance, and demoralizing conditions. In particular, he noted the migration of young Indian women to thickly populated settlements. "The amount and dreadful character of Social Evil reported to exist amongst them is deplorable," he bemoaned in his account to the secretary of the Admiralty. He could not praise Metlakatla highly enough for its efforts in improving the condition of the natives.[29]

Yet for all these outward signs of peace, violence erupted at Metlakatla between the internal factions in 1882, and Bishop Ridley appealed to Victoria for aid. No British warship then being available for service, the captain of the United States Revenue Cutter *Oliver Wolcott* placed his ship at the authorities' disposal, an act which brought protests from the Victoria *Colonist,* which objected to the use of a foreign vessel to control British subjects. The Metlakatla Indians had "openly boasted," the *Oliver Wolcott*'s commander wrote Washington headquarters, that no British gunboat would be sent to punish them "whatever acts they might commit." The appearance of the revenue cutter was a source of great wonder to them, he said, and they realized that help would always be forthcoming to whites whose lives and security were threatened. It was his opinion that this knowledge would spread from tribe to tribe and be greatly conducive to the general good.[30] The revenue cutter carried two magistrates to Metlakatla. The "supposed rioters," including Duncan, were summoned at a board of enquiry but the case was dismissed.[31]

Now matters had been intensified at the mission, and the lines of difference were sharply drawn. Colonial authorities could hardly ignore the crisis that had led to riot. For these reasons and no doubt to counter the accusations of the Victoria press, the Royal Navy began a more constant watch over the affairs at Metlakatla. Rear-Admiral Algernon Lyons, the commander-in-chief, made a cruise "to the somewhat celebrated mission-ary station" in the summer of 1883, and he found the rival factions de-feating the efforts of Christianity and the advancement of civilization. Lyons regarded the situation as serious enough to warrant the British Columbia government appointing an intelligent stipendiary magistrate for Metlakatla, a step he recommended to the lieutenant-governor.[32] This was done, but Duncan and his followers refused to accept the authority of Joseph McKay, a seasoned, ex-company trader, who took up his duties as government agent in the fall of 1883. This, they said, would have recognized the Dominion's rights to jurisdiction over the Metlakatlan's affairs. At bottom, they denied that the Dominion could reserve, survey, and appropriate land which the Indians claimed title to by aboriginal right.

Because of the growing crisis in 1884, a nine-day royal commission made a full enquiry into the difficulties at Metlakatla. Captain Charles B. Theobald of the corvette *Satellite,* sent in support of the enquiry, was convinced that the problems of internal division could only be solved in one of two ways: either by buying the land not marked off as Indian re-serve by the dominion authorities or by force of arms. He explained to the Admiralty the Indian position on crown land as follows. The Indians say "How can the Queen own the land? She has never paid for it! She has not got it by conquest! Therefore she must have stolen it. Our Fore-fathers have lived here from time immemorial and handed the land down to us. The Queen has had no one of her Forefathers living here. Why do you tell us the land is the Queen's?"[33]

To the Indians Theobald made the following careful rejoinder:

> The land belongs to the Queen in this way. She holds it in trust for the Indians and the white men to protect *all* from foreign aggres-sions. The Indian Reserves (which are very large) have been marked off so that no white man can come and live there without assent from them, but though the Indian reserves belong to them it still be-longs to the Queen in the following way, that the Queen will pro-tect the Indian reserves from any warlike or aggressive proceedings from their powers but the Queen will never take the Reserve away from the Indians.[34]

Theobald must have wondered how effective this reasoning was. In fact, to his commander-in-chief, he admitted difficulty in explaining this mat-ter to the Tsimshian, a problem compounded by the intricacies of their language.

Captain Theobald saw the matter essentially as one with religious roots. Though dominion policy forbade the existence of two or more churches of different denominations in the same Indian village, in actuality two were here—though both were nominally Anglican. Theobald blamed the Church Missionary Society for attempting to remove Duncan and for bringing in Bishop William Ridley who was not from the Church Missionary Society. He found the place in a state of seige, with the bishop's house stoutly fortified by barricades and defended by special constables. The Metlakatla brass band escorted the Canadian commissioners to the *Satellite* to the tune of "Rule Britannia," while at other times played "God Save the Queen." This formed a distinctly happy contrast, Theobald noted, to the ship's arrival when only "Yankee tunes" had been played. Similarly, an English flag was hoisted over their own tribal flag where previously none had flown.

Theobald did not conclude on the basis of these few promising signs that all was well at Metlakatla. Rather, he thought they masked the cross-currents of Indian loyalties and uncertainties. He classified matters there as "very grave," warranting firm action and justice. The presence of a British warship proved useful on this occasion, he stressed in his report to his superior. But this was not a situation into which any ship's commander would have wished to be drawn.[35] "I sincerely trust," Rear-Admiral Baird reported to the Lords of the Admiralty in solemn tones, "it will not fall to the lot of Her Majesty's Navy to take any part in coercing these unfortunate Indians regarding their Religion, or into following any particular Clergyman or Missionary they have no inclination for."[36]

With the dominion government determined to pursue a policy of full survey, a two-acre portion of Metlakatla known as Mission Point became the centre of Indian resistance. In sending the *Satellite* there in 1885 Baird cautioned her commander against using coercive measures. The admiral considered the survey a dominion matter and felt that force should not be used, unless Ottawa was prepared to use Canadian forces to quell any disturbances which might arise in parts of British Columbia where Indians were settled. In his opinion, the whole question should be investigated as to Indian rights and proclamations made on the subject of Indian title and legal rights. On no account could the captain of the *Satellite* act in response to any Canadian request, Baird instructed Captain Arthur H. Alington, "unless with my sanction, or if you are ordered to do so direct from the Admiralty."[37] A proponent of minimum intervention, he was not about to be sucked into the vortex of a problem of the Dominion's making.

As for Duncan, now in Victoria, he urged that "warlike armaments" were no remedy for Indian complaints that instead required patience and just dealing. Sending a gunboat to Metlakatla would not solve the problem, he advised the government, and he offered to go north with a commissioner to bring peace in order to avoid another expensive rebellion such as that which had just occurred in the Canadian Northwest. In his view the authorities had been too eager to listen to reports, false in themselves, that came from persons who had their own "hypocritical ends to serve." Yet surely he must have known why he was not listened to when he concluded, cynically, "The peaceful measures I proposed were, however, rejected and the ship of war has gone."[38] The authorities would no longer hear him out; he had lost all credibility as a peacemaker. Governments now saw him as a troublemaker, resisting the law for his own, self-serving ends.

The ship Duncan had referred to was H.M.S. *Cormorant,* and she had been sent from Esquimalt bearing Judge Harrison, a stipendiary magistrate, the superintendent of provincial police, H.M. Roycraft, two constables, and an Indian department lawyer, on the request of the province of British Columbia "to carry out the law." The captain of the *Cormorant,* Commander J.E.T. Nicholls, had permission to land an armed force of marines and sailors in support of the police if necessary and if requested.[39] The ultimate object of the civil authorities was to dismantle a house erected by "Duncan Indians" on Mission Point to enable the survey of seventy thousand acres alloted by the Dominion to proceed. Rear-Admiral Sir Michael Culme Seymour, Bart., who adhered to a tough policy was a different man from his more cautious predecessor, Baird. He believed that British law had to be enforced to prevent further disturbances and, moreover, that the Indians needed to know that it would be enforced. "It is quite clear to my mind," he advised the Admiralty, "that unless the law is enforced at once and the Indians made to understand that it will be enforced, there are likely to be further difficulties." Seymour was obviously agreeable to supplying aid to both civil powers involved—the provincial government in charge of justice and the dominion government in charge of administering the Indian Act.[40]

On the *Cormorant's* arrival at the settlement on 2 November 1886, Commander Nicholls proceeded close to the town so as to be in a position to use force if required. Two days later, a steamer from Victoria brought an injunction from the Superior Court of British Columbia ordering the removal of the mission house and the arrest of the ringleaders. Thus, civil officials enjoined Duncan's Indians to leave the Mission Point house, constables pulled down this point of Indian resistance, and the police chief arrested several Indians for stopping the survey. A five-day trial followed, and the accused were found guilty or taken to Victoria for trial. In all, eight were convicted.

In making his report to Rear-Admiral Seymour on this display of force, Commander Nicholls described the reasons for their militancy. The "offenders" had told him that they were compelled to stop the survey because their previous petitions and deputations had gone unheeded.[41] Furthermore, they said they were unaware they were breaking the law by keeping surveyors off the land they considered their own, since they had signed no treaty relinquishing title. The Indians grievously complained of attempts made by both the dominion and provincial governments "to take from us by force, part of our patrimony, and the inheritance from our fathers." "We firmly believe that these lands are ours," they continued passionately, "and that those who would take them from us, have no legal title to them, and are acting illegally." They pointed out that they had not surrendered the land; indeed, they said that Lord Dufferin had told them that in every other Canadian province, Indian title had been acknowledged and that no government, federal or provincial, had ever claimed the right "to deal with an acre until a treaty had been made." These Indians sought legal aid. They wanted the courts to decide the issue and offered to abide by the ruling. "Instead of doing this they try to force us, to frighten us and to force us to give up our rights."[42]

The Indians were truly sorry that they had broken the law, Commander Nicholls wrote, explaining further that they did not believe the presence of a British warship was necessary since they had no intention of resisting the authorities. They considered the Cormorant's presence intimidating, an attempt on the authorities' part to coerce them. "On the other hand," Nicholls reasoned, "it may be said that this line was taken since they found themselves in the wrong and on the weaker side, and it is a fact that a very great number of Indians were assembled on the arrival of the Cormorant, and that their gestures and behaviour were at first far from being either friendly or humble."[43]

This was the last exhibition of naval power employed at Metlakatla. For good or ill, the difficulties and divisions had been brought to a peaceful solution, much to the satisfaction of Commander Nicholls. "There appears to have been a great deal of excitement about the matter here," he concluded his report to Rear-Admiral Seymour, "and great relief experienced at its pacific termination."[44]

The authorities, civil and naval, could be relieved because by this time Duncan had decided to move his people to Annette Island, Alaska, where a new and better Metlakatla might be founded. There were ironies to this migration of 1887, the British philanthropist and partisan to the Duncan cause, Sir Henry Wellcome, wrote: "In this the fiftieth year of the reign of Queen Victoria, when her loyal and frugal subjects, the Metlakatlans would gladly and joyously join in the jubilee, they are expatriated, and, driven by the oppression of her unworthy representatives, to seek in a foreign land, freedom of worship, and homes that shall be secure to their children, and their children's children."[45] For them it was entirely appropriate that at their last Christmas they sang "Hold the Fort" instead of "God Save the Queen" and they raised no British flag for the jubilee. Of Old Metlakatla's 948 people, 823 followed their fifty-five-year-old leader to build a new Christian industrial town. Yet it too was not without interfactional rivalries and government involvement.[46] This migration, the only major movement of Indians from British Columbia's borders in modern times, removed the problem from British Columbian, Canadian, and Admiralty jurisdiction and responsibility. Old Metlakatla remained a shadow of its former self, the uncontested seat of Bishop Ridley, and a testament to the control asserted by dominion authorities over aboriginal land in British Columbia. The surveyors whose chains represented such an alien culture could now complete their work without interruption. Ships of the Royal Navy watched the peaceful progress of the remnant mission and others in the area.[47]

On the other side, some Indians who remained behind resented the treatment they had received at the hands of authorities. For instance, the Port Simpson Indians explained in their testimony before the "Commission Appointed to Enquire into the Condition of the Indians of the Northwest Coast" in 1888 that they were heart-broken about unkept promises and the appearance of gunboats. They thought Dr. Powell was "ashamed to come up here" and that he had therefore sent Indian agent Joseph McKay as his deputy. McKay had listened to them and agreed that their claims for land were just. But he had never returned, they complained, and they suspected it was because the Indian view was not agreed to by the government. They knew of the visit of warships to Metlakatla, of the Dominion's insistence that "not one inch of the ground" belonged to the Tsimshians, and of the Mission Point dispute. "All this sending of warships and putting Metlakatla people in gaol, and the way we were treated about our land, cause us great trouble and make our hearts weak," they told the commissioners. As for themselves, they were proud that the government had "never sent a warship to us." As an index of their law-abiding ways, they explained that the Port Simpson judge would be unemployed if it were not for the fact that the government had given the Hudson's Bay Company a license to sell liquor to "bad white men" who sold it to the Indians.[48] Broken promises, gunboats, coercion, and fluctuating government policies—all took a toll on the Indians.

"It is painful, and yet indisputable fact," the Church Missionary Society's *Intelligencer* reported in 1867, "that colonization brings with it many dangers to the heathen race in whose country it is carried on."[49] It is no less true that in their own way the men and women of the Church Missionary Society were agents of change, contributing to the modification of Indian lifestyles. The problems evolving at Metlakatla, for all that settlement's good intentions, represented the breakdown of ancient

Indian identities, will, economy, and energy and the establishment of new values and modes of conduct. The society, William Duncan, and Bishop Ridley were all answering Heaven's Command in their several ways. Some naval officers, such as Collins and Theobald, also worked towards this end within the service's limits. Others, such as Prevost and Richards, were anxious to foster missions by using their influence with government or by writing impassioned letters to the Lords of the Admiralty. Generally speaking, the naval service exercised a silent mode of conduct in support of missionaries on the same frontier.

13

New Zones of Influence: Nass, Kimsquit, and Skeena

O N THE REMOTE and rugged reaches of British Columbia's northern coastline, authorities and the Navy continued to be drawn into intertribal violence, as they continued their efforts to investigate cases of piracy and murder among the Indians. On the northern coast, from Vancouver Island to southeastern Alaska, during the 1860's and 1870's, most Indian crimes against Indians went undetected and unpoliced. Though security for all races constituted an official and high-minded objective of English law in British Columbia, in fact this frontier was too remote, too extensive to police. As late as 1869, a British Columbia colonial official wondered why missionaries did not establish their Indian village settlements closer to Victoria so that appropriate protection could be provided.[1] There was much missionary work to be done near the southern settlements, but missionaries, particularly Anglicans and Methodists, were taking their creeds to the far frontier, particularly to the Tsimshian living near the mouths of the Skeena and Nass Rivers. In these circumstances, the 1869 complaint did not disclaim responsibility, but only admitted that authority in the north was little more than a ghostly presence — a magistrate, an Indian constable, a missionary, or an Indian agent being the only representative of law. These on the spot authorities could not count on the regular appearance of one of Her Majesty's ships of war, for the diverse and far-flung demands on the squadron's limited and overextended resources did not allow that. In consequence, the authorities were obliged to meet the needs of the day as they arose. Such was the case of crimes involving the Nishga, the Kimsquit, and the Tsimshian.

The Nishga, "people of the Nass," inhabited the long, mountainous and in some places lava-bedded valley of their great river. The Nass, deriving from the Tlingit word meaning stomach, or cache, was then as now a great food depot. The Nass rises in the Skeena Mountains and pursues a course of 236 miles south and west to reach the Pacific at Portland Canal and its extension Observatory Inlet. Its tidal estuary enters the Observatory Inlet at Nass Bay, in 55°N., some fifty miles from Chatham Sound and the open Pacific. At the river mouth, broad mudflats and sandbars warn mariners of a silted stream of fluctuating depth, depending on the strength of spring freshets. Within the estuary, the navigation is difficult and dangerous, and the channel at low water is barely sufficient for large canoes. A pair of bold white cliffs serve as forbidding gates to the river. The entrance is sufficiently wide for navigation but soon constricts about fifteen miles upstream at Greenville and the Lower Nass villages and is even more narrow, following the windings of the river another twenty-eight miles at Aiyansh. In 1793 Captain George Vancouver had missed Nass Bay; but shortly thereafter a British maritime fur trader, Charles Bishop, made contact with the Nishga near the river entrance. "It is a doubt with us," he wrote, "wither these People had ever seen a Vessel before. They wore, by far, the most savage wild appearance I have ever seen."[2]

Then as now the Nishga were passionate defenders of their concept of property: the river and the waters drained between the great snow-crowned mountains flanking the heavily-forested valley on either side being theirs by right of occupation since the first man, Wu-Gat, who was placed in the Nass valley when it was still in darkness. The Nishga zealously guarded their valley's resources, which gave them their reason for being, their items of trade and strength, and their precious independence.

On the lower, tidal reaches of the Nass, silver shoals of oolachen or "candlefish" moved from the salt sea into the northern river, pursued by hungry sea lions, killer whales, porpoises, and hair seals, while above the churning surface of tidal waters sea gulls screamed and dived for the rich harvest which appeared annually in late February or in early March and continued until May. Each year the Nishga were joined in the oolachen catch by Haida, Tlingit, and Tsimshian; and at the river estuary an industry yielded an extracted oil or grease which served as a food preservative and an equally valuable trade item. Each year from distant quarters coast and interior Indians came to barter for the oil. Here the Nishga also fished for salmon and halibut; on land they smoked or dried fish, prepared meat and berries with grease, and exploited the rich shellfish and seaweed places for barter and food items. In this locale, where kinship ties were rigidly defined and strong hereditary chieftainships emerged, few places were unoccupied or unclaimed at the time Euro-

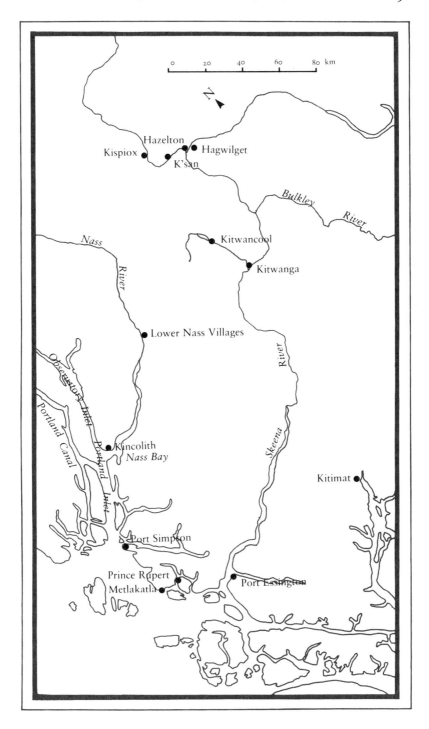

peans arrived. Sections of the lower river and its banks were clearly divided among the various lineages, not always peaceably. Various Nishga households zealously watched over their ancestral preserves, on guard as much against ancient enemies as new foes. In the late nineteenth century the Nishga did not constitute a nation, for each tribe was a separate political entity with its own village.[3] Here, where constant raids and counterraids, forays, and attacks occurred, internecine violence constituted a way of life. The Nishga held the upper reaches of the Nass against all intruders, while they permitted the Tsimshian, to whom they considered themselves related in language, to retain fishing stations and claims on the lower stretches of the river.

At the tidal estuary on a rocky point near the seasonal Nishga village Ewen Nass, the Hudson's Bay Company had erected Fort Nass in 1831, although they subsequently abandoned it three years later in favour of a better location for coastal navigation, Fort Simpson at what was then known as McLoughlin's Bay. The Company's removal from Ewen Nass had been partly caused by Nishga arrogance and hostility, and it left the Nishga undisturbed for a generation, except for the occasional visit of company traders in the *Beaver*.[4]

Before the late 1860's ships of the Royal Navy were seldom seen on the Nass, and then only at the river mouth. In 1862 the surveying vessel H.M.S. *Hecate,* Captain George Henry Richards commanding, had made a cursory reconnaisance of Nass Bay and the river estuary, and her officers had advised William Duncan of the prospects of establishing a mission there. Duncan had visited the river on several occasions beginning in April 1860. He had made friends with a chief named Kahdoonahah at the Lower Nass villages who eagerly awaited the Church Missionary Society's permanent mission.[5] While the Catholics and the Methodists had begun to push into the upper reaches of the Nass Valley, Duncan was unable until 1864 to send a missionary to the Lower Nass villages. In July of that year R.R.A. Doolan, B.A., and Robert Cunningham, arrived at the villages, selected a site for a house and schools, and began their work. The missionaries were altogether horrified by the prevalence of liquor feasts and the entrenched power and the aloof and lofty disposition of the local chiefs. Polygamy and child deaths were other problems and, in addition, Doolan who was left alone when Cunningham returned to Metlakatla, did not know much of the Nishga tongue.[6]

But the principal difficulty was the presence of whiskey schooners and unscrupulous traders at the river mouth, and in the 1860's the Navy began to police the traffic. Certain Nishga chiefs promised to obey the law, and not commit murders.[7] In December 1865 H.M.S. *Clio,* Captain Nicholas Turnour, was patrolling the mouth of the Skeena and making arrests. News of this raced through the Nishga villages. Apprehension and fear spread that a gunboat would pay them a visit in order to apprehend two witnesses. "Great excitement in the camp on account of the news about the man-of-war," Doolan recorded nervously in his journal on 6 December, "the mission house full of Indians, and a perfect babel of tongues." The possible appearance of the gunboat sufficed to deter a local chief, Claythas, from threatening to shoot someone and thereby wipe out the disgrace of his brother's death. On the other hand another chief, Ndah, had exhorted still other chiefs to seize the man-of-war if it came up river and take vengeance on the white man. The other chiefs would hear none of this and told Ndah that they were no fools: they would not risk their lives for the sake of saving a murderer. At this Ndah became apologetic and preached peace and even said that he was afraid that the others would deliver him up to the warship when it came.[8]

Doolan was anxious that a gunboat visit the Lower Nass villages for there was much liquor being sold there and the presence of a ship, he reasoned, would produce a very beneficial effect among the Nishga. But the gunboat did not come, and on 18 April 1866 he recorded despondently "the camp is flooded with whiskey," some Indians being opposed to it and others in favour of it. Doolan grew depressed and lonesome. He feared that the old quarrels between the Nishga and the Tsimshian would be perpetuated, and in consequence the bitter intertribal rivalries between the two peoples would grow into violence.[9] He waited long and impatiently for a gunboat to appear on the river, and at last it came.

On 28 September Lieutenant D'Arcy Anthony Denny, commanding the gunboat *Forward,* entered the Nass and anchored near the remnants of the Old Hudson Bay Company fort at Ewen Nass. In the ship's gig, Denny with an Indian guide, and accompanied by Doolan, who was pleased by the Navy's support, went fourteen miles upriver to the Lower Nass villages and the head of navigation. The Lower Nass villages were three in number and were named Kit-min-i-ook, Kit-luh-kum-ka-dah and Kut-a-kauze, the south, middle and north villages respectively, and at the time boasted a population of about 400. Two of them stood on islands and were isolated from one another, except by water, at high tide. They were the beginning of the Nishga settlements on the river, and upstream along the river banks stood many other villages whose locations are known but which have now been reclaimed by the dark forest.

The Hudson's Bay Company agent there, Robert Cunningham, previously assistant to William Duncan, was pleased to see a man-of-war's boat, though no "outrages" had been committed lately. Yet some of the chiefs "were inclined to be insolent" and had threatened to shoot him. "The Indians," Denny reported, with perceptive understanding, "had so often been told that a Man-of-War would come up the River, and never having seen one, they began to doubt the possibility of a vessel coming up and consequently were rather inclined to treat the Queen's authority with contempt. In fact two or three of the Chiefs had openly boasted that they would resist a War Ship and that they would traffic in liquor and get drunk as often as they pleased."[10] This was just the sort of challenge that Denny liked.

The captain of H.M.S. *Forward,* Lieutenant Denny, shared one characteristic with his fellow officers Captain Nicholas Turnour of the *Clio* and Commander John Pike of the *Devastation,* and with his commanding officer Rear-Admiral Denman: he was decidedly a no-nonsense type. Neither was he a neophyte in the naval service, being a sixteen-year veteran and a seasoned gunboat commander, coming to British Columbia waters fresh from a testing tour of duty in command of the paddle-wheel gunboat *Coromandel* on China rivers and coasts. He was a hard-nosed career professional, both spirited and determined; and he operated from a strict and disciplined mindset of legalistic rationality. He thought that the best way to make recalcitrant Indians into good and obedient subjects of Her Britannic Majesty Queen Victoria was to bring them on board ship and give them a sound flogging.[11]

At the Lower Nass villages he had observed the "insolent bearing" of some of the Nishga. He therefore determined to "show the flag" at the villages, and to attempt the risky ascent of the turbulent river in the *Forward.* He decided to return downriver to his vessel. He carefully sounded the river on the way down in the ship's gig, reached and rejoined his ship. At 2 p.m. on the 30th, having loaded the guns and prepared for action, he weighed anchor and steamed slowly up the river with the first of the flood tide. For miles, through the slate-girt channel, the vessel was in but eight to twelve feet of water, but at five p.m. the gunboat arrived at the head of navigation river without having once touched ground. Denny and the *Forward* were now at, or more correctly, below the Lower Nass villages. Denny anchored one hundred and fifty yards from the nearest village and eight hundred from the farthest, "all in good range" of the ship's guns.[12]

He notified the chiefs to assemble next day at Trader Cunningham's house and said that if they failed to do so he would consider them "enemies." He fired four blank guns (twenty-four pounders) "to give them an idea of what they might expect." The next morning, October 1st, he landed with all the officers and ten armed men and went to Cunningham's house. All the chiefs except "the two most obnoxious ones" met with Denny. He told them that he had come merely on cordial terms and that only those who acted contrary to law need be afraid.

> I said I could easily see who the evil disposed were, for with all their bragging they had made themselves scarce directly the Gun Boat

made her appearance, and the next time I came up, I should know how to deal with them. I then spoke to them on the subject of trafficking in whisky, which was illegal and pointed out to them how it led to all the disgraceful murders and bloodshed in the Country, and told them in future any cases of the kind would be promptly punished.[13]

He explained the friendly wish of government and warned that he could easily destroy the villages. Two or three of the principal chiefs replied, saying "how happy they were to hear me talk so peacefully" and gave long speeches testifying to their goodness and willingness to support laws and keep order. He then attended dances given by the chiefs and in the evening he fired a twelve-pounder rocket "to show them how easily their Huts could be burnt down by those destructive missiles."[14] The day "ended with great rejoicings on their part."

Denny thought the ship's visit would do a great deal of good, because it had weakened the influence of the disaffected chiefs "who being great Bullies, were very much feared by the peacefully disposed portion." These recalcitrants would become despised, he believed, while the majority would find it in their interest to stop liquor feasts, often the cause of murder. On 2 October he weighed anchor and proceeded cautiously and safely downriver to continue his round of duty to Fort Simpson, Metlakatla, Bella Bella, Fort Rupert, Comox, Nanaimo, and thence to Esquimalt after a seven-week voyage of 1,300 miles.[15]

For two years after the *Forward*'s visit, affairs on the Nass remained quiet, but in June 1868, during Rear-Admiral Hastings' visit to Metlakatla in H.M.S. *Zealous,* Duncan pressed on him all the sordid details of the murder of three Nishga of the Kincolith mission on 28 April. Kincolith, "place of scalps," was an ancient native site on Nass Bay where, in July 1867, ten months after Denny's visit, the Church Missionary Society had established its new Nass mission. The Society had abandoned its attempts at the Lower Nass villages, where Doolan's enterprise had been hindered by extremely cold winters, five months of frozen river, an equally distressing summer period of mosquitoes, the prevalence of whisky and, above all, the unwavering resistance of the chiefs. The new mission was under the charge of the medical missionary, the Reverend Robert Tomlinson, Doolan having gone to England and then warmer Spanish climes, never to return. The Kincolith mission had begun with 33 Nishga, and the Church Missionary Society hoped that it would be the successful Nishga equivalent of the Tsimshian-dominated Metlakatla. Kincolith's progress depended heavily on peace existing among the Indians both there and nearby. Thus the murder of three Kincolith Indians nine months after its founding was an alarming blow to the mission, and

Tomlinson thought its future in doubt.[16]

Duncan had already written of this to Governor Seymour on 16 May, noting the panic-stricken nature of the besieged "little band" at Kincolith Christians in the face of the murders and their determination to abide patiently under the law. At the same time he appealed to Seymour, they "look to Your Excellency to avenge their loss."[17] Seymour told the Colonial Office that Rear-Admiral Hastings was cruising in that locale and would doubtless investigate the case. The Duke of Buckingham, secretary of state for the colonies, taking no chances that the matter would be overlooked, wrote to the Admiralty on this subject, one which he classified as "of great moment." In his opinion these infant Christian native settlements "should not be allowed to be destroyed."[18]

The facts of the case, as Hastings discovered, were that on 28 April, at a "liquor feast" at the Lower Nass villages given by the Nishga chiefs to the chiefs and principal men of the Fort Simpson Tsimshian, or Kinnakanyeak as they were called, a "drunken riot" had occurred during which two Kincolith chiefs and one Kinnakanyeak man and two Nishga Indians lost their lives. On the same day, a party of Kinnakanyeak who had been at the feast started down river. Unable to take revenge, they "devised the diabolical design of making a tour down the river and murdering every Nishga they might meet," Tomlinson said.[19] They met two Hagwilgets who were guests of the Nishga during the fishing season but who had not been at the feast and killed them in revenge. Furthermore, when they got near the Kincolith mission and met four mission Indians who were fishing, they killed three of them and carried away the fourth, a child, who was later set free.

Hastings was reluctant to interfere. Not knowing Seymour's position and, of course, not being in direct communication with London, he could not have known of Buckingham's anxiety. He knew that this was the first case of "outrage" against the Indians "attached to our Missions" and required full and patient investigation. Awaiting Seymour's instruction for intervention, Hastings was nonetheless willing to act by sending the gunvessel *Sparrowhawk*, Commander Edwin Porcher, to secure the murderers "and to take such measures as circumstances will dictate." He had Duncan's advice that the murderers could be secured at Port Simpson and that Duncan could supply witnesses.[20]

When the *Sparrowhawk* called at Metlakatla on 4 July, Tomlinson, the missionary at Kincolith, fearing that disturbances between neighbouring tribes threatened his charges and himself, solicited Commander Porcher to interfere. Porcher, unwilling to be drawn into what has been called "a Corsican vendetta," decided that it was politic to refer the matter to the colonial government. This was done, but Hastings was uncertain if any action was contemplated by the governor, an obvious indication that Seymour had no firm hand on colonial affairs.[21] By this time, as previously mentioned, Seymour was severely debilitated by drink, a fact not well known in official or public circles at the time, or if so largely covered up, even after his death on 10 June of the following year.[22] But while the Admiralty kept forwarding to the Colonial Office successive reports from Hastings urging action, Seymour failed to act.

Seymour had received from Lord Granville, the secretary of state for the colonies in Gladstone's first administration, an unduly sharp reprimand. The governor had sent London an "unsatisfactory" report on the state of the northern Indian problem, and he had not shown initiative in dealing with the Indians.[23] In the decided opinion of the Colonial Office, the Indians had placed themselves under British sovereignty and law and were thus as much entitled to redress of grievance as whites.[24] In these circumstances, Seymour had no option but to act immediately, and on 17 May 1869 he left Esquimalt in H.M.S. *Sparrowhawk* with the civil authority in the person of the chief commissioner of lands and works, Joseph Trutch, and his private secretary, Lowndes. On the way, the *Sparrowhawk* called at Metlakatla where Duncan was embarked as interpreter.

The *Sparrowhawk* arrived off of Kincolith on 30 May. The ship's gig ascended the Nass above Kincolith: at various villages Trutch and others told the belligerents that the governor was much grieved at the "evil work" that had been going on between the Nishga and Tsimshians and that he intended to make them friends. The Nishga agreed to come down the river to the *Sparrowhawk* and then go to Fort Simpson in the gun-vessel. It was understood that their differences with their rivals would be healed. They reached Fort Simpson on 2 June, and at 10 a.m. the Tsimshian chiefs were brought on board and placed opposite the Nishga chiefs on the quarter-deck, in Seymour's presence. For two hours they talked, discussing all the details of the hostilities and of amounts owing each other for injuries done. Peace was restored and the act consecrated by blowing the sacred swan's down over each other's heads and signing an agreement of peace certified by the governor.

On this occasion the British authorities acted adroitly as peacemakers. Seymour took the opportunity to tell them that he had allowed them for the last time to compensate each other in the age-old way for murder and theft. In future, they must live according to English law, and if they took each other's lives the governor would use every means at his disposal to apprehend and punish them. The Nishga and Tsimshians now exchanged gifts, mixed together with the greatest cordiality, and, after feasting, departed "much satisfied" at the conference's proceedings.[25]

The British officials found this mode of conflict-resolution more agreeable than bombarding and burning villages and canoes. To Trutch a "happy contrast" existed between the 1869 proceedings on the Nass and the previous and all too customary use of force on "the authority of Government" by which there was perhaps, he argued, an unnecessary loss of life, impoverishment, and sometimes destruction of tribes. Trutch, perhaps mirroring Seymour's opinion or indeed defending his superior against possible censure from London, was critical of certain tactics employed by the Navy on previous occasions, and in his report at the conclusion of the voyage, he took the opportunity of pointing out the obvious advantages of Seymour's mode of proceedings. It was, Trutch said, a highly creditable last act before Seymour's death and one representative of his high administrative skills. By the same token, however, because the governor had given the problem his personal attention, it was now necessary that English law had to be enforced among the natives "at whatever cost." Trutch recommended that a warship should visit periodically the various settlements, missions, and Indian villages in order to provide protection for the scattered settlers and missionaries and to keep the "wild tribes" under control. On these expeditions a duly authorized colonial agent ought to bear responsibility for whatever actions might be required. This was necessary, he wrote, "for Officers in command of Her Majesty's Ships, although holding Commissions as Justices of the Peace, may reasonably be supposed to be disinclined to take decisive action in police matters which can hardly be considered within their proper jurisdiction, and which may involve questions of material importance and great pecuniary interest to the Colony."[26]

Trutch correctly understood that this matter was a colonial responsibility. Colonial authorities wanted to share in the implementation of Indian policy, and they did not believe that the Royal Navy officers, no matter how well intentioned, ought to have full control in such delicate matters. Such a position would doubtless have been welcomed by naval officers on the Pacific Station who were too often accustomed to acting without support of an economy-minded colonial government and then being blamed for unsanctioned "brutal" actions.

Nevertheless, the peace which Seymour and his self-congratulatory subordinates had laboured to effect proved fragile on the northern coast. Subsequently, gunboats bearing marines, police superintendents, constables, and militia had to enforce the queen's warrant. They did so by show of force if possible, by armed intervention if necessary.[27]

Among the last cases of sanctioned use of violence by the Royal Navy against Northwest Coast Indians occurred in 1877 at Kimsquit, north of Bella Coola and near where the North West Company explorer Alexander Mackenzie had reached Pacific tidewater in 1793. Once again the authorities used force as a last resort, when the commanding officer of the warship thought it necessary to teach recalcitrant natives that crimes against white people and property would be repaid in kind by the

destruction of native houses and other material possessions. The Kimsquit affair offers another case of "forest diplomacy" in which the Navy,
on government request, employed violent techniques of retribution that
officials believed, perhaps correctly in this case, that the Indians fully
understood in advance of the use of force.

In early 1873 the *George S. Wright,* a 116-foot steamer of American registry carrying mail and cargo for the North Pacific Transportation Corporation, vanished without trace during her voyage from Kluvok,
Alaska, to Nanaimo. Anxious friends and family of the vessel's crew
feared the fate of survivors "at the hands of the murderous savages of the
North Coast." American government officials tended to ignore pleas for
aid of American shipping on the British Columbia coast, for various vessels had been lost on that dangerous shoreline. However, officials at Victoria, answering a request from the United States consul resident there,
despatched H.M.S. *Petrel* from Esquimalt to search the northern coast
near Cape Caution. Cape Caution, the mainland cape off the north end
of Vancouver Island, had been well named by Captain George Vancouver. In the 1870's no lighthouse aided mariners on that particularly hazardous section of the seaboard. In Queen Charlotte Sound strong gales,
high seas and thick weather frequently harried mariners. Near the cape a
long spit and rocky shallows now marked on charts as Wright Bank lay
in wait for the unsuspecting navigator or for a ship in distress.

On instructions from government, H.M.S. *Petrel* scoured the Cape
Caution shoreline. Firing guns and rockets by day and night to get the
attention of anyone fortunate enough to have survived the wreck, she
looked in at every cove and river mouth. Her men combed every beach
and reef for wreckage. H.M.S. *Rocket* joined the search but again without success. Nor could Indians interrogated by the Navy provide any useful clues. As the summer months wore on remains of two people and
various scraps of wreckage were discovered. This news pushed Mrs.
John Sutton, wife of the *George S. Wright's* chief engineer, to urge that
the Port Townsend revenue cutter *Lincoln* be sent to search Queen Charlotte Sound. Told by American authorities that the *Lincoln* was too small
to be risked in such treacherous seas, Mrs. Sutton would not be denied.
She wired President Ulysses S. Grant, and afterwards the *Lincoln* was
sent to search Queen Charlotte and Milbanke Sounds. Her skipper
conjectured that the *George S. Wright* had struck the Sea Otter Group
and had sunk without trace.[28] Two years later, in 1875, information from
Indian sources filtered through to Victoria that a makeshift European-
built shelter had been seen on the rocky coast. Shortly thereafter the remains of a U.S. Army officer, Major Walker, a passenger on the *George
S. Wright,* were found near Sitka. Despite these finds the mystery remained unsolved.

Nineteen months later, in mid-February 1877, five years after the wreck, the most important clue to the ship's fate came to light. Alfred Dundower, the captain of the trading sloop *Ringleader* and a highrank- ing Tsimshian and promoter of the Methodist mission at Port Simpson established in 1873, reported at Victoria that Charley Hemsett, a Bella Bella chief, had told him that an Owikeno Indian named Billy Coma, who had been a coal passer in the *George S. Wright,* had actually sur- vived the wreck and was living at Nanaimo.[29] Chief Hemsett related that after the *George S. Wright* had been swamped by mountainous seas, Coma and fourteen whites had miraculously reached two small islands in Queen Charlotte Sound. That night their campfires had attracted some Owikeno Indians of the Heiltsuk dialect of the Northern Kwakiutl who landed from their canoes and slit the throats of the survivors. Detective work by Chief Constable Steward led to the discovery of Coma in Nanaimo. Apparently Coma's Owikeno blood had saved him. The Owi- kenos had released Coma, warning him that they would kill his father if authorities learned of the tale of the ship's crew and passengers.[30]

On the strength of this information, Lieutenant Charles Reynold Harris, commanding H.M.S. *Rocket,* was instructed to determine once and for all the disappearance of the *George S. Wright* and the fate of her survivors. In compliance with a requisition from the lieutenant-governor of British Columbia, the *Rocket* steamed from Esquimalt on 14 March 1877, carrying Dundower and Sergeant Bloomfield of the Victoria police. Both men played important roles in subsequent events: Dundower as in- terpreter between the authorities and the natives; Bloomfield as repre- sentative of the civil power.

The *Rocket*'s voyage north through the Inland Passage was no easy one in that season. Frequent fogs and heavy winds plagued her. Under stress of heavy weather the *Rocket* found various refuges at Safety, Tak- ush, and Beaver Harbours. At Fort Rupert the *Rocket* embarked George Hunt as interpreter. And at various coves officials gathered fragments of information from chiefs and other Indians. Near Bella Bella the chief Hempsett, who had told Dundower about Coma, was brought on board. On his recommendation the authorities detained a Kitimat woman near Kikeis as a suspect. For eight days the *Rocket* cruised as Harris, Dun- dower, and Bloomfield interrogated potential witnesses and used the In- dians in custody in an attempt to reconstruct the fate of the *George S. Wright.* Farther south, at Alert Bay, the search for Billy Coma, now van- ished from Nanaimo, continued without success.[31]

Forced to follow new paths of inquiry, Lieutenant Harris once more shaped a course northward, again through thick fog. At Cape Caution a landing party searched for wreckage. At Oweekano village, River's Inlet, the Navy seized a chief and two other natives. At the next river north they captured another Owikeno Indian. In each case the interpreter,

George Hunt, took the captain's message to the village. Although some of the Owikeno suspects had been captured, two Kimsquit Indians still had to be found. Lieutenant Harris possessed enough information to suspect that they lived fifty miles away on the upper reaches of Dean Channel. He determined to navigate the long, labyrinthine and steep-faced passage of Burke, Labouchere, and Dean Channels to their village.

From the open Pacific the voyage to Kimsquit consumed the whole day. But towards sunset, on 28 March, the *Rocket* anchored behind the Kimsquit village, which faced the river but backed on Dean Channel. This peaceful row of cedar shelters stood near the head of the channel, a long arm of water dwarfed by lofty snow-capped mountains. Surrounded by brooding rain forest and confining mountains, Kimsquit lay near the mouth of Dean River. The village could only be approached by a steam-powered vessel from either the Dean River or the channel, here reduced to a narrow fairway by the river delta.

Kimsquit, meaning "narrow" or "canyon," was one of some forty-five villages of the Bella Coola Indians, linguistically an isolated enclave of Salish-speaking people.[32] The Kimsquit lived far off the beaten tracks of coastal traders. At Kimsquit huge red and black graphic designs of the raven as well as animals and fish appeared on the fronts of the great houses propped up on pilings and lining the river bank. Until this time, the Kimsquit had had virtually no contact with the white world except in the form of the Hudson's Bay Company. One company trader, Pyms Nevins Compton, the sole known white visitor there in the 1860's, categorically dismissed the Kimsquit as the most uncivilized natives he had ever met. He deplored their filth and found the great piles of human excrement deposited at the very doorways of their houses particularly disgusting. In his view it was fortunate that the air was cold and pure, which kept them healthy. Yet for all their barbaric ways, Compton allowed that the Kimsquit were "a moderately healthy and happy race."[33]

The Kimsquit were a tightly-knit people whose interwoven ancestries were tied together by sentiment and pride of lineage. As such they sported a heady disdain for outsiders.[34] Here, as in nearby Bella Coola where the great and powerful chief Potles held sway, a cultural trait among the head chief and the leading village chiefs was their aggressive arrogance towards foreigners. They bitterly resented any outside intrusion. Not far from Kimsquit some of their ancestors nearly a century before had harassed Alexander Mackenzie's party and stolen some of his property. Zealously protective of their village rights and economy, the Kimsquit, like other Bella Coolas, readily fought other village peoples. Each village remained autonomous, ruled by a strong chief without whose authority nothing could be done. This explains why the Kimsquit paid little attention to the threats of officials. For their part, the British knew nothing of the subtle characteristics and orderings of Kimsquit chieftainship. To them a chief was simply a chief, irrespective of rank. Not armed with the ethnologist's data or the anthropologist's insights, the British acted both as circumstances warranted and their own inclinations dictated.

Soon after the *Rocket* anchored, Harris sent George Hunt to bring the Kimsquit chiefs to the ship. The Indians told him that very few of their people were in camp and that the principal chiefs were away at the neighbouring villages of Bella Coola and Kitlope. However, they expected the head chief to return that night and promised to come to the warship in the morning. But the next day they did not appear, and consequently Harris sent Sergeant Bloomfield, Hunt, and Dundower to the village. The Indians categorically denied that any chiefs were there, saying that the head chief had not returned. Bloomfield, however, found four "chiefs" in camp and later that day he told them that they were to give up the Kimsquit Indians who had been at the wreck of the *George S. Wright.*[35]

At first the Kimsquit denied any knowledge of the wreck. Then, in a sudden about face, they admitted that two of the Indians wanted were dead and that another was at Victoria. Eventually they confessed that three men and one woman who had been at the *George S. Wright*'s wreck were indeed in camp.[36]

The police now tried to arrest all the suspects. They succeeded in capturing two of them who had decided to flee the village that night. But in the act of seizing the suspects one of them, an old man, threatened to shoot Alfred Dundower and his son, perhaps because the father had told the authorities in Victoria about the wreck. In the scuffle the old man seized Dundower's gun and, in Harris's words, "called up the camp to resist by force."[37] Now Harris and the police had in their custody no less than six village chiefs and two suspects. Yet they still wanted the old man and the woman. Harris warned the hostages that unless the two suspects on shore came on board the ship by nine o'clock the next morning the village would be burnt. The six chiefs agreed to deliver the old man and the woman. On this promise, four of them were allowed to return on shore while two others were kept as hostages on board the *Rocket.*[38]

Harris now began his patient wait, but when no Indians appeared by the appointed time, he weighed anchor and steamed to a position off the village where the *Rocket*'s guns could be trained on the village. In a last, desperate attempt to seize the suspects, Harris sent an armed gig and galley to arrest the offenders. The landing party found the village nearly deserted, with only two chiefs and a few others remaining. They could not find the suspects. The British gave those who stayed behind the final warning, their characteristic imperial fiat—unless they surrendered the offenders, the village would be fired into and burned.[39]

After the boats returned to the ship, the British began the process of intimidation. Harris ordered his gun crews to fire blank charges from the *Rocket*'s "great guns"[40] and then to fire two twenty-pounder shells, one on either side of the village. Harris calculated that this display of fire-power would bring an instant response from the chiefs in their custody. He was dead right. Absolutely certain about the damage that shells would do to their village they promised that they would bring back the guilty if the village was not fired and burned. Harris then sent hostages to shore in the ship's gig. When they reached the beach the hostages called to two Indians who, evidently terrified by the firing, fled into the bush. A sub-lieutenant, A.R.F. Bailey, and the police sergeant, Bloomfield, made a last minute search of the village to see that no inhabitants remained. Then the warship's guns began firing—first blank cartridges, then shells around the outskirts of the village, and lastly shells into the village itself. In one last final act of punishment, Harris sent the gig in to burn the houses of the old man who had threatened Dundower's life. The action complete, the *Rocket* steamed down Dean Channel, leaving Kimsquit engulfed in flames and smoke.[41]

On the *Rocket*'s return voyage various chiefs, informants and witnesses were taken to their villages. The *Rocket* searched Cape Caution again, but only a portion of a mast was found. The *Rocket*'s last port-of-call before returning to Esquimalt on 6 April was Nanaimo. Here she took on coal and, in yet an altogether different form of gunboat diplomacy, lingered for two days on the local sheriff's request to protect property of Dunsmuir, Diggle and Company, then being struck by certain coal miners.[42]

In Victoria Lieutenant Harris brought four prisoners to trial, two Owikenos and two Kimsquit Indians. These men had admitted finding a portion of the shipwreck near Cape Caution and were suspected of knowing more about it. Harris believed that the resistance made to lawful authority by the Kimsquit pointed to guilty knowledge on the part of their tribe.[43] However, even his painstaking efforts had not solved the mystery of the wreck of the *George S. Wright* and the fate of her cargo and crew. "It is evident," he painfully admitted to his commander-in-chief, "that all the Indians from Alert Bay north were aware of a great deal more in connection with this matter than they would reveal." "There is," he complained, "the greatest difficulty in getting an Indian to tell the same story twice on this subject."[44]

Much time had been spent on the costly expedition, much coastline had been searched, and many places and tribes had been visited, but ultimately the authorities were thwarted in exacting justice. The Navy had carried out retribution, it is true, under the assumption that the Kimsquit were guilty. However, the Crown never proved its case against the four brought to trial: conclusive evidence was wanting. As for the Kimsquit tribe, those who returned to their burned village found no shelter. In keeping with this society's traditions, if their village was attacked they all suffered equally. They endured two terrible winters there.[45] The settlement, which probably numbered one hundred or more before the shelling, was uninhabitable and was abandoned, and its population dispersed to other settlements.

If last in this account, the Skeena River and its peoples, Indian and white, are by no means of least importance. From the outset of contact between the two peoples there had been cordial relations. The People of the Skeena, the Tsimshian, ranked among the most populous and progressive of the Northwest Coast peoples. By the facts of geography their river, "the river of mists," gave them a central location on the northern Northwest Coast. At the mouth of their fish-rich river, where several villages stood, and up the river's estuary and on its many tributaries, the Tsimshian lived a comparatively tenuous existence, for the Haida, Tlingit, and Kwakiutl were among their testy neighbours. And, among their own kin were clans and subsepts, to say nothing of intervillage rivalries and linguistic and regional groupings, such as the Nishga and Gitksan.

On the coast near Skeena mouth the Tsimshian were prosperous and active traders, not only with other Indians but with competing Yankee, Russian and Hudson's Bay Company merchants. In 1834 the Bay traders built a new fort, Port Simpson, on Chatham Sound and about seventy miles north of the mouth of the Skeena River. It grew into a place of great congregation for the various Indian peoples of the Northwest Coast and for many years in the early colonial history of British Columbia was that jurisdiction's largest settlement. This "London of the Northwest Coast," was but one of many Tsimshian communities, for up the Skeena at various places where mountain or valley stream joined the Skeena or on some isolated interior bench of land that offered a good site for human occupation other Tsimshian villages stood—Kitwanga, Kispiox, and Kitwancool to name but three. Another, lying beneath the celebrated mountain Rocher de Boule and not far from where the Bulkley River merges with the Skeena, was Gitanmaax, an ancient Tsimshian village of the Gitksan. And nearby at the river forks, which stood at the extremity of steam navigation upriver 200 miles from the Pacific, sits Hazelton, perched precariously on a bench of land sufficiently broad for the Hudson's Bay Company to erect in 1868 a trading post and to found, nearby, a settlement where side by side Indians and whites lived, in the main, peaceful and secure.

Through the valley of the Skeena passed a parade of European pioneers—explorers, gold seekers, missionaries, prospectors, telegraph linesmen and government agents. Disease and liquor had come that way, too. Near the river mouth William Duncan of the Church Missionary Society reigned supreme at Metlakatla, and nearby The Reverend Thomas Crosby, a Canadian Methodist, was developing a successful mission at Port Simpson; and in 1887, when Duncan departed for Alaska, Crosby's mission became the focal point of Tsimshian Christian activities on or near the river's lower reaches. Upriver some 200 miles the Roman Catholics were well established: the Oblates under Father A.G. Morice had worked westwards from Fort St. James, through Babine Lake, to Moricetown and the Carriers at Hagwilget, near Hazelton. In the early 1860's when traders and gold seekers arrived, the contact between whites and Indians became violent on occasion, primarily because whites infringed on native ways. There was inter-Indian violence as well, as in the case of the Nishga-Tsimshian quarrels of 1869. But the Tsimshian, unlike the Nishga or the Kimsquit, had a longstanding history of interaction with whites, and in many cases they had shown their willingness to adapt to European ways, including law. Indeed it was this Tsimshian adaptability or progressive nature which had led Prevost to believe that the Tsimshian would make good Christians.[46] Gradually the predominant early economy of fur trading gave way to fishing. The export of salmon in sealed tin cans revolutionized Indian communities and incomes, and new settlements such as Port Essington, fourteen miles from the Pacific on the Skeena, were forged into existence. Founded in 1871 by former Church Missionary Society worker and Hudson's Bay Company servant Robert Cunningham, Port Essington near the Tsimshian hunting camp Spokeshute, was a shipping and canning centre of the lower Skeena.[47] Here Indian and Chinese toiled side by side in canneries, earning wages of a cash-based economy that in its own way was subverting traditional Indian community practices and principles of property and wealth.

The Tsimshian did not resist by force the arrival of the whites, but as the century moved on towards its conclusion they grew frustrated by government's unwillingness to compensate them for land taken. They did not mind sharing their land and resources with the government, but they lived with deep-seated and disturbing memories of broken promises. They therefore refused to accept an Indian agent among them, and as such counted as the only British Columbia Indians to so resist. Their resentments were acute, and in these circumstances a problem broke at Hazelton, in 1888.

The "rebellion" or "Skeena War," as it is sometimes called, was neither unannounced nor unexpected. In 1873, the lieutenant-governor of British Columbia, Trutch, and the Attorney General, J.F. McCreight, visited the Skeena in H.M.S. *Scout* in August 1873 in order to appease outraged Kitsegukla Indians. In 1884, government was well aware of the possibility of rebellion on the Skeena. Time and again, magistrates and naval officers warned of such a possibility. The Navy wearied of "acting as policeman," and Lords of the Admiralty waited longingly for Canada and British Columbia to exercise their own maritime influence on the Northwest Coast. If Port Simpson were in danger, the Lords of the Admiralty told the Colonial Office (for Canadian consumption), then the Dominion government should garrison the place and make it safe against Indian assault. As to charges from the British Columbia government that Port Simpson stood unprotected from Indian assault, and that Victoria was obliged to request support from a United States revenue vessel the *Oliver Wolcott*, Their Lordships were quick to point out that the request from local authorities lacked specific details as to the nature of the impending attack and the assailants.[48] Ministers of the Crown in Whitehall perceptively understood that the province and Canada wanted the Navy's shield. In response to earlier troubles, governmental inquiries into Indian affairs had been made—in 1878, again in 1883, and once again in 1887. In the last two instances, the commissioners had recommended the appointment of an Indian agent for the Skeena. In 1887 the North West Coast Agency was established at Metlakatla under Charles Todd.[49] But for the interim the Upper Skeena had no resident agent, no "man on the spot"—to advise or to mediate.

To this date warships had seldom if ever been above the Skeena River mouth, which was unsurveyed and unmarked. The Navy's attention had been confined to Metlakatla and to the coast. But in 1888 the threat of "insurrection" on the Skeena brought H.M.S. *Caroline*, Captain Sir William Wiseman, a good distance upriver to Port Essington, and there to conduct gunboat diplomacy in the characteristic fashion.

To the authorities the pattern of stimulus and response was by now altogether familiar. News of a rather wild and desperate sort reached Victoria that there was a native uprising on the Skeena. The particulars appeared to be that hostile, well-armed Indians had killed a constable and were "closely investing," or laying siege to, the Hudson's Bay Company post at Hazelton. The Lieutenant-Governor of British Columbia, The Hon. Hugh Nelson, appealed passionately to Wiseman, the senior naval officer at Esquimalt, to take Canadian militia to the Skeena River to quell the rising. Carefully weighing the merits of the case on the basis of the scanty evidence available, Wiseman concluded that the cause was just and that lives were in danger, and he informed the Admiralty that he would provide aid. To the lieutenant-governor he said that he could not remain absent from Esquimalt indefinitely and he regretted that the Canadian government could not supply the requisite transport. In fact, as he knew, Hazelton was so far inland from the coast that a warship would be of "no active assistance" whatsoever.[50] It is of interest to note that the Colonial Office knew little about the matter until so informed by the Secretary of the Admiralty. Indeed, the Colonial Office wrongly thought the problem might have "to do with the old Metlakatla troubles."[51]

In Victoria, meanwhile, the Dominion's Indian Superintendent, Dr. Powell, refused to be dragged into the quarrel. To his way of thinking the Skeena business was a matter for the provincial Department of Justice, and that law must be exercised by authorities, not Indian agents. It was a fine point, and a correct one too. So, although the premier and attorney-general of the province, Alex Davie, appealed for Powell to go to Skeena where he would be, in Davie's words "first authority," Powell declined to be involved, and even cautioned his deputy, Charles Todd, to exercise the most careful discretion so that Indian Affairs was not misrepresented as the Provincial Police or the Canadian Militia.[52] In any event on 16 July the *Caroline* left Esquimalt with a contingent of eighty officers and men of "C" battery, Royal Garrison Artillery, under Colonel Holmes, and a party of twelve police under Superintendent of Provincial Police, H.W. Roycraft, for Port Essington. Every man was equipped with a 50-pound pack, a 45 calibre Martini-Henry rifle, 40 rounds of ammunition, and a bush knife. Sent ahead with ten tons of food and 18,000 rounds of ammunition was the supply ship *Barbara Boscowitz*. It was estimated it would take three weeks to quell the rising, and to report on the event the Victoria *Colonist* sent a "war correspondent."[53]

At Port Essington, Robert Cunningham provided details about developments at Hazelton. The child of Kitwancool Jim or Kamalmuk, a Hazelton chief, had died. Encouraged by his wife, Sunbeam, Kitwancool Jim had shot a medicine man, Neetuh, in retaliation. Four police were sent to arrest Kitwancool Jim but he escaped and was shot dead by a constable by the name of Green. The local Indians were indignant and took up arms. Whites in the area had scurried to refuge in the hastily fortified Hazelton HBC post awaiting relief. To this information was added the advice of a part native Methodist minister, The Reverend William Henry Pierce, who told Wiseman not to send a force to secure Kitwancool Jim: a special constable would do just as well![54] Thus only additional police were sent from the *Caroline* to investigate and to bring this turmoil to a peaceful conclusion. The fault, the serving magistrate, Captain Fitzstubbs concluded, was Green's: he had killed Kitwancool Jim when he had only intended to wound him. In Powell's view the constable's killing of Kitwancool Jim was "a great blunder."[55]

Even at Port Essington where the *Caroline* lay peacefully, the imperial presence was being established, the imperial authority being exercised. This was the first time a gunboat had come so far upriver. Cunningham was glad of the security afforded to the community and his interests by the vessel. In his opinion, the ship's presence made a great impression on the Indians, "most of whom had never seen a man-of-war before" and were decidedly of the opinion that "they were out of reach of one." To many of the Indians the ship was a curiosity, and they took particular interest in the machine guns, fired and on display for their edification and amusement.[56] One night the ship's search light was thrown on the settlement, and was "a great source of alarm to them," Wiseman recorded. Meanwhile, the Royal Garrison Artillery set up camp at Soldier's Point and made preparation for a field expedition. It was all part of exercising power and extending the frontier.

The judge, Captain Napoleon Fitzstubbs, a twenty-year veteran in the Police, now took law to the frontier. He went to the various villages of the upper Skeena, including Kitwancool, and he told assembled chiefs that British, not Indian, law must prevail. At these meetings news was presented that the chief of the Gitanmaax, Gethumuldoe, had during the winter held consultations with other Indians as to whether or not the whites should be exterminated. But at these meetings, plans to mount a massacre were ended when an old chief pointed out the folly of killing men from whom the Indians got food and clothing. Again the economic realities of the transition attendant with settlement, colonization and trade underscored Indian responses.[57]

From these peoples the authorities clearly grasped the Indian complaint. The Indians asserted that their law and not that of the government was to be administered. They acted with haughty demeanor in a manner so hostile that the authorities considered that armed force was necessary. The Indians, the authorities attested, would submit under force. Indeed, as the official report on the Skeena affair noted, before the *Caroline* arrived at Port Essington with the militia and special investigators were sent upriver to Hazelton, the Indians were threatening. Afterwards, "a complete change came over them." To conclude the affair, all the chiefs, thirteen in number, were assembled at Hazelton on 8 August, and Police Superintendent Roycraft took pains to detail the new legalities under which the natives would be obliged to live, whether they wished to or not. In asking them to abide by British law he said, "I must ask you to remember that before you came under the British law one tribe was always in danger of being massacred by some other tribe and that there was continual warfare between all the tribes: slaves were taken: but now you all live in peace and quietness because of the Queen's care."[58] The chiefs promised obedience, and the party returned downriver, the intemperate and careless Constable Green their prisoner.[59] The *Caroline* steamed to Esquimalt with the militia, the officers in charge thoroughly pleased with the results of this display of power, which was defrayed by the public purse in the amount of $65,000.

In 1890 the Upper Skeena or Babine Agency was established with head-quarters at Hazelton. Yet here and elsewhere along the Skeena, Indians remained apprehensive about the role of agents, and the Kitwancool band adamantly refused to give any details to government about their reserve requirements.[60] Nor would they allow any land to be surveyed for a reserve for them: that would have been tantamount to acquiescence. Government's need to survey lands for the Grand Trunk Pacific Railway and for settlement in the Skeena Valley, led to increased resistance by peoples such as the remote and aloof Kitwancool, who remained solidly opposed to any governmental "progress" as long as the question of title remained unresolved. Like the Nishga, the Kitwancool insisted that they had never been party to any relinquishment of their land rights. They were prepared to back this insistence with force if necessary. As late as 1927 a detachment of Royal Canadian Mounted Police established local headquarters at Kitwanga in order to institute proceedings against the nearby Kitwancool who had obstructed government surveyors. No wonder even today the white stranger walking in this village inspecting totem poles and tomb stones meets a stoney silence that in itself speaks volumes. And to this day these people cling tenaciously to their hereditary rights.

The "Skeena war," like the Nass River penetration and intimidation by H.M.S. *Forward* or the Kimsquit destruction by H.M.S. *Rocket,* were all part of a gunboat frontier. The Navy constituted the cutting edge of an imperial instrument dedicated to establishing the rule of law on behalf of the British Empire, Canada and British Columbia. At the Lower Nass villages, Kimsquit and Port Essington, and even upriver at distant Hazelton, the imperial tide had risen quickly to lap against these settlements as, at other times, it had at so many other places on the Northwest Coast.

Meanwhile in England, Oscar Wilde was writing pensively:

> Set in this stormy Northern sea,
> Queen of these restless fields of tide
> England! what shall men say of thee,
> Before whose feet the worlds divide?

And England had reason to pause, for the Empire was an English product which changed England itself. These little wars of the frontier, these parades of power—countless in number, puzzlingly insignificant in the amalgam but vitally illuminating in their individual particularities of character, circumstance and place—were episodes of Empire whose legacies of distrust and regret linger where Northwest Coast peoples gather still.

14

Retrospect

AFTER 1890 SHIPS of the Royal Navy were never again obliged to take punitive action against Indians for piracies, thefts, or murders, and they no longer intervened by force in tribal or intertribal quarrels. Their role on the Northwest Coast was more peaceful than at any time since their predecessors began calling in Puget Sound and Vancouver Island in the mid 1840's in support of British interests.

What accounts for the end of retributive action? Why were there no more of these "savage wars of peace," as Rudyard Kipling called them?

The answer to these questions cannot be found in the simple statement that the Navy had established a Britannic peace. Yet it can be said that the Navy contributed to the imperial process whereby a peace was established on the Northwest Coast. Gunboats were the symbols of Empire and of the colonial governments in Victoria and New Westminster and of their provincial and Canadian successors after 1871. They were the armed might of the fragile system of magistrates and police superintendents that were extending English law on this populous Indian frontier. Their work was continued by agents, magistrates, militia and police.

The young naval commanders and lieutenants who did the bulk of the work were, in fact, bona fide justices of the peace. They were, more than anything else in that time and place, amphibious policemen pursuing policies of minimum intervention and acting in the awkward and inexperienced role of sailor-diplomats. Seldom, if ever, did they act on their own initiative. Rather, responding to requests of civil authority, they would arrive on the scene to make a show of force and, thereafter, would exact justice by peaceful means if possible and by violent measures if necessary. They attempted also to check a nefarious liquor traffic. They helped stamp out slavery by stopping intertribal marauding. They assisted missionaries, protected shipping, secured settlers, and, in general, preserved law and order where and when they could. They were, in short, servants of an imperial cause, guardians of a British peace, and, in their own, reluctant way, pathfinders of empire.

Paradoxically, their methods sometimes had to be warlike. Their strategy was to force the Indian tribes to deal with the white man on the white man's terms. They focused their attention on the chiefs whom they would convince or compel to abide by the new rule of law. They developed military tactics which were semi-aboriginal. The policy of retributive justice prevailed—at Newitty, Kuper Island, Ahousat, and Kimsquit, to cite but four cases. Such a policy was intended to teach the Indians a lasting lesson and to remind them that the Crown had superior force at its disposal. This was called "keeping the Indians in awe" of British power. It reflected a British appreciation of the warlike characteristics and the fighting capabilities of the native peoples. The ultimate arbiter of empire is the power wielded by the ruler, and in this particular case the British held the upper hand with their gunboats. They provided the technological advantage, the seaborne variant of Hilaire Belloc's:

> Whatever happens we have got
> The Maxim gun, and they have not.

A gun-carrying steamer, as a veteran of the Burma River wars, Colonel W.F.B. Laurie of the Royal Marines, said, was a powerful " 'political persuader,' with fearful instruments of speech, in an age of progress! "[1]

If the gunboat was a precise instrument of Empire in certain instances it was not without it's limitations in others. The effectiveness of well-drilled crews and naval weaponry that a gunboat commander had at his disposal had obvious limits. Indian resistance was strong and competent. The influence of one of Her Majesty's ships spread no farther inland from salt water or river fairway than the range of shot, shell or rocket; it penetrated no deeper than the endurance of foot-sore landing parties slogging through wet bush.

Gunboat diplomacy could be foiled by the skill of the Indians and their knowledge of terrain. Chapchah of Clayoquot escaped capture and trial, as did the Hesquiat chief Matlahaw, Father Brabant's attempted murderer. Acheewun of the Lemalchi forced the Navy to frustrating limits before he was flushed out of his Galiano mountain hideaway. Sometimes the Navy possessed insufficient evidence to act against suspects, as in the case of the great Haida chief Edenshaw during the *Susan Sturgis* affair. Men like Admirals Moresby and Denman, Captains Prevost and Pike,

Lieutenants Verney and Lascelles acquired a healthy respect for Indian abilities to evade capture. In many cases the forests and mountains provided all the cover that the Indians required.

For the men who made and carried out the decisions, this type of forest diplomacy must have been distasteful. All too frequently naval officers have been classified among what the distinguished jurist and parliamentarian Sir William Harcourt called "the warlike classes," that is, armed agents of empire bullying their way in scrapes with natives and extending British domains in distant places. With few exceptions they were Victorian men of conscience, and some experienced officers like Fairfax Moresby and Joseph Denman could be both high-handed and high-minded. "These wretched creatures," a ship's captain wrote plaintively of his punitive expedition in the Pacific Islands, "have been hunted and worried till it will be long before they settle again . . . I regret that my whole voyage in these islands has been one of apparently ruthless destruction, but no other course has been possible."[2] Another, John Moresby, wrote his memoirs some years after the 1853 Cowichan expedition and recalled that as a young gunnery lieutenant the excitement of the event served to suppress any twinge of conscience. Only later did he realize the meaning of the barbarities that he was undertaking for Queen and Country. The expedition was, he wrote, "one of the myriad tragedies of the red man's collision with civilization."[3]

"Send a gunboat!" had become a common cry on the Northwest Coast and almost everywhere where British overseas interests were threatened in one way or another. The Foreign Office might ask the Board of Admiralty to browbeat the Manchus or suppress Malay pirates. The Colonial Office might badger Their Lordships to help a governor or consul in a tight scrape with a foreign foe or an internal enemy. The Archbishop of Canterbury might request aid for a missionary in trouble in Borneo. The British Museum might appeal for protection for harried archeologists in North Africa. In the same year Their Lordships received Governor Douglas's request for more ships of war to reinforce besieged British authority during the Fraser River gold rush, secretaries at the Admiralty had to deal with a flood of correspondence dealing with other requests, all of them granted, from New Zealand, Panama, Kuria Muria Islands, Honduras, Siam, Brazil, Sarawak, Alexandria, Vera Cruz, Morocco, and Newfoundland. Such demands seemed incessant, a Foreign Office secretary complained. British agents of empire liked the sense of security supplied by the white ensign. Even in places where no treaty ties bound native to national interests, "claims of humanity" obliged the British to yield assistance.[4]

These demands for "showing the flag," putting down rebellions, or intimidating natives meant continual drains on the Treasury in spite of

RETROSPECT

213

parliamentary objections. In 1871, for instance, half of the naval expenditures went for policing the seas. If economies were to be affected, said the penny-pinching Mr. G.J. Goschen, M.P., First Lord of the Admiralty during Gladstone's 1868 administration, overseas squadrons would have to be reduced and fewer duties undertaken for humanity in every corner of the earth. "The fact is," he groaned, "that half of our expenditure is not for war service in the strict sense, but keeping the policy of the seas and protecting semi-barbarous and barbarous men against kidnapping and various forms of outrage. Philanthropy decidedly costs money."[5] Not least among the results of gunboat diplomacy was the effect on the morale of the service itself, for this was not war with a capital "W" but the day to day work of "a World Police Force."[6] As the century came to an end, the Admiralty was already bound on a course of replacing its *Kingfishers* and *Ringdoves, Sparrowhawks* and *Pheasants* with capital ships and cruisers more appropriate to meeting the military threat of rival nations closer to home. The time had arrived, the foreign secretary said in 1893, when the British could not "afford to be the Knight Errant of the World, careering about to address grievances and help the weak."[7] In actuality and of necessity, the British were obliged to cling to the practice of gunboat diplomacy almost as long as the Empire continued and used warships as shows of force against recalcitrant Pacific islanders as late as the 1940's.[8] The principle of these operations remained the same; enforce law and order through the threatened use of legalized state violence.[9]

For most of the nineteenth century, Britons, with their abiding faith in law, their unending quest for freedom of the seas and free trade, and their passionate concern for spreading Christianity and civilization as they knew it, had not shied away from their colonial responsibilities no matter how remote from the home islands. Without much success parliamentarians in Westminster had tried to shift the burdens of local naval and military defence to the colonial governments. More often than not colonial politicians had avoided the issue of responsibility by pleading financial insolvency as was the case with the colonies of Vancouver Island and British Columbia. Even British Columbia's entry into Canadian Confederation in 1871 had brought no change in the dogged dependence of British Columbia and Canada on British naval strength. Secure behind the mighty shield of the world's premier naval service, Canadian governments were hardly moved to undertake security measures of their own. Thus, from the days of the Hudson's Bay Company monopoly and of the settlement of Vancouver Island and British Columbia, the Royal Navy provided a continual presence and security, uninterrupted by the several political and constitutional changes that took the area from Indian lands to Canadian province. Apart from paying for a few bunkers full of coal, such a service cost the local taxpayer not one penny.[10]

In the interim, however, Indian policy had changed. Its origins in Hudson's Bay Company treatment of Indians—of intervention only when natives interfered with whites—grew into an unwritten policy for the colony of Vancouver Island, as the instances of Fort Rupert and Cowichan reveal. But the growth of settlement meant that calls came from Saltspring, Comox, and elsewhere for gunboat protection. And, since these little beachheads of civilization had to be protected against the depredations of "savages," ministers in Whitehall delegated responsibility to the Crown's local representative to conduct operations and reprisals as he saw fit. At the same time, both the Colonial Office and the Admiralty monitored abuses of power by reading respectively the regular despatches from the colonial capitals and Pacific Station headquarters. When abuses occurred, they issued stern admonitions to governors or commanders that their actions were out of keeping with metropolitan intentions.

On the other hand, London fortunately found in James Douglas a willing supporter of a firm and paternalistic Indian policy. His advice on tactics and conduct that the Navy should employ in these seaborne cases of forest diplomacy became standard practice. His predecessor, Blanshard, and his successors, Kennedy, Musgrave, and Seymour, lacked his experience with Indians. Nonetheless, they employed gunboat diplomacy. Perhaps they were less skilled practitioners of an Indian policy that after 1871 became Ottawa's responsibility. The young Dominion had no experience in the treatment of Indians west of the Rockies and scant interest in heeding the province's pleas for a suitable policy for British Columbia Indians. Governor Douglas's noble intention of 1861 for financially compensating Indians for loss of title[11] has been avoided by a long succession of colonial, provincial, and dominion governments. The Indians' several concerted attempts to bring their grievances to court were continually thwarted by the inconsistencies of the very laws to which they had voluntarily entrusted themselves. They saw governments and white men breaking promises made to them on various occasions such as the Royal Navy's great tour to Indian villages in 1860.

In spite of these shifts and changes the Indians had made advances in accommodating themselves to the new order of things. Those who resisted the new imperium and who are the subject of the gunboat actions described in these pages were few in number and the small minority of natives. Most adjusted to English law both quickly and readily, and in some cases were aided by missionaries who promised the kingdom of heaven and the freedom of the individual. Some offered resistance. The Cowichan chief Techamalt, in complaining of white abuses against Indian property, defiantly boasted that if Governor Seymour sent a gunboat, he would "fetch his friends from all parts, and hold the lands

against him."[12] However, a general Indian rising never occurred at Cowichan Bay. Nor did it happen elsewhere. A gathering of war canoes at
some convenient spot along the coast lay beyond the realm of possibility.
This was not because the Indians had no claims to injustice, and not because they could not paddle or sail there, but because, as the Indian commissioner Powell put it in 1874, they were insufficiently united. Indian
strength and morale was also greatly reduced by disease and alcohol.[13]
Divided by lineage and language, geography, and rivalry, the various
tribes responded to the growing authority of government in their several
separate ways. The Indians, the Haida Methodist minister Peter Kelly
rightly boasted, had been "a law unto themselves."[14] But as the nineteenth century wore on, their old codes of conduct gave way to a new
legal system brought to them by police, magistrates, agents, and gunboats, to a new economic order, and to an evangelical Christian mission
movement. The corresponding damage to native morale may be imagined. Injustices in the management of reserves further deepened Indian
discontent and resentment about white exploitation of aboriginal land
without compensation.

Now only the last fragments remain of an Indian culture that existed at
many places along the Northwest Coast at the time of the white man's
coming two centuries ago. Approaching Ninstints or Skedans in the
Queen Charlotte Islands the seafarer sees but sad remnants of Haida
poles, cracked and bleached by wind and weather, carrying their secrets
across the years. Old mortuary and memorial poles totter at drunken
angles, proudly resisting the inevitable. Others have succumbed and lie
rotting on the ground. Their ranks are not filled. Moss covers the great
beams and house posts. The brooding forest has all but reclaimed the
land. Great canoes no longer line the beaches. The once secure lords of
the coast have vanished in the imperial process by which whites attempted to remake the New World in the image of the Old.

Appendix I

Governors of Vancouver Island and British Columbia, 1849–1871

COLONY OF VANCOUVER ISLAND
1849–1866

Blanshard, Richard
Governor, 1849–51   Sworn in   March 11, 1850

Douglas, James
Governor, 1851–64   Commissioned   May 16, 1851

Lieutenant-Governor,   Commissioned   July 29, 1852
Queen Charlotte Islands

Kennedy, Arthur Edward
Governor, 1864–66   Sworn in   March 26, 1864

CROWN COLONY OF BRITISH COLUMBIA
1858–1866

Douglas, James
Governor, 1858–64   Sworn in   November 19, 1858

Moody, Col. Richard Clement
Lieutenant-Governor   Commissioned   September 21, 1858

Seymour, Frederick
Governor, 1864–66   Sworn in   April 21, 1864

UNITED COLONY OF BRITISH COLUMBIA
1866–1871

Seymour, Frederick
Governor, 1866–69   Commissioned   October 24, 1866

Musgrave, Anthony
Lieutenant-Governor, 1869   Sworn in   August 23, 1869

Musgrave, Anthony
Governor, 1869–71   Sworn in   January 10, 1870

Appendix II

Statutory Provisions on Liquor Relating to British Columbia Indians, 1850–1876

The first statutory and regulatory provision of the government of the Colony of Vancouver Island provided for controls over the importation and sale of spirituous liquors. This enactment, The Proclamation of 13 May 1850 (found in GR 771, P.A.B.C.), applied equally to natives and whites. The preamble to this proclamation, written by Governor Richard Blanshard, specifies the rationale of the measure: "the free and unrestricted traffic in spirituous liquors has caused and does still cause great damage and inconvenience to the Inhabitants of Her Majesty's Colony of Vancouvers Island, by debauching and corrupting the population, both native and Immigrant." The proclamation provided regulations for specified volumes and sale of imported liquors. It also established penalties for unlawful offences. The intention was to prevent smuggling and lessen social evils attendant on such illegal importations.

Some indication of Governor Blanshard's concern respecting liquor consumption is given in his letter to the secretary of state for war and the colonies, Earl Grey, 10 July 1850 (*Vancouver Island Dispatches,* p. 3), reporting among other things riotous conduct by miners and labourers at Fort Rupert which might lead to serious consequences with the "numerous, savage, and treacherous" Indian population. "I would strongly recommend," he wrote, "a duty be imposed on the importation and manufacture of ardent spirits, as their introduction tends to demoralize the Indians to a most dangerous degree." Blanshard held that he had no power to impose such a duty, as free trade had been proclaimed in the colony, and he requested Grey's early advice on the matter. No further references to liquor are given in Blanshard's subsequent dispatches. Grey did not consider the matter further, but the proclamation remained in effect.

Periodically during the colonial period of Vancouver Island and British Columbia history the provisions of Blanshard's liquor proclamation were strengthened. Gradually, however, the legislation became discriminatory — that is, it differentiated between Indians and whites. Whatever the merits of the case, by the mid-1850s, it was widely accepted in official circles in the colony that the gift, barter, or sale of spirituous liquors to native peoples was damaging to the Indians themselves and dangerous to the security of settlers.

On 3 August 1854 the Council of the Colony of Vancouver Island approved legislation laid before the Council by Governor James Douglas "prohibiting the Gift or Sale of Spirituous Liquors to Indians" (C.O. 306/1, Vancouver Island Acts, pp. 27–8; *Minutes of the Council of Vancouver Island, 1851–61*, Victoria: Archives of British Columbia Memoir No. 2 [1918], p. 25). This legislation, introduced for the peace, order and security of the colony, included a terse rationale: "many complaints had been made of excesses committed by drunken Indians, which could not otherwise be checked without endangering the peace of the Colony." This enactment was strengthened by "An Act for better prohibiting the Sale or Gift of Intoxicating Liquors to the Indians, 2 November 1860," or more commonly, the Vancouver Island *Indian Liquor Act, 1860* (C.O. 306/1, p. 77).

An attempt to legalize the sale of liquor to Indians in 1861 was led by Attorney-General George H. Cary on the grounds that it had "been found that any attempt to check the sale of liquor was useless" (*British Colonist,* 6 August 1861). In 1866 another attempt was undertaken in the Vancouver Island Legislative Assembly, but it was defeated. Making legal the sale of liquor to natives, Governor Arthur Kennedy wrote to the secretary of state for the colonies, would have allowed the natives to "execute their own laws, that is, to murder each other without let or hindrance when inflamed by drink" (Kennedy to E. Cardwell, 24 January, 13 February, and 21 March 1866, C.O. 880/5, no. 37).

Meanwhile, as in the Colony of Vancouver Island, the earliest proclamation of James Douglas, issued two months before he formally became governor of the Crown Colony of British Columbia, was an order relating to intoxicating liquors. Dated 6 September 1858 and issued at Fort Hope, the "Proclamation respecting Sale or Gift of Intoxicating Liquor to Indians" had the standard provisions. Its preamble recited the rationale: "It has been represented to me that spirituous and other intoxicating liquors have been sold to the Native Indians of Fraser River and elsewhere, to the great injury and demoralization of the said Indians: and also thereby endangering to the Public Peace, and the lives and property of Her Majesty's subjects and others in the said Districts" (Proclamation of 6 September 1858, P.A.B.C.; also H. Merivale to Admiralty, 26 January 1859, Adm. 1/5721). The proclamation announced that the sale or gift of such liquors was contrary to law, strictly prohibited, and punishable, on conviction, by a fine of a minimum of £5 and a maximum of £20. This statutory provision was based on the dual purpose of such measures: protection of natives and preservation of peace and order. It served as the basis of the tougher *Indian Liquor Ordinance, 1865* (C.O. 61/1, British Columbia Acts and Ordinances, pp. 183–4).

In 1867 the liquor regulations of Vancouver Island and British Columbia were repealed and redefined. After the union of the two colonies in 1866, it was expedient to consolidate the previous laws of the separate jurisdictions and to amend them. The Vancouver Island *Indian Liquor Act, 1860* and the British Columbia *Indian Liquor Ordinance, 1865* were repealed. The new ordinance, No. 85 and effective 2 April 1867, was entitled "An Ordinance to assimilate and amend the Law prohibiting the sale or gift of Intoxicating Liquor to Indians" (C.O. 61/1, pp. 266–7; also *Laws of British Columbia* [Victoria, 1871], pp. 249–53). It imposed a penalty of $500 for selling liquor to Indians. Persons found in Indian dwellings with liquor were, upon conviction, punishable: they were liable to a fine not exceeding the same amount and imprisonment not exceeding six months. A second offence could bring twelve months' imprisonment with hard labour. Offenders under age sixteen could be privately whipped. Licensed wholesale or retail vendors infringing this ordinance were liable to forfeiture of their licences. They were to be denied a new licence for two years from date of conviction.

Unlike previous ordinances, the 1867 ordinance established rights of search and details of manifests of lading. Vessels on the coast, lakes, rivers, or streams were to be confiscated if it were proven before a magistrate that they were guilty of carrying intoxicating liquors to Indians. One-third of any pecuniary penalty was to go to the informer. Customs officers, police inspectors, government agents specifically commissioned, and Royal Navy officers on full pay possessed full power to search for liquor on ships, boats, canoes, and other vessels. They could, "upon reasonable ground" in suspected cases, detain and seize such shipping, bringing the vessel to a colonial port for further investigation and adjudication. Masters of ships possessing liquors not adequately accounted for would be required to forfeit the cargo and pay a penalty not exceeding $1,000. All coasting vessels bound for ports to any part of the colony's coast or to any place on the coast of Alaska had first to make a declaration of cargo and possess a customs officer's permit to carry such liquors. Penalties of up to $500 for obstructing the law were provided for by the ordinance. The fines and penalties applied to males and females, to one person or to a party, and to corporate bodies as well as individuals. However, the authorized prescription of liquor to Indians for medicinal use was allowed.

Under the Terms of Union of the United Colony of British Columbia and the Dominion of Canada, effective 20 July 1871, federal authority over Indians and lands reserved for Indians was established. Provincial regulation against Indian liquor consumption and trading in spirituous liquors was superseded by section 12 of the *Act providing for the organization of the Secretary of State of Canada, and for the management of Indian and Ordnance Lands* (Statutes of Canada, 31 Vict., chap. 42, 1868). This legislation specified that:

> No person shall sell, barter, exchange or give to any Indian man, woman or child in Canada, any kind of spirituous liquors, in any manner or way, or cause or procure the same to be done for any purpose whatsoever;—and if any person so sells, barters, exchanges or gives any such spirituous liquors to any Indian man, woman or child as aforesaid, or causes the same to be done, he shall on conviction thereof, before any Justice of the Peace upon the evidence of one credible witness, other than the informer or prosecutor, be fined not exceeding twenty dollars for each such offence, one moiety to go to the informer or prosecutor, and the other moiety to Her Majesty to form part of the fund for the benefit of that tribe, band or body of Indians with respect to one or more members of which the offence was committed; but no such penalty shall be incurred by furnishing to any Indian in case of sickness, any spirituous liquor, either by a medical man or under the direction of a medical man or clergyman.

Modifications to these provisions were made in *An Act to Amend Certain Laws Respecting Indians, and to Extend Certain Laws Relating to Matters Connected with Indians to the Provinces of Manitoba and British Columbia, 1874* (Statutes of Canada, 37 Vict., chap. 21) and in section 79 of *The Indian Act, 1876* (Statutes of Canada, 39 Vict., chap. 42).

The above statutory and regulatory provisions—dating from 1850 and continuing after 1876—show a clear continuity of executive authority. Such proclamations, ordinances, and statutes were based on executive and legislative assumptions about what was best for society, whether under British colonial or, after 1871, Canadian authority. These provisions remained until 1956 when under revisions to the Indian Act (Statutes of Canada, 4–5 Eliz.II, chap. 40), two major changes occurred: firstly, provincial legislation was made operative allowing Indians to purchase and possess intoxicants, and, secondly, local option was possible "with the wishes of the band" and under which, in 1964, new regulations were first proclaimed in force on 11 British Columbia reserves (*Canada Gazette,* Part 1, 27 June 1964, p. 1892; also *The Canada Statute Citator* (Agincourt, Ontario: Canada Law Book Co., 1971, p. 90–12a).

Abbreviations

Adm.	Admiralty Papers, P.R.O.
B.L.B.	Bancroft Library, Berkeley, California
B.L.	British Library, London
C.M.S.A.	Church Missionary Society Archives, London
C.O.	Colonial Office Papers, P.R.O.
F.O.	Foreign Office Papers, P.R.O.
H.B.C.A.	Hudson's Bay Company Archives, Winnipeg
M.M.B.C.	Maritime Museum of British Columbia, Victoria
N.M.M.	National Maritime Museum, Greenwich
P.A.B.C.	Provincial Archives of British Columbia, Victoria
P.A.C.	Public Archives of Canada, Ottawa
P.R.O.	Public Record Office, London

Notes

NOTES TO CHAPTER ONE: DWELLERS ALONG THE SHORE

1. Great Britain, Admiralty, *Vancouver Island Pilot*, pt. 1 (London, 1861) [comp. George Henry Richards, R.N.], p. 3. These population figures are from Wilson Duff, *The Indian History of British Columbia. Vol. 1: The Impact of the White Man* (Victoria, B.C.: Provincial Museum, Anthropology in British Columbia Memoir, 1964), ch. 2. See also, Herbert C. Taylor, Jr., "Aboriginal Populations of the Lower Northwest Coast," *Pacific Northwest Quarterly* 54 (1963): 158–65.

2. Instructions to James Cook, 30 July 1768, are in the Public Record Office, London, Admiralty Papers, Adm. 2/1332, pp. 160ff.; those for 6 July 1776 are in ibid., pp. 284–96.

3. This armament was later reduced in the case of the *Forward* in 1869 to four 24-pounders, making her not therefore a fighting vessel of the original description (Rear-Adm. G. F. Hastings to Sec. of the Admiralty, 7 and 27 May and 6 August 1868, Adm. 1/6056).

4. But even the *Clio,* 400 horsepower, sent in 1865 to northern British Columbia waters, had a difficult voyage, causing the commander-in-chief to note that it was evident that a ship needed "great steam power and hardiness" for the navigation of the treacherous, open waters north of Vancouver Island (Rear-Adm. the Hon. Joseph Denman to Sec. of the Admiralty, 27 November 1865, Adm. 1/5924).

5. John C. Beaglehole, ed., *The Journals of Captain James Cook on His Voyages of Discovery, Vol. 3: The Voyage of the* Resolution *and* Discovery, *1776–1780,* 2 pts. (Cambridge: Hakluyt Society, extra ser. no. 36, 1967), pt. 1, pp. 297–99, 306.

6. Ibid., p. 306.

7. Numerous are the cases of trade in which no violence occurred, of course, but there was an undeniable pattern of violence. In-depth, systematic investigations of these incidents would reveal a great deal. An example of this type of useful inquiry is Jean Brathwaite and W.J. Folan, "The Taking of the ship *Boston*: An ethnohistoric Study of Nootkan-European Con-

flict," *Syesis,* 5 (1972): 259–77.

8. On one occasion, in 1811, John Jacob Astor's vessel, the *Tonquin,* trading at Clayoquot, was boarded by several hundred armed Indians. Twenty-three traders and two hundred Indians died in the affair when the ship's magazine blew up and the ship sank. The dispute developed over prices, the captain's impatience, insults, and provocation (Edmund Hayes, "A Search for the *Tonquin"* [unpublished manuscript, 1973]; Gabriel Franchère, *Journal of a Voyage on the North West Coast of North America During the Years 1811, 1812, 1813 and 1814,* ed. W. Kaye Lamb [Toronto: Champlain Society, 1969], pp. 123–28).

9. Quoted in F. W. Howay, "Indian Attacks Upon Maritime Traders of the Northwest Coast, 1785–1805," *Canadian Historical Review* 6 (1935): 305. See also S. W. Jackman, ed., *The Journal of William Sturgis* (Victoria: Sono Nis Press, 1978), p. 15.

10. Lord Grenville to Admiralty, 11 February 1791, in *Report of the Provincial Archives. . . 1913* (Victoria, 1914), p. V47.

11. George Vancouver, *Voyage to the North Pacific Ocean,* 3 vols. (London, 1796), 3: 306–7; Edmond S. Meany, ed., *Vancouver's Discovery of Puget Sound* (Portland, Ore: Binfords & Mort, 1957), p. 162; and Alexander Begg, *History of British Columbia From its Earliest Discovery to the Present Time* (Toronto: William Briggs, 1894), p. 82.

12. *Physician and Fur Trader: The Journals of William Fraser Tolmie* (Vancouver: Mitchell Press, 1963), p. 175.

13. F. W. Howay, "A List of Trading Vessels in the Maritime Fur Trade, 1820–1825," *Transactions of the Royal Society of Canada,* 3d ser., section 2 (1934): 12.

14. See Barry M. Gough, *Distant Dominion: Britain and the Northwest Coast of North America, 1579–1809* (Vancouver: University of British Columbia Press, 1980).

15. When Dr. John Helmcken recounted to Captain George Wellesley of H.M.S. *Daedalus* how he had demanded that the Newitty should surrender the murderers of three English seamen in 1850 "in the name of King George," Wellesley attempted to correct him. "King George? Why, he has long been dead. You should have demanded them in the name of Her Majesty the Queen." "Oh," replied Helmcken, "these fellows know nothing about King William or Queen Victoria; King George is still the great chief in these regions, and we are all King George men and the *Daedalus* King George's ship" (John T. Walbran, *British Columbia Coast Names 1592–1906* [1909; reprint ed., Vancouver: J. J. Douglas, 1971], p. 128). The anomalous association remained at least until the late nineteenth century.

16. Francis Ermatinger, "Notes Connected with Clallum Expedition," transcript, Special Collections, University of British Columbia Library; E.E. Rich, *The History of the Hudson's Bay Company, 1670–1870,* 2 vols. (London: Hudson's Bay Record Society, 1958, 1959), 2: 623, 641; Walbran, *British Columbia Place Names,* pp. 40–41.

17. Joseph Needham calls this West-

ern European characteristic (a view shared by European America) "spiritual pride." In his *Within the Four Seas: The Dialogue of East and West* (London: George Allen and Unwin Ltd., 1969), pp. 11 ff. he analyses how this preconception was not limited to law and order but extended to politics, institutions and technology.

18. W. Ross Johnston, *Sovereignty and Protection: A Study of British Jurisdictionalism in the Late Nineteenth Century* (Durham, N.C.: Duke University Press, 1973), ch. 1.

19. Quoted in ibid., p. 15.

20. Quoted in ibid., p. 15.

21. John S. Galbraith, *Hudson's Bay Company as an Imperial Factor, 1821–1869* (Berkeley and Los Angeles: University of California Press, 1957), p. 340.

22. David T. McNab, "Herman Merivale and Colonial Office Indian Policy in the Mid-Nineteenth Century," *Canadian Journal of Native Studies,* 1, (1981):281.

23. One accounting lists 230 "little wars" of the good queen's reign exclusive of major and minor naval confrontations (Bryon Farwell, *Queen Victoria's Little Wars* [London: Allen Lane, 1973], pp. 364–71). See also, John Cell, "The Imperial Conscience," in Peter Marsh, ed., *The Conscience of the Victorian State* (Syracuse: Syracuse University Press, 1979), pp. 173–79.

24. Quoted in James Morris, *Heaven's Command: An Imperial Progress* (New York: Harcourt Brace Jovanovich, 1973), p. 86.

NOTES TO CHAPTER TWO: TIDE OF EMPIRE

1. John Moresby, *Two Admirals: Admiral of the Fleet Sir Fairfax Moresby (1787–1877) and His Son, John Moresby,* new and rev. ed. (London: 1913), pp. 102–3.

2. Governor George Simpson, "Character Book, 1832," in Glyndwr Williams, ed., *Hudson's Bay Miscellany, 1670–1870* (Winnipeg: Hudson's Bay Record Society, 1975), pp. 204–5; Margaret A. Ormsby, *A Pioneer Gentlewoman in British Columbia: The Recollections of Susan Allison* (Vancouver: University of British Columbia Press, 1976). p. 6. For other views on Douglas at this time, see Barry M. Gough, "Sir James Douglas as

Seen by his Contemporaries: A Preliminary List," *BC Studies,* no. 44 (Winter 1979–80): 32–40.

3. Henry J. Warre Papers, vol. 2, p. 1246, P.A.C.

4. James Douglas, pocket diary, 16 March 1843, P.A.B.C; Douglas to G. Simpson, 10 March 1843, D. 5/8 H.B.C.A.

5. Simpson to Governor and Committee, 1 March 1842, D. 4/111, ff. 42–67a, in Glyndwr Williams, ed., *London Correspondence Inward from Sir George Simpson, 1841–1842* (London: Hudson's Bay Record Society, 1973), p.111.

6. Reports of Lieutenants Warre and Vavasour, F.O. 5/457, p. 122; also

Bertold Seemann, *Narrative of the Voyage of H.M.S. Herald...1845 –1851*, 2 vols. (London, 1853), 1: 102–3.

7. On the Songhees or Lekwungen, see Franz Boas, "Second General Report on the Indians of British Columbia," *Report of the British Association for the Advancement of Science* 60 (1890): 563–82; and Charles Hill-Tout, "Report on the Ethnology of the Southeastern Tribes of Vancouver Island, British Columbia," *Journal of the Royal Anthropological Institute* 37 (1907): 306–74; Warre papers, vol. 2, p. 1239, P.A.C.

8. See W. Kaye Lamb, ed., "Five Letters of Charles Ross, 1842–44," *British Columbia Historical Quarterly* 7 (1943): 103–18.

9. "Recollections of Six Months in Puget Sound," *Nautical Magazine* 21 (1852): 318.

10. He has been written large in the mythology of Indian aggressiveness. Howard O'Hagan described him as "a hunchback" who controlled the dangerous waters outside of Cowichan Bay and "a man whose twenty-year record of pillage, rape, murder, and torture is probably unequalled on the West Coast north of the tropics. At one time, with confederates, he held under seige the entrenched forces of the mighty Hudson's Bay Company" (Howard O'Hagan, *Wilderness Men* [New York: Doubleday, 1958], pp. 200, 209–10). For another view, see B.A. McKelvie, *Tales of Conflict* (Vancouver: Vancouver Daily Province, 1949), pp. 36–39.

11. "King Freezy" as he was called by the whites owing to his frizzled hair, an inheritance from his Kan-

aka or Hawaiian progenitor, was very friendly to the whites. But he was "in disgrace" with the Royal Navy, having walked off with the *Thetis*'s cashbox on the pretext of taking it to show his wife (W.H. Hills Journal, mss. 1436/1, Mitchell Library, Sydney, Australia, p. 138).

12. Wilson Duff, " The Fort Victoria Treaties," *BC Studies* 3 (1969): 3–57; Roderick Finlayson, "History of Vancouver Island and the Northwest Coast," typescript, P.A.B.C., pp. 19–22.

13. Seemann, *Voyage of H.M.S. Herald*, 1: 102.

14. Lieutenant James Wood, R.N., for instance, obtained from Roderick Finlayson an enumeration of Vancouver Island tribes with a total native population of 11,463 (encl. in Wood to Sec. of the Admiralty, 19 September 1848, Adm. 1/W33).

15. Rear-Adm. Sir George Seymour to Capt. J.A. Duntze, 14 January 1846, Adm. 1/5561.

16. See Gloria Griffien Cline, *Peter Skene Ogden and the Hudson's Bay Company* (Norman: University of Oklahoma Press, 1974), for an account of the Cayuse War. This ominous disturbance modified company activities. The interior brigade began using the Similkameen Valley, thereby avoiding the Cayuse Country where the U.S. Cavalry was conducting its pacification. Fort Yale grew in importance. The Lower Fraser supplanted the Columbia as the company's waterway to the interior.

17. Quoted in F.V. Longstaff and W. Kaye Lamb, "The Royal Navy on the Northwest Coast, 1813–1850," pt. 2, *British Columbia Historical*

Quarterly 9 (1945): 123–24; for another version, see Robin A. Fisher, *Contact and Conflict: Indian-European Relations in British Columbia, 1774–1890* (Vancouver: University of British Columbia Press, 1977), p. 40. Finlayson's account does not, however, specify the Songhees as the Indians in question; they were probably the transient Flattery and Clallums, as the Fort Victoria Journal entry for 24 August 1848 indicates.

18. At the same time, on the south side of the Strait of Juan de Fuca tensions continued. The captain of H.M.S. *Pandora*, who visited Fort Nisqually in 1848, found it heavily defended against the Indians of upper Puget Sound. Indian "bravado" had driven many settlers back to the Columbia River. He thought the Company's influence was in question. He also found that measles and influenza had killed one-fifth of the Indian population of Puget Sound and the Strait of Juan de Fuca that year (Lt. James Wood to Sec. of the Admiralty, 19 September 1848, Adm. 1/W33).

19. Shepherd to officer-in-charge, Fort Victoria, 12 May 1849, B. 226/6/2 fols. 18d–19. H.B.C.A.; Hornby to J. Parker, 29 August 1849, *Report of the Provincial Archives. . . 1913*, p. V74.

20. J. Pelly to B. Hawes, 22 November 1849, A. 8/6, fols. 14–15; A. Barclay to Sec. of the Admiralty, 22 November 1849, A. 8/17, fol. 46, H.B.C.A. On company officials' requests for naval support, see Barry M. Gough, *The Royal Navy and the Northwest Coast of North America, 1810–1914: A Study of British Maritime Ascen-*

dancy (Vancouver: University of British Columbia Press, 1971), p. 88, n. 24; and A. Colvile to Earl Grey, 18 December 1850, *Report of the Provincial Archives. . . 1913*, p. V80.

21. Statement of Lt. Dundas, R.N. [to B. Hawes], 30 May 1848, C.O. 305/1, fols. 220–24; *Report from the Select Committee on the Hudson's Bay Company* (London, 1857), pp. 291–92.

22. R.M. Martin, *The Hudson's Bay Territories and Vancouver Island* (London, 1848); J.E. Fitzgerald, *An Examination of the Charter and Proceedings of the Hudson's Bay Company With Reference to the Grant of Vancouver's Island* (London, 1849), pp. 135, 153.

23. Lincoln noted that Sir George Simpson's *Narrative of a Journey Round the World. . . 1841 and 1842* (2 vols. [London, 1847] contained the following remark: "In the absence of any other means of obtaining redress, our people had recourse to the law of Moses, which, after the loss of several lives on the side of the natives, brought the savages to their senses, while the steamer's mysterious and rapid movements speedily completed their subjugation. In fact, whether in matters of life or death or of petty thefts, the rule of retaliation is the only standard of equity which the tribes on this coast are capable of appreciating" (Great Britain, *Hansard's Parliamentary Debates*, 3d ser., 106 [1849]: 562).

24. Draft of grant, encl. in order-in-council, 4 September 1848, B.T. 1/470/2506. In seeking the charter, Sir John Pelly of the Company had written to Earl Grey on 24

October 1846 urging that the government consider whether "the object of colonization, embracing as I trust it will the conversion to Christianity and the civilization of the native population, might not be most readily and effectually accomplished through the instrumentality of the Hudson's Bay Company" (F.W. Howay and E.O.S. Scholefield, *British Columbia from the Earliest Times to the Present,* 4 vols. [Vancouver: S.J. Clarke, 1914], 1:498). For Grey's views, see his *Colonial Policy of Lord John Russell's Administra-*

tion, 2 vols. (London, 1853), 1:13.

25. Grey, *Colonial Policy,* 1: 27. See also W. P. Morrell, *British Colonial Policy in the Mid-Victorian Age: South Africa, New Zealand and the West Indies* (Oxford: Clarendon Press, 1969), passim, especially p. 2. W. E. Gladstone ("Memorandum on Colonies," Gladstone Papers, Add. MSS 44,738, B.L., fols. 236–38) believed that colonies should be abandoned to colonists who would develop their native policies as part of self-government.

NOTES TO CHAPTER THREE: "THIS MISERABLE AFFAIR"

1. J[ohn] K[east] L[ord], "How We Went to Fort Rupert and Made a Strange Purchase," *Once a Week* 24 June 1865, pp. 19–20.

2. Later called Tahsis (Frederick Webb Hodge, *Handbook of American Indians North of Mexico,* 2 pts. [New York: Pageant Books, 1959], pt. 2, p. 744).

3. Lord, "How We Went to Fort Rupert," pp. 19–20.

4. J.S. Helmcken, "Fort Rupert in 1850...," *Victoria Daily Colonist,* 1 January 1890, p. 4, reprinted in Dorothy Blakey Smith, ed., *The Reminiscences of Doctor John Sebastian Helmcken* (Vancouver: University of British Columbia Press, 1975), appendix. Quotations from original newspaper article.

5. The first independent settler estimated the Kwakiutl at Fort Rupert at 1,500 (W. Colquhoun Grant, "Description of Vancouver Island," *Royal Geographical So-*

ciety Journal 27 [1857]: 293).

6. The territorial aggrandizement of the Kwakiutl "at the expense of their less warlike neighbours" is discussed in Herbert C. Taylor, Jr., and Wilson Duff, "A Post-Contact Southward Movement of the Kwakiutl," *Research Studies* 24 (1956): 56–66; Walbran, *British Columbia Coast Names,* pp. 184–85; Helmcken, "Fort Rupert."

7. J.K. Nesbitt, " Capt. Porcher of Sparrowhawk Studied Indians and Coral," *Victoria Daily Colonist, Islander* (supplement), 3 September 1967, p. 2.

8. Patricia M. Johnson, "Fort Rupert, B.C.," *The Beaver* 302 (1972): 4–15. Also John Keast Lord, *The Naturalist in Vancouver Island and British Columbia,* 2 vols. (London, 1866), 1: 162–64; Charles E. Barrett-Lennard, *Travels in British Columbia* (London, 1862), pp. 67–69.

9. Guetela, Komkutis, Komoyue,

and Walaskawakiutl (Hodge, *Handbook of American Indians*, pt.1, p. 744).

10. According to one anthropologist, the building of Fort Rupert helped reduce warfare among the Kwakiutl. As they themselves said, "the white man came and stopped [the stream] of blood with wealth." Between 1849 and 1865, when the last of their wars occurred, their potlatches as "wars of property" gradually supplanted "wars of blood" (Helen Codere, *Fighting With Property: A Study of Kwakiutl Potlatching and Warfare, 1792-1930*, Monographs of the American Ethnological Society, vol. 18 [1950]: 11-25).

11. Fort Rupert Journal, 4 September 1849, B.185/a/1 H.B.C.A. See also, W. Kaye Lamb, "The Governorship of Richard Blanshard," *British Columbia Historical Quarterly* 14 (1950): 8.

12. Helmcken, "Fort Rupert."

13. Andrew Muir, Diary, P.A.B.C.

14. J. Helmcken to R. Blanshard, 2 July 1850, CAA 40.3 R2, P.A.B.C.

15. This and the preceding paragraph are based on the survey of these events in Johnson, "Fort Rupert," p. 10. See also Helmcken, "Fort Rupert," and Andrew Muir, Diary, P.A.B.C.

16. Howay and Scholefield, *British Columbia*, 3:1135.

17. The two tribes were Tla-tli-si-kwila and Ne-kum-ke-lis-la, according to G. M. Dawson. This description of the Newitty is taken from George Mercer Dawson, "Notes and Observations on the Kwakiool People of the Northern Part of Vancouver Island," *Proceedings and Transactions of the Royal Society of Canada*, ser. 1

vol. 5, sec 2 (1887): 69-72. Also, James Douglas, Diary of a Trip to Sitka, 6-21 October 1841, AB HO, D75.4A, fol.6, and "Original Indian Population: Vancouver Island [c.1840]," B20 1853, fol. 17; both in Private Papers of Sir James Douglas, Second Series, P.A.B.C. In the last-named reference the Newitty are called "Tlatlas heguilla or Nawity-Quaghenil," the first of which corresponds to Dawson's aforecited name.

18. Fort Rupert Journal, 30 March 1850, B.185/a/1, H.B.C.A.; Blanshard to Rear-Adm. T. Phipps Hornby, [?]October 1850, PH1/3/5, N.M.M.

19. Andrew Muir, who was there, wrote: "Mr. Blenkinsop offered the Indians 10 blankets for each of their heads should they bring back only their heads. Was ever such barbarity heard of giving these blood hounds 10 blankets for one white man's head, these savages who care no more about taking of a man's head than you should do of taking a meal of meat. Surely these things will not pass without punishment" (Diary, P.A.B.C.).

20. J. Douglas to A. Barclay, 5 October 1850, extract, A.8/6, f.148, H.B.C.A.; Blenkinsop to Helmcken, 21 September 1887, AE H37, B61, P.A.B.C.; Helmcken, "Fort Rupert."

21. Beardmore's Account of his Journey to Newitty, in Vancouver Island, Magistrate's Court, Fort Rupert, Diary, 27 June-20 August 1850, by J. S. Helmcken, J. P., CAA 40.3 R3, P.A.B.C.

22. J. Helmcken to R. Blanshard, 17 July 1850, CAA 40.3 R2, P.A.B.C.

23. Ibid.

24. Blanshard to Helmcken, 5 August

1850, private, in Lamb, "Governorship of Richard Blanshard," p.13.

25. Douglas to Blenkinsop, 20 September 1850, B.226/6/3, ff. 12d–13d, H.B.C.A.

26. Douglas to Blenkinsop, 27 October 1850, B.226/6/3 f. 14d, H.B.C.A. His predecessor, Captain W. H. McNeill, had left for the Queen Charlotte gold discoveries in April 1850 to protect company interests there.

27. Blanshard to Grey, 18 August 1850, C.O. 305/2.

28. The place has been variously spelled Newittie, Nahwitti, Newitty, Newity, and otherwise.

29. Blanshard to Grey, 19 October 1850, in *Vancouver Island Despatches, Governor Blanshard to the Secretary of State, 1849–1851*, (New Westminster-Government Printing Office [1863]), p. 5.

30. In 1892 Helmcken recalled: "It shows too how quarrels were settled Indian fashion by payment of damages. This Indian idea of law — indeed it is their law — of payment applies even to persons killed, as shown too by their offer to pay for the murdered men at Newittie. This Indian law was often acted on at Fort Rupert and suited very well. — none other would — or could — have been put in force. Douglas perhaps might have landed and seized the Indian here at Newittie — but I do not believe even he would have tried" (Helmcken, *Reminiscences*, pp. 142–3).

31. Captain G. G. Wellesley to Blanshard, 13 October 1853, *Vancouver Island Despatches*, p. 6.

32. Blanshard to Rear-Admiral Phipps Hornby, [?] October 1850, PHI/3/5, N.M.M.

33. Blanshard to Rear-Admiral Fairfax Moresby, 27 June 1851, noted in Adm. 50/260, p. 90.

34. Christopher Lloyd, *The Navy and the Slave Trade: The Suppression of the African Slave Trade in the Nineteenth Century* (London: Longmans Green & Co., 1949), pp. 192, 195, 198, 203–4, 229. See also G. S. Graham, *Great Britain in the Indian Ocean: A Study of Maritime Enterprise, 1810–1850* (Oxford: Clarendon Press, 1967), pp. 198–200.

35. Lt. E. Lacy to Capt. E. G. Fanshawe, 21 July 1851, encl. no. 2, in Blanshard to Grey, 4 August in 1851, *Vancouver Island Despatches*, p. 13.

36. Ibid.

37. Helmcken, "Fort Rupert,"

38. Douglas to Blenkinsop, 1 July 1851, Fort Victoria, B.226/6/3, ff. 111d–12d; Douglas to Ogden, 6 August 1851, B.226/6/3, ff. 116–17; Douglas to Grey, 31 October 1851, A.8/6, f.244, H.B.C.A. See also Moresby to Blanshard, 27 June 1851, copy, encl. in Hawes to Pelly, 8 October 1851, A. 8/6, f. 191 H.B.C.A. Moresby to Secretary of the Admiralty, 27 June 1851, copy, encl. in Hawes to Pelly, 8 October 1851, A. 8/6, H.B.C.A. ff. 190–91 H.B.C.A.; Blanshard to Grey, 4 August 1851, in *Vancouver Island Despatches*, p. 12.

39. Helmcken, "Fort Rupert."

40. Hubert Howe Bancroft, *History of British Columbia, 1792–1887* (San Francisco: History Company, 1887), pp. 274–75.

41. See footnote 30, above.

42. Helmcken, "Fort Rupert."

Helmcken wrote his account of the whole affair to correct Bancroft. George Blenkinsop wrote to him, "I am heartily glad you have lade bare to the public in plain unmistakeable language those proceedings which Bancroft so wilfully and maliciously represented" (Blenkinsop to Helmcken, 24 February 1890, Beaver Harbour, AE H37 B61, P.A.B.C.). In another letter to Helmcken (21 April 1890, ibid.) he said he thought Bancroft "a profound hater of our country and fully upholds the French in terming it 'Perfidious Albion'"; see also Blenkinsop to Helmcken, 21 September 1887, AE H37 B61, P.A.B.C.

43. Fisher, *Contact and Conflict*, p. 51.

44. Pelly to Grey, 14 January 1852, A.8/6, f. 224, H.B.C.A.

45. On this point, generally, see Wilcomb E. Washburn, *The Indian in America* (New York: Harper & Row, 1975), pp. 17–18. For Jews and Indians alike, mercy was a latter-day Christian corruption (ibid.).

46. Fisher, *Contact and Conflict*, p. 52. Compare, however, the opinion of Helmcken that it was vital to secure the deserters: "These were of great importance at Fort Rupert at the time, for if more had deserted the place would have been without defenders against the three thousand Indians outside" (Smith, ed., *Reminiscences of Doctor John Sebastian Helmcken*, p. 107).

47. Douglas to Earl Grey, 31 October 1851, quoted in Derek Pethick, *James Douglas: Servant of Two Empires* (Vancouver: Mitchell Press, 1969), p. 97.

48. One historian has classified Douglas's methods as "more subtle" than Blanshard's (Arthur S. Morton, *A History of the Canadian West to 1870–1871*, 2d ed. [Toronto: University of Toronto Press, 1973], pp. 762–63).

49. Douglas to Blenkinsop, 15 August 1851, B. 226/6/3, ff. 119–20d; Douglas to J. Work, 4 June 1852, B.226/6/4, f. 99; Douglas to Blenkinsop, 27 October 1850, B.226/b/3, f. 14d; and Pelly to Grey, 14 January 1852, A.8/6, f. 226; Barclay to Douglas, 26 September 1851, B.226/b/5a, f. 18d, H.B.C.A.

50. Grey to Blanshard, 20 March 1851, in Howay and Scholefield, *British Columbia*, 1: 523–24.

51. For Blanshard, this was the last of several indignities. He had agreed to serve as governor without pay. Perhaps Blanshard expected that when settlements had advanced he could look forward to a salary similar to those enjoyed by other junior colonial governors. In any case his conception of the dignity and status of a governor was not above reason, and great was his disappointment to find on his arrival at Fort Victoria that no residence was available and that he would have to be reliant on the kindness of Captain Johnstone of H.M.S. *Driver* for "bed and board." Douglas must have known that Blanshard had been promised one thousand acres of land, but he did nothing to accord the queen's representative the courtesy he deserved, even denying him one hundred acres as a settler. Blanshard's rudimentary residence took months to complete. He had no office and no

clerical assistance from the Company. (He did have a personal servant.) He paid all expenses out of his own pocket at the rate of £1,100 per annum, and he was obliged to buy all necessities from the Company store at a high markup above London prices. He was ignored and snubbed by Douglas and associates; not surprisingly some early settlers recalled him as being a very lonely man who took long walks— perhaps for solace (Diary of James Anderson, P.A.B.C.; see also

Lamb, "Governorship of Richard Blanshard," pp. 25–37.)

52. Law Officers of the Crown to Lord Clarendon (F.O.), 28 July 1853, encl. in R. Osborne (Adm.) to Rear-Admiral D. Price, 9 August 1853, Adm. 172/3, no. 6. The original report of the Law Officers is in F.O. 83/2314, pp. 188–89.

53. Minute by Herman Merivale, 19 July 1852, on J. Douglas to Earl Grey, 15 April 1852, C.O. 305/3.

54. Rich, *History of the Hudson's Bay Company*, 2: 761.

NOTES TO CHAPTER FOUR: THE SMOULDERING VOLCANO

1. Richard C. Mayne, *Four Years in British Columbia and Vancouver Island* (London, 1862), p. 54.

2. Douglas to Tolmie, 5 November 1852, in Charles B. Bagley, ed., "Attitude of the Hudson's Bay Company During the Indian War of 1855–1856," *Washington Historical Quarterly* 8 (1917): 293.

3. Douglas to Tolmie, 17 November 1853 [1852], ibid.

4. Ibid.

5. Colvile to Sir John Pelly, 15 October 1849, in E. E. Rich, ed., *London Correspondence Inward From Eden Colvile, 1849–1852* (London: Hudson's Bay Record Society, 1956), p. 5.

6. Moresby, *Two Admirals*, p. 109. Likely this is the same Cowichan chief sketched by Paul Kane as "Saw-se-a" (J. Russell Harper, ed., *Paul Kane's Frontier* [Toronto: University of Toronto Press, 1971], p. 262).

7. Douglas, Diary, 3–25 January 1853, Private Papers, 2nd ser., B20

1853, fol. 32, P.A.B.C.

8. Moresby, *Two Admirals*, p. 110.

9. Douglas, Diary, 3–25 January 1853, Private Papers, 2nd ser., B20 1853, fols. 34–35, P.A.B.C.

10. Douglas to J. Tod (member, Council of Vancouver Island), 7 January 1853; copy, ibid., fol. 38.

11. Douglas to A. Barclay, 20 January 1853, quoted in B.A. McKelvie and W.E. Ireland, "The Victoria Voltigeurs," *British Columbia Historical Quarterly* 20 (1956): 227.

12. Kuper to Moresby, 4 February 1853, in W. Kaye Lamb, ed., "Four Letters Relating to the Cruise of the *Thetis*, 1852–1853," *British Columbia Historical Quarterly* 6 (1942): 201.

13. Douglas to A. Barclay (Sec. H.B.C.), 20 January 1853, ibid., 204–6. Moresby, *Two Admirals*, p. 107.

14. W.H. Hills Journal, mss. 1436/1, Mitchell Library, Sydney, Australia, pp. 156–60.

15. Douglas to Barclay, 20 January 1853, in Lamb, "Four Letters," 204–6.

16. Sub-encl. 2, copy of letter to T. Banister, n.d., in H. Labouchere to Douglas, 8 July 1856, Great Britain, *Parliamentary Papers, 1863* (H. of C. 507), 47–48, Sir G. Grey to Douglas, 3 August 1855, C.O. 410/1; Willard E. Ireland, "Pre-Confederation Defence Problems of the Pacific Colonies," Canadian Historical Association, *Annual Report 1941* (Toronto, 1941), 46; Howay and Scholefield, *British Columbia*, 1: 535.

17. "No man in his right senses would ever suppose that the Governor of a British province would be guilty of the monstrous outrage of arming a horde of savages and letting them loose upon the defenceless frontier of a neighbouring and friendly state" (Douglas to Tolmie, 13 June 1854, in Bagley, "Attitude of the Hudson's Bay Company," p. 294).

18. Tilton to Douglas, 1 November 1855, Winlock Miller Collection, Western Americana, Item 475, Beineke Library, Yale University.

19. Douglas to Tilton, 6 November 1855, and invoice of Sundries shipped for Puget Sound as per request of Major Tilton, ibid.

20. Douglas to Tilton, 19 November, 1855, ibid.

21. Tolmie to Tilton, 30 October 1855, ibid. Fort Nisqually became the haven for several settlers sent there by Tilton for protection (Tolmie to Tilton, 9 March 1856, ibid.).

22. Fear of a raid by "British Indians" provided one of the reasons for the American occupation in 1859 (see Brig. Gen. W. S. Harvey to Col. S. Cooper, 29 August 1859, in "Pig War National Historical Park," U.S. Senate, 89th Cong., 1st Session, S.489 (1965), pp. 199–200; see also James O. McCabe, *The San Juan Water Boundary Question* [Toronto: University of Toronto Press, 1964],pp. 46, 50, 51, 54).

23. Douglas to Colonial Office, 19 May 1856, quoted in Lelah Jackson Edson, *The Fourth Corner: Highlights from the Early Northwest,* 2d ed. (Bellingham: Whatcom Museum of History and Art, 1968), p. 72; Norman R. Hacking and W. Kaye Lamb, *The Princess Story: A Century and a Half of West Coast Shipping* (Vancouver: Mitchell Press, 1974), pp. 52–53; minute by H. Merivale, 17 February 1858, on J. Douglas to H. Labouchere, 7 December 1857, C.O. 305/8. Douglas finally received a draft from the Treasurer of the United States for $8,306.66, "a trifling discrepancy" to the final bill sent Washington, D.C. (Edson, *Fourth Corner,* p. 73).

24. Clarence B. Bagley, *History of Seattle,* 2 vols. (Chicago: S. J. Clarke, 1916), 1: 53–66; *Dictionary of American Biography* 11: 182–83, and 16: 542–53; and George Fuller, *A History of the Pacific Northwest,* 2d ed. rev. (New York: Alfred A. Knopf, 1966), p. 237. A concise account of the U.S. Navy's role in quelling Indian resistance is given in Robert E. Johnson, *Thence Round Cape Horn: The Story of United States Naval Forces on Pacific Station, 1818–1923* (Annapolis, Md.: United States Naval Institute, 1963), p. 107. Details with respect to the

U.S.S. *Massachusetts*'s retaliatory action are to be found in Edson, *Fourth Corner*, pp. 64–9, and Lottie Roeder Roth, *History of Whatcom County*, 2 vols. (Chicago and Seattle: Pioneer Historical Publishing Company, 1926), 1: 61–63.

25. R. S. Swanston to Banister, 4 January 1856, encl. in Labouchere to Douglas, 8 July 1856. Great Britain, *Parliamentary Papers*. 1863 (H. of C. 507), 47.

26. Rear-Adm. H. W. Bruce to Sir Charles Wood (First Lord of the Admiralty), 18 September 1855, Add. MSS. 49,549, B.L.

27. *Minutes of the House of Assembly of Vancouver Island, 1856-1858*, Archives Memoir No. 2 (Victoria, B.C., 1918), p. 15; Douglas to W. G. Smith, 19 July 1856, B. 226 /6/13, f. 69, H.B.C.A.

28. Bruce to R. Osborne, 6 September 1856, Adm. 1/5672, Y136.

29. The following account is based on Bruce to R. Osborne, 6 September 1856; Douglas to Bruce, 5 September 1856; Capt. G. Patey to Bruce, 6 September 1856; and Cdr. M. Connolly to Bruce, 6 September 1856; all in Adm. 1/5672. Log of Lambton Lorraine, 25–31 August 1856, OA 20–5, T731L, P.A.B.C.

30. Connolly's orders, dated 31 August 1856, Cowichan Bay, on board H.B.C. Steam Vessel *Otter*, Adm. 1/5672.

31. Walbran, *British Columbia Coast Names*, pp. 310–11. The Victoria militia played no significant role in this expedition. Annie Deans learned from a friend, perhaps Captain Houston, that 700 to 800 Indians approached the governor and naval party. The assailant, she wrote, was prepared to shoot

Douglas "but he was aware he has got a great dare over the indian when he is speaking to them so he walked up to the indian speaking all the time till he got within 5 or 6 paces of him when the indian cocked his gun at the Gove[r]nor when two indians laid hold of the gun and would not let him fire so some of the officers laid hold of him and one of them got his hand cut with his knife and Captain [sic] Houston got knocked over. ... the[y] asked him wither [sic] he would be Shot or Hanged so he prefared [sic] Hanging." Therefore, two block and tackles were rigged to a branch of an oak tree and he was let drop. Then his mother blew into his nostrils and "was feeding him with salmon." Then the field piece crews practised shooting to frighten the Indians and then re-embarked (Annie Deans to friends, 1 October 1856, EB D343A, P.A.B.C.).

32. Walbran, *British Columbia Coast Names*, pp. 310–11.

33. These opinions are given in the documents cited in note 29 above. Also, Admiralty Minute, 13 November 1856, Adm. 1/5672, Y136.

34. Douglas to Tolmie, 6 September 1856, B.226/b/12, f. 108, H.B.C.A.

35. Rear-Adm. H. W. Bruce to Sir Charles Wood, 16 April 1856, Add. MSS 49,549, B.L.

36. Bruce to Wood, 18 September 1855, ibid. Italics in original. Bruce also reported to Wood: "Mr. Douglas, the Hudson's Bay Company's Officer and Govr. is a man of clear views, and ability and decision of character" (Bruce to Wood, 22 September 1856, ibid.).

37. "A Scotchman who had been forbidden to remain there, on ac-

count of the late tragical event, applied to me for leave to return; he holds an expensive piece of land from an Indian Chief on the terms of—'giving him two blankets, and *accepting one of his daughters.*' I asked him how he should act, were an Indian warrior to demand the girl at the peril of his life; his instant reply to which was—'Give her up to be sure'; adding that in the case where the Englishman was shot, the Indian girl refused to be parted from him" (Bruce to Wood, 22 September 1856, ibid.).

38. Douglas to Tolmie, 30 May 1854, and 28 April 1856, Hudson's Bay Correspondence, Western Americana Collection, Beineke Library, Yale University, item 263, pp. 56, 65. James G. Swan, *Almost out of the World* (Tacoma: Washington Historical Society, 1971), pp. 31–35, and 96100, gives important American perspectives on the northern Indians in Victoria.

39. Richard Byron Johnston, *Very Far West Indeed: A Few Rough Experiences on the North-west Pacific Coast* (London, 1872), p. 38; Journal of W.J. Walker, acting mate, H.M.S. *Dido*, 17 July–September 1855, Historical Notes, vol. 1, pp. 900–10, M.M.B.C.; G.F.G. Stanley, ed., *Mapping the Frontier: Charles Wilson's Diary*

of the Survey of the 49th Parallel, 1858–1862, While Secretary of the British Boundary Commission (Toronto: Macmillan, 1970), pp. 46–47; Walbran, *British Columbia Place Names,* p. 463.

40. Swan, *Almost out of the World,* p. 99.

41. Stanley, ed., *Mapping the Frontier,* p. 46.

42. Mayne, *Four Years in British Columbia,* pp. 76–78.

43. Ibid., p. 77.

44. Ibid.

45. Capt. DeCourcy to Rear-Adm. R.L. Baynes, 10 March 1859, copy, C.O. 60/5; and J. Work to T. Fraser, 31 March 1859, B. 226/b/17, f. 124, H.B.C.A.; Baynes to Sec. of Admiralty, 3 and 8 July, 1860, Y129 and 131 respectively, Adm. 1/5736, p. 2; Journal of R.C. Mayne, 1857–60, EB M45A, P.A.B.C.

46. See Chapter 6, pp. 000–000.

47. Barclay to Douglas, [?] December 1849, A.11/72, H.B.C.A.

48. Duff, "The Fort Victoria Treaties," pp. 3–57.

49. *British Colonist,* 26 February 1859.

50. Quoted in F.E. LaViolette, *The Struggle for Survival: Indian Cultures and the Protestant Ethic in British Columbia* (Toronto: University of Toronto Press, 1961), pp. 104–5.

NOTES TO CHAPTER FIVE: POLICY MAKING

1. As the Duke of Newcastle stated, government intervention was necessary for the protection of the aborigines against the Americans

to prevent "cruelties and horrors that had been perpetrated in the early days of our colonies" and in the western United States (Great

Britain, *Hansard's Parliamentary Debates*, 3d ser. [1858]: cols. 2101–2).

2. Matthew Macfie, *Vancouver Island and British Columbia: Their History, Resources, and Prospects* (London, 1865), pp. 461–62.

3. For example, Rev. Thomas Crosby, *Among the An-ko-menums, Or Flathead Tribes of Indians of the Pacific Coast* (Toronto: Wm. Briggs, 1907), pp. 88–90; Medical Officers' Journals, R.N. Hospital, Esquimalt, 1872, p. 8 and Table 3; 1873, p. 30; and 1875, p. 35, micro. Oregon Historical Society, Portland.

4. The charter of grant issued to the Hudson's Bay Company specified that the type of government established in Vancouver Island "would conduce greatly to the maintenance of peace, justice, and good order, and the advancement of colonization and the promotion and encouragement of trade and commerce in, and also to the protection and welfare of the native Indians residing within that portion of Our territories in North America called Vancouver's Island" (Vancouver's Island, Royal Grant, C.O. 880/2, No. 45, p. 6). Sir E. Bulwer Lytton (sec. of state, colonies) to Douglas, 31 July 1858, in British Columbia, *Papers Connected with the Indian Land Question, 1850–1875* (Victoria, 1875), p. 12.

5. Herman Merivale to Sir E. Bulwer Lytton, 7 August 1858, Bulwer Lytton Papers, D/EK 101, Bulwer Lytton Papers, Hertfordshire Records Office.

6. Policy exists in anticipation of the future or in explanation of the past" (John W. Cell, *British Colonial Administration in the Mid-Nineteenth Century: The Policy-Making Process* [New Haven: Yale University Press, 1970], p. 285).

7. Douglas to Lord Stanley (C.O.), 15 June 1858, no. 26, in B.C. Papers, pt. 1, *Parliamentary Papers*, 1858 (Cmd. 2476), 16.

8. See Thomas A. Rickard, "Indian Participation in the Gold Discoveries," *British Columbia Historical Quarterly* 2 (1938): 11–18.

9. Evidence of Chief John Tedlenitsa of the Coteau tribe, in deposition to Sir Wilfrid Laurier, 27 April 1916, in Borden Papers, MG 26 H1(a), vol. 38, pp. 16394–5, P.A.C.

10. Capt. J. C. Prevost to Rear-Adm. R. L. Baynes, 10 January 1859, copy, C.O. 60/5.

11. See also, Barry M. Gough, "'Turbulent Frontiers' and British Expansion: Governor James Douglas, the Royal Navy and the British Columbia Gold Rushes," *Pacific Historical Review* 41 (1972): 15–32; "Keeping British Columbia British: The Law-and-Order Question on a Gold Mining Frontier," *Huntington Library Quarterly* 38 (1975): 269–80; and "The Character of the British Columbia Frontier," *B.C. Studies* 32 (Winter 1976–77): 28–40.

12. Capilano village was at Homulcheson Creek, now called Capilano Creek. Musqueam means "up the slough." This chief Ki-ap-a-lano, not to be confused with the chief of the same name who had met Captain George Vancouver, 13 June 1792, was an old man and of impressive height. He had led his tribe to victory over the famed Eclataws. He was the son

of a Squamish father and a Musqueam mother. Captain Richards spelled his name Ki-ap-a-lano (see Major J. S. Matthews, *Conversations with Khahtsahlano* (Vancouver: Brock Webber Ltd., 1967) and James W. Morton, *Capilano: The Story of a River* (Toronto: McClelland and Stewart, 1970), chap. 2.

13. Extract of a letter from Capt. Richards, Port Moody, Burrard Inlet, 21 August 1859, encl. in R. L. Baynes to J. Douglas, 26 August 1859, F1212a 24, P.A.B.C.

14. Ibid.

15. Ibid.

16. Ibid.

17. David Walker, M.D., to the Hon. Colonial Secretary, British Columbia, 21 October 1864, F1214, P.A.B.C.

18. In 1861, Lieutenant Charles Robson of the *Forward* bought wood there and was obliged to pay for it. "King George's Name passes very current on the Coast, but I assure you, sir, the mind of the Savage is penetrable only through the all powerful medium of the everlasting Pattach (gifts)," and he asked that captains be able to buy powder, tobacco, blankets and vermillion as trade items of exchange (Lt. C. R. Robson to Rear-Adm. R. L. Baynes, 27 January 1861, encl. in Maitland to Sec. of the Admiralty, 13 April 1861, Adm. 1/5761, Y144).

19. Journal of John Gowlland, 14 August 1860, MSS 830/2, Mitchell Library, Sydney, Australia (micro 447-A, P.A.B.C.).

20. Ibid., 8 April 1862.

21. R. L. Baynes to J. Douglas, 4 September 1860, copy, encl. in Baynes to Sec. of the Admiralty, 10 September 1860, Adm. 1/5736, pt. 2, Y152.

22. "They replied [in answer to Captain Richard's demand that they should not retaliate but trust to British law] it was an Indian custom to kill all they could, if one of their people were killed, that they were not worse than the other tribes; that what I said was 'good'—and if the others would leave off murdering, they would" (Richards to Baynes, 17 August 1860, encl. in Baynes in Sec. of the Admiralty, 10 September 1860, ibid.

23. Ibid.

24. Ibid.

25. Baynes to Sec. of the Admiralty, 10 September 1860, ibid.

26. Baynes to Douglas, 4 September 1860, copy, encl. in Baynes to Sec. of the Admiralty, 10 September 1860, ibid.

27. Ibid.

28. Report of Proceedings, Turnour to Arthur Kennedy, 29 December 1865, F1209a, 2. Carey's report is printed in McKelvie, *Tales of Conflict*, pp. 82–83.

29. *British Colonist*, 5 and 6 January 1866.

30. Ibid.

31. Minutes of 12 and 17 January 1866, Vancouver Island Assembly Minute Book, CAA 20.sA 6, and Minutes of 17 January 1866, Vancouver Island Executive Council, CAA 20.3A 1, P.A.B.C. Also, *British Colonist*, 12 and 18 January 1866.

32. Johan Adrian Jacobsen, *Alaskan Voyage, 1881–1883: An Expedition to the Northwest Coast of America*, trans. Erna Gunther (Chicago: University of Chicago Press, 1977), p. 32.

NOTES TO CHAPTER SIX: OF SLAVES AND LIQUOR

1. John Keast Lord, *The Naturalist in Vancouver Island and British Columbia,* 2 vols. (London, 1866), 2: 21, 23; see also *Physician and Fur Trader,* pp. 299, 308, 313.

2. F.O. 5/457, fols. 86–88, quoted in G.P.V. Akrigg and Helen B. Akrigg, *British Columbia Chronicle, 1778–1846: Adventures by Sea and Land* (Vancouver: Discovery Press, 1975), p. 385.

3. For a more detailed analysis of the prevalence of Indian slavery, see Barry M. Gough, "Send a Gunboat! Checking Slavery and Controlling Liquor Traffic Among Coast Indians of British Columbia in the 1860's," *Pacific Northwest Quarterly* 69 (1978): 159–61. Professor D. H. Mitchell of the University of Victoria informs me that in some Northwest Coast tribes slaves may have reached 25 per cent of the population.

4. James Douglas to Governor and Committee, 18 October 1838, B.223/b/20, H.B.C.A., in E. E. Rich, ed., *The Letters of John McLoughlin, First Series, 1825–38* (London: Hudson's Bay Record Society, 1941), p. 238.

5. Lord, "How We Went to Fort Rupert...," pp. 19–21.

6. Mayne, *Four Years in British Columbia,* pp. 74, 208–9.

7. Ibid., pp. 210, 212.

8. Ibid., p. 209.

9. See, for instance, Rear-Adm. the Hon. G. F. Hastings to Sec. of the Admiralty, 17 June 1868, Adm. 1/6056, Y79.

10. James Cooper (harbour master at Esquimalt) to Acting Colonial Secretary, 10 October 1860, F347, 26a, P.A.B.C.

11. Ibid.

12. Ibid.

13. Ibid.

14. Ibid.

15. Wilson Duff to Barry Gough, 6 December 1970. In 1868, Rear-Admiral the Hon. George F. Hastings proceeded to Kitkatla to free two Fort Rupert Indians who had been in slavery since childhood and had been sold and resold in Alaska until 1866 when, having escaped to freedom, they were captured by the Kitkatlas and sold to Chief Sebassah for 110 blankets. Hastings freed them without indemnification to Sebassah, giving them the choice of a return to Fort Rupert or Metlakatla. They chose the former and he took them there (Hastings to Sec. of the Admiralty, 17 June 1868, Adm. 1/6056, Y79).

16. Attempts to ban the sale of liquor to Northwest Coast Indians date back to Baranov's controls in the 1790's. But smugglers were artful dodgers (Roland L. De Lorme, "Liquor Smuggling in Alaska, 1867–1899," *Pacific Northwest Quarterly* 66 [1975]: 145–52).

17. Gilbert M. Sproat, *Scenes and Studies of Savage Life* (London, 1868), pp. 278–85.

18. Edwin M. Lemert, *Alcohol and the Northwest Coast Indians,* in *University of California Publications in Culture and Society,* vol. 2, no. 6 (1954), pp. 326, 334–35.

19. "I am sorry to say that there are many here," wrote a Nanaimo

citizen to the editor of the *British Colonist* (17 September 1865), "who would like to see the Indian prohibition law abolished.... Remove this restraint... and the whole country will soon be set on fire with insensible chain-lightning and rot-gut by scores who would rejoice in having an opportunity to do such a fiendish work."

20. As late as 1904 the cry against whisky sellers existed. One writer estimated that between 1858 and 1870, 100,000 Indians died directly from use of alcoholic spirits (D.W.H[iggens]., in *Victoria Semi-Weekly Colonist,* 25 March 1904).

21. Journal of Commodore the Hon. John Spencer, March 1863, Adm. 50/311, p. 3; Jean Usher, *William Duncan of Metlakatla: A Victorian Missionary in British Columbia* (Ottawa: National Museum of Canada, 1974), pp. 80–81. In 1853, according to Captain Prevost of H.M.S. *Virago,* "not a drop of grog can be purchased [at Port Simpson] at any price" (Prevost to Moresby, 23 July 1853, Adm. 1/5630, Y73). However, at that place officers of the *Virago* traded rum for marten and bear skins (Fort Simpson Journal, 17 June and 11 July 1853, B.201/ a/7, H.B.C.A.).

22. Alexander Rattray, *Vancouver Island and British Columbia* (London, 1862), p. 172.

23. Sir William R. Kennedy, *Sporting Adventures in Pacific* (London, 1876), p. 191.

24. Rear-Adm. Baynes to Sec. of Admiralty, 10 September 1860, Adm. 1/5736, pt. 2, Y168.

25. Lemert, *Alcohol,* pp. 307–8.

26. James Gilchrist Swan, "Washington Sketches," 1878, PB20, p. 9, Bancroft Collection, Bancroft Library, Berkeley. Also J. Ross Browne, *Crusoe's Island: A Ramble in the Footsteps of Alexander Selkirk* (New York, 1864), pp. 270–83. Traders told Commander Pike at Fort Rupert in 1863 they "did not deny having broken the law alleging as a justification that they had sold better spirits than the other traders" (Pike to Spencer, 28 April 1863, and Spencer to Sec. of the Admiralty, 4 May 1863, Adm. 1/5829, Cap. S89).

27. Sproat, *Savage Life,* p. 284.

28. Frederick Whymper, *Travel and Adventure in the Territory of Alaska* (London, 1868), p. 36; Kennedy to E. Cardwell, 24 August 1865, C.O. 880/5, no. 37; "An Act prohibiting the Gift or Sale of intoxicating Liquors to Indians," passed and published 3 Aug. 1854, C.O. 306/1, pp. 27–28. For B.C. a similar measure was effected by proclamation, 6 September 1858. In his journal dated 10 April 1866, the Rev. Robert R.A. Doolan of the Church Missionary Society's Nass River mission noted that five vessels "keep in Russian waters, so our laws cannot touch them" (Doolan Journal, 4 and 10 April 1866, C C2/o 7/15, C.M.S.A.).

29. See Kennedy's letters to Edward Cardwell, 24 January, 13 February and 21 March 1866, in C.O. 880/5, no. 37. Also, *British Colonist,* 23 February and 7 April 1866. The move to legalize the sale of liquor to Indians in 1861 was led by Attorney-General George H. Cary on the grounds that it had

"been found that any attempt to check the sale of liquor was useless" (*British Colonist,* 6 August 1861).

30. "An Ordinance to Assimilate and Amend the Law prohibiting the Sale or Gift of Intoxicating Liquor to Indians," 1867, C.O. 61/1, pp. 266–67, repealing "The Indian Liquor Ordinance, 1865 [for B.C.]," ibid., pp. 183–84, and "The Indian Liquor Act, 1860 [for Vancouver Island], C.O. 306/1, p. 77.

31. Cdr. John W. Pike to Rear-Adm. Sir T. Maitland, 7 October 1862, F1219, P.A.B.C. This view was supported by James Cooper (Cooper to Colonial Secretary, 17 October 1862, F1210/3, P.A.B.C.).

32. The rates of trade were: ½ pint liquor for a mink skin, ¼ gallon for a marten or bear, and ½ gallon for a blanket (Pike to Maitland, 7 October 1862, F1219, P.A.B.C.).

33. Pike to Commodore the Hon. John Spencer, 4 April 1863, and Pike to Customs Collector, New Westminster, 4 April 1863, both in F1210, 5a; Cooper to Colonial Secretary, 17 October 1862, F1210/3, P.A.B.C.

34. Customs Consolidation Act, 1853, 16 and 17 *Vict.,* c. 107. Pike to Colonial Secretary, 8 June 1863, and appended documents, F1210/7, P.A.B.C.

35. Draft of reply, on Pike to J. Douglas, 28 April 1863, F1210/5a, P.A.B.C.; Journal of Rear-Admiral John Kingcome, 23 September 1863, Adm. 50/311.

36. *British Colonist,* 14 May 1863.

37. Walbran, *British Columbia Coast Names,* pp. 95–96.

38. R.R.A. Doolan to Church Missionary Society, 26 Oct. 1864, C C2/o 7/3; and Doolan, Journal, 6 December 1865, C C2/o 7/13, p. 19, C.M.S.A.

39. Doolan, Journal, 5 April 1866, C C2/o 7/15, C.M.S.A. The Nass remained one profitable market for whiskey sellers, but there were convictions. See, for example, Conviction of William John Stephen of the schooner *Nanaimo Packet,* 4 June 1869, CB 30.3, St.4, P.A.B.C.

40. Vice-Admiral C.F. Hillyar to Secretary of the Admiralty, 26 August 1873, Adm. 1/6263, Y124.

41. *British Colonist,* 11 January 1866, and Walbran, *British Columbia Coast Names,* p. 96. See, for a view of Begbie's views on liquor and Indians, David R. Williams, *"The Man for a New Country": Sir Matthew Baillie Begbie* (Sidney, B.C.: Gray's Publishing, 1977), pp. 107–8.

NOTES TO CHAPTER SEVEN: AMONG THE VIKINGS OF THE NORTH PACIFIC

1. John R. Swanton, *Contributions to the Ethnology of the Haida,* in *The Jesup North Pacific Expedition,* vol. 5, pt. 1 (New York: American Museum of Natural History, 1905), p. 16.

2. There were, in actuality, four divisions of Haida peoples, each of which was linguistically and geographically distinct, though they were culturally very similar. There were: the Northern Haida living

mainly on the northern shores of Graham Island; the Central Haida living on south Graham Island, on Moresby, and other nearby islands, the Southern Haida living on the southern portion of Moresby and on other islands; and the Kaigani (Alaskan) Haida who had migrated to the Alexander Islands during the eighteenth century (Margaret Berlin Blackman, "The Northern and Kaigani Haida: A Study in Photographic Ethnohistory" [Ph.D. dissertation, Ohio State University, 1973], pp. 7–8).

3. William H. Collison, *In the Wake of the War Canoe* (London: Seeley, Service & Co., 1915), p. 88; see also Charles Harrison, *Ancient Warriors of the North Pacific* (London: H.F. & G. Whitherby, 1925), passim.

4. Robert Haswell's log of the first voyage of the *Columbia* [June 1789], in F.W. Howay, ed., *Voyages of the "Columbia" to the Northwest Coast, 1787–1790* (Boston: Massachusetts Historical Society, 1941), p. 95. For a somewhat similar British view, see [William Beresford], *A Voyage Round the World...in 1785, 1786, 1787 and 1788...by George Dixon* (London, 1789), pp. 217–20; and James C. Prevost to Rear-Adm. Fairfax Moresby, 7 June 1853, in Moresby to Sec. of the Admiralty, 13 October 1853, Adm. 1/5630, Y73.

5. Prevost to Moresby, 23 July 1853, encl. in Moresby to Sec. of the Admiralty, ibid.

6. John R. Henderson, "Haida Culture Change: A Geographical Analysis" (Ph.D. diss. Michigan State University, 1972), p. 62.

7. Diary of Surgeon Henry Treven,

R.N., in H.M.S. *Virago,* 1852–54, M.G. 24, F40, p. 325, P.A.C.

8. Gough, " 'Turbulent Frontiers' and British Expansion," pp. 15–32.

9. This had not been the case when the *Una* visited there in 1851; see Capt. McNeill's report, in Thomas A. Rickard, *Historic Backgrounds of British Columbia* (Vancouver: privately printed, 1948), pp. 293–94. On 18 August 1850, a Haida took gold to Fort Simpson to trade; the Company valued it at $16,000 per ton, and in March 1851 the company ship *Una,* Capt. William Mitchell, went to Gold Harbour to mine the precious metal. The Haida became uneasy and objected to the whites taking their metal, and this forced Mitchell to load the ore into the *Una* and sail for Fort Victoria. Her capture by Indians at Neah Bay is a well-known incident of local history (*Queen Charlotte Islands Papers* [1853], Cmd. 788, p. 1).

10. Capt. Augustus L. Kuper to Rear Adm. Fairfax Moresby, 20 July 1852, in W. Kaye Lamb, ed., "Four Letters," pp. 192–99.

11. Ibid.

12. Kuper to Moresby, 4 February 1853, ibid., p. 202.

13. To the end of his life Edenshaw claimed that his name was "Captain Juglass" (Walbran, *British Columbia Coast Names,* pp. 162–63). He was also a notorious slave-trader (J.H. Van den Brink, *The Haida Indians* [Leiden: Brill, 1974], p. 39). Born about 1812, he became Chief Edensa in 1841, was baptised Albert Edward Edenshaw (taking an English royal name) in 1884, and died in 1894. For further particulars on Eden-

shaw, the *Susan Sturgis* affair, and related perceptions, see my "New Light on Haida Chiefship: the Case of Edenshaw," forthcoming in *Ethnohistory*, 29, 2 (1983).

14. Capt. James C. Prevost to Rear-Adm. Fairfax Moresby, 23 July 1853, encl. in Moresby to Sec. of the Admiralty, 13 October 1853, 23 July 1853, Adm. 1/5630, Y73.

15. Ibid.; see also testimony of Rooney, in Kathleen E. Dalzell, *The Queen Charlotte Islands, 1774–1966* (Terrace, B.C.: C.M. Adam, 1968), pp. 67–77; "Statement of Edenshaw, Chief of North Island," in "Account of the Plunder of the 'Susan Sturges,' " *Nautical Magazine* 23 (1854): 210–11. Edenshaw later told Collison that when the *Susan Sturgis* was captured he prevented the slaughter of the whites. Other Haida told him that it was on Edenshaw's orders that the schooner was attacked and burned (Collison, *In the Wake of the War Canoe,* p. 111). This is further evidence that the piracy was carefully planned and skilfully executed.

16. Opinion of Sir John Pakington, sec. of state for the colonies, reported in H. Merivale to Admiralty, 13 May 1852, Admiralty Correspondence, I, P.A.B.C.; and Pakington to Douglas, September 1852, in *Queen Charlotte Islands Papers* (1853), Cmd. 788, pp. 17–18.

17. Treven Diary, p. 297, P.A.B.C.

18. Prevost to Moresby, 23 July 1853, Adm. 1/5630.

19. Treven Diary, pp. 300, 303, P.A.B.C.

20. Ibid., p. 300, P.A.B.C; Prevost to Moresby, 23 July 1853, Adm. 1/5630.

21. Prevost to Moresby, 23 July 1853, Adm. 1/5630.

22. Prevost to Moresby, 7 June 1853; Prevost to Moresby, 23 July 1853; Moresby to Sec. of the Admiralty, 10 October 1853; and Admiralty Board Minute, 7 January 1854, all in Adm. 1/5630.

23. Stafford to Moresby, 24 June 1852, Adm. Corr., Vol. I; and Capt. Houston to Moresby, 23 July 1853, in Journal and Letterbook of H.M. Ship *Trincomalee,* OA 20.5, T731 H, P.A.B.C.

24. Houston to Moresby, 2 January 1854, Houston letterbook, P.A.B.C.

25. Quoted in Corday McKay, *Queen Charlotte Islands* [Victoria: Department of Education, 1953], p. 44.

26. Houston to Moresby, 2 January 1854, Houston letterbook, P.A.B.C.

27. Henderson, "Haida Culture Change," pp. 58–59.

28. Francis Poole, *Queen Charlotte Islands: A Narrative of Discovery and Adventure in the North Pacific* (London, 1872), pp. 67–68, 107, 156.

29. Cited in Henderson, "Haida Culture Change," abstract.

30. A.F. Poole, "Two Years amongst the Indians of Queen Charlotte's Islands," *Mission Life* 3 (1868): 106–7.

31. R.C.P. Bayle had first made the suggestion in 1854 (Henderson, "Haida Culture Change," pp. 81–82).

32. Ibid., p. 91.

33. Collison, *In the Wake of the War Canoe,* pp. 166. Prevost was also there, in H.M.S. *Satellite,* in 1859. Prevost had dispensed New Testa-

ments published by the Naval and Bible Society, London, at the islands. In one of them, given to Edenshaw's elder son, the young chief George Cowhoe, Prevost had written providentially on the end papers, "I trust that the bread cast upon the waters will soon be found." Cowhoe's New Testament bore an inscription with that date in Prevost's hand (ibid., pp. 173, 257).

34. Dalzell, *Queen Charlotte Islands,* p. 68.

35. Quoted in ibid., p. 67.

36. Memoirs of Capt. P. Hankin, R.N. EBH 19A p. 39, P.A.B.C.; see also, Mayne, *Four Years in British Columbia,* p. 186.

37. See, for instance, the case of the sloop *Thornton,* in which Captain Warren and his crew defended his becalmed vessel in Queen Charlotte Sound with a rapid fire from Henry repeating rifles (George Nicolson, *Vancouver Island's West Coast, 1762–1962* [Victoria: 1965], pp. 76–77).

38. See, for instance, the stories which are told each generation about Charles Blake, Barney Goldsworthy, and other ex-sailors-turned-gold-seekers who fell into Haida hands as retold in *Western Living* (Vancouver), April 1975, 6–9; and *Victoria Daily Colonist, Islander,* 27 July 1975, 10–11.

39. Molyneux St. John, *The Sea of Mountains: An Account of Lord Dufferin's Tour through British Columbia in 1876,* 2 vols. (London: Hurst and Blackett, 1877), 1: 229.

40. In 1860, for instance, H.M.S. *Alert's* visit to Tanu (Laskeek) extracted the promise that such expeditions and the taking of slaves would stop (James Cooper to Acting Colonial Secretary, 10 October 1860, F 347, 26a, P.A.B.C.).

NOTES TO CHAPTER EIGHT: PIRACY AND PUNISHMENT

1. The views of the Rev. A.J. Brabant on the Ahousat and Clayoquot are in Walbran, *British Columbia Coast Names,* p. 94.

2. Richard J. Cleveland, *A Narrative of Voyages and Commercial Enterprises* (London, 1842), p. 18.

3. Fisher, *Contact and Conflict,* pp. 13–17; Howay, "Indian Attacks upon Maritime Traders," pp. 287–309.

4. John Gowlland Journal, 18 May and 2 June 1861, micro. 447-A, P.A.B.C. See also Barrett-Lennard, *Travels in British Columbia,* pp. 41–42 and 133–35. In a society where revenge constituted the chief motivation for warfare and where whites failed to acknowledge native societal norms and interfered with them, tribes naturally retaliated for actions taken against them. See Philip Drucker, *The Northern and Central Nootkan Tribes* (Washington, D.C.: Smithsonian Institution, Bureau of American Ethnology, Bulletin 144 [in 81st Cong., 1st sess., H. Docs., vol. 49, p. 332–35]); John Edwin Mills, "The Ethnohistory of Nootka Sound" Ph.D. diss., University of Wash-

ington, 1955), ch. 3; Vincent A. Koppert, *Contributions to Clayoquot Ethnology* (Washington, D.C.: Catholic University of America Anthropological Series No. 1, 1930), ch. 8.

5. John Boit's log, *Proceedings of the Massachusetts Historical Society* 53 (1920): 228.

6. This prodigious worker directed the patient survey of Vancouver Island which resulted in no less than thirty-six charts and the first *Vancouver Island Pilot* (1864). In 1863 he became Admiralty Hydrographer, a post he held until 1874 (rear-admiral 1870; knighted 1877). At the time of his death in 1900 he was Admiral Sir George H. Richards, K.C.B., F.R.S. When he quit Vancouver Island for London, he told Governor Douglas that the published data from the surveys would "prevent a recurrence or lessen the frequency of disasters which have annually befallen vessels navigating in that boisterous neighbourhood." He was given a vote of thanks by the Vancouver Island Legislative Assembly (Llewellyn S. Dawson, *Memoirs of Hydrography* 2 vols. [Eastbourne, England: H.W. Keny, 1885], 2: ch. 3; R.W. Sandilands, "The History of Hydrographic Surveying in British Columbia," mimeo. [Victoria: Canadian Hydrographic Service, 1965], pp. 16, 19).

7. Rear-Adm. Baynes to Douglas, 31 October 1859, F1212a, 27, P.A.B.C.

8. Douglas to Tolmie, 17 September 1852, Western Americana Collection, Item 263, p. 43, Beineke Library, Yale University; Nicolson,

Vancouver Island's West Coast, pp. 73–74.

9. Prevost to Capt. M. deCourcy, Senior Officer, Vancouver Island, 11 March 1859, encl. in deCourcy to Douglas, 12 March 1859, F 1218, P.A.B.C.; see also, R. Bruce Scott, *Barkley Sound: A History of the Pacific Rim National Park Area* (Victoria: n.p., 1972), pp. 43–47.

10. Robbers Bay has since disappeared from pilot and chart. At that time Barkley Sound was also known, by the Indians, as Nitinat, and is not to be confused with the tidal river "False Nitinat" which now bears the name Nitinat.

11. Swell, referred to in British sources as "Swale," suffered for his friendship to whites. On 10 March 1861, while travelling in a canoe between Neah Bay and Port Townsend, he was set upon by some native rivals and brutally murdered. Swell was "the nearest thing to a white man of any Indian on Fuca's Straits," local Indian Agent Colonel Michael T. Simmons is reported to have said. Swell's people plotted and took revenge while James Swan hoped for a better Indian policy to stop murders and revenge for murders. Swan, *Almost Out of the World,* pp. 70, 100–104. Swan knew Swell well; consequently I have used his spelling of the name in preference to the British "Swale."

12. *British Colonist,* 19 February 1859. Gowlland Journal, 18 May 1861.

13. Prevost to DeCourcy, 11 March 1859, F 1218, P.A.B.C.

14. Ibid.

15. In fact, he wrote to the Church Missionary Society, complaining

that liquor was the principal poison at Barkley Sound and that local Indian women were working as prostitutes in Victoria. He hoped that the recently appointed Indian agent, William Banfield, would become a supporter of the Society (Prevost to Henry Venn, 21 November 1859, C C2/o, 13/4, C.M.S.A.). Banfield had advised Prevost that the West Coast Indians greatly needed missionary help. The Ohiet, he reported, were prepared to receive a missionary teacher (William Banfield to Prevost, 30 October 1850, C C2/o, 13/12, C.M.S.A.). Two years later, in Victoria, Edward Cridge pressed the Society to do the same (Cridge to Secretary, C C2/o, 5/1, C.M.S.A.). But, for reasons of manpower, the Society was unable to meet the request and (to use Cridge's exalted prose) "send large reinforcements to this outpost of the Redeemer's Kingdom, and drive Satan from his long-established seat."

16. Prevost to DeCourcy, 11 March 1859, F 1218, P.A.B.C.

17. Drucker, *Northern and Central Nootkan Tribes*, pp. 254–56.

18. Journal of Rear-Admiral Sir Thomas Maitland, 5 August 1862, Adm. 50/311.

19. Prevost had advice from Banfield that Indians on the West Coast, "five months shut up in their strongholds... are apt to forget that chastisement might come, when their avarice and cupidity are tempted by the sight of civilized commodities thrown unprotected on their shores, by stress of wind and weather" (W.E. Banfield to Capt. J.C. Prevost, 17

September 1859, Ohiet, Barkley Sound, C C2/o 13/11, C.M.S.A.). Banfield regarded most of these Indians as quiet, subservient, and unlikely to be dangerous or expensive to the government, but he thought they were liable to be incited to war "by some ambitious, restless, subordinate chief" (Banfield to Prevost, 30 October 1859, C C2/o 13/12, C.M.S.A.). Gilbert M. Sproat, "The West Coast Indians in Vancouver Island," *Transactions of the Ethnological Society of London*, new ser., 5 (1867): 245.

20. Sproat, *Savage Life* and, by the same author, *British Columbia: Information for Emigrants* (London, 1873), p. 7.

21. Banfield to the Colonial Secretary, 6 September 1860, P.A.B.C.

22. Sproat, "West Coast Indians," p. 245.

23. See below, n. 35.

24. Scott, *Barkley Sound*, pp. 65–66, and Walbran, *British Columbia Coast Names*, pp. 31–32.

25. James Douglas to Rear-Adm. Kingcome, 10 September 1863, Admiralty Correspondence, vol. 3, P.A.B.C.; Journal of Rear-Adm. John Kingcome, 11 and 12 September 1863, Adm. 50/311. The Nootkas killed the Indian crew-member who was a Clayoquot because they feared he would implicate them in the crime; the vessel was chopped in pieces and the cargo distributed among the Indians (*British Colonist*, 21 April 1863).

26. Walbran, *British Columbia Coast Names*, p. 14; and information from Leonard Clay, 24 August 1976.

27. See *Victoria Daily Colonist*, 20

October 1864; Journal of Rear-Adm. the Hon. Joseph Denman, 17 September 1864, Adm. 50/312.

28. Pike to Rear-Adm. Denman, 27 September 1864, encl. in Denman to Sec. of the Admiralty, 30 September 1864, Adm. 1/5878, Y117.

29. In June 1861, when H.M.S. *Hecate* had visited Echachets village, Clayoquot Sound, the Indians feared that the vessel's visit was intended to introduce a disease among them "as had once been done at Cape Flattery by the Americans, killing hundreds of the natives." The chief became convinced that British intentions were peaceable. (Gowlland Journal, 27 June 1861).

30. Pike to Rear-Adm. Denman, 27 September 1864, encl. in Denman to Sec. of the Admiralty, 30 September, Adm. 1/5878, Y117.

31. "Rockets are very useful for setting places on fire and are especially valuable against savage tribes," wrote Captain H. Garbett, R.N. in his *Naval Gunnery* (London, 1897, pp. 260–62), "They are fired by friction tube from a trough on land or a tube in boats." The Hale 24-pounder rocket was a standard article of British naval armament for use during the Victorian reign. They used high-pressure gas in the tail, generated by internal combustion. Though not particularly accurate, the rocket's main use was as a bombarding weapon against a wide general target. The projectile's noise, "produced an awe-inspiring effect on bush tribes, to whom the prolonged and diabolical howl as they soared overhead almost suggested the wail of the last trumpet in the sky" (G.A. Ballard, "War Rockets in the Mid-Victorian Fleet," *Mariner's Mirror* 31 [1945]: 174).

32. Christopher Lloyd, *The Navy and the Slave Trade: The Suppression of the African Slave Trade in the Nineteenth Century* (London: Longmans Green, 1949), pp. 92–97.

33. Gough, *The Royal Navy and the Northwest Coast*, ch. 9.

34. Denman to Sec. of the Admiralty, 15 September 1864, Adm. 1/5878, Y107.

35. He was referring to the case of the sloop *Random* where some native constables had been fired on and one killed near Port Simpson. The *Grappler* was sent to investigate (Denman to Sec. of the Admiralty, 30 September 1864, Adm. 1/5878, Y117).

36. Denman to Sec. of the Admiralty, 15 September 1864, Adm. 1/5878, Y107.

37. Kennedy entered the army as an ensign in the 68th Regiment, May 1827. He was promoted lieutenant February 1832 and captain June 1840. Retired on half pay in 1840, he "sold out" in 1848. He was engaged during the Irish famine, 1846–47, under the commissioners of public works in Ireland (See *Colonial Office List for 1865* [London, 1865], p. 196). Colonial perceptions of Kennedy are given in Sproat, *Savage Life,* p. 62, and Walbran, *British Columbia Coast Names,* p. 282.

38. Gov. A.E. Kennedy to Rear-Adm. Denman, 27 September 1864, in Denman to Sec. of the Admiralty, 12 October 1864, Adm. 1/5878, Y133.

39. This account of proceedings is based on Journal of Rear-Admiral Denman, 1–3 October 1864, Adm. 50/312; Denman to Sec. of the Admiralty, 12 October 1864, Adm. 1/5878, Y133; *Sutlej*'s log (Adm. 53/8837), and *Devastation*'s log (Adm. 53/8594) for 2–13 October 1864; and Kennedy to E. Cardwell, 14 October 1864, and enclosures, C.O. 305/23.

40. Gowlland Journal, 23 July 1861. Testimony of Enquiokshittle, 5 October 1864, encl. in Denman to Sec. of the Admiralty, 12 October 1864, Adm. 1/5878, Y133. In 1885, when Dr. William W. Walkem visited Ahousat, an Indian told him that he did not understand how the captain of the *Kingfisher* "was induced to come in shore, as Chapchah was noted all over the west coast as a "mesatche man" (bad man), and that he remembered the occasion well, though he was a little boy" (W. W. Walkem, *Stories of Early British Columbia* [Vancouver: News-Advertiser, 1914, p. 13).

41. I have not been able to determine precisely what small arms the bluejackets and marines had; likely they were the small bore Enfield rifle and the Deane and Adam's muzzle loading, percussion-capped revolver, certainly better in accuracy than the trade musket. In the mid-1860's advances were being made in breech-loading and new rifles such as the Snider, Martini Henry, and later the Lee-Metford and Lee-Enfield (.303) were introduced (Sir William Laird Clowes, *The Royal Navy: A History,* 7 vols. [London: Sampson Low, Marston, and Co., 1897–

1913], 6: 202; 7: 50).

42. Denman to the Sec. of the Admiralty, 8 November 1864, Adm. 1/5878, Y129.

43. Denman to Sec. of the Admiralty, 12 October 1864, Adm. 1/5878, Y133.

44. Kennedy to Denman, 14 October 1864, Adm. 1/5878.

45. Great Britain, Statutes at Large, 6 and 7 *Vict.* c. 22 (1843). Minute by H. Merivale, 6 March 1852, on Douglas to Grey, 16 December 1851, and J. Pakington to Douglas, 18 March 1852, C.O. 305/3, fols. 78–81. For court proceedings, see *British Colonist,* 20 October 1864. On 26 January 1865, the Legislative Council of British Columbia passed the Native Evidence Ordinance, and it was effective 8 February 1865. This ordinance was brought forward in order to deal with the question of competence of aborigines to give evidence "by reason of their imperfect comprehension of the obligations now necessary to give validity to their testimony." Under this, natives and half-breeds could be examined in all civil and criminal proceedings, the judge, at his discretion, waiving the standard oath and in such an instance being obliged to tell the witness that proven false evidence would result in a perjury charge being laid ("Indian Evidence Ordinance, 1865," C.O. 61/1, p. 149).

46. Denman to Kennedy, 18 November 1864, R45/829 (Attorney-General), P.A.B.C.

47. Sproat, *Savage Life,* pp. 201–2.

48. Ibid., pp. 196–97.

49. Charles Moser, *Reminiscences of the West Coast of Vancouver Is-*

land (Victoria: Acme Press, 1926), p. 190.

50. Ibid., pp. 25–26.

51. Walbran, *British Columbia Coast Names*, p. 14.

52. Ibid., p. 190; and John Jacobson to Willard Ireland, 24 November 1960, Ahousat, Historical Notes, vol. 1, 900–910, M.M.B.C.

53. Admiralty Board Minute, 14 December 1864, on Denman to Sec. of the Admiralty, 13 October 1864, Adm. 1/5878, Y133.

54. Colonial Office Papers to the Admiralty for 1865, 5 January 1865, Adm. 1/5950; noted in Index 12368, Adm. 12/765.

55. R. Maynard, "Memoranda of a trip round Vancouver Island and Nootka Island on board H.M.S. *Scout*, Captn Price, A.D. 1866," EB D16m, P.A.B.C.; Hankin Memoirs, EB H19 A, P.A.B.C.; Walbran, *British Columbia Coast Names*, pp. 225–26.

56. Denman to Sec. of the Admiralty, 19 October 1864, Adm. 1/5878, Y165.

57. A.J. Brabant, Misc. Papers, ED B72-4, p. 45, P.A.B.C.

58. *Colonial Office List for 1865* (London 1865) p. 217; R.R.A. Doolan to H. Venn, 1 April 1864, C C2/o 7/1, C.M.S.A.

59. Victoria newspapers long complained that the local executive's actions were inadequate for protecting shipping and that a gunboat should be sent (see *British Colonist*, 31 July 1869, and *Evening News*, 26 April 1869).

60. Cdr. H.W. Mist to Capt. W.H. Edge, 11 May 1869, encl. in Hastings to Sec. of Admiralty, 29 June 1869, Adm. 1/6092.

61. Ibid. Also, Maurice de Baets, *The Apostle of Alaska: Life of the Most Reverend Charles John Seghers*, trans. Mary Mildren (Paterson, NJ: St. Anthony Guild Press, 1943), p. 85.

62. Capt. Edge to Rear-Adm. Hastings, 13 May 1869, encl. in Hastings to Sec. of Admiralty, 29 June 1869; Admiralty Minute, 3 August 1869; and Hastings to Secretary of Admiralty, 14 October 1869, all in Adm. 1/6092.

63. Brabant's view of the *John Bright* episode is in A.J. Brabant, Misc. Papers, ED B72.4, pp. 41–48, P.A.B.C.

64. Walbran, *British Columbia Coast Names*, pp. 241–42. When Capt. James Colnett of the trader *Argonaut* investigated the death of Thomas Hudson and five companions near Hesquiat in 1790, he was told by the Indians that they had drowned and that when the bodies reached the beach they were stripped of clothes and thrown to the crows (Warren L. Cook, *Flood Tide of Empire: Spain and the Pacific Northwest, 1543–1819* [New Haven: Yale University Press, 1973], pp. 292–93).

65. A case of flogging in which an Indian chief was totally demeaned before his kinsmen is described in J.C. Sabben, Journal of H.M.S. *Termagant* and *Clio*, 20 August 1860, EB Sal, P.A.B.C. In another case, a Sheshat was released from flogging when three chiefs brought seal skins as compensation (*Report of the Columbia Mission* [London, 1860], p. 88). In 1867, flogging was ordered stopped (see below, p. 000, n. 11).

66. Rear-Adm. Denman to Lt. Denny, 3 September 1866, copy, C.O. 60/30.

NOTES TO CHAPTER NINE: POLICING THE PASSAGE

1. Vancouver, *Voyage*, 1:328; C.F. Newcombe, ed., *Menzie's Journal of Vancouver's Voyage* (Victoria: Archives of British Columbia, Memoir 5. 1923), p. 77; Cdr. J.C. Prevost to Rear-Adm. F. Moresby, 7 June 1853, copy in Moresby to Sec. of the Admiralty, 13 October 1853, Adm. 1/5630, Y73; Francis Poole, *Queen Charlotte Islands: A Narrative of Discovery and Adventure in the North Pacific* (London, 1872), pp. 174–75. Discovery Passage remains "the main ship channel leading NW from the north end of the Strait of Georgia." "In the vicinity of Cape Mudge, the tidal streams attain velocities of from 5 to 7 knots, the flood flowing south and the ebb north." These cause back eddies (*Sailing Directions, British Columbia Coast, vol. 1* [8th ed., Ottawa: Information Canada, 1973], p. 195).

2. Dawson, "Notes and Observations on the Kwakiool," p. 74; Taylor and Duff, "Post-Contact Southward Movement of the Kwakiutl," pp. 56–66; Helen Codere, "Kwakiutl," in Edward H. Spicer, ed., *Perspectives in American Indian Culture Change* (Chicago Press, 1961), pp. 435–54.

3. Gowlland, Journal, 20 April 1860; James C. Prevost to Moresby, 7 June 1853, Adm. 1/5630, Y73; Mayne, *Four Years in British Columbia*, p. 245; James Douglas Journal, 1840, pp. 9, 11, B.L.B.; Taylor and Duff, "Post-Contact Southward Movement of the Kwakiutl," p. 62; Barrett-Lennard, *Travels in British Columbia*, p. 37; Thomas Crosby, *Up and*

Down the Pacific Coast (London: Missionary Society of the Methodist Church, 1914), p. 367.

4. Prevost to Moresby, 7 June 1853, Adm. 1/5630, Y73.

5. Mayne, *Four Years in British Columbia*, pp. 75, 245–46.

6. W. Hales Franklyn to Lt. Robson, 16 May 1861, encl. in Maitland to Sec. of the Admiralty, 24 May 1861, Adm. 1/5761, Y165.

7. Robson to Maitland, 20 May 1861, encl. in Maitland to Sec. of the Admiralty, 24 May 1861, Adm. 1/5761, Y165.

8. Ibid.

9. *British Colonist*, 18 April and 21 and 22 May 1861; Mayne, *Four Years in British Columbia*, p. 75; Macfie, *Vancouver Island and British Columbia*, p. 459; Walbran, *British Columbia Coast Names*, p. 186.

10. Robson to Maitland, 20 May 1861, encl. in Maitland to Sec. of the Admiralty, 24 May 1861, Adm. 1/5761, Y165.

11. Maitland to Sec. of the Admiralty, 24 May 1861, Adm. 1/5761, Y165.

12. Maitland to Senior Member of the Council, Victoria, 21 May 1861, F1206/4, P.A.B.C.; Work to Maitland, 21 May 1861, encl. in Adm. 1/5761, Y165; Douglas to Maitland, 24 June 1861, encl. in Maitland to Sec. of the Admiralty, 11 July 1861, Adm. 1/5761, Y222.

13. Maitland to Sec. of the Admiralty, 26 August 1861, Adm. 1/5761, Y309.

14. Maitland Journal, 2 August 1862, Adm. 50/311. See pp. 000–000.

15. Spencer Journal, 13 April 1863, Adm. 50/311.

16. Douglas to Rear-Adm. John King-

come, 10 September 1863, Adm.
Corr. 3, P.A.B.C.; and Denman to
Sec. of the Admiralty, 27 Novem-
ber 1865, Adm. 1/5924, Y145.

17. Henry Wakeford (Acting Col.
Sec.) to Gov. A.E. Kennedy, 28
March 1865, in C.O. 880/5, no. 37
(1856–66), p. 11.

18. In 1863 Commander John W.
Pike, R.N., and Lieutenant Edmund H. Verney, R.N., held
"Commissions as Justices of the
Peace on the Coast Service" (Howay and Scholefield, *British Columbia*, 2:160).

19. Details of the island's early pio-
neer history are to be found in
A.F. Flucke, "Early Days on Salt-
spring Island," *British Columbia
Historical Quarterly* 15 (1951):
161–202; Charles C. Irby, "The
Black Settlers on Saltspring Island,
Canada, in the Nineteenth Cen-
tury," *Association of Pacific Coast
Geographers 1974 Yearbook*
(Corvallis: Oregon State Univer-
sity Press, 1974): 35–44; and Erica
Roberts, *Saltspring Saga* (Ganges,
B.C.: Driftwood, 1962).

20. Roberts, *Saltspring Saga*, p. 9.

21. Flucke, "Early Days on Saltspring
Island," p. 164; and Irby, "Black
Settlers on Saltspring Island," p.
40. Though whites claimed that
Indians had never been there before, this was disputed by Mayne
(*Four Years in British Columbia*,
p. 165). Wayne P. Suttles lists
three villages: one on the north
shore of Fulford Harbour, another
on the south shore of Fulford Harbour, and a third on Ganges Harbour ("Economic Life of the Coast
Salish of Haro and Rosario
Straits" [1951], in *Coast Salish and
Western Washington Indians*

[New York and London: Garland
Publishing, 1974], p. 81).

22. Marie A. Stark Wallace, Sylvia
Stark's Story, typescript, n.d., EE
St. 2, p. 20, P.A.B.C.; Crawford
Kilian, *Go Do Some Great Thing:
The Black Pioneers of British Co-
lumbia* (Vancouver: Douglas and
McIntyre, 1978), ch. 9.

23. Walbran, *British Columbia Coast
Names*, pp. 117–18, 199–200; and
Roberts, *Saltspring Saga*, ch. 4.
Mayne (*Four Years in British
Columbia*, pp. 246–48) tells of the
visit by H.M.S. *Satellite* to Ganges
Harbour to check intertribal vio-
lence.

24. *British Colonist*, 12 July 1860;
Walbran, *British Columbia Coast
Names*, pp. 117–18.

25. Wallace, Stark Story, p. 22, P.A.
B.C.; Robin W. Winks, *The
Blacks in Canada* (New Haven
and London: Yale University
Press, 1971), p. 278.

26. Testimony of John Henley, un-
dated, encl. in Lascelles to Commodore the Hon. J.W.S. Spencer,
25 April 1863, encl. in Spencer to
Sec. of the Admiralty, 4 May 1863,
Cap. S89; Pike to Spencer, 8 May
1863, encl. in Spencer to Sec. of
Admiralty, 14 May 1864, Cap.
S90; all in Adm. 1/5829.

27. Douglas to Spencer, 9 May 1863,
encl. in Spencer to Sec. of the
Admiralty, 14 May 1863, Adm.
1/5829, Cap. S90.

28. *British Colonist*, 16 April and 6, 8,
16, 25 May 1863; also Walbran,
British Columbia Coast Names, p.
118.

29. Douglas to Newcastle, 21 May
1863, C.O. 305/20.

30. Mayne, *Four Years in British Columbia*, pp. 152, 396; Maitland

Journal, 24 August 1862, Adm. 50/311.

31. *British Colonist,* 10 April 1863. Walbran incorrectly gives the date as November 1862 (Walbran, *British Columbia Coast Names,* p. 299).

32. *British Colonist,* 15 April 1863.

33. Suttles, "Economic Life of the Coast Salish," pp. 378–79.

34. Lieut. the Hon. Horace D. Lascelles to Commodore the Hon. J.W.S. Spencer, 25 April 1863, encl. in Spencer to Sec. of the Admiralty, 4 May 1863, Adm. 1/5829.

35. Ibid. Also, Seaman's report in *British Colonist,* 27 April 1863.

36. Commodore the Hon. J.W.S. Spencer to Sec. of the Admiralty, 4 May 1863, Adm. 1/5829, Cap. S89.

37. Douglas to Newcastle, 21 May 1863, C.O. 305/20.

38. Douglas to Spencer, 9 May 1863, encl. in Spencer to Sec. of the Admiralty, 14 May 1863, Adm. 1/5829.

39. Ibid.

40. Cdr. J.W. Pike to Commodore the Hon. J.W.S. Spencer, 26 May 1863, F1210/6, P.A.B.C.

41. Ibid.

42. Ibid.

43. *British Colonist,* 22 May 1863; and Walbran, *British Columbia Coast Names,* p. 301. Cf. R. Kenryn ("Over the Foreyard," *Vancouver Daily Province,* 17 November 1936), who makes the unsubstantiated charge that the article so offended the Navy that the *Forward* returned and dealt with the Lemalchi in such a fashion "that they never again broke into open revolt."

44. Letter from S. Harris, 25 April 1863, In *British Colonist,* 27 April 1863; Cdr. J.W. Pike to Commodore the Hon. J.W.S. Spencer, 26 May 1863, Adm. 1/5826.

45. *British Colonist,* 27 May 1863.

46. Cdr. E. Hardinge to Commodore the Hon. J.W.S. Spencer, 8 June 1863, encl. in Spencer to Sec. of the Admiralty, 13 June 1863, Adm. 1/5826.

47. "Indians of the Lamalcha tribe detained and sent to Victoria at the pleasure of His Excellency the Governor," encl. in ibid.

48. *British Colonist,* 10 June 1863.

49. "*Regina vs. Whan-uch:* Prisoner was convicted of assisting Pollak in killing Frederick Marks and Mrs. Caroline Harvey, on Kulman (or Saturna) Island. Evidence of Nuchuss, an Indian woman, was to effect that Pollak, since shot, killed Marks, while the accused stabbed Mrs. Harvey. Both bodies were weighted with stones and sunk—Verdict, Guilty; sentenced to hang, July 4. *Regina vs. Quah-ah-ilton, She-nall-ou-ouck, Ot-chee-wun:* Evidence of Horace Smith, superintendent of police, told of fight in Village Bay, Kuper Island, when sailor, Gliddon was killed. All found guilty—sentenced to hang, July 4" (Notes of Chief Justice Cameron, entered in record of assizes, June 17 et seq, 1863, in McKelvie, *Tales of Conflict,* p. 97).

50. Walbran, *British Columbia Coast Names,* p. 299. In 1877 the Penelukuts protested against their lands being taken and were classified as "offenders gainst the law" and a gunboat was recommended to be sent. "It is true kindness to

check it [Indian resistance], for the practice is sure to get the Indians into trouble," Gilbert Malcolm Sproat said (A.C. Anderson and A. McKinlay to A.C. Elliott, Provincial Secretary, Victoria, 7 January 1877; and Sproat to Elliott, 28 January 1877, Indian Reserve Commission, 1876–78, Instructions, Reports and Memoranda, Misc. 19, Legislative Library, Victoria).

51. Douglas to Rear-Adm. J. Kingcome, 6 July 1863 and 10 February 1864, Adm. Corr. 3, P.A.B.C.; see also Kingcome Journal, 28 May 1864, Adm. 50/311. In 1870 a request from Mayne Island settlers for a gunboat to "teach the Indians a lesson" was denied by the colonial authority: see Marie Anne Elliott, "A History of Mayne Island," M.A. thesis, University of Victoria, 1982, pp. 15–16.

52. As has been claimed in E. W. Wright, *Lewis and Dryden's Marine History of the Pacific Northwest* (Portland, OR; 1895), p. 176.

53. Roberts, *Saltspring Saga,* p. 40

NOTES TO CHAPTER TEN: THE PULLS OF ALASKA

1. Hector Chevigny, *Russian America: The Great Alaskan Venture, 1741–1867* (New York: Ballantine, 1973), pp. 85–91; see also Clarence L. Andrews, *The Story of Sitka* (Seattle: Lowman and Hardon, 1922), pp. 20–25. Cf. P. A. Tikhmenev, *A History of the Russian-American Company,* trans. and ed. by Richard A. Pierce and Alton S. Donnelly (Seattle: University of Washington Press, 1978), pp. 65–66. In describing the inveterate hatred of the Kolosh for the Russians, Captain Pavel Nikolaevich Golovin of the Imperial Russian Navy reported to St. Petersburg that in 1855 the Kolosh attacked Sitka but did not succeed, and the reason for their attack seems to be the fluctuations and reversal of policies of allowing them to settle near the fort's walls. See *The End of Russian America: Captain P. N. Golovin's Last Report, 1862,* by Basil Dmytryshyn and E. A. P. Crownhart-Vaughan (Portland Oregon Historical Society, 1979), pp. 28–29.

2. Maitland had taken part in several actions: Malabar 1838, Scinde and Persian Gulf 1839, Canton and Chusan 1840, and Amoy and Shanghai 1841. He succeeded to the earldom of Lauderdale in 1863. At his death in 1878 he was Admiral of the Fleet, K.C.B., G.C.B.

3. Rear-Adm. Sir T. Maitland to Sec. of the Admiralty, September 1862, Adm. 1/5790, pt. 1, Y246. In 1863 the Admiralty sent the 17-gun screw-sloop *Cameleon* from England to provide further protection for British subjects expected on the northern coast during the mining season (Gough, *Royal Navy,* pp. 147–48).

4. W. H. McNeill and Francis A. Dobbs to J. Douglas, 2 August 1862, and testimony by Charles Neslar, 26 August 1862, encl. in Maitland to Sec. of the Admiralty, 3 September 1862, Adm. 1/5790, pt. 1, Y246.

5. Governor J. Douglas to Rear-

Adm. Sir T. Maitland, 29 August 1862, encl. in Maitland to Sec. of the Admiralty, 2 September 1862, ibid.

6. Cdr. J. W. Pike to Rear-Admiral Sir T. Maitland, 6 October 1862, and Furuhjelm to Maitland, 25/6 September 1862, encl. in Maitland to Sec. of the Admiralty, 2 December 1862, ibid., Y306.

7. Cdr. J. W. Pike to Rear-Admiral Sir T. Maitland, 6 October 1862, in Maitland to Sec. of the Admiralty, 2 December, ibid.

8. George Davidson, *The Alaska Boundary* (San Francisco: Alaska Packers Association, 1903), pp. 111–12. Davidson is wrong, however, in asserting (p. 111) that Pike sought Furuhjelm's *permission* to enter the Stikine. He asked only if he could cooperate with the Russians. Admittedly the Russians were jealous of their rights, but Furuhjelm's own letter to Admiral Maitland, cited in note 6 above, makes clear his own cooperative spirit.

9. J. Cooper to Colonial Secretary, 17 October 1862, F1210/3; Cdr. J. W. Pike to Rear-Adm. Maitland, 7 October 1862, F1219; and draft of Douglas's reply on Pike to Douglas, 28 April 1863, F1210/5a, all in P.A.B.C.

10. Cdr. J. W. Pike to Rear-Adm. Sir T. Maitland, 6 October 1862, and Capt. G. H. Richards to Rear-Adm. Sir T. Maitland, 24 September 1862, encl. in Maitland to Sec. of the Admiralty, 1 December 1862, Adm. 1/5790, pt. 1, Y328. The bringing of chiefs on board ship after securing them by armed force, a colonial official observed, "placed the Commander in a position to treat with Indians 'bona fide' as the superior power and to make terms in accordance with the demands of Justice." The display of force intimidated the old chief Allanlahhah, for "in every direction the old man turned, a twenty-four pounder besides other arms was too formidable for him to view with calmness, what appeared such stern reality" (J. Cooper to Colonial Secretary, 17 October 1862, F1210/3, P.A.B.C.).

11. H. Hammond (F.O.) to Undersecretary of State, Colonial Office, 9 December 1867, C.O. 60/30.

12. Report in *San Francisco Bulletin*, printed in *British Colonist*, 8 July 1868; Johnson, *Thence Round Cape Horn*, p. 131.

13. Cdr. Henry Glass, "Naval Administration in Alaska," *Proceedings of the United States Naval Institute* 16 (1890):2.

14. Roland L. De Lorme, "Liquor Smuggling in Alaska 1867–1899," *Pacific Northwest Quarterly* 66 (1975): 145–52.

15. Jeanette Paddock Nichols, *Alaska: A History of its Administration, Exploitation, and Industrial Development during its First Half Century under the Rule of the United States* (Cleveland: Arthur H. Clark, 1924), pp. 59–65, provides a useful review of administrative history and argues (p. 61, n. 61) "The navy was better adapted to Alaska than the army because the only punishable offences were in violation of laws regarding commerce, customs, and navigation, and Alaska had approximately 25,000 miles of coast line from which evil-doers could choose for their operations." See also Hubert Howe Bancroft, *History of Alaska* (San Francisco:

History Publishing Co., 1886), pp. 612, 618.

16. Quoted in Margan B. Sherwood, "Ardent Spirits: Hooch and the *Osprey* Affair at Sitka," *Journal of the West* 4, (1965): 323.

17. Quoted in Madge Wolfenden and J. H. Hamilton, "The Sitka Affair," *The Beaver* 17 (1955–56): 4.

18. Rear-Adm. A.F.R. de Horsey to Sec. of the Admiralty, 22 May 1879, Adm. 1/6489, Y62.

19. Report of Capt. H. A'Court, quoted in *Reports of Captain L. A. Beardslee, U.S. Navy, Relative to Affairs in Alaska*, typescript, Historical Notes, vol. 2, M.M.B.C. See also Sir William Laird Clowes, *The Royal Navy: A History*, vol. 7 (London: Sampson Low, Mars-

ton, and Co., 1903), 310–11.

20. On Beardslee's work in Alaska, see Lt. J. G. Mel Crain, "When the Navy Ruled Alaska," *U.S. Naval Institute Proceedings*, 81 (1955): 198–203. Also, Cdr. L. A. Beardslee, "Report on the Operations of the *Jamestown* in connection with the Indian Tribes," 47th Cong., 1st sess., Sen. Exec. Doc. 71 (1879).

21. Glass, "Naval Administration," p. 4.

22. Sherwood, "Ardent Spirits," pp. 335, 337–38; see also Johnson, *Thence Round Cape Horn*, p. 136, and Andrews, *Story of Sitka*, pp. 82–84.

23. Quoted in Crain, "When the Navy Ruled Alaska," p. 200.

NOTES TO CHAPTER ELEVEN: "THE CUSTOMARY AUTHORITY" UNDER DOMINION AUSPICES

1. The controversy began soon after the constitutional changes were effected; see British Columbia, *Papers Connected with the Indian Land Question, 1850–1875* (Victoria: Queen's Printer, 1875) and *Report of the Royal Commission on Indian Affairs for the Province of British Columbia*, 4 vols. (Victoria: Acme Press, 1916). See also, Fisher, *Contact and Conflict*, ch. 7; Cail, *Land, Man, and the Law* chs. 11 and 12; and LaViolette, *Struggle for Survival*, ch. 4.

2. The terms of union are in Howay and Scholefield, *British Columbia*, 2:697.

3. British North America Act, 1867; copy in ibid., 2:697–713.

4. Fisher, *Contact and Conflict*, p. 172.

5. Ibid., ch. 7, passim.

6. I. W. Powell to the Right Hon. the Superintendent-General of Indian Affairs, 1 April 1880, Victoria, R.G. 10, vol 3698, file 15,927, P.A.C.

7. Duncan C. Scott, "Indian Affairs, 1867–1912," in Adam Short and Arthur G. Doughty, eds., *Canada and Its Provinces*, 23 vols. (Toronto: Glasgow Brook, 1914), 7:621; also, Douglas Leighton, "A Victorian Civil Servant at Work: Lawrence Vankoughnet and the Canadian Indian Department, 1874–1893" in Ian A. L. Getty and Antoine S. Lussier, eds., *As Long as the Sun Shines and Water Flows* (Vancouver: University of British Columbia Press, 1983), pp. 104–19.

8. On Powell, see B.A. McKelvie, "Lieutenant–Colonel Israel Wood Powell, M.D., C. M.," *British Columbia Historical Quarterly* 11 (1947): 33–54.

9. Joseph W. Trutch to Sir John A. Macdonald, 14 October 1872, in Sir Joseph Pope, *Correspondence of Sir John A. Macdonald* (Toronto: Oxford University Press, 1921), pp. 183–85; also Cail, *Land, Man, and the Law*, pp. 297–99.

10. Fisher, *Contact and Conflict*, p. 180.

11. I. W. Powell's diaries, P.A.B.C., contain numerous references to gifts.

12. Kimberley to Dufferin, 4 February 1873, draft, and Admiralty to Colonial Office, 5 February 1873, C.O. 42/722, pp. 57–65.

13. Admiralty to Colonial Office, 28 February 1873; Colonial Office Minutes, 3 March 1873; and Kimberley to Dufferin, 6 March 1873, ibid., pp. 62–79.

14. Colonial Office Minutes, 14 November 1873, on Admiralty to Colonial Office, 11 November 1873, encl. in Commander-in-Chief, Pacific, to Admiralty, 11 October 1873, ibid., pp. 138–40.

15. Memo of David Laird, Department of the Interior, 11 April 1874; and Powell to Minister of the Interior, 6 April 1874, R.G. 10, vol. 3608, file 3163, P.A.C.

16. Report of Privy Council, approved by Governor-General in Council, 29 April 1874, R.G. 10, vol. 3608, file 3163, P.A.C.

17. ibid.

18. Minutes by Lord Carnarvon and others, 11 May 1874, telegram to Lieutenant-Governor of British Columbia, 11 May 1874, C.O.

42/731, PP. 77–87; Admiralty to Colonial Office, 30 July 1874, Ibid., pp. 128–31.

19. Gilbert Malcolm Sproat to R.G.W. Herbert, 29 March 1876, C.O. 42/745, pp. 113–15. A sketch to Sproat's career is found in T. A. Rickard, "Gilbert Malcolm Sproat," *British Columbia Historical Quarterly* 1 (1937):21–32.

20. Gilbert Malcolm Sproat to Superintendent-General of Indian Affairs, 6 September 1879, R. G. 10, vol. 3698, file 15,927, P.A.C.

21. Powell was correct in his allegation against Sproat. At the time Sproat had said that force must be used: "It is a true kindness to check it [Indian resistance], for the practice is sure to get the Indians into trouble" (see Sproat to A. C. Elliott, 28 January 1877, in Original Instructions, Reports and Memoranda of the Indian Reserve Commission, 1876–78, Misc. 19, Legislative Library, Victoria). "It will probably be a mere police affair," Sproat's colleagues wrote, "but in these matters a demonstration of force is often useful and we would therefore recommend the Senior Officer of H.M. Ships at Esquimalt be requested if convenient, to send a gunboat" (A. McKinlay and A. C. Anderson to A. C. Elliott, 7 January 1877, ibid.).

22. Powell to the Right Hon. the Superintendent-General of Indian Affairs, 1 April 1880, Victoria, R. G. 10, vol. 3698, file 15,927, P.A.C.

23. Ibid.

24. Executive Council Minutes of 5 October 1882, W. J. Armstrong (Clerk, Executive Council) to Hon. Secretary of State, Ottawa,

6 October 1882, and Report, Privy Council of Canada, 17 November 1882, encl. in Governor General to Earl of Kimberley, 20 November 1882, C.O. 42/772, pp. 377–84.

25. Gough, *Royal Navy*, ch. 10.

26. Admiralty to Colonial Office, 14 March 1883, and Lord Derby to Marquis of Lorne, 26 March 1885, draft, C.O. 42/775, pp. 261–64.

27. Lyons to Admiralty, 13 August 1883, copy, ibid.

28. The *Sir James Douglas* was launched in Victoria on 7 January 1865. Refitted and lengthened (to 116 feet) in 1883, this propeller-driven vessel was replaced by the *Quadra* in 1892 and broken up. At the time of writing, another *Sir James Douglas* works the customary beat of the lighthouse tender and working vessel made famous by her predecessor.

29. Peter O'Reilly to Superintendent-General of Indian Affairs, 14 May 1886, R.G. 10, vol. 3698, file 16,018; Edward Dewdney to L. Vankoughnet, 16 May 1889, R.G. 10, vol. 3815, file 56,546; and O'Reilly to Superintendent General of Indian Affairs, 4 June 1889, R.G. 10, vol. 3814, file 56,936, P.A.C.

30. Vankoughnet to Dewdney, 5 December 1889, draft; Telegram to A.W. Vowell, 7 December 1889; C. Todd to H. Moffatt, 20 September 1889; L. Vankoughnet to E. Dewdney, 8 January 1890; Vowell to Vankoughnet, 10 March 1890; Vowell to Deputy Superintendent, 5 March 1894; Todd to Vowell, 9 April 1894 and 16 April 1894; all in R.G. 10, vol. 3614, file 56,936, P.A.C. The *Vigilant* was sold at a public auction by the Indian Department in 1901, converted into a tug by her new owner, Captain Young, a New Westminster cannery operator, converted to diesel in 1929, and disappeared from the historical record in 1938.

31. On the *Boxer*'s 1873 cruise, see *Daily British Colonist*, 18 June 1873; see also, Leigh Burpee Robinson, "To British Columbia's Totem Land: — Expedition of Dr. Powell in 1873," *Canadian Geographical Journal*, 24, 2 (1942): 80–93.

32. A. Davie to Powell, 15 July 1888, R.G. 10, vol. 3802, file 49,774, P.A.C.

NOTES TO CHAPTER TWELVE: AT HEAVEN'S COMMAND

1. Quoted in Margery Perham, *Colonial Reckoning: The Reith Lectures 1961* (London: Collins Fontana Library, 1963), p. 78.

2. Usher, *William Duncan*, p. 9.

3. Joseph Trutch, the lieutenant-governor of British Columbia, felt the missionary pressure to be unwarranted and of considerable nuisance value. He noted that only two missions, Metlaktla and St. Mary's (later Mission), had shown any notable success, while there were many failures (Joseph W. Trutch to Secretary of State for the provinces [Joseph Howe], 26 September 1871, in British Columbia, *Papers Connected with the Indian Land Question 1850–1875* [Victoria: Queen's Printer, 1875], p. 99).

4. A.J. Brabant, *Mission to Nootka,*

1874–1900: Reminiscences of the West Coast of Vancouver Island, ed. Charles Lillard (Sidney, B.C.: Gray's Publishing, 1977), pp. 24–27.

5. De Baets, *The Apostle of Alaska,* p.110.

6. Brabant, *Mission to Nootka,* pp. 41–48.

7. Ibid., p. 98.

8. [James Charles Prevost], "Vancouver's Island," *Church Missionary Intelligencer* 7 (1856): 167–68.

9. Phyllis Jane Wetherell [Bultmann], "The Foundation and Early Work of the Church Missionary Society," *Historical Magazine of the Protestant Episcopal Church* 18 (1949): 350–71. The C.M.S. transferred its Canadian enterprises to the missionary arm of the Anglican Church of Canada in 1920 (ibid., p. 357).

10. Usher, *William Duncan,* p. 147, n. 97.

11. [Prevost], "Vancouver's Island," pp. 167–68.

12. Most missionaries and ministers who came to colonial British Columbia did so in merchantmen. On at least one other occasion, however, the Lords of the Admiralty provided transport. The Rev. W. Burton Crickmer, M.A. (Oxon), arrived in Victoria on Christmas Day 1858, having been brought out in H.M.S. *Plumper.* He represented the Church of England's Colonial and Continental Church Society (Frank A. Peake, *The Anglican Church in British Columbia* [Vancouver: Mitchell Press, 1959]. p. 21).

13. Prevost to Henry Venn, 12 August 1857, C C2/o 13/1, C.M.S.A.

14. Not to be confused with the first Fort Simpson on the Nass.

15. Pilfering had been an age-old problem for the company at Fort Simpson. "The propensity of the Indians to theft," one company servant noted in 1835, might have "led to quarrels but as the guns command the situation, I think the natives may be deterred from stealing." Of the Indian plunder of the *Vancouver*'s wreck in 1835, he noted: "It is a pity there were not means of compelling them to give back the property or something in lieu of it and at the same time of punishing them effectually for what they have been guilty of. But were we to go there we would not be able to do anything by force, and until we [can] do so it is deemed better to say nothing on the subject, further than that it will not be dropped. Should the steamboat [*Beaver*] come, they might probably be punished effectually" (Henry Drummond Dee, ed., *The Journal of John Work, January to October, 1835* [Victoria: King's Printer, Archives of British Columbia Memoir 10, 1945], pp. 18, 22). A typical view of white-Indian tensions there is Rev. W. H. Pierce, *From Potlatch to Pulpit: The Autobiography of Rev. William Henry Pierce,* ed. Rev. J. P. Hicks (Vancouver: Vancouver Bindery, 1933), p. 168.

16. The views of John Work, H. G. Barnett, and J. W. McKay respectively; quoted in Usher, *William Duncan,* p. 37.

17. Frederick E. Molyneux St. John, *The Sea of Mountains: An Account of Lord Dufferin's Tour Through British Columbia in 1876,* 2 vols. (London, 1877), 1: 301–7, and Dufferin's Speech, 20 September 1876, quoted in Usher,

William Duncan, p. 1. In 1875, the Rev. G. Mason eulogized this model Christian utopia before the Mechanics' Literary Institute in Victoria as follows (ibid.):

There is a happy spot of busy life
Where order reigns where hushed the din of strife,
Harmonious brethren neath paternal rule,
Play their glad task in Methlacatla's school,
There Duncan holds supreme his peaceful throne,
His power unquestioned, and their rights his own.
Anvil and hammer, saw and wheel resound,
And useful arts of industry abound,
While faith and knowledge find an altar there.

18. Quoted in Henry S. Wellcome, *The Story of Metlakatla,* 4th ed. (London, 1887), p. 80.

19. Mayne, *Four Years in British Columbia,* p. 210.

20. Richards to Rear-Adm. Baynes, 17 August 1860, encl. in Baynes to Sec. of the Admiralty, 10 September 1860, Adm. 1/5736, pt. 2, Y152.

21. That is, that cited in note 20 above.

22. Mayne, *Four Years in British Columbia,* pp. 210–12. See also, Journal of William Duncan, 19 August 1860, published in *Church Missionary Record,* March 1861, p. 98.

23. Stock, *The History of the Church Missionary Society,* 3:251; see also Peake, *Anglican Church,* pp. 90–92.

24. "Extract... of Proceedings... from Lieut. Denny," 24 October 1866, encl. in Pacific Station Letter No. 153, 9 November 1866, Adm. 1/5969.

25. Rogers to Sec. of the Admiralty, 24 July 1868, Adm. 1/6072.

26. Ibid.

27. Seymour to the Duke of Buckingham, 30 November 1868, C.O. 60/33.

28. Usher, *William Duncan,* p. 80.

29. Rear-Adm. Arthur A. Farquhar to Sec. of Admiralty, 11 October 1873, Adm. 1/6263, Y116. A copy of this report was sent to the Colonial Office and thence to the Governor General of Canada for information of the Department of the Interior (see R.G. 10, vol. 3,604, file 2,753).

30. Based on Usher, *William Duncan,* p. 122.

31. Wellcome, *Story of Metlakatla,* p. 221.

32. Elsewhere during his tour of inspection he found the Methodist missionary the Rev. Thomas Crosby doing well at Duncan's old station at Port Simpson while at Sitka a motley collection of three hundred whites, both Russian and American, U.S. Marines, and traders were living in close proximity to eight hundred Indians. At Wrangell, Alaska, an undefended settlement, six or seven hundred Indians, and a transient population of gold seekers interested in the Cassiar gold diggings in British Columbia were mixed together. Perhaps Rear-Admiral Lyons was mindful of past troubles at Sitka, when in 1879 H.M.S. *Osprey* had provided a deterrent to civil unrest (Rear-Adm. A. Lyons to Sec. of the Admiralty, 13 August 1883, Adm. 1/6666, Y44).

33. Capt. Charles B. Theobald to Rear-Adm. John K. E. Baird, 1 December 1884, Esquimalt, Admiralty Correspondence, vol. 6,

no. 8, P.A.B.C.

34. Ibid.

35. Ibid.

36. Baird to Sec. of Admiralty, 26 December 1884, Adm. 1/6715, Y61.

37. See extracts from and to H.M.S. *Satellite*, 19 February, 8 March, 30 April 1885, encl. in Baird to Sec. of the Admiralty, 15 May 1885, Adm. 1/6762, Y49; also "Extract of Memorandum to H.M. Ship *Satellite*." 30 April 1885, encl. in Evan Macgregor to Colonial Office, 3 July 1885, C.O. 42/782, pp. 61–65.

38. Wellcome, *Story of Metlakahtla*, pp. 482–83.

39. Instructions to Cdr. J.E.F. Nicolls from Rear-Adm. M. Culme Seymour, 21 October 1886, Adm. Corr., vol. 6, no. 8, P.A.B.C. Sir Henry Wellcome, in supporting Duncan, quotes from the Victoria *Industrial News*, 30 October 1886, that the *Cormorant*'s commander had instructions from Chief Justice Sir Matthew Begbie that if the Indians resisted Duncan was to be seized and to be conveyed to Victoria and tried for conspiracy (Wellcome, *Story of Metlakahtla*, pp. 323–24). I have not been able to verify this.

40. Memorandum by Culme Seymour, 23 October 1886, in Adm. 1/6813, Y64. Copy sent to Colonial Office, 19 November 1886, C.O. 42/786, p. 219.

41. The Indians petitioned Commander Nicholls for protection of their legal rights against the civil authorities. The petition, dated 3 November 1886, was signed by Paul Legaic, Alfred Dudoward and three others for the people of Metlakatla and Fort Simpson (encl. in Admiralty to Colonial Office, 17 Dec. 1886, C.O. 42/786, pp. 248–50). This petition is printed in the Victoria *Daily Colonist,* 17 November 1886; also in Wellcome, *Story of Metlakahtla*, pp. 428–29.

42. Memorandum by Cdr. J. Nicolls, "The Metlakahtla Trouble," encl. in Nicolls to Rear-Adm. Culme Seymour, 22 November 1886, Adm. Corr., vol. 6, no. 8, P.A.B.C.

43. Cdr. Nicolls to Rear-Admiral Culme Seymour, 22 November 1886, ibid.

44. Ibid.

45. Wellcome, *Story of Metlakahtla*, p. 346.

46. In 1908 two forces—one led by Duncan who was pastor, magistrate, and commercial leader, and the other, a group of Metlakatlans seeking a secular, more technical training than Duncan's school offered—began contesting for the control of New Metlakatla. Sir Henry Wellcome, a British philanthropist, backed Duncan's fight to retain control of the mission whereas the United States government supported the progressive Indian cause ("The Sir Henry S. Wellcome Papers," *Preliminary Inventories, No.* 150 [Washington, D.C.: National Archives and Record Service, 1963], pp. 103. Duncan died at New Metlakatla in 1918. This phase of the Duncan drama has been told in several works, including John W. Arctander, *The Apostle of Alaska: The Story of William Duncan of Metlakahtla* (New York: Fleming H. Revell Co., 1909) [a partisan account]; and William Beynon, "The Tsimshians of Metlakahtla, Alaska," *American Anthropologist* 43 (1941): 83–88.

47. Rear-Adm. Culme Seymour found Metlakatla this way during his coastal tour of 1887 (see Culme Seymour to Sec. of the Admiralty, 5 August 1887, Adm. 1/6865, Y105).

48. *Papers Relating to the Commis-* *sion Appointed to Enquire into the Condition of the Indians of the North-west Coast* (Victoria: Queen's Printer, 1888), pp. 41–44.

49. "Christian Missions in British Columbia," *Church Missionary Intelligencer* 3(1867): 240.

NOTES TO CHAPTER THIRTEEN: NEW ZONES OF INFLUENCE: NASS, KIMSQUIT, AND SKEENA

1. Statement of Joseph Trutch, 22 June 1869, in *Report and Journal of Proceedings of Governor Seymour to the North-West Coast in Her Majesty's Ship Sparrowhawk* (Victoria: Queen's Printer, 1869).

2. *Vancouver Island Pilot Supplement* (London, 1883), pp. 112–14; Vancouver, *Voyage,* 2: 379; Walbran, *British Columbia Place Names,* pp. 351–52; Michael Roe, ed., *The Journal and Letters of Captain Charles Bishop on the North-West Coast of America, in the Pacific and in New South Wales, 1794–1799* (Cambridge: Hakluyt Society, 1966), p. 76.

3. Viola E. Garfield, "The Tsimshian and Their Neighbours," in *The Tsimshian Indians and Their Arts,* pp. 13–15. Also E. Sapir, "A Sketch of the Social Organization of the Nass River Indians," Canada, *Geological Survey Museum Bulletin No. 19* (Ottawa: King's Printer, 1915).

4. Walbran, *British Columbia Coast Names,* pp. 394–97; and Hubert Howe Bancroft, *History of the Northwest Coast,* 2: 623–25.

5. On Duncan and the Nass, 1860, see *Church Missionary Record,* Mar. 1861, 91–99, and *Church Missionary Intelligencer,* 1 (1865): 110–17. "Captain Simpson's Report of his Voyage to Nass," 23 September 1830, B.223/c/1, fols. 19–24d, H.B.C.A., in E. E. Rich, ed., *The Letters of John McLoughlin . . . First Series, 1825–38* (Toronto: Champlain Society for the Hudson's Bay Record Society, 1941), pp. 305–13. On the Company's use of liquor in expediting a safe withdrawal from Ewen Nass, see *Journals of William Fraser Tolmie,* pp. 282–83 and 290–91.

6. R. Cunningham, Journal, 4 Dec. 1862, C C2/o 6/3, and R. R. A. Doolan to C.M.S. 26 Oct. 1864, C C2/o 7/3, C.M.S.A. Collison, *In the Wake of the War Canoe,* p. 267.

7. The "undersigned Chiefs of the Nishka tribe of Indians at Nass River" who signed the promise at Fort Simpson, 22 September 1862, were Kintsahdah, Alnshaktahan, Ahwah, Shahoowha, Neeashkinwaht, Kithron, Naywun, Kamighyan, Pellahshkah, and Yay (Subenclosure no. 1, in Cdr. J. Pike to Rear-Adm. Maitland, 7 October 1862, Adm. 1/5790, pt. 1).

8. Doolan Journal, 6 December 1865 and 8 and 29 January, 1866.

9. Doolan Journal, 18 April 1866, C. C2/o 7/14, C.M.S.A.

10. Extract from a letter of Proceedings received from Lt. D'A. A. Denny, 24 October 1866, Adm. 1/5969. Also Doolan to Church Missionary Society, 20 October 1866, C C2/o 7/9, C.M.S.A.

11. Walbran, *British Columbia Coast Names*, pp. 137–39. Denny had to be checked in his flogging practices; he and other commanders were cautioned against "exercising any such irregular power or authority." The change came as a result of a complaint from the Colonial Office (Colonial Office Papers of the Admiralty for 1867, Adm.1/6026, noted in Adm.12/796, Index 12599.

12. Proceedings, Lt. D'A. A. Denny, 24 October 1866, Adm. 1/5969.

13. Ibid.

14. Ibid.

15. Ibid.

16. Rear-Adm. George Hastings to Sec. of the Admiralty, 16 June 1868, Adm. 1/6056, Y76. Much of Duncan's information came from Tomlinson (see Tomlinson's Journal, 16 May, 4 July 1868, C C2/o 16/22, C.M.S.A.).

17. W. Duncan to F. Seymour, 16 May 1869, copy, Adm. 1/6071 (quoted in Akrigg and Akrigg, *British Columbia Chronicle, 1847–1871*, pp. 363–64).

18. Akrigg and Akrigg, *British Columbia Chronicle, 1847–1871*, p. 364.

19. Journal of R. Tomlinson, 16 May 1868, C C2/o 16/22, C.M.S.A. Rear-Admiral Hastings, he wrote, expressed "the warmest attachment to the mission work among the people and assured us of his support (Ibid., entry for 4 July).

However, under entry for 25 July 1870 (ibid.) Tomlinson complained that government policy was not well developed, and that the government would do nothing to help the mission.

20. Hastings to Sec. of the Admiralty, 16 June 1868, Adm. 1/6056, Y76.

21. Hastings to Sec. of the Admiralty, 10 August 1868, Adm. 1/6056, Y100; Howay and Scholefield, *British Columbia*, 2: 288.

22. Akrigg and Akrigg, *British Columbia Chronicle, 1847–1871*, p. 376.

23. He went to Bentinck Arm in 1864 to deal with the murder of the Waddington party and visited Metlakatla in 1867, and he knew that naval assistance was needed to suppress the whisky sellers (Margaret Ormsby, "Frederick Seymour, the Forgotten Governor," *BC Studies* 22 [1974]: 22).

24. Ibid., p. 23.

25. Statement of Joseph Trutch, 22 June 1869, in *Report and Journal of... Sparrowhawk* : Rear-Adm. Hastings to Sec. of Admiralty, 27 July 1869, Adm. 1/6092; "Visit of His Excellency, Governor Frederick Seymour to the North-West Coast," in "Historical Notes," vol. 2, M.M.B.C.

26. Statement of Joseph Trutch, 22 June 1869, in *Report and Journal*, pp. 1–2.

27. As at the Skeena River mouth in 1872 when H.M.S. *Boxer* and *Scout* settled differences between natives and whites (Farquhar to Sec. of the Admiralty, 23 September and 31 October 1872, Adm. 1/6231, Y125, Y149).

28. Report of Proceedings of H.M.S. *Petrel*, 30 April 1873, Adm. 1/6263, Y59; Wright, *Lewis and*

Dryden's Marine History, p. 205.

29. Alfred's last name is also spelled Dudoward; his native name was Nih-now-wo.

30. "Loss of the *Geo. S. Wright*," *Daily Colonist* supplement, 9 April 1961.

31. Details of H.M.S. *Rocket*'s proceedings are encl. in Lt. C.R. Harris to Rear-Adm. Algernon F.R. de Horsey, 10 April 1877, encl. in de Horsey to Sec. of the Admiralty, 22 May 1877, Adm. 1/6414, Y84. Copies of these documents were sent to the Colonial Office, which sent copies to Ottawa (C.O. 42/752, pp. 44–57).

32. This site corresponds to the village traditionally known as *Annttitix* (T.F. McIlwraith, *The Bella Coola Indians*, 2 vols. [Toronto: University of Toronto Press, 1948], 1: 15).

33. Pyms Nevins Compton, "Aboriginal British Columbia," P–C 39, Hubert Howe Bancroft Collection, B.L.B.

34. McIlwraith, *Bella Coola*, passim.

35. *Rocket*'s Proceedings, Adm. 1/6414, Y84.

36. Ibid.

37. Ibid.

38. Ibid.

39. Ibid.

40. These were probably the new pattern 7-in. muzzle-loading guns (Rear-Adm. P. W. Brock, H.M.S. *Rocket* Dossier, p. 3, M.M.B.C.).

41. *Rocket*'s Proceedings, Adm. 1/6414, Y84.

42. Ibid. On another occasion, H.M.S. *Grappler* was dispatched with a force of militia to break the strike. The four-month strike was broken at a public cost of $18,000 (Paul A. Phillips, *No Greater Power: A Century of Labour in British Columbia* [Vancouver:

B.C. Federation of Labour and Boag Foundation, 1967], p. 7).

43. 23a The Owikeno, in about 1848, had suffered grievously at the hands of the Bella Bellas and had never forgotten it (Walbran, *British Columbia Coast Names*, p. 368). Could it be that Hemsett, a Bella Bella. chief, was trying to keep the blood feud alive by blaming the Owikeno? The Owikeno may have been involved in other piracies (ibid., pp. 347–48), but by and large these people were neither traditionally warlike nor traditionally maritime. See Ronald L. Olson, "Social Life of the Owikeno Kwakiutl," *Anthropological Records*; 14,3 (1950–60): 213–59.

44. Harris to de Horsey, 10 April 1877, Adm. 1/6414, Y84.

45. I owe this information to Mr. Jefferay V. Boys, former Indian Commissioner for British Columbia and the Yukon.

46. Usher, *William Duncan*, p. 27.

47. Sandra McHarg and Maureen Cassidy, *Early Days on the Skeena River* (Hazelton: Northwest Community College, 1982), p. 23. R. Geddes Large, *The Skeena: River of Destiny* (Vancouver: Mitchell Press, 1957), chs. 7 and 8.

48. Admiralty to Colonial Office, 14 March 1883, and Lord Derby to the Marquis of Lorne, 26 March 1883 (draft), C.O. 42/775, pp. 261–4.

49. Douglas Hudson, "Reserves and Indian Agents: The Extension of Government Control over Indian People in Northwestern British Columbia, 1880–1930," ms. 1978; LaViolette, *Struggle for Survival*, p. 125 n. 40 and p. 126.

50. Sir W. Wiseman to Rear Admiral Algernon C. F. Heneage, 8 August

1888, encl. in Admiralty to Colonial Office, 28 August 1888, C.O. 42/797, pp. 60–67.

51. C.O. minute, 19 September 1888, on ibid.

52. A. Davie to I. W. Powell, 15 July 1888, and Powell to Davie, 16 July 1888, R.G. 10, vol. 3802, file 49,774, P.A.C.

53. Wiseman to Heneage, 8 August 1888, copy, C.O. 42/797. Also Ian Johnson, "The Gitksan Rising of 1888," ms., 1983. Cecil Clark, *Tales of the British Columbia Provincial Police* (Vancouver: Mitchell Press, 1971), pp. 28–33. The "war correspondent's report" is in *Victoria Colonist*, 30 July 1888.

54. Pierce, *Potlatch to Pulpit,* p. 60.

55. Powell to Superintendent-General of Indian Affairs, 31 July 1888, R.G. 10, vol. 3802, file 49,774, P.A.C.

56. Wiseman to Heneage, 8 August 1888, copy, C.O. 72/797, pp. 60–67.

57. *Victoria Colonist*, 16 August 1888.

58. Enclosed in Report of a Committee of the Hon. Exec. Council, approved by Lt. Gov. 18 October 1888, encl. in Lt. Gov. H. Nelson to Sec. of State, Ottawa, R.G. 10, vol. 3802, file 49,774, P.A.C.

59. Ibid.

60. Wilson Duff, ed. *Histories, Territories, and Laws of the Kitwancool* (Victoria: Anthropology in British Columbia Memoir No. 4, 1959), p. 12.

NOTES TO CHAPTER FOURTEEN: RETROSPECT

1. Col. W.F.B. Laurie, *Our Burma Wars and Relations with Burma* (London, 1880), p. 109; quoted in Daniel R. Headrick, *The Tools of Empire: Technology and European Imperialism in the Nineteenth Century* (New York: Oxford University Press, 1982), p. 54.

2. Quoted in Anthony Preston and John Major, *Send a Gunboat! A Study of the Gunboat and its Role in British Policy, 1854–1904* (London: Longmans, 1971), p. 8.

3. Moresby, *Two Admirals,* p. 107.

4. Preston and Major, *Send a Gunboat,* pp. 37–38.

5. Quoted in C. J. Bartlett, "The Mid-Victorian Reappraisal of Naval Policy," in K. Bourne and D. C. Watt, eds., *Studies in International History: Essays Presented to W. Norton Medlicott* (London: Longmans, 1967), p. 205.

6. Vice-Admiral Humphrey H. Smith, *A Yellow Admiral Remembers* (London: Edward Arnold, 1932), p. 54.

7. Marquess of Crewe, *Lord Rosebery*, 2 vols. (Toronto: Macmillan of Canada, 1931), 2: 426.

8. In 1947 ships of the Royal Navy and Royal Australian Navy were employed to check "Marching Rule," a quasi-nationalist movement in the Solomon Islands involving terrorism and robbery (Peter Worsley, *The Trumpet Shall Sound: A Study of "Cargo" Cults in Melanesia*, 2nd ed. [New York: Schockan Books, 1970], pp. 178–79; *Pacific Islands Monthly*, October 1947, p. 71).

9. "It will, I think be conceded," a Western Pacific high commission-

er wrote on 8 December 1911, "that one of the cardinal principles upon which the administration of a new country should be based is that the 'Pax Britannica' must be enforced. It is useless to endeavour to educate a savage people in order to lift them to a higher plane of civilization unless it is demonstrated that the Government can and will make the King's peace respected" (May to L.V. Harcourt, 8 December 1911, Western Pacific High Commission, IC 2161/1911, quoted in James Boutilier, "Killing the Government: Imperial Policy and the Pacification of Malaita," in Margaret Rodman and Matthew Cooper, eds., *The Pacification of Melanesia* [Ann Arbor: University of Michigan Press, 1979], p. 44).

10. In 1912 the Admiralty estimated that British taxpayers had spent £25–30 million in keeping ships in Canadian waters in the period 1851–1901. But this was only an approximation. "Mere statements of the cost of keeping certain ships near Canada, or of the expense of certain naval establishments in Canada, are no measure of the value of the naval defence by which her territory and interests have been protected. The British Navy as a whole and the sea power which its supremacy ensures, and not the squadrons on the North American or Pacific Stations, have given Canada the security she has enjoyed. This truth should never be darkened by detail" (*British Naval Expenditure in Aid of the Dominion of Canada during the Nineteenth Century*, secret, printed at the Foreign Office, 26 October 1912, copy in Borden Papers, MG 26 H1[a], vol. 123, p. 66804, P.A.C.).

11. LaViolette, *Struggle for Survival*, p. 105.

12. Quoted in ibid., p. 113.

13. The great smallpox epidemic of 1862 reduced native numbers by as much as a third: by rough approximation, in 1885 the British Columbia Indian population numbered 28,000 whereas in 1835 it had been 70,000 (Duff, *Indian History of British Columbia*, p. 39).

14. *Claims of the Allied Indian Tribes of British Columbia, as set forth in their Petition Submitted to Parliament in June, 1926: Report and Evidence* (Ottawa, 1927), p. 224, quoted in LaViolette, *Struggle for Survival*, p. 103.

Bibliography

The sources for this book are primarily the In-letters of admirals and ship captains to the Secretary of the Admiralty (Adm. 1 series and related correspondence and minutes), journals of Commanders-in-Chief, Pacific (Adm. 50), and ship's logs (Adm. 53), all in the Public Record Office, London. I have published a full list of Pacific Station records and related documents in the *Journal of Pacific History* 5 (1969): 146–53, and to this the reader is referred for a full list of commanders-in-chiefs' papers and allied documents. No less important for this book is the precious, hitherto largely unused Ships' Letters (F) Series in the Provincial Archives of British Columbia, Victoria. This series and the Admiralty Correspondence in the same repository contain letters from commissioned officers to the colonial governments and, in some cases, drafts of replies. These richly supplement the Adm. 1 series as well as the two Colonial Office series (305: Vancouver Island; and 60: British Columbia). Statutes and ordinances are found in C.O. 306/1 (Vancouver Island) and C.O. 61/1 (British Columbia).

For the "national period," that is, after 1871, the Adm. 1 series is supplemented by documents in the Pacific Station Records deposited in the Public Archives of Canada. The relationship of the Canadian and British governments to Indian affairs in British Columbia is based on the C.O. 42 series, particularly the correspondence between the Colonial Office and the Admiralty and also involving the Governor General of Canada. Department of Indian Affairs correspondence is to be found in the still largely unmined R.G 10 (Black [i.e., Western] series). The files of the *British Colonist* of Victoria, B.C., contain a wealth of information; and readers of my footnotes will note my indebtedness to that important chronicle as well as to Captain John T. Walbran's *British Columbia Coast Names, 1592–1906*, first published in 1909 (first reprinted 1971), a most reliable work which includes Indian testimony. I have found George Nicholson's *Vancouver Island's West Coast, 1762–1962* (first printed in 1962) useful and interesting but often inaccurate and unreliable. The many dossiers on ships on Pacific Station prepared by Rear-Admiral P. W. Brock, C. B., D.S.O., are always of value to the student interested in technical data on a particular ship, as well as on her career and her history; the originals are in the Maritime Museum of British Columbia, Victoria, and copies are deposited in the Provincial Archives, Victoria, in Special Collections, The University of British Columbia Library, Vancouver, and in the National Maritime Museum, Greenwich.

Rather than repeat in a list all sources used in this volume which are, in any case, given in the footnotes in full on the first time of use, I list here the major printed works. Many of the related anthropological studies read in conjunction with this work do not appear in the footnotes; a partial list of them appears in Duff, *Indian History of British Columbia, vol. 1*, pp. 111–17. Unless otherwise noted, the books were published in London, England. For books published after 1900 the name of the publisher is provided, here and in the notes.

Barrett-Lennard, Charles Edward. *Travels in British Columbia, With the Narrative of a Yacht Voyage Round Vancouver's Island*. 1862.

Begg, Alexander. *History of British Columbia from Its Earliest Discovery to the Present Time*. Toronto: William Briggs, 1894.

Brabant, Augustin J. *Vancouver Island and Its Missions, 1874–1900*. In Charles Moser, *Reminiscences of the West Coast of Vancouver Island*. Victoria: Acme Press, 1926.

———. *Mission to Nootka, 1874–1900: Reminiscences of the West Coast of Vancouver Island*, Ed. Charles Lillard. Sidney, B.C.: Gray's Publishing Ltd., 1977.

Cail, Robert E. *Land, Man, and the Law: The Disposal of Crown Lands in British Columbia, 1871–1913*. Vancouver: University of British Columbia Press, 1974.

Clowes, Sir William Laird. *The Royal Navy: A History*. 7 vols. Sampson Low, Marston and Company, 1897–1913.

Collison, William H. *In the Wake of the War Canoe*. Seeley, Service & Co., 1915.

Duff, Wilson. *The Indian History of British Columbia, Volume 1: The Impact of the White Man*. Victoria: Anthropology in British Columbia, Memoir 5, 1964.

Fisher, Robin. *Contact and Conflict: Indian-European Relations in British Columbia, 1774–1890*. Vancouver: University of British Columbia Press, 1977.

Gough, Barry M. *Distant Dominion: Britain and the Northwest Coast of North America, 1579–1809*. Vancouver: University of British Columbia Press, 1980.

———. *The Royal Navy and the Northwest Coast of North America, 1810–1914: A Study of British Maritime Ascendancy*. Vancouver: University of British Columbia Press, 1971.

———. "Send a Gunboat! Checking Slavery and Controlling Liquor Traffic among Coast Indians of British Columbia in the 1860s," *Pacific Northwest Quarterly*, 69, 4 (Oct. 1978), 159–68.

_____"Official Uses of Violence against Northwest Coast Indians in Colonial British Columbia," in James W. Scott, ed., *Pacific Northwest Themes: Historical Essays in Honor of Keith A. Murray* (Bellingham, Wa. 1978), 43–70.

Great Britain, Admiralty. *Vancouver Island Pilot. 1861 and 1864, and Supplement 1883.*

_____. *British Columbia Pilot.* 1888.

Headrick, Daniel R. *The Tools of Empire: Technology and European Imperialism in the Nineteenth Century.* New York, Oxford University Press, 1982.

[Helmcken, John Sebastian]. *The Reminiscences of Doctor John Sebastian Helmcken,* Ed. Dorothy Blakey Smith. Vancouver: University of British Columbia Press, 1975.

Howay, F. W., and E.O.S. Scholefield. *British Columbia from the Earliest Times to the Present,* 4 vols. Vancouver: S. J. Clarke, 1914.

Lamb, W. Kaye, ed. "Four Letters relating to the Cruise of the *Thetis,* 1852–53," *British Columbia Historical Quarterly,* 6, 3 (July 1942): 189–206.

LaViolette, Forrest E. *The Struggle for Survival: Indian Cultures and the Protestant Ethic in British Columbia.* Toronto: Univerity of Toronto Press, 1961.

Lord, John Keast. *The Naturalist in Vancouver Island and British Columbia.* 2 vols. 1866.

Macfie, Matthew. *Vancouver Island and British Columbia: Their History, Resources, and Prospects.* 1865.

McNab, David. "Herman Merivale and the Native Question, 1837–1861," *Albion,* 9, 4 (Winter 1977): 359–84.

_____. "Herman Merivale and Colonial Office Indian Policy in the mid-Nineteenth Century," *Canadian Journal of Native Studies,* 1, 2 (1981): 277–302.

Mayne, Richard Charles. *Four Years in British Columbia and Vancouver Island.* 1862.

Moresby, John. *Two Admirals: Admiral of the Fleet Sir Fairfax Moresby (1786–1877) and His Son, John Moresby.* New and rev. ed., 1913.

Ormsby, Margaret A. *British Columbia: a History.* Toronto: Macmillan of Canada, 1958.

Pethick, Derek. *James Douglas, Servant of Two Empires.* Vancouver: Mitchell Press, 1969.

Poole, Francis. *Queen Charlotte Islands: A Narrative of Discovery and Adventure in the North Pacific.* 1972.

Preston, Anthony, and John Major. *Send a Gunboat! A Study of the Gunboat and Its Role in British Policy, 1854–1904.* Longmans, 1971.

Rattray, Alexander. *Vancouver Island and British Columbia.* 1862.

Rich, E. E. *The History of the Hudson's Bay Company, 1670–1870.* 2 vols. Hudson's Bay Records Society, 1958–1959.

Sage, Walter N. *Sir James Douglas and British Columbia.* Toronto: University of Toronto Press, 1930.

Sproat, Gilbert M. *Scenes and Studies of Savage Life.* 1868.

Usher, Jean. *William Duncan of Metlakatla: A Victorian Missionary in British Columbia.* Ottawa:

National Musems of Canada Publications in History, No. 5, 1974.

Walbran, John T. *British Columbia Coast Names, 1592–1906: Their Origin and History*. Ottawa: Government Printing Bureau, 1909, 1st reprint ed., Vancouver: J. J. Douglas, Ltd., 1971.

Wellcome, Sir Henry. *The Story of Metlakahtla*, 4th ed. 1887.

Index

Individual Indian cultural and linguistic groups appear under the heading "Indian cultures, groups, and languages, names of." Topics incorporating names of Indian groups or ships (e.g., "Ahousat incident," "Hesquiat [village]," or "*Susan Sturgis* affair") are listed alphabetically in the index itself, not the sub-indexes. Individual ships appear under "ships' names."

Aberdeen, Lord, 116
Aborigines' Protection Society, 17, 86, 166
Acheewun, xv, 143, 144, 145–46, 211
A'Court, Captain H. Holmes, 156–57
Active Pass, 145
Admiralty Inlet, 125
Admiralty, Lords Commissioners of the, xiv, 27, 76, 165, 212, 214
  and African slave trade, 44, 116
  and Ahousat incident, 118, 121, 123
  and Cape Mudge incident, 1861, 136, 137
  and *Clio* incident, 84
  and Cowichan expedition, 1856, 66, 67
  early directives of, on Indian relations, 10, 15
  and gunboat availability, 30, 63, 117, 124, 164, 168
  and gunboat costs, 12, 213, 266
  and *John Bright* affair, 127, 128
  and the Haida, 96, 102
  and the limits of colonial control, 48, 206
  and Kincolith murders, 196
  and Lemalchi incident, 142
  on liquor traffic, 93
  and missionary activity, 176–77, 184, 185, 188, 259
  and Stikine expedition, 151
Ahousat (village), 123. *See also* Ahousat (Indians); Ahousat incident
Ahousat incident, 117–21, 124. *See also* Chapchah; Denman, Joseph; Kennedy, Arthur; Pike, John; *Devastation; Forward; Kingfisher; Kinnaird; Sutlej*
Aiyansh, 190
Alaska, xv, 154–55, 199, 255
  and Anglo-American relations, 148, 154–57, 158, 169
  Russia in, 148–50, 151–52
  site of New Metlakatla, 186
Alberni, 114
Alberni Canal, 108, 112, 113
Alcohol. *See* Liquor
Alert Bay, 180, 200, 203
Alexander Islands, 243
Allanlahhah (Indian chief), 255
Allen, Charles Wilson, 144
Allison, Susan, 21
Allwheuck (Lemalchi murder suspect), 143–44
American-Indian wars, British involvement in, 58–62, 155–58
Americans, 15, 16, 77–78, 248. *See also* Alaska; United States; Washington (American capital); Washington Territory; American-Indian wars; Anglo-American relations
Amphritrite Point, 108
Andrieff (Russian engineer), 152
Angeline (daughter of Chief Seattle), 58

Anglicans. *See* England, Church of
Anglo-American Relations, 10, 16, 30, 50, 67
Anglo-Russian Treaty, 93, 149–50
Anietsachist, John (Hesquiat murder suspect), 127
Annahootz (Indian chief), 155–56
Annette Island, 186
Annttitix. *See* Kimsquit (village)
Arlington, Captain Arthur H., 184
Astor, John Jacob, 109, 226

Babine Agency. *See* Upper Skeena Agency
Babine Lake, 205
Bailey, R. F., 203
Baird, Rear-Admiral John K. E., 184
Ball, H. M., 126
Bancroft, Hubert Howe, 45–46, 233
Banfield, William, 113, 114, 247
Banfield Creek, 115
Baranov, Alexander, 148–49, 240
Baranov Island, 148
Barber, Henry (Harry), 148
Barkley Inlet. *See* Robbers Bay
Barkley Sound, 108, 109, 113, 246, 247
    and Ahousat incident, 115
    and *Swiss Boy* affair, 111, 112
Barrett-Lennard, Charles, 35
Bartlett, John, 15
Bawden Bay, 116
Bay Islands, 125
Baynes, Rear-Admiral Sir Robert Lambert, 79, 81, 111
    on Indian administration, 82, 84
    on liquor control, 90, 91
Beacon Hill, 24, 70
Beale Cape, 108
Beardmore, Charley, 35, 39, 41
Beardslee, Commander Lester A., 157
Beaver Harbour, 33, 81, 179, 200
Bedwell Harbour, 139
Bedwell Sound, 119, 120
Beecher Bay, 23
Begbie, Chief Justice Matthew, 94, 261
Bella Bella, 195, 200
Bella Coola, 201, 202
Bellingham, 79
Bellingham Bay, 59
Belloc, Hilaire, 211
Bentinck Arm, 263
Bering Sea, 168
Bilateral descent, 8. *See also* Kwakiutl; Salish
Bishop, Charles, 190
Bishops Cove, 93
Blacks, 138, 139
Blaine, 141

Blake, Charles, 245
Blakow-Coneehaw (Indian chief), 99. *See also* Edenshaw
Blanshard, Governor Richard, xiv, 32, 50, 125, 219, 233–34
    on admissibility of Indian testimony, 121
    and Fort Rupert, 33, 40, 41
    on genocide by colonization, 29, 98
    as Governor of Vancouver Island, Colony of, 30, 217
    inexperience of, 30–31, 214
    and liquor act, 220
    and Newitty incident, 42, 43, 45, 46, 48
Blenkinsop, George, 231
    labour problems of, 39
    and Fort Rupert Kwakiutl, 39–40
    and Newitty incident, 41, 45, 46, 47, 233
Bloomfield, Sergeant, 200, 202, 203
Board of Admiralty. *See* Admiralty, Lords Commissioners of the
Boas, Franz, 38
Boit, John, 109
"Boston men," 16. *See also* Americans
Boulder Point, 125
Brabant, Father Augustin Joseph, 122–23, 127
    attack on, by Hesquiat chief, 174–75, 211
    and the *Boxer,* 173–74
Brady, Bill, 139–40
British Colonist, 145. *See also Victoria Daily Colonist, The*
    on Indian incidents, 83, 124, 127, 146
    on liquor control, 93, 241
British Columbia, 104, 124, 125, 161, 168, 213
    as crown colony, 77, 218
    described, 4, 9
    expansion of, 21, 30, 150
    Indians of, and policing of, 19, 106, 154, 164, 166, 170, 190
    Legislative Council of, 249
    and liquor control, 85, 89, 90–91, 219–23
    and Metlakatla, 183, 187
    and slavery, 85, 86
British North America. *See* Canada, Dominion of
British North America Act, 1867, 161
British Parliament Select Committee, 18–19, 29
Brown, Peter, 51
Browne, J. Ross, 90
Bruce, Rear-Admiral H. W., 62, 63

on agricultural potential, Vancouver
Island, 67–68, 72
on Cowichan expedition, 66
Bruce, Mount, 65, 66
Buckingham, Duke of, 124, 196
Bull Harbour, 44
Burke Channel, 9, 201
Burnaby, Robert, 79
Burnaby Island, 104
Burrard Inlet, 78
Burton, Lieutenant A. A., 43
Bute Inlet, 6, 165

Cadboro Bay, 23
California, 9, 39
Cameron, Chief Justice David, 121
Camosack Harbour. See Camosun
Harbour
Camosun Harbour, 20–21, 23–24
Campbell River, 132
Canada, Dominion of, 162, 169, 170, 183,
213
incorporation of British Columbia
into, 161
conflicts of, with British Columbia,
161, 165
Canadian Northwest, 185
Canadian Pacific Railway, 165
Candlefish. See Oolachan
Canneries, fish, 205
Canoes, 6–7
Canton, 14
Cape Mudge incident, 1860, 132–34. See
also Robson, Charles R.; Lekwiltok;
Forward
Cape Mudge incident, 1861, 134–37. See
also Robson, Charles R.; Haida;
Forward; Laurel
Capilano (village), xvi, 238
Capilano Creek, 238
Capitalist economy, 164
"Captain Juglass," 243. See also
Edenshaw, Albert Edward
Carey, Lieutenant Charles J., 82
Cariboo, the, 104
Carnarvon, Lord, 165
Cary, Attorney-General George H., 220,
241–42
Cassiar, 150, 260
Catface Point, 120, 123
Caution, Cape, 199, 200, 203
Catholics. See Roman Catholics
Cayuse War, 60
Chackloff, Lieutenant M., 152, 153
Chambers, Alexander J., 83
Chapchah, xv, 119–23, 211. See also
Ahousat incident

Chatham Sound, 190, 204
Cheealthluc (Songhees chief), 25, 27, 228
Chemainus (town), 130, 139, 144, 145,
146, 167
Chemainus Bay, 142, 143
Chief Jim (Fort Rupert Kwakiutl), 82
Childers, Hugh C. Erskine, 127
Christensen, John, 125, 126
Church of England. See England, Church
of
Church Missionary Intelligencer, 176, 187
Church Missionary Society, 176, 180, 187,
205
on liquor traffic, 94, 246–47
and Fort Simpson mission, 177
in Metlakatla conflict, 181, 184
and Nass River mission, 192, 195, 241
Clans, 8. See also Haida; Tlingit;
Tsimshian
Clayoquot (village), 113, 211, 226
Clayoquot Sound, 108, 173
Ahousat, incident at, 114–20, 122, 124,
248
hazards of, 111
wreck of John Bright at, 125
Clythas (Nishga chief), 193
Clio affair, 82–84. See also Chief Jim;
Kennedy, Arthur; Turnour,
Nicholas; Fort Rupert Kwakiutl;
Fort Rupert; Ku-Kultz; Clio
Clover Point, 144
Coal, 33, 49, 68
Coast Range, 4
Collins, Lieutenant-Commander William,
174, 175, 188
Collison, W. H., 96, 105, 106, 244
Colnett, Captain James, 250
Colonial and Continental Church Society,
259. See also England, Church of
Colonial Office, 61, 91, 125, 212, 214
and Douglas, James, 61, 62, 111
and gunboat availability, 30, 164, 169
and Hudson's Bay Company, 32, 72
and Indian incidents, 27–28, 47, 84,
123, 127, 137, 140, 196, 207
Indian policy of, 17, 121, 164, 166,
197, 263
ignorance of, of local difficulties, 48,
76
policies of, toward colonies, 27–28,
29–30, 75
and self-government, 18, 165–66, 206
Colonist, The. See Victoria Daily Colonist,
The
Columbia River, 4, 25, 85, 177, 228, 229
Columbia Valley, 20
Colvile, Eden, 54

Coma, Billy, 200
Combie, Peter, 126
Comiaken Hill, 65
Commerell, Cape, 40
Commission Appointed to Enquire into
    the Condition of the Indians of the
    Northwest Coast, 187
Commissioner of Indian Affairs for British
    Columbia. See Indian Affairs,
    Commissioner of, for British
    Columbia
Comox, 34, 137, 214
Comox Harbour, 132
Compton, Pyms Nevins, 83, 201
Confederate raiders, 117
Congregationalists, 173
Connolly, Amelia, 21
Connolly, Commander Matthew, 63,
    64–65, 66, 67. See also Cowichan
    expedition, 1856
Connolly, William, 21
Cook, Captain James, 10, 15, 16, 108–9
Cooper, James, 92
Copper, 14, 104
Copper Islands, 180
Cormorant Islands, 180
Corvettes, 12. See also ships' names
Council of the Colony of Vancouver
    Island. See Vancouver Island,
    Council of the Colony of
Courtenay, Captain George, 26
Cowhoe, George, 245
Cowichan (village), xv, 72
    Indian incidents at, 51, 137, 139, 141,
        144, 145
    and Indian policy, 75, 214
Cowichan Bay, 54, 64, 67, 215, 228
Cowichan expedition, 1853, 51–58, 212.
    See also Douglas, James; Kuper,
    Augustus; Moresby, John; Beaver;
    Recovery; Thetis
Cowichan expedition, 1856, 63–67. See
    also Connolly, Matthew; Douglas,
    James; Haverfield, J. T.; Scott,
    Edward; Tathsalut; Otter;
    Trincomalee
Cowichan Harbour, 130, 139
Cowichan River, 51–53, 54
Cowichan Valley, 140
    agricultural potential of, 54, 67, 68
Cowlitz Valley, 20
Crease, H. P. P., 126
Crickmer, Reverend W. Burton, 258
Cridge, Edward, 247
Crimean War, 12, 58, 63
Crosby, Reverend Thomas, 205, 260
Customs Act of 1868 (United States), 155

Cunningham, Robert, 192, 193, 205, 207
Cypre River. See Trout River
Cypress Bay, 119, 120

Dalles, The, 58, 85
Davie, Attorney-General Alex, 170, 207
Davis, General Jefferson C., 155
Dean Channel, 9, 165, 201, 203
Deans, Annie, 236
de Cosmos, Amor, 163
de Horsey, Rear Admiral Algernon, 156
Denman, Rear-Admiral the Hon. Joseph,
    86, 115, 124, 194, 211, 212
    and Ahousat incident, 117–21, 122–23
    biography of, 116–117
Denman, Lord Chief Justice Thomas, First
    Baron (Joseph's father), 116
Denman Island, 130
Denny, Lieutenant D'Arcy Anthony, 128,
    181, 263. See also Nass River
    penetration
    and Nass River penetration, 193,
        194–95
Discovery Passage, 130, 132, 251
Diseases, 80–81, 205, 215. See also
    Smallpox; Syphilis
Dixon, George, 15, 96
Dixon Entrance, 6, 148
Dodds Narrows, 33, 145
Dominion. See Canada, Dominion of
Dominion of Canada. See Canada,
    Dominion of
Doolan, Robert R. A., 94, 241. See also
    Nass River penetration
    and Nass River penetration, 192,
        193, 195
Douglas, James, xiv, 67–68, 125, 138, 153,
    161, 233, 234, 246. See also
    Connally, Matthew; Kuper,
    Augustus; Pike, James; Powell,
    Isaac; Stevens, Isaac; British
    Columbia; Canada, Dominion of;
    Vancouver Island; Victoria;
    Washington Territory; Admiralty,
    Lords Commissioners of; Colonial
    Office; Foreign Office; and
    individual Indian incidents
    biography of, 20–21
    criticisms of administration of, 58, 62
    and Indian incidents, 84, 236
        of Ahousat, 114, 139
        in Cowichan expedition (1853), 51,
            54–57
        in Cowichan expedition (1856),
            64–65
        of Cape Mudge (1861), 136–37
        of Lemalchi, 140, 142

of Newitty, 42–43, 46–47, 232
of *Swiss Boy,* 111, 113
in Washington Territory, 59–61, 158
Indian policies of, 48, 49, 77–78, 82, 117
in admissibility of Indian testimony, 121
in appointing Indian agents, 80
compared to Charles Wood's, 164
and land, 70–72
mentioned in Sproat-Powell exchange, 167
and slavery, 86–87
mining policies of, 77–78, 98, 212
and missions, 177, 179
offices held by, 50, 88, 217
security policies of, against Indians, 2(62–63, 104, 132, 134, 150, 151, 152
Douglas, William, 99
Dowson, Richard, 34
Drake, Sir Francis, 172
Dudoward, Alfred. *See* Dundower, Alfred
Dufferin, Lord, 164, 179, 186
Duncan, William, 172, 188, 192, 193, 260.
    See also Prevost, James; Richards, George; Ridley, William; Metlakatla; New Metlakatla; Church Missionary Society
    biography of, 177
    disputes of, with Church Missionary Society, 180–81
        with provincial authorities, 182, 183, 184–85
    early missionary activities of, 177–78
    and Kincolith murders, 196, 197
    and liquor trade, 94
    and Metlakatla, 178–79, 205
    move of, to New Metlakatla, 186–87
    and Richards, George, 153, 179–80
Dundas, Lieutenant Adam, 29
Dundas Island, 92, 153, 178
Dundower, Alfred, 200, 202, 203, 261, 264
Dunsmuir, Diggle and Company, 203
Duntze, Captain John, 26

Earl Grey, 46, 219
    and Blanshard, 30–31, 47–48
    colonial policy of, 17, 18, 30
    and Hudson's Bay Company, 229
    and Vancouver Island, Colony of, 28
Ea-qui-ok-shittle (Indian witness, *Kingfisher* piracy), 118
East Indian Company, 14
Echachets (Indian village), 248
Edensa. *See* Edenshaw, Albert Edward
Edenshaw, Alfred Edward, xv, 88, 99, 243, 245

and changes among Haida, 105, 106, 107
and *Susan Sturgis* affair, 100, 101, 103, 211, 244
Edenshaw, Henry, 106
Edenso. *See* Edenshaw
Edge, William, 127
Elliott Bay, 60
England. *See* Great Britain
England, Church of, 105, 173, 176, 189, 259. *See also* Colonial and Continental Church Society
Esperanza Inlet, 108
Esquimalt, 116, 137, 140, 177, 185, 257
    Island campaigns from, 83, 111, 117, 118, 127, 142, 195
    naval fleet at, 25–26, 50, 63, 125, 168
    northern campaigns from, 151–52, 155, 156, 182, 200, 206, 207
Estevan Point, 125, 173, 198
Evening Express, 144
Evening News, 126
Ewan Nass (Nishga village), 192
Executive Council, Colony of Vancouver Island, 90–91

False Nitinat, 246
Fanshawe, Captain Edward G., 44, 45
Farquhar, Rear-Admiral Arthur A., 182
Finlayson, Roderick, 24, 25, 26, 228. *See also* Songhees (Indians)
Firearms, described, 15, 249
Fisher, Robin, 46–47
Fitzgerald, James Edward, 29
Fitzstubbs, Captain Napoleon, 207, 208
"Flying Squads," 137
Flattery, Cape, 4, 108
Flogging, 128, 250, 263
Foreign Office, 30, 86, 116, 154, 212
    and Russia, 149, 151, 156
    and Treaty of Washington, 25
Forest diplomacy, described, 25, 55, 199
Fort Bellingham, 61
Fort Durham, 22
Fort Gamble, 62
"Fort Go Ahead." *See* Fort Rupert
Fort Hope, 220
Fort Langley, 129, 132, 141
Fort McLoughlin, 22
Fort Nanaimo, 129–30. *See also* Nanaimo
Fort Nass, 192
Fort Nisqually, 59, 62
Fort Rupert, xv, 71, 132, 180, 182, 231, 240. *See also* Fort Rupert Kwakiutl (Indians); Newitty (Indians); *Clio* affair; Ku-Kultz; Newitty incident described, 35, 38

economic base of, 33, 49, 214
as embarkation point, 151, 195, 200
labour unrest at, 38–39, 219, 233
liquor traffic at, 93, 241
Indian unrest nearby, 39–40, 81–82,
  82–84, 86–87, 149, 158, 230, 232
Fort St. James, 21, 205
Fort Simpson, 70, 177, 195, 197. *See also*
  Duncan, William; Tsimshian
  (Indians); Metlakatla; Nass River
  penetration; Stikine expedition
  and Haida, 100, 243
  Indian-white relations at, 149, 150, 151,
    153, 259, 261
  and missionary work, 176, 177–78
  as trading post, 22, 98, 178, 259
Fort Stelacoom, 58
Fort Stikine, 150
Fort Vancouver, 58
Fort Victoria, 33, 51, 98, 233, 243
  description of, 21–22, 109
  and Indian unrest, 25, 26, 27, 56, 71–72
  visits of, by Indians, 68–69, 70, 95
Fort Yale, 228
Franklyn, William Hayes, 134, 135
Fraser River, 4, 34, 141, 143, 228
  and Fort Langley, 129
  gold rush to, 77–78
Freezy. *See* Cheealthluc
Friday (Indian interpreter), 118, 119
Friendly Cove, 174
Fulford Harbour, 252
Furuhjelm, Johann, 150, 151, 152, 255

Gabriola, 130
Galiano Island, 130, 145, 211
Gallows Point, 57
Ganges, 139
Ganges Harbour, 138, 252
Gem. *See* Chief Jim
George (Ohiet headman), 112, 113
George III, 226, 239
Georgia, Strait of, xv, 3, 9, 75, 130
  as Indian passage, 138
  and protection from Indians, 129, 147
Gethumuldoe (Indian chief), 208
Gitanmaax (Gitksan village), 204
Gitkins (Haida chief), 104
Gladstone, William E., 30, 123, 197, 213
Glenelg, Lord, 19
Glidden, Charles, 141, 253
gold, 68
  discovery of, along Fraser River, 77–78
  on Queen Charlotte Islands, 95, 98,
    99, 102, 104, 108
  in Stikine territory, 150–53
Gold Harbour, 96, 98, 99, 243

Goldsworthy, Barney, 245
Goletas Channel, 33, 41
Golovin, Captain Pavel Nikolaelovich, 254
Gordon, George, 33
Gordon Channel, 33
Goschen, G. J., 213
Gough, Edwin, 134–35
Government House, 137
Graham Island, 96, 99, 243
Grand Trunk Pacific Railway, 209
Grant, George Munro, 3
Grant, Ulysses S., 199
Granville, Lord, 197
Gravesend, England, 33
Great Britain, 10, 17, 95, 209. *See also*
  Admiralty, Lords Commissioner of
  the; Colonial Office; Foreign Office;
  England, Church of; Royal Navy
  and Russia, 149
  disengagement of, from Canada, 161
Green, Constable, 207, 208
Greenville, 190
Gulf Islands, 75, 130
Gunboat diplomacy, 113, 173–75, 210,
  212–13
  decline of, 168–69, 170–71
  techniques described, 13–14

Hagwilget, 205. *See also* Hazelton;
  "Skeena War"
Hankin, Phillip, 118, 123–24
Hanna, James, 15
Harcourt, Sir William, 212
Hardinge, Commander Edward, 145
Hare, Richard, 165
Haro Strait, 23, 130
Harris, Lieutenant-Commander Charles
  Reynold, 175, 200, 201. *See also*
  Kimsquit incident
Harrison, Judge, 185
Harvey, Caroline, 140, 253. *See also*
  Lemalchi incident
Hastings, Rear-Admiral the Hon. George,
  181, 195, 196, 197, 240. *See also*
  "Skeena War"
Haswell, Robert, 96
Haverfield, Lieutenant J. T., 26–27, 64
Hazelton, 204, 209
  and "Skeena War," 205, 206, 207, 208.
  See also "Skeena War"
Hecate Strait, 6, 9, 95
Helmcken, Dr. John Sebastian, 32–33, 38,
  39, 41, 232. *See also* Fort Rupert;
  Newitty incident
  and Newitty incident, 42, 43, 46, 226,
    233
Hemsett, Charley, 200, 264

Henley, John, 139
Herbert Arm, 116, 120
Hesquiat (village), 125, 173, 175, 177, 250.
    See also Brabant, Augustin Joseph;
    Matlahaw; John Bright affair
Hesquiat Harbour, 108, 125, 173
Hill's Bar, 78
    incident at, 77–78
Hillyar, Rear-Admiral Charles F., 164
Holmes, Colonel, 207
Holy Communion, 181
Homulcheson Creek. See Capilano Creek
Hooch. See Hoochinoo
Hoochino, 90, 177
Hood Canal, 62
Hope Island, 44
Hornby, Rear-Admiral T. Phipps, 27, 43
Hornby Island, 92–93, 130, 134, 135
Hot Springs Cove, 111
Hoth-lu-arta (Indian suspect, Kingfisher
    piracy), 115
House of Commons, 31
    Committee on Aborigines of, 17
Houston, Captain Wallace, 236. See also
    Haida; Cowichan expedition, 1856
    and Cowichan expedition, 1856, 64,
    66, 67
    and Haida, 102–3, 103–4, 106
Howay, Judge F. W., 16
Howe Sound, 78
Hudson, Thomas, 250
Hudson's Bay Company, 21, 31, 85, 104,
    138, 141. See also Douglas, James;
    Colonial Office; Individual posts
    American accusations against, 59, 60,
    103
    Board of Management of, 103
    decline of, 82, 84
    and defence, 16, 27–28, 30, 32, 35, 50,
    166
    employees of, 134–35, 152, 177, 205
    Indian relations of, 24, 40, 51, 72,
    204, 214
    and Indian unrest, 27, 98, 100, 111,
    149–50
    investigations of, 17, 18–19, 77–78, 201
    as monopoly, 213, 234
    posts of, 105, 129, 192, 206, 207
Humukanis (Indian village), 115
Hunt, George, 200, 201, 202
Hu-saw-i, 87

Imperial Russian Navy, 254
Indian Affairs for British Columbia,
    Commissioner of, 162
Indian Affairs, Department of, 162, 165,
    167, 169

Indian cultures, groups, and languages,
    names of
Ahousat, xv, 109, 113, 114, 211
    and Ahousat incident, 115–21, 122,
    123, 124, 249. See also Chapchah;
    Ahousat incident
Alaska Haida. See Kaigani
Athabaskan, 9. See also Carrier;
    Kootenay; Thompson River Indians
Barkley, 108
Bella Bella, 40, 68, 129, 200, 264
Bella Coola, 9, 198, 201
Cape Flattery. See Makah
Capilano, 78, 79
Carrier, 21, 205
Central Haida, 243
Chemainus, 143, 146
Cherokee, 139, 141
Cheyenne, 7
Chinook, 33, 85
Clallam, 17, 25, 26, 90
Clatsop, 17
Clayoquot, xvi, 108, 109, 120, 123. See
    also Ahousat incident
    and property, 121
    and murders, 111, 247
Coast Salish, 9, 34, 132
Comox, 9, 75, 94, 132, 147, 195
Couteau, 78
Cowichan, 9, 94, 147, 169, 214. See
    also Cowichan expedition, 1856;
    Cowichan expedition, 1853
    attack by, on Fort Victoria, 25
    and Cowichan expedition, 1853,
    51–57
    and Cowichan expedition, 1856,
    63–67
    claims of, on Saltspring Island, 138
    murder by, of Bill Brady, 139
    and Powell visit, 165
Cowitzen. See Cowichan
Crow, 7
Dwamish, 58
Echachets, 116
Eclataws, 137, 238
Flattery. See Makah
Fort Rupert Kwakiutl, 34, 81–82, 230.
    See also Fort Rupert; Ku-Kultz;
    Newitty; Clio incident; Newitty
    incident
    and Clio incident, 82, 84
    fears of unrest of, 40, 43
    intertribal conflict of, 41–42
    missions among, 179, 180
    and slavery, 86
Fort Simpson Tsimshian. See
    Kinnakanyeak

Ginakangeek. *See* Kinnakanyeak
Gitanmaax, 208
Gitksan, 9, 204
Hagwilgets, 196
Haida, xv, 71, 96–98, 132, 190, 211, 243. *See also* Edenshaw, Alfred Edward; Central Haida; Kaigani; Kloo; Masset; Northern Haida; Skidegate; Southern Haida; Cape Mudge incident; *Susan Sturgis* affair
and Cape Mudge incident, 136
change among, 105, 106, 107
clans of, 8
described, 7, 95–96, 242
and Fort Victoria, 27, 68
missionaries among, 180, 215
pacification of, 87, 102–3
predatory reputation of, 40, 41, 43, 61–62, 103–4, 129, 204
and *Susan Sturgis* affair, 98–100, 176, 244
Haisla, 9
Halkomelem, 9
Heiltsuk, 9, 200
Hesquiat, 9, 122, 128, 211. *See also* Brabant, Augustin Joseph; *John Bright* affair; Smallpox
and Brabant, 173
and *John Bright* affair, 125–27
smallpox epidemic among, 174
Interior Salish, 9
Kaigani, 148, 243
Kakes, 155
Kitsatis, 155–56
Kimsquit, 189, 205, 211. *See also* Kimsquit affair
described, 201–2
and the *George S. Wright,* 201, 203–4
Kincolith, 196. *See also* Kincolith murder
Kinnakanyeak, 153, 196
Kitimat, 200
Kitkatla, 240
Kitsegukla, 205
Kitwancool, 208, 209
Kloo, 104
Kokwantons, 156
Kolosh, 148, 254
Kootenay, 9
Kwakiutl, 9, 95, 130, 204, 231. *See also* Fort Rupert Kwakiutl; Heiltsuk; Haisla; Lekwiltok; Owikeno; Southern Kwakiutl
and Beaver Harbour, 35–38
numaym of, 8

Kyuquot, 109, 173
Lekwiltok, 130, 132–34, 136. *See also* Cape Mudge incident, 1860
Lemalchi Salish, xv, 8, 130
and Lemalchi incident, 140–47, 211. *See also* Acheewun; Lemalchi incident
Makah, 26, 85, 111, 112
Masset, 9, 100, 101–2, 106
Milbanke, 40
Musqueam, 78, 79, 143, 238, 239
Nanaimo, 51, 56–57, 86, 147
Ne-kum-ke-lis-la, 231
Newitty, 39, 226, 231. *See also* Newitty incident
and Newitty incident, 40–45
as slave traders, 85
Nishga, xv, 9, 92, 189, 209. *See also* Kincolith murders; Nass River penetration
described, 190–92
and Kincolith murders, 195–96, 197
and meeting with Denny, 194–95
missions among, 180, 192
polygamy among, 192
rivalry with Tsimshian, 204, 205
Nisqually, 58, 60, 62
Nootka, 108, 114, 247. *See also* Ahousat; Barkley; Clayoquot; Hesquiat; Kyoquot; Makah; Ohiet; Quatsino
described, 6, 7, 8
trade of, with whites, 15, 109
Northern Haida, 242
Ohiet, 109, 247. *See also Swiss Boy* affair
murder of Banfield by, 114
and *Swiss Boy* affair, 111, 112, 113
Owikeno, 200, 201, 203, 264. *See also* Kimsquit incident
Penelukuts, 130, 138, 143, 146, 253. *See also* Lemalchi incident
Pentlatch, 9
Puyallup, 62
Quatsino, 40, 108
Saanich, 71
Salish, 78, 128, 130, 132, 201. *See also* Capilano; Chemainus; Coastal Salish; Comox; Cowichan; Halkomelem; Inland Salish; Kimsquit; Lemalchi; Musqueam; Nanaimo; Penelukut; Saanich; Somenos; Squamish; Stalo; Straits Salish
Sechart, 109
Sechelt, 9
Semiahmoo, 141

Sheshat, 111, 112, 113–14, 250. *See also Swiss Boy* affair
Skidegate, 9, 88, 135
Somenos, 63
Songhees, 25, 26
  migration of, to Fort Victoria, 23–24
  relations, intertribal, 68, 69, 71
  and reserves, 71, 162
Southern Haida, 243
Southern Kwakiutl, 8
Squamish, 9, 78, 239
Stalo, 78, 129
Stikine, 59, 68
Straits Salish, 9, 23, 26
Suquamish, 58
Thompson River Indians, 78
Tla-tli-si-kwila, 231
Tlingit, 7, 190, 204. *See also* Kakes; Kolosh; Kiksatis; Stikine
  and Sitka, 148, 149
  social organization of, 8
Tongass, 68
Tsimshean. *See* Tsimshian
Tsimshian, xv, 68, 88, 92, 148, 190, 200, 204. *See also* Gitanmaax; Gitksan; Hagwilget; Kinnakanyeak; Kitimat; Kitkatla; Kitwancool; Nishga; Tongass; Kincolith murders
  and land, 183, 187
  missions to, 177–80, 181, 189, 205
  and Prevost's opinion, 176, 178–79
  relations of, with Nishga, 192, 193, 197, 205
  social organization of, 7, 8, 9, 204
  unrest among, 27, 95, 151, 189
Ucluelet, 109
Yaculta, 130
Indian Department. *See* Indian Affairs, Department of
Indians, 13, 30, 75, 205. *See also* Douglas, James; Colonial Office; Hudson's Bay Company; Indian cultures, groups, and languages
  and liquor, 87–94, 221–23
  of Northwest Coast, 6, 7–9, 28, 68–70
  policy toward, 76–77, 214
Ingraham, Joseph, 15
Inland Passage, 4–6, 9
Iomo (Indian interpreter), 141, 142, 146
Iron, 14

Jacobson, Johan Adrian, 84
Japan, 14
Japanese Current, 4
Jefferson, Chief, 135, 136

Jewitt, John, 109
John Bright affair, 125–28. *See also* Hesquiat (Indians); Mist, Captain Henry Wentworth; Seymour, Frederick; *John Bright; Sparrowhawk*
Johnstone, Captain Charles Richardson, 233
Johnstone Strait, 9, 93, 132
Juan de Fuca, Strait of, 9, 108, 128, 229, 246
  and British-American crisis, 25
  and Fort Victoria, 22
Justice, Department of, 207

Kahdoonahah (Indian chief), 192
Kalmalmuk. *See* Kitwancool Jim
Kamchatka, 14
Katkinna (Hesquiat chief), 127. *See also John Bright* affair
Katlean (Kiksatis chief), 155–56
Kelly, Peter, 215
Kendrick, John, 15
Kennedy, Governor Arthur Edward, 83–84, 123, 125, 214, 217
  and admissibility of Indian testimony, 122
  Ahousat crisis, 117–21
  biography of, 248
  and liquor control, 91, 220
Kennedy, Captain Sir William R., 90
Ki-ap-a-lano, 78, 79, 238
Kikeis, 200
Killonecaulla (Newitty suspect), 41
Kimberley, Earl of, 164
Kimsquit (village), xvi, 198, 201, 204, 209, 264
Kimsquit incident, 198–204. *See also* Dundower, Alfred; Harris, Charles Reynold; Bella Coola; Kimsquit (Indians); *George S. Wright; Rocket*
Kindred, 8. *See also* Kwakiutl; Salish
Kincolith (village), 195
Kincolith murders, 195–98. *See also* Duncan, William; Hastings, George; Porcher, Edwin; Seymour, Frederick; Tomlinson, Robert; Trutch, Joseph; Kincolith (village); *Sparrowhawk*
King Freezy. *See* Cheealthluc
King George. *See* George III
"King George" (Clallam chief), 27
"King George Men," 16, 57
Kingcome Inlet, 6
Kipling, Rudyard, 210
Kispiox, 204
Kitgen. *See* Gitkins (Haida chief)

Kitkatla, 41, 240
Kitlope, 202
Kit-luh-kum-ka-dah (village), 193
Kit-min-i-ook (village), 193
Kitwancool (village), 204
Kitwancool Jim, 207
Kitwanga, 204, 209
Kiusta, 99
"Klale stone," 33
Klatsmick (Ohiet chief), 114, 115. See also
    Ahousat incident
Kluvok, Alaska, 199
Knight Inlet, 6, 182
Koksilah River, 54
Konyil (Haida chief), 87
Kou Island, 155
Ku-Kultz, 34, 35, 38, 49. See also Clio
    incident
    destruction of, 81, 83
Kung, 99, 105
Kuper, Captain Augustus, 51, 57, 98, 99,
    106
Kuper Island, 129, 130, 211, 253. See also
    Lemalchi incident
    and Lemalchi incident, 141, 145
Kyuquot Sound, 108, 174

Labouchere, Henry, 19
Labouchere Channel, 201
Lacy, Lieutenant Edward, 44–45. See also
    Newitty incident
Ladysmith, 130
Lake Hill, 51
Lander, Judge Edward, 60
Lascelles, Lieutenant the Hon. Horace D.,
    121, 144, 212. See also Lemalchi
    incident
    and Brady murder, 139
    in Lemalchi incident, 141, 142, 143
Laskeek (Haida village), 87, 245
Laskeek Harbour, 104
Lasqueti Island, 130
Laurie, Colonel W. F. B., 211
Law Officers of the Crown, 48
Legaic, Paul, 261
Legislative Assembly, of Vancouver Island.
    See Vancouver Island, Legislative
    Assembly of
Legislative Council of British Columbia.
    See British Columbia, Legislative
    Council of
Legislative Council of Vancouver Island.
    See Vancouver Island, Legislative
    Council of
Lekwungen. See Songhees
Lemalchi Bay, 130, 141, 146, 253. See also
    Lemalchi incident

Lemalchi incident, 149–47. See
    also Acheewun; Allwheuk; Douglas,
    James; Harvey, Caroline; Lascelles,
    Horace D.; Marks, Frederick; Pike,
    James; Pusey, Lieutenant;
    Shahkutchsus; Skullowayat;
    Devastation; Forward; Grappler;
    Topaze
Lennard Island, 108
Leschi (Nisqually chief), 38, 58
Lincoln, Earl of. See Newcastle, Duke of
Lineages, 8. See also Kimsquit; Nishga
Liquor, 15, 105, 106, 136, 192, 205, 211
    attempts to regulate, 87–94
    in British Columbia, statutory
    provisions of, 219–223
Lisianskii, Captain Iu. F., 149
London, 20, 172, 198
Lookinglass, Chief, 45
Lord, John Keast, 34, 35, 38
Lords of the Admiralty. See Admiralty,
    Lords Commissioners of the
Lords Commissioners of the Admiralty.
    See Admiralty, Lords
    Commissioners of the
Lorraine, Sir Lambton, 64, 67
Lower Nass Villages, 193, 194, 195. See
    also Kincolith murders; Nass River
    penetration
Lowndes (private secretary of Seymour),
    197
Lynn Canal, 35
Lyons, Rear-Admiral Algernon, 169, 183,
    260

McCauley, George, 138
McCreight, J. F., 205
Macdonald, Sir John A., 162, 163
Macdonald, Captain William, 64–65
Macfie, Matthew, 76
McKay, Joseph, 183, 187
Mackenzie, Alexander, 198, 201
McLoughlin's Bay, 192
McNeill, Captain William H., 39, 103, 232
McNeill Harbour, 38–39

Maitland, Rear-Admiral Sir T., 136, 137,
    154, 254
    and the Stikine, 150–51, 152
Maksutoff, Prince, 152
Maloney, Captain Maurice, 60
Manhouisaht Village, 111
Maquinna (Nootka chief), 15
Marks, Frederick, 140, 253. See also
    Lemalchi incident
Marks, Mrs. Frederick, 140, 147. See also
    Lemalchi incident

Martin, Mungo, 38
Martin, Richard Montgomery, 29
Marktosis (Ahousat village), 114, 118, 119, 123
Mason, Reverend G., 260
Masset (village), 88, 96, 105, 180
Matilda Creek, 114, 115, 116, 118, 119
Matlahaw (Hesquiat chief), 174, 175, 211
Matrilineal descent, 8. *See also* Haida; Tlingit; Tsimshian
Mayne, Commander Richard Charles, 69–70, 86–87, 132, 134, 179, 180
Mayne Island, 130, 140, 142, 254
Mayers, Christian, 140
Meares, John, 15
Mechanics' Literary Institute, 260
Melville Island, 178
Memaloose. *See* Smallpox
Merivale, Herman, 47
Methlacatla. *See* Metlakatla
Methodists, 173, 189, 192, 200, 205, 215
Metlakatla, xv, 94, 158, 172, 192, 205, 206, 240. *See also* Duncan, William; Ridley, William; New Metlakatla
and colonial authority, 181, 182, 183, 185–86
conflict in, 180–86
described, 178–79, 180
evaluations of, 180, 258, 260
and land tenure, 183, 185–86, 187–88, 261
visitors of, 187, 195, 196, 263
Milbanke Sound, 9, 16, 22, 199
Militia, Canadian, 163, 170, 207
Mill, John Stuart, xiv
Miners Bay, 140, 142
Ministers of the Crown, 206
Mission (town). *See* St. Mary's
Mission Point, 184, 185, 187
Missionaries, 86, 173, 180. *See also* Brabant, Augustin Joseph; Duncan, William; Morice, A. G.; Prevost, James; Richards, George; Tomlinson, Robert; Metlakatla
Mist, Commander Henry Wentworth, 126, 128
Mitchell, Captain William, 243
Mitchell Inlet. *See* Gold Harbour
Mitrapolsky, N. G., 156
Molyneux St. John, Frederic, 179
Montague Harbour, 145. *See also* Acheewun
Moody, Col. Richard Clement, 217
Mooyahhat, 118, 119
Moresby, Rear-Admiral Sir Fairfax, 57, 175, 177, 211, 212. *See also* Cowichan expedition 1853; Newitty

incident; *Susan Sturgis* affair
and anti-slavery campaigns, 86, 116
and Newitty incident, 43–44, 46, 47
and *Susan Sturgis* affair, 101, 102
Moresby, Lieutenant John, 51, 55, 57, 212. *See also* Cowichan expedition, 1853
Moresby Island, 104, 139, 243
Morice, Father A. G., 205
Moricetown, 205
Moss, Morris, 83
Moyeha. *See* Mooyahhat
Mudge, Cape, 69, 130. *See also* Cape Mudge incident, 1860; Cape Mudge incident, 1861
as Indian passage, 129
police actions at, 132–37
Muir, Andrew, 39, 231
Muir, John, 38, 39
Muir, Michael, 39
Musgrave, Governor Anthony, 218

Naden Harbour, 99
Nahpook, 118
Nahtay, 118
Nahwitti. *See* Newitty (village)
Naikoon. *See* Rose Point Spit
Nanaimo, 56, 76, 139. *See also* Cowichan expedition, 1853; Lemalchi incident; Kimsquit incident
and coal, 49, 203
and Cowichan expedition, 1853, 51, 55, 57
and Kimsquit incident, 199, 200
land treaty at, 71, 75
protection of, against Indians, 34, 134, 137, 150, 182, 195, 240
Nass Bay, 190, 192, 195
Nass River, xvi, 87, 92, 169, 180, 192. *See also* Nishga (Indians); Nass River penetration
described, 4, 190
missionary activity along, 189
Nass River penetration, 192–95. *See also* Cunningham, Robert; Denny, D'Arcy Anthony; Doolan, Robert R. A.; Nishga (Indians); *Forward*
Native Evidence Ordinance, 121–22, 249
Naval and Bible Society. *See* Naval and Military Bible Society
Naval and Military Bible Society, 175, 245
Navy Department (United States), 155, 157
Ndah (Nishga chief), 193
Neah Bay, 112, 243, 246
Needham, Joseph, 226
Neetuh (Indian murder victim), 207
Nelson, Hugh, 206
Nelson, Horatio, 10

Nestecanna (Haida chief), 88, 99–100
New Archangel. *See* Sitka
New Caledonia. *See* British Columbia
New Metlakatla, 261. *See also* Duncan, William; Metlakatla
New Testaments, 244–45
New Westminster, xv, 81, 124
    as capital, British Columbia, 75
    and liquor, 92, 93, 94, 157
New York Times, 157
Newcastle, Duke of, 29, 140, 237
Newittie. *See* Newitty (village)
Newitty (village), 40, 104, 211, 232
Newitty incident, 41–48. *See also* Blanshard, Richard; Blenkinsop, George; Fanshawe, Edward G.; Helmcken, John Sebastian; Lacy, Edward; Newitty (Indians); Newitty (village); *Daedalus; Daphne*
    background of, 32–41
    evaluation of, 48–49
Newity. *See* Newitty (village), 232
Nicholls, Commander J. E. T., 185–86, 261
Nih-now-wo. *See* Dundower, Alfred
Ninstints (village), 215
Nitinat, 246. *See also* Barkley Sound; False Nitinat
Nootka Sound, 10, 14, 108, 172, 174
North America, 9
North Coast, 70
North Pacific, storms of, 4
North Pacific Transportation Corporation, 199
North Pender Island, 130
North West Coast Agency, 206
North West Company, 16, 21, 198
Northwest Coast, 3, 12, 16, 177, 209
    gunboat incidents along, 16, 17, 22
    and Royal Navy, 9–10, 210
    trade along, 14, 204
Northwest Passage, 149
Nouetsat (village), 174

Oak Bay, 139
Oblate Order, 205
Observatory Inlet, 190
Ocean to Ocean, 3
Ogden, Peter Skene, 26
O'Hagan, Howard, 228
Ohiet (village), 111. *See also Swiss Boy* affair
Old Metlakatla. *See* Metlakatla
Old Shakes (Stikine Indian), 151
Old Wale (Kwakiutl chief), 41
Oolachan, 178, 190
Opetchesaht, 112
Oregon, 16, 17, 23, 26, 60

Oregon Treaty (Treaty of Washington, 1846), 20, 25, 149, 176
Osborne Bay, 143, 145
Ottawa, 162, 165, 170, 172, 184, 214. *See also* Powell, Isaac Wood; Canada, Dominion of
Owekeeno, xvi, 200
Oyster Bay, 145

Pacific Ocean, described, 3, 4
Pacific Mail Steamship Company, 38
Pacific Station, 117, 168, 182, 198, 214
Pacific Station (United States), 154
Palmerston, Lord Henry John Temple, 116
Pax Britannica, 19, 172
Peace, Justice of the, 198
Pelly, Sir John, 28, 46, 229
Pender Island, 137, 139
Pierce, Reverend Henry William, 207
Pierce County, 59
Piers Island, 139
Pike, Commander John, 194, 211
    and Ahousat incident, 115–17, 119
    and Brady murder, 139
    and Lemalchi incident, 142, 144
    and liquor trade, 92–94, 241
    Stikine expedition of, 151–54, 255
Pollak (Indian suspect), 253
Poole, Francis, 104, 105
Porcelain, 14
Porcher, Captain Edward Augustus, 35, 196
Port Alberni, 113
Port Colbourne, 163
Port Effingham, 109
Port Essington, 205, 206, 208, 209
Port Hardy, 33
Port Highfield, 150, 152, 153
Port Ludlow, 125
Port McNeill, 33
Port Orchard, 111
Port Roberts, 94
Port San Juan, 108, 112
Port Simpson, 85, 204. *See also* Prevost, James; Tsimshian; Fort Simpson; Stikine expedition
    and gunboats, 88, 169
    Indian relations in, 92, 106, 206
    liquor traffic in, 89, 91, 241
    mission at, 200, 205, 260
Port Townsend, 69, 90, 246
Portland, 155
Portland Canal, 22, 93, 148, 190
Portland Inlet, 9
Portland Island, 139
Potlatches, 38
Potles, 201

Powell, Israel Wood, 162–63, 215, 207
  biography of, 163
  exchange with Sproat, 167–68, 257
  Indian policies of, 162, 163–64, 170
  and Brabant, 173, 174
Presbyterians, 123, 173
Prevost, Captain James Charles, 130, 132,
  176, 211, 247. *See also* Duncan,
  William; Haida; *Susan Sturgis*
  affair; *Swiss Boy* affair
  and the Haida, 96–98, 106
  Susan Sturgis affair of, 100, 101, 102
  and liquor traffic, 241, 246–47
  missionary activities of, 105, 175–77,
  177–78, 205, 244
  and *Swiss Boy* affair, 111–13
PRIVY COUNCIL, 162
Property, Indian conceptions of, 109,
  112–13, 190
Protection Island, 57
Provincial Police, 207
Public Works, Department of, 165
Puget Sound, 24, 35, 72, 154
  British interests in, 20, 210
  described, 3, 111, 129, 150
  Indian revolt around, 58, 59, 62, 229
Puget's Sound Agricultural Company, 22
Pusey, Lieutenant, 145

Quadra Island, 9, 69, 130, 132
Quamichan. *See* Cowichan River
Quatsino (village), 114
Quatsino Sound, 108
Queen Charlotte Islands, xv, 30, 70, 77,
  87, 95–107, 215
  described, 4, 9, 95, 108
  gold discovery at, 96, 98, 232
  missions on, 105–6, 180
  Prevost's visit of, 100–102, 105, 106
Queen Charlotte Sound, 95, 199
Queen Charlotte Strait, 9, 23
Queen Charlotte Islands, 105
Queen Charlotte Mining Company, 104

Redfern, Thomas, 175
Redoubt St. Dionysius, 150. *See also*
  Wrangell
Refuge Cove, 173
Reserves, Indian, 24, 71, 162, 183
Richards, Captain George Henry, 87,
  105, 153
  and Indian pacification, 78, 107,
  153–54, 239
  on Indian-white relations, 79–80,
  81–82
  and missions, 179–80, 188
  surveys by, 109, 192, 246

Ridgeway, Joseph, 176
Ridley, Bishop William, 181, 182, 184,
  187, 188. *See also* Duncan, William;
  Metlakatla; Church Missionary
  Society
River's Inlet, 200
Robbers Bay, 111, 246
Robinson, Captain, 61
Robson, Lieutenant Charles R., 134, 135
  136, 239, 204. *See also* Cape Mudge
  incident, 1860; Cape Mudge
  incident, 1861
Rockets, description of, 248
Rocky Mountains, 85
Roebuck, John, 29
Roman Catholics, 173, 174, 192, 205
Rooney, Matthew, 99–100
Rose Point Spit, 100, 103
Royal Canadian Mounted Police, 171, 209
Royal Engineers, 78
Royal Garrison Artillery, 207, 208
Royal Marines, 12, 120
Royal Navy, xv, 214. *See also* Admiralty,
  Lords Commissioners of the;
  *Individual Naval Officers; Individual
  ships*
  as colonial police, 32–33, 76, 86, 87–88,
  125, 162, 165, 191–92, 210
  and Indian pacification, 10, 81–82, 105,
  115, 157–58, 170
  Indian policies of, 57–58, 76, 122–23,
  128, 137, 198
  and missionaries, 173, 175–78, 182–83
Roycraft, H.M., 185, 207, 208
Rupert's Land, 17
Russian America, 68, 148, 149, 154, 177.
  See also Alaska; Sitka
Russian American Company, 148, 151, 152
Russian-American Treaty, 149–50
Russian-British Treaty. *See* Anglo-Russian
  Treaty
Russians, 10, 16, 30, 102, 158
  Indian attack of, 155
  and Indian trade, 15, 204

Saanich (village), 51
Safety Harbour, 200
St. Mary's, 258
Saltspring Island, 130, 138, 214
  Indian unrest at, 134, 135, 137, 140,
  144, 147
San Francisco, 59, 98, 101, 107, 157
  and British ships, 58
  and Pacific Mail Steamship Company,
  38
San Juan Island, 23, 60, 67
Sansun, Lieutenant Arthur, 51, 56, 58

Saturna Island, 130, 140, 141
Scanlan, Tim, 173, 174
Scott, Duncan Campbell, 64, 170
Scott, Cape, 108, 109, 112
Scott Channel, 33
Sea Otter, 14, 105
Sea Otter Group, 99
Seattle, Chief, 58
Seattle, 60
Seattle War, 60–61
Sebessa, 41, 43, 240
Seghers, Father Charles, 127, 173, 175
Septs, 38. See also Kwakiutl
Seven Sisters Hill, 34
Seymour, Governor Frederick, 181, 217, 218. See also John Bright affair; Kincolith murders
  and Indian unrest, 125, 126, 196–97, 198, 214
Seymour, Rear-Admiral Sir Michael Culme, 185, 186, 262
Seymour Narrows, hazards of, 4–6, 33
Shahkutchsus (Indian suspect), 143
Shark Cover, 139
Shepherd, Captain John, 27
Shelter Inlet, 118
Ship's Names
  Active, 59
  Alert, 70, 81, 87, 88
  Alaska, 157
  Alexander, 152–53
  Argonaut, 250
  Barbara Boscowitz, 207
  Beaver, 33, 103. See also Cowichan Expedition, 1853; Washington Territory
    and Cowichan expedition, 1853, 51 54, 57, 63
    as "floating general store," 22, 96, 98, 192
    and Washington Territory, Indian uprising in, 59, 60, 61
    military functions of, 12, 17, 39, 41, 50, 259
  Boston, 226n7
  Boxer, 13, 164, 173, 174, 175
    as patrol boat, 170, 182, 263
  Cameleon, 114, 145, 146, 254
  Caroline (steam warship), 170, 206, 207, 208
  Caroline (trading schooner), 178
  Chatham, 15
  Chichagoff, 150
  Clio, 13, 94, 192, 194, 225. See also Clio incident
    and attack of Port Rupert Kwakiutl, 82–84

  Constance, 26
  Cormorant, 12, 38, 113. See also Metlakatla
    and Metlakatla, 185–86, 261
  Coromandel 194
  Daedalus, 12, 226. See also Newitty incident
    and Newitty incident, 42, 43
  Daphne, 12. See also Newitty incident
    and Newitty incident, 44, 45, 46
  Decatur, 60
  Devastation, 12, 113, 139, 194. See also Ahousat incident; Lemalchi incident; Liquor; Stikine expedition
    and Ahousat incident, 114–20
    and Lemalchi incident, 142–43
    liquor control by, 92–94
    Stikine expedition of, 151–54
  Discovery, 10, 15
  Driver, 12, 40, 233
  Dryad, 150
  Eagle, 111
  England, 39, 40–41
  Explorer, 92–93
  Fisgard, 26
  Forward, 124, 128, 134, 139, 144, 181, 239, See also Ahousat incident; Cape Mudge incident, 1860; Cape Mudge incident, 1861; Lemalchi incident; Nass river penetration
    and Ahousat incident, 121
    Cape Mudge incidents, 132, 135, 136
    as fighting vessel, 12–13, 117, 225
    and Lemalchi incident, 140, 141, 143 145–47
    Nass River penetration, 193, 194, 195, 209
  Ganges, 70
  George S. Wright, 199, 200, 202. See also Kimsquit incident
  Georgiana, 98
  Grappler, 12–13, 124, 132, 264. See also Lemalchi incident
    and Indian unrest, investigation of 114, 117, 248
    and Lemalchi incident, 142, 143
  Hamley, 92
  Hecate, 87, 109, 154, 192, 248
    and Haida 104, 153
  Inconstant, 27
  John Bright, 123, 125, 126, 128. See also John Bright affair
  Jamestown, 157
  Kingfisher (gunvessel), 125, 175, 213
  Kingfisher (trading schooner) 93, 114, 115, 118, 119, 121, 249. See also

Ahousat incident
Kinnaird, 118. See also Ahousat in-
    cident
Komagata Maru, 171
Langley, 93
Laurel, 134, 135, 136
Lincoln, 199
Massachusetts, 59, 62, 158
Modeste, 28–29
Monarch, 63
Morning Star, 111
Myrmidon, 13, 94, 165
Nanaimo, 242
Native, 151
Neva, 149
Norman Morison, 33, 41
Oliver Wollcott, 155, 206. See also
    Sitka
    and Sitka, 156, 157
    and Metlakata, 158, 182
Osprey, 155, 156, 157, 260. See also
    Sitka
Otter, 12, 34, 50, 58
    and Cowichan incident, 1856, 63–64
    and Indian uprising, 59–60, 61
Pandora, 228
Pensacola, 154
Petrel, 93, 164, 199
Pheasant, 13, 213
Plumper, 78, 81, 132, 179, 259
    and Indian unrest, 70, 87
Portland, 175
President, 59, 63
Quadra, 258
Rainbow, 170
Random, 117, 248
Recovery, 51, 63, 99
Reindeer, 90, 164
Ringdove, 13, 213
Ringleader, 200
Rocket, 13, 125, 167, 170, 174–75. See
    also Kimsquit incident
    and Kimsquit incident 199, 200,
    201–3
Resolution, 10
Royal Charlie, 70
Rynda, 153
Santiago, 172
Satellite, 176, 177, 183, 184. See also
    Swiss Boy affair
    and Swiss Boy affair, 111, 112
Scout, 123, 164, 205, 263
Sir James Douglas (Indian affairs ship),
    169, 258
Sir James Douglas (modern vessel), 258
Sparrowhawk, 13, 125, 181, 213
    and John Bright affair, 126, 127

and Kincolith murders, 196, 197
Surprise, 115, 125
Susan Sturgis, 101, 102, 103, 106,
    107, 211. See also Susan Sturgis
    affair
    piracy of, 98–100, 176, 244
Sutlej, 13, 124. See also Ahousat crisis
    and Ahousat incident, 118, 119, 120
Swiss Boy, 111–13, 121. See also Swiss
    Boy affair
Tenedos, 164
Termagant, 70, 87
Thetis, 100, 228. See also Cowichan
    Expedition, 1853
    and Cowichan expedition, 1853, 51,
    54, 55
Tonquin, 109, 226
Topaze, 142, 145. See also Lemalchi in-
    cident
Trader, 114
Tribune, 69
Trincomalee, 12, 202. See also
    Cowichan expedition, 1856
    and Cowichan expedition 1856, 63,
    64, 67
Una, 98, 243
Unicorn, 148
Vancouver, 103, 259
Vigilant, 169–70, 258
Virago, 12, 176, 241. See also Susan
    Sturgis affair
    and Susan Sturgis affair, 100, 101
William and Anne, 16
Zealous, 195
Shunaseluk (Indian suspect), 146
Shushartie Bay, 41
Siam-a-sit (Indian suspect), 56
Siktokkis (Ahousat village), 118
Similkameen Valley, 228
Simmons, Colonel Michael T., 246
Simpson, George, 21, 22–23
Sitka, 102, 137, 150, 260
    under American jurisdiction, 154, 158
    and Indian crisis, 155–57
    and Tlingit wars, 148, 149, 254
    and white-Indian relations, 92, 102,
    152
Sitka Sound, 148
Skayutlelt (Tlingit chief), 148
Skedans (village), 215
Skeena Mountains, 190
Skeena River, 4, 89, 204, 205, 263. See
    also "Skeena war"
    Indian unrest in, 87, 151, 170, 206
Skeena Valley, 209
"Skeena War," 205–9 See also Cunning-
    ham, Robert; Green, Constable;

Holmes, Colonel; Wiseman, Sir
William; *Caroline*
Skidegate (village), 99, 182
Skullowayat (Indian suspect), 144
Slavery, 87–89, 211, 240
    functions of, 85–86
Sloops, 12. *See also* ships' names
Smallpox, 80, 81, 105, 174, 178, 266
Smith, Adam, 10–12
Smith, Horace, 139, 142, 253
Smith, Marius, 165
Sne-ny-mo. See Nanaimo
Snooks (Indian desperado), 152
Soldier's Point, 208
Somenos Fields, 66
Songhees Point, 24
Soseiah (Cowichan chief), 54, 234n6
South Pender Island, 130
Spencer, Commodore the Hon. J. W. S.,
    140, 142
Spokeshute, 205
Sproat, Gilbert, 11, 113, 122
    and exchange with Powell, 166–67, 257
Sque-is (Indian suspect), 55
Sta Stas Eagles, 99
Sta Stas Shongaith (Edenshaw's lineage),
    99
Stamp, Captain Edward, 113
Stark family, 138
State Department (United States), 156
Steamships, 12. *See also* ships' names
Steilacoom, 60
Stephen, William John, 242
Stephens Island, 178
Stevens, Isaac, 58, 59, 61
Stevenson, Captain James, 115
Steward, Chief Constable, 200
Stewart, Lieutenant, 120
Stikine (town), 98
Stikine Expedition, 151–54. *See also*
    Douglas, James; Furuhjelm, Johann;
    Maitland, T.; Pike, John; Richards,
    George; *Devastation; Hecate*
Stikine River, 4, 22, 93, 149, 150. *See also*
    Stikine expedition
    and Anglo-Russian tensions, 137, 151,
    152
    and Indian relations, 92, 151–54, 255
Stikine Territory, 150–51
Stockade, 141
Strait of Georgia. *See* Georgia, Strait of
Strange, James, 15
Sturgis, William, 15
Supreme Court (of Victoria), 121–22
Suchkool, 115
Sunbeam (Kitwankool Jim's wife), 207
Superior Court of British Columbia, 185

Suquash (Indian sealing site), 33
Sutton, Mrs. John, 199
Swale. *See* Swell
Swan, James Gilcrist, 68, 246
Swanston, R.S., 62
Swanton, John, 95
Swell (interpreter and pilot), 111, 112, 246
Swinhon. *See* Songhees
Swiss Boy affair, 111–13
Syphilis, 80, 81

Tackshicoate (Newitty suspect), 41
Tahsis, 230
Taku Inlet, 22
Takush Harbour, 200
Tanu. *See* Laskeek
Tathlasut (Somenos chief), 63, 66. *See
    also* Cowichan expedition, 1856
Tawankstalla (Newitty suspect), 41
Tcoosma (Kwakiutl chief), 82
Techamalt (Cowichan chief), 214
Texada Island, 130
Thatcher, Henry K., 154
Theobald, Captain Charles B., 183–84,
    188
Thetis Island, 130, 143
Thornberg, Frederick Christian, 113
"This Miserable Affair." *See* Newitty
    Incident
"Tillicums" (Haida people), 136
Tilton, James, 59, 61
Tishtan (Lemalchi suspect), 143
Tlolemistin (Indian), 71
Todd, Charles, 17, 206, 207
Tolmie, William Fraser, 16, 59, 60, 67
Tomlinson, Robert, 195–96, 263
Toquart, 115
Totem poles, 7, 105
Townissim (Hesquiat), 174
Trader Barney, 111
Treasury Department, (United States) 154,
    155
Treaty Eight, 71,
Treven, Henry, 101, 106
Trevor Channel, 111
Trinidad Bay, 6
Trout River 119, 120
Trutch, Joseph William, 162, 163, 167–68,
    197, 205. *See also* Kincolith murders
Tsqulotn (Indian village), 132
Tsukmeen (Indian village), 143
Tuan. *See* Saltspring Island
Tugwell Island, 178
Turnour, Captain Nicholas Edward
    Brooke, 82–84, 192, 194. *See also Clio*
    incident
Tsouhalem (Cowichan chief), 25

Uchucklesaht (Indian village), 112
United Kingdom. *See* Great Britain
United States, 16, 29, 68, 75, 155
 and Alaska, 148, 149, 154–58
 and New Metlakatla, 261
 and *Swiss Boy* affair, 111
 and Treaty of Washington, 25
Upper Skeena Agency, 209

Vancouver, George, 15–16, 109, 130, 190, 199
Vancouver Island, xv, 17, 21, 77, 124, 130, 213
 colony status of, 28, 32, 217
 geography of, 3, 68, 109–11, 246
 Legislative Assembly of, 62, 91, 163, 246
 Legislative Council of, 58, 136
 security measures of, 27, 48, 67, 150, 164, 210
Vankoughnet, Lawrence, 162, 169
Vargas Island, 114
Vavasour, Lieutenant Mervin, 23
Venn, Henry, 176
Verney, Lieutenant Edmund Hope, 142, 179, 212
Vesuvius Bay, 138
Victoria (Queen of England), 19, 128, 194, 226
Victoria, xv, 28, 114, 139, 172, 185
 as administrative centre, 75, 130, 161, 162
 liquor trade in, 91
 and gunboat diplomacy, 63, 124, 181
 Indian incidents, public opinion of, 115, 121, 125, 126, 140
Victoria Harbour, 68, 69
Victoria Daily Colonist. the, 46, 182, 207. *See also British Colonist,* the
Village Bay. *See* Lemalchi Bay
Virago Sound, 102
Voltigeurs, 50, 146

Waddington, Alfred, xv, 165, 263
Walbran, Captain John, 34–35, 127
Waldron Island, 140

Walkem, W. W., 175, 249
Walker, David, 80, 199
Walleshuk (Indian suspect), 146
War Department (United States), 154
War for the Union, 117
Warre, Lieutenant, Henry J., 23, 24
Washington (capital, United States), 61, 154
Washington Territory, 50, 69, 92, 125
 Indian revolt in, 59–61
Washington Territory Volunteers, 60
Washington, Treaty of. *See* Oregon Treaty
Wellesley, Captain George Grenville, 42, 45, 48, 226. *See also* Newitty incident
Weah (Masset Haida chief), 100
Weldon (shipmaster, *Swiss Boy*), 111
Wellcome, Sir Henry, 186, 261
Westminster, 213
Whidbey Island, 24
Wha-latl. *See* Swell
Whisky. *See* Liquor
White River, 58
Whitepine Grove, 120
Wicanninnish (Indian chief), 15
Wilberforce, William, 44
Wilde, Oscar, 209
Willamete Valley, 20
William IV, 226
William, Thomas, 63
Wilson, Charles William, 69
Wiseman, Captain Sir William, 206. *See also* "Skeena War"
Wood, Sir Charles, 67, 177
Wood, Lieutenant James, 228
Work, John, 136
Wrangell, 150, 260
Wrangell Island, 150, 152
Wright Bank, 199
Wu-Gat, 190

Yaculta Rapids, 132
Yaculta Village. *See* Tsqulotn
Yakutat Bay, 6
Young, Captain, 258